MISSILE HAPPY!

Volume 3

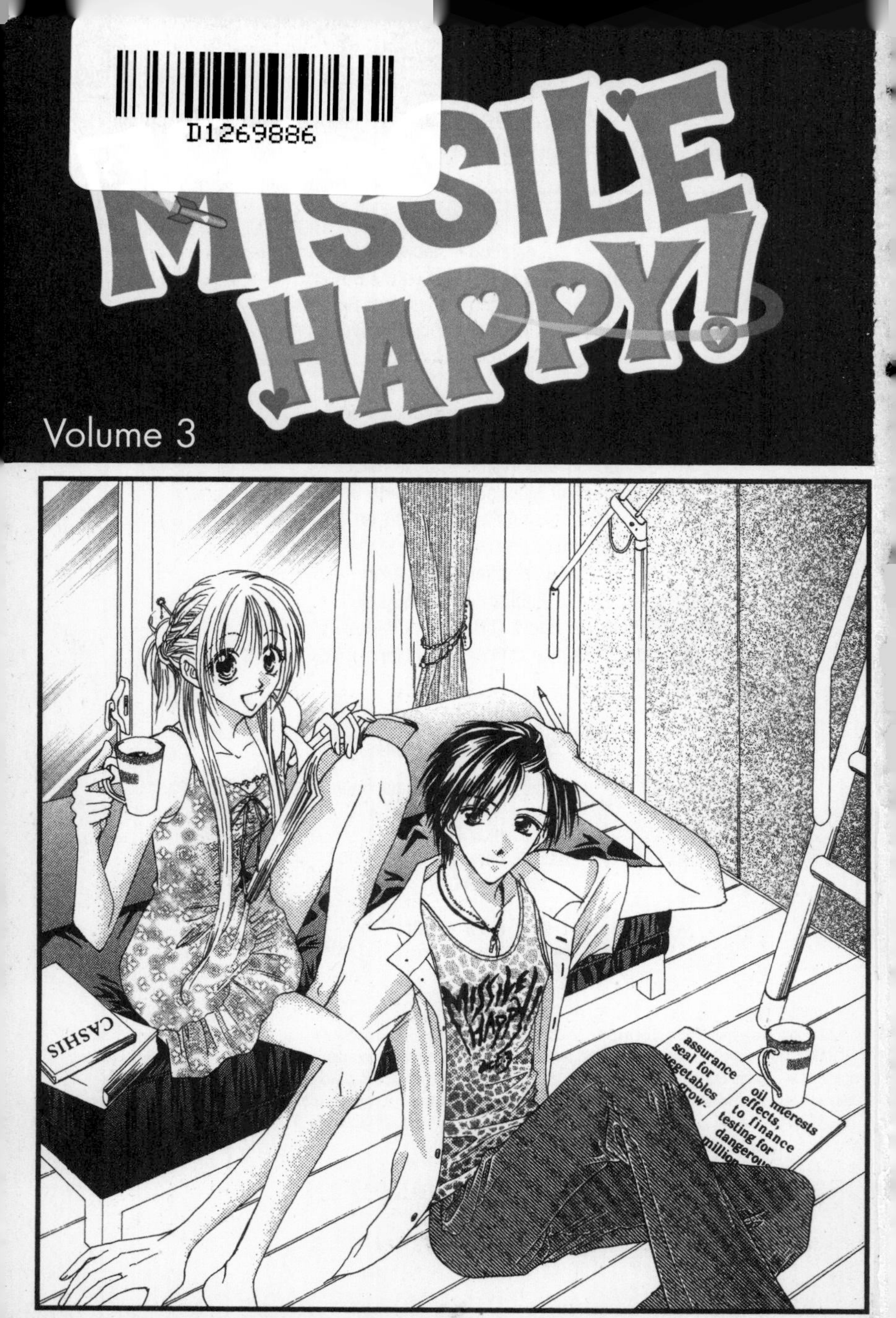
CASHIS
MISSILE HAPPY!
assurance
seal for
vegetables
grow-
oil interests
effects,
to finance
testing for
dangerous
million

Missile Happy! Volume 3
Created by Miki Kiritani

Translation - Angela Liu
English Adaptation - Christine Boylan
Retouch and Lettering - Star Print Brokers
Production Artist - Vicente Rivera, Jr.
Graphic Designer - John Lo

Editor - Hyun Joo Kim
Digital Imaging Manager - Chris Buford
Pre-Production Supervisor - Lucas Rivera
Production Manager - Elisabeth Brizzi
Managing Editor - Vy Nguyen
Creative Director - Anne Marie Horne
Editor-in-Chief - Rob Tokar
Publisher - Mike Kiley
President and C.O.O. - John Parker
C.E.O. and Chief Creative Officer - Stu Levy

A  Manga

TOKYOPOP Inc.
5900 Wilshire Blvd. Suite 2000
Los Angeles, CA 90036

E-mail: info@TOKYOPOP.com
Come visit us online at www.TOKYOPOP.com

ISBN: 978-1-59816-934-8

First TOKYOPOP printing: June 2008
10 9 8 7 6 5 4 3 2 1
Printed in the USA

MISSILE HAPPY!™

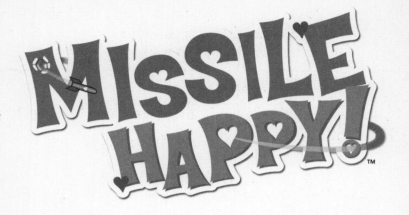

VOLUME 3

MIKI KIRITANI

TOKYOPOP®

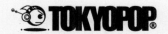

HAMBURG // LONDON // LOS ANGELES // TOKYO

CONTENTS

CHAPTER 9 7

CHAPTER 10 47

CHAPTER 11 85

CHAPTER 12 125

LOVE'S SLAVE 165

EXTRA: THE SLEEPING AFTERWORD-KIRIKIRI MY ROOM 197

PREVIOUSLY IN

MISSILE HAPPY!™

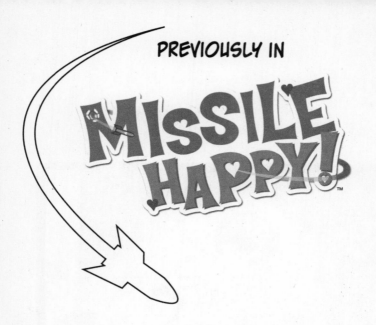

HONESTLY, MIKAKO'S INTENTION OF BARGING IN ON ROU'S HOUSE WAS TO STOP HIS ARRANGED MARRIAGE MEETING WITH HER OLDER SISTER, MEGUMI. BUT AFTER LIVING WITH HIM FOR A FEW DAYS, SHE LEARNS THAT ASIDE FROM BEING EXTREMELY WEALTHY, ROU IS ALSO CUTE, SMART AND WONDERFUL! WHAT MORE COULD A THIRD-YEAR JUNIOR HIGH SCHOOL GIRL WANT IN A GUY? MEGUMI, BEING THE CLEVER AND KIND SISTER THAT SHE IS, STEPPED ASIDE TO LET MIKAKO HAVE ROU AND FELL IN LOVE WITH ROU'S OLDER BROTHER, SEI, HERSELF. MIKAKO AND ROU ARE STILL LIVING TOGETHER, BUT NOW THAT THEIR OLDER SIBLINGS HAVE MOVED RIGHT NEXT DOOR TOGETHER, WHAT LOVELY CRISIS WILL OCCUR NEXT?

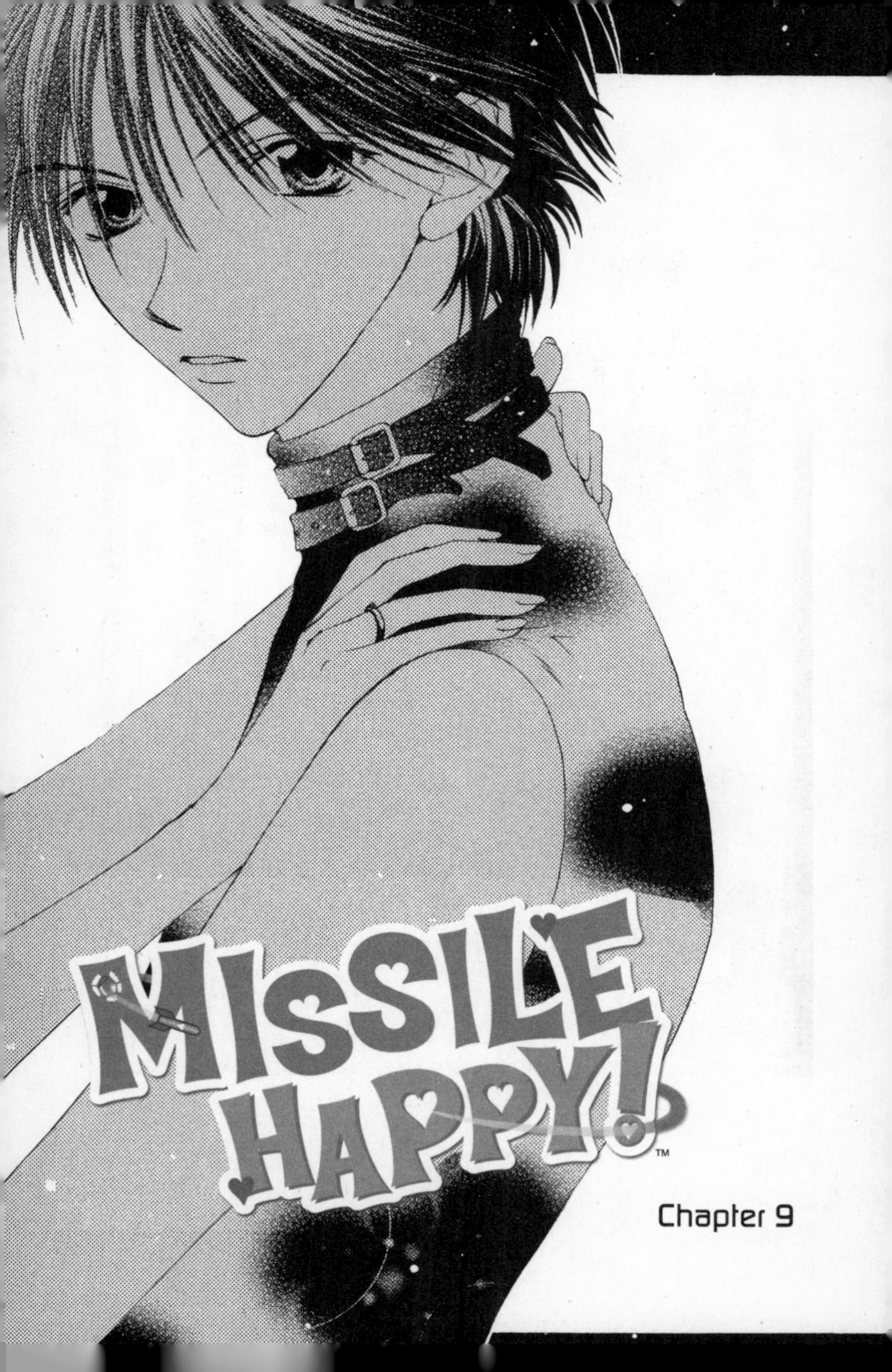
MISSILE HAPPY!™
Chapter 9

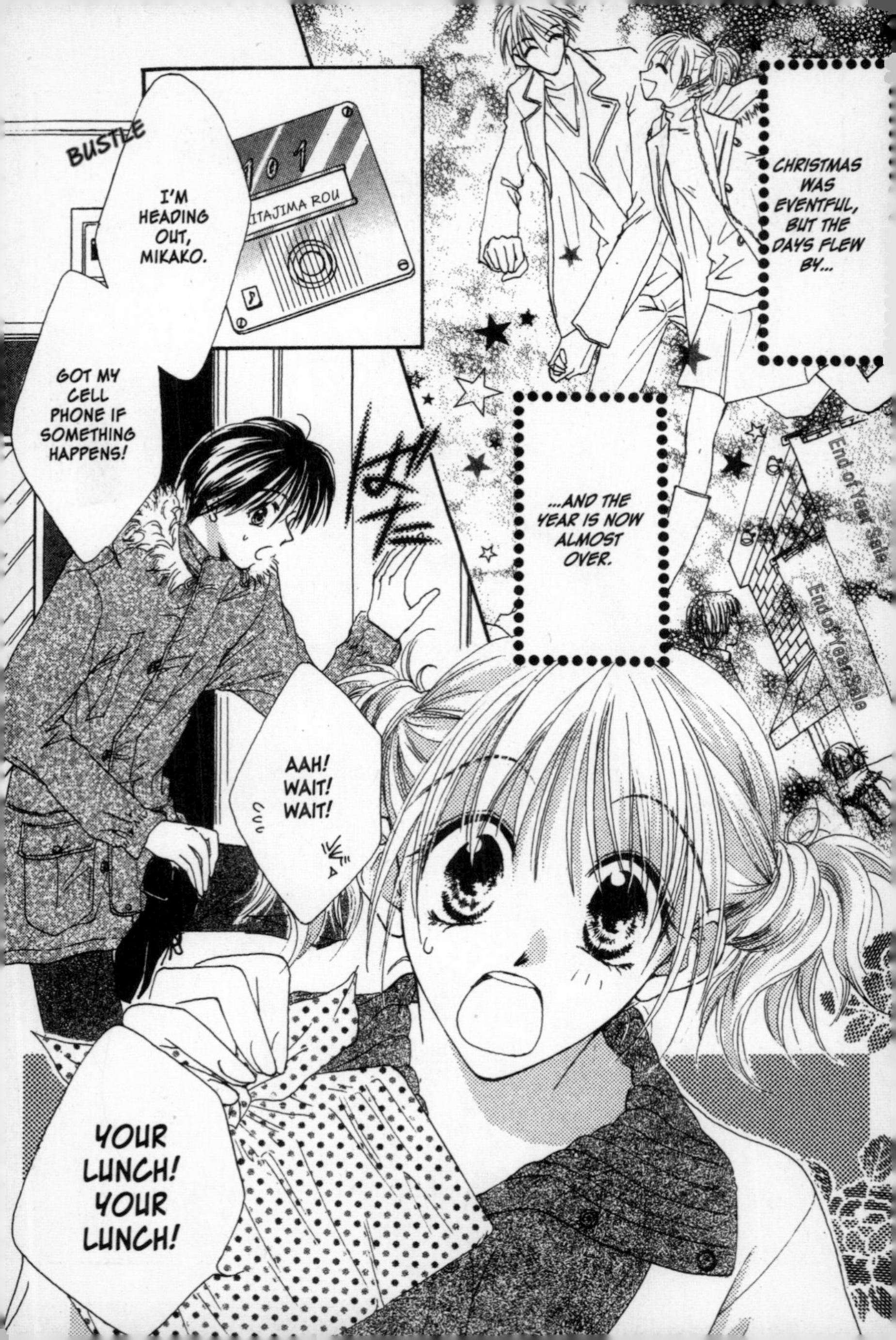
CHRISTMAS WAS EVENTFUL, BUT THE DAYS FLEW BY...
End of Year Sale
End of Year Sale
...AND THE YEAR IS NOW ALMOST OVER.
BUSTLE
101
ITAJIMA ROU
I'M HEADING OUT, MIKAKO.
GOT MY CELL PHONE IF SOMETHING HAPPENS!
AAH! WAIT! WAIT!
YOUR LUNCH! YOUR LUNCH!

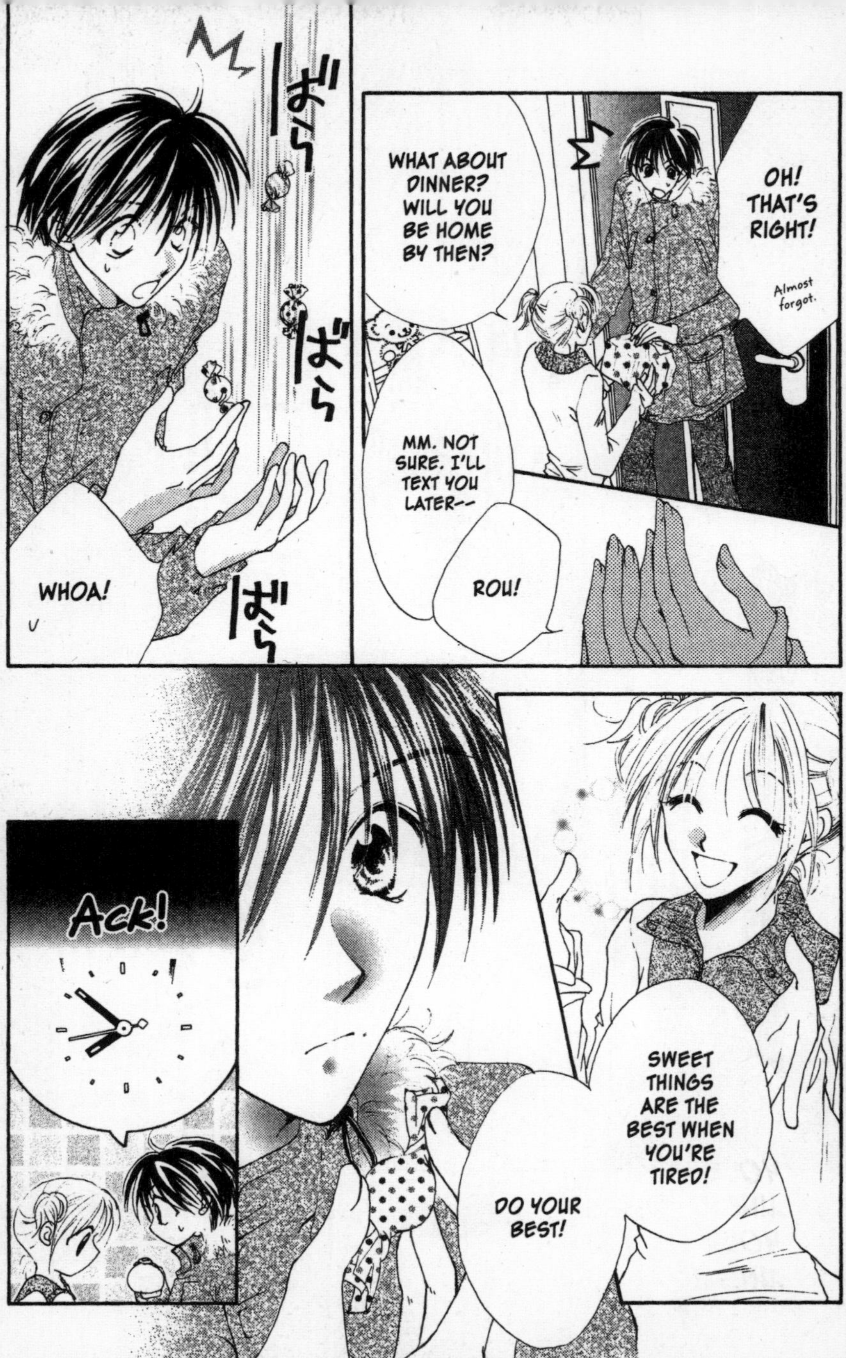
OH! THAT'S RIGHT!
Almost forgot.
WHAT ABOUT DINNER? WILL YOU BE HOME BY THEN?
MM. NOT SURE. I'LL TEXT YOU LATER--
ROU!
ばら
ばら
ばら
WHOA!
SWEET THINGS ARE THE BEST WHEN YOU'RE TIRED!
DO YOUR BEST!
Ack!

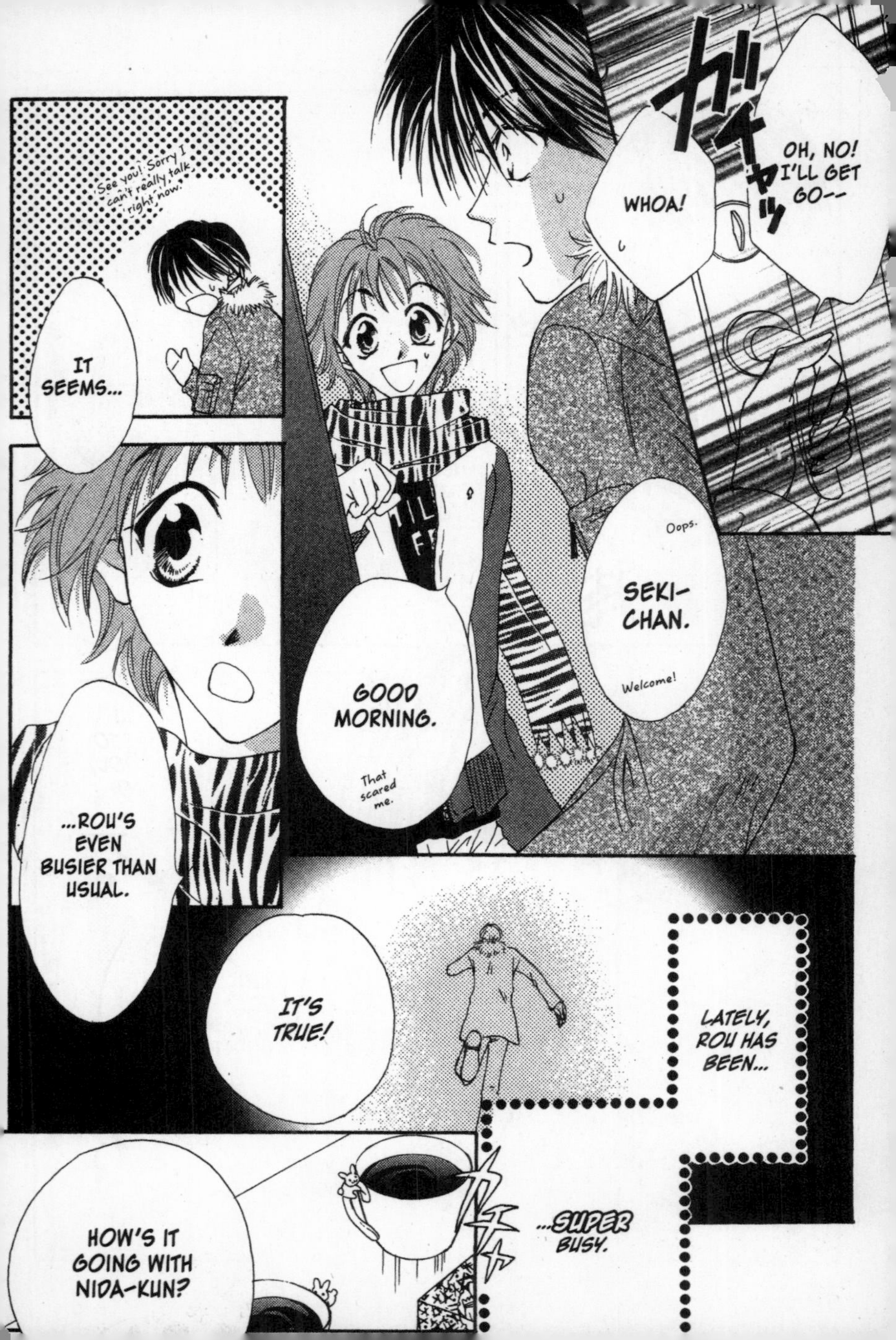
ガチャッ
OH, NO! I'LL GET GO--
WHOA!
SEKI-CHAN.
Oops.
Welcome!
GOOD MORNING.
That scared me.
See you! Sorry I can't really talk right now.
IT SEEMS...
...ROU'S EVEN BUSIER THAN USUAL.
LATELY, ROU HAS BEEN...
...SUPER BUSY.
IT'S TRUE!
HOW'S IT GOING WITH NIDA-KUN?

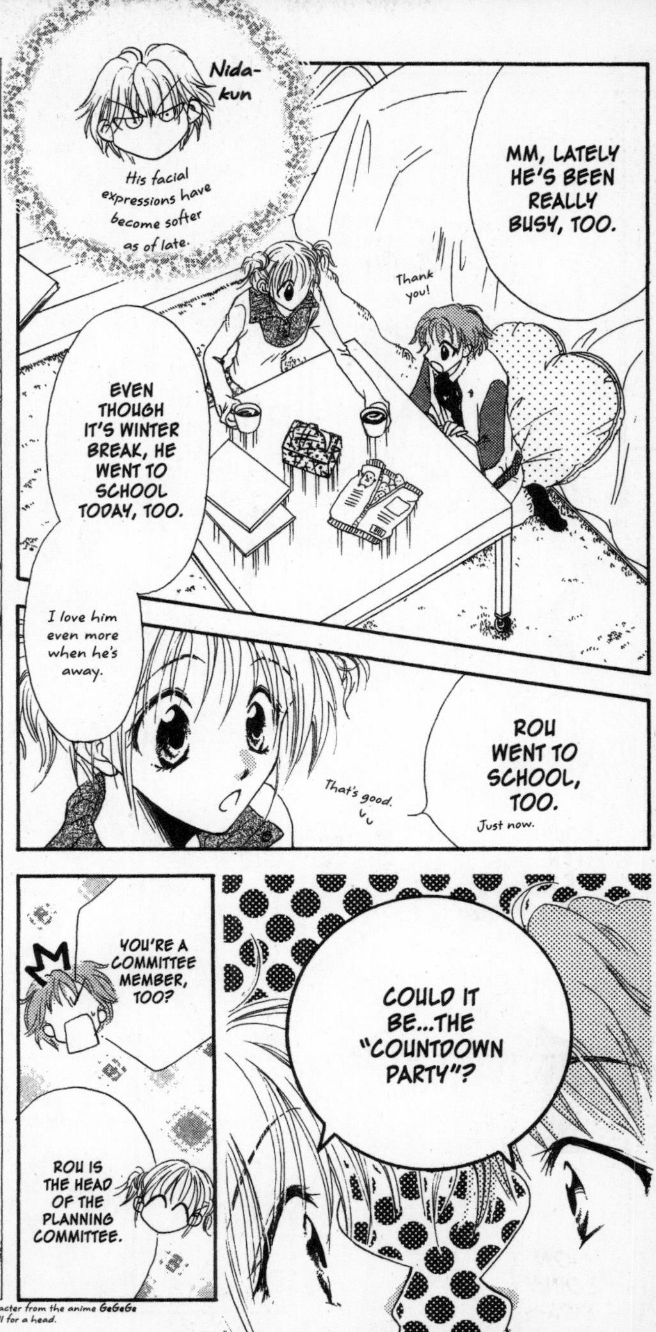
Nida-kun
His facial expressions have become softer as of late.
MM, LATELY HE'S BEEN REALLY BUSY, TOO.
Thank you!
EVEN THOUGH IT'S WINTER BREAK, HE WENT TO SCHOOL TODAY, TOO.
ROU WENT TO SCHOOL, TOO.
Just now.
That's good.
I love him even more when he's away.
COULD IT BE...THE "COUNTDOWN PARTY"?
YOU'RE A COMMITTEE MEMBER, TOO?
ROU IS THE HEAD OF THE PLANNING COMMITTEE.

GREETINGS

It's the third volume! The **third** volume! Hello! My younger sister said to me in Eyeball Geezer's* voice...

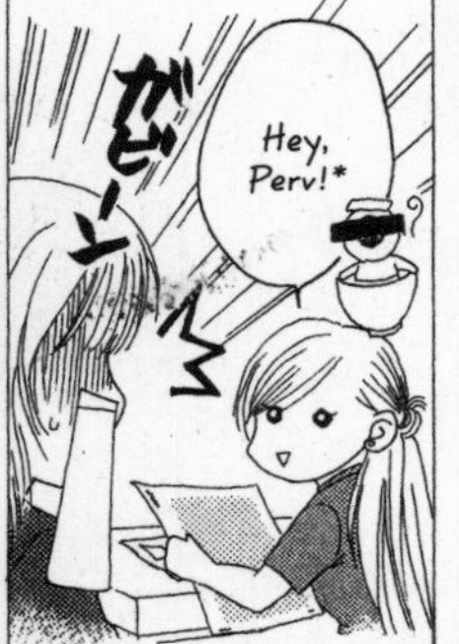
Hey, Perv!*

I am the Kiritani that gets that phrase...a lot. Is that okay?

Thank you very much for picking up Missile Happy! volume 3. To publish three volumes within a year! This year, in January, I received the Athena Award. It was a good year... I got to do the cover for the Hana to Yume magazine, too!

So. The third volume. I will be very happy if you enjoy it even a little bit. This time, I have nine of these 1/4 spaces. Will I be able to fill them all? I hope it works like the side garnish on sashimi.

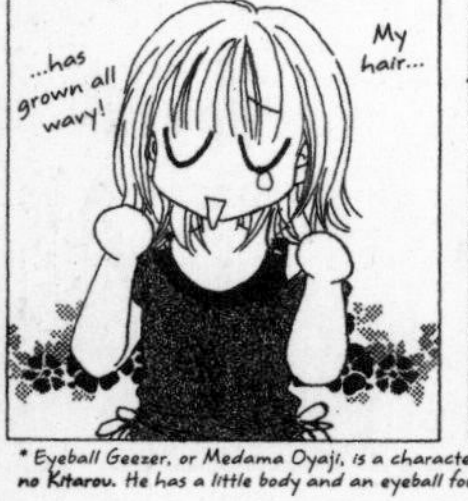
My hair...
...has grown all wavy!

* Eyeball Geezer, or Medama Oyaji, is a character from the anime *GeGeGe no Kitarou*. He has a little body and an eyeball for a head.

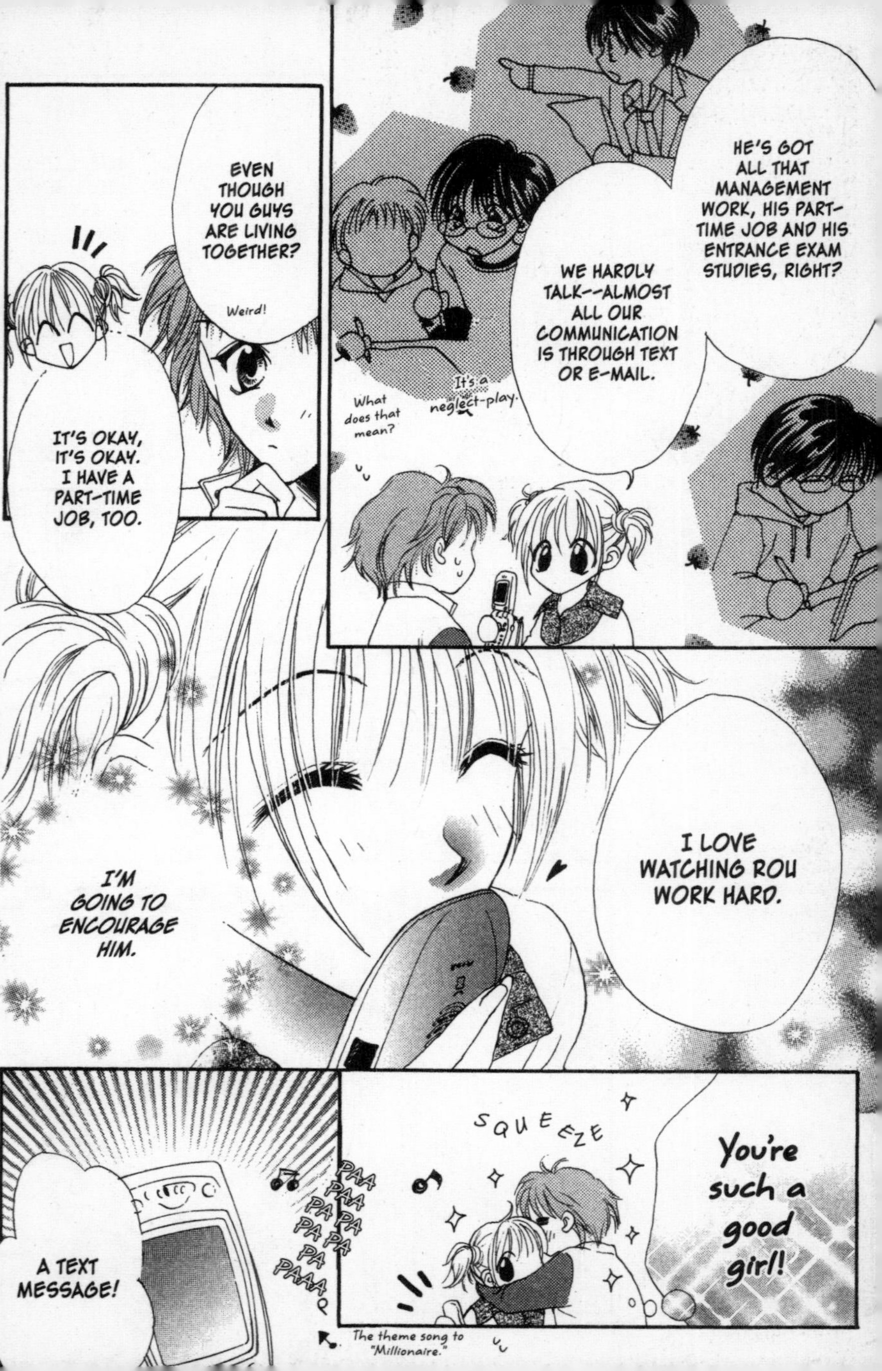
HE'S GOT ALL THAT MANAGEMENT WORK, HIS PART-TIME JOB AND HIS ENTRANCE EXAM STUDIES, RIGHT?
WE HARDLY TALK--ALMOST ALL OUR COMMUNICATION IS THROUGH TEXT OR E-MAIL.
It's a neglect-play.
What does that mean?
EVEN THOUGH YOU GUYS ARE LIVING TOGETHER?
Weird!
IT'S OKAY, IT'S OKAY. I HAVE A PART-TIME JOB, TOO.
I LOVE WATCHING ROU WORK HARD.
I'M GOING TO ENCOURAGE HIM.
You're such a good girl!
SQUEEZE
PAA PAA PA PA PA PA PA PAAA
The theme song to "Millionaire."
A TEXT MESSAGE!

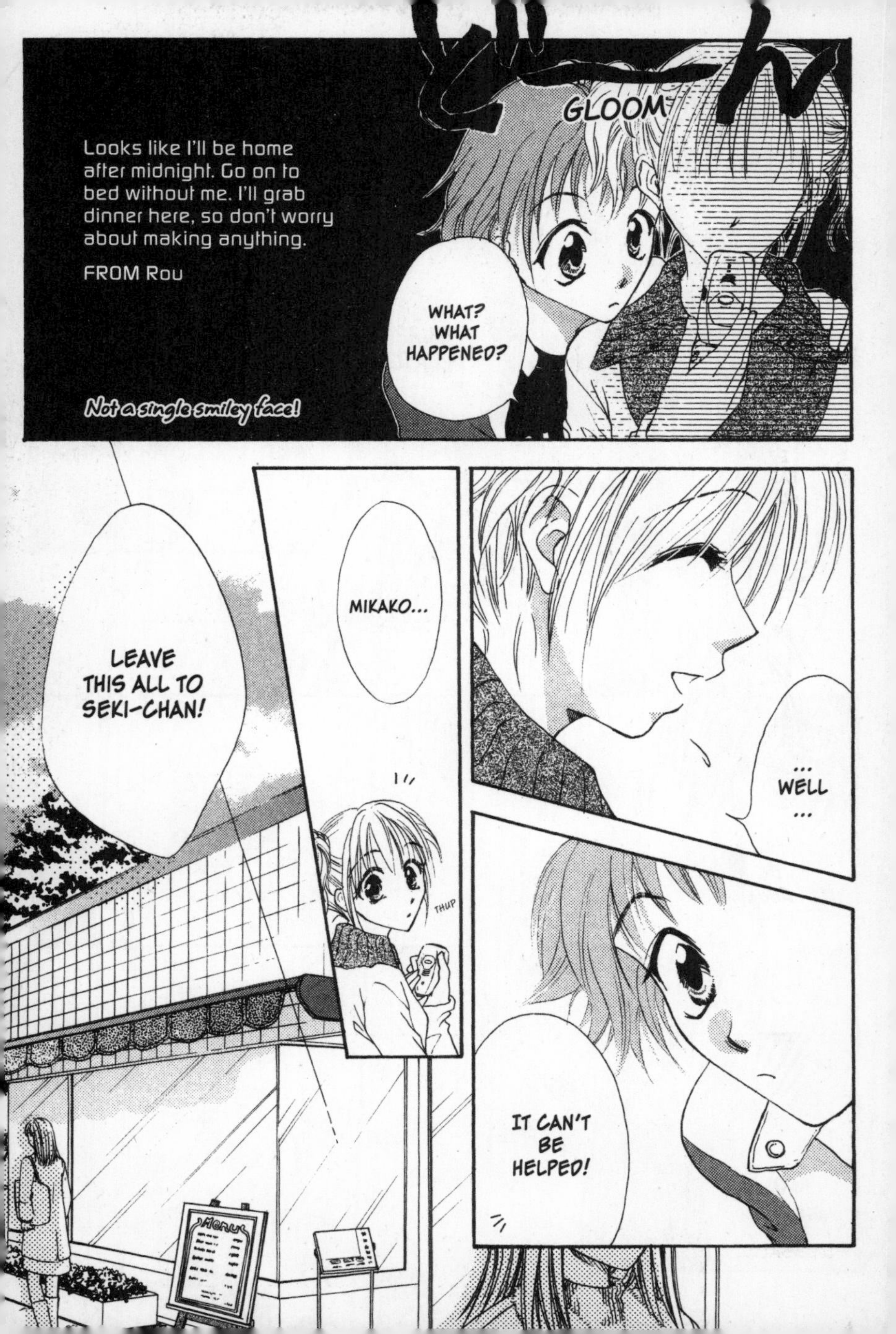
GLOOM
Looks like I'll be home after midnight. Go on to bed without me. I'll grab dinner here, so don't worry about making anything.
FROM Rou
WHAT? WHAT HAPPENED?
Not a single smiley face!
... WELL ...
IT CAN'T BE HELPED!
MIKAKO...
THUP
LEAVE THIS ALL TO SEKI-CHAN!

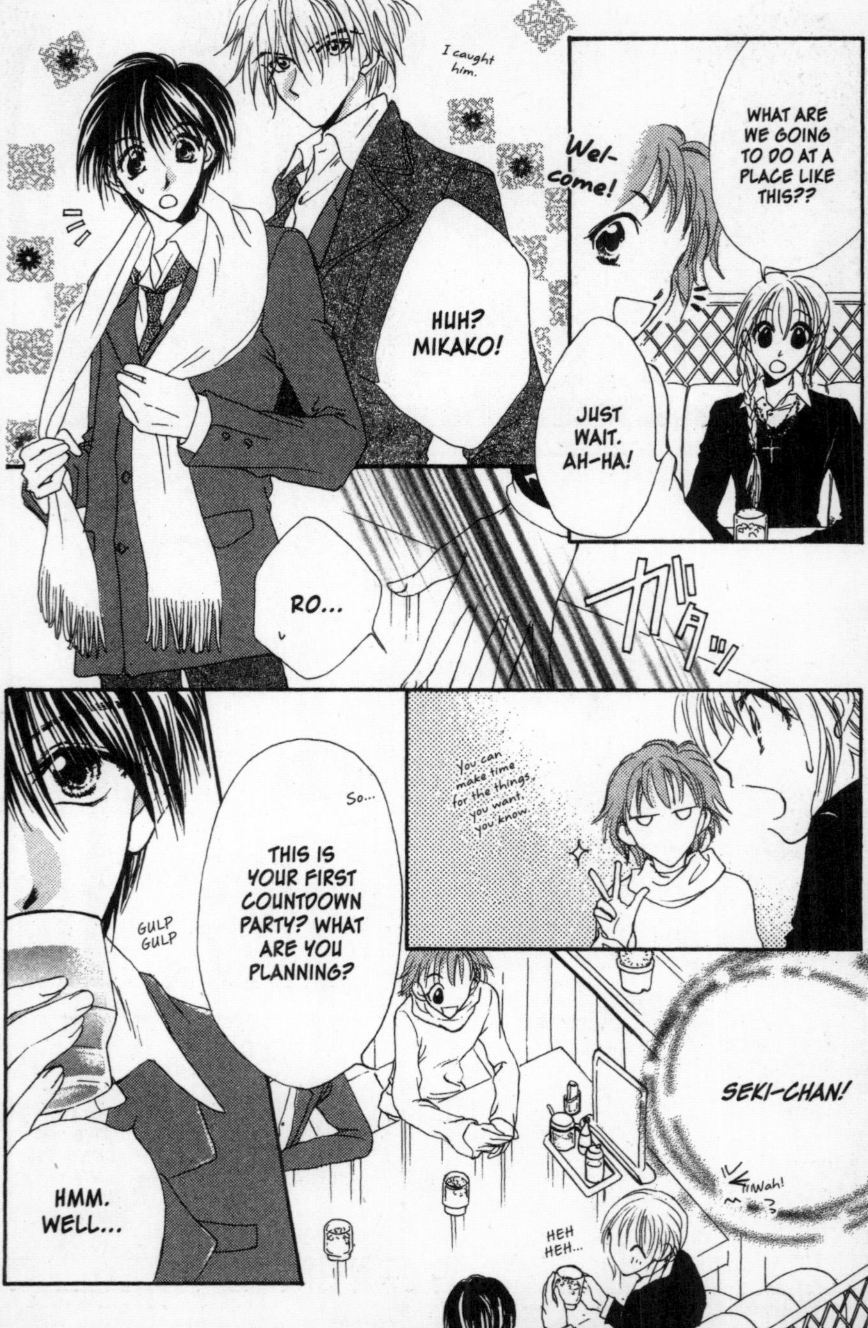

Wel-
come!
WHAT ARE WE GOING TO DO AT A PLACE LIKE THIS??
JUST WAIT. AH-HA!
ガタッ
I caught him.
HUH? MIKAKO!
RO...
You can make time for the things you want, you know.
SEKI-CHAN!
Wah!
HEH HEH...
So...
THIS IS YOUR FIRST COUNTDOWN PARTY? WHAT ARE YOU PLANNING?
GULP GULP
HMM. WELL...

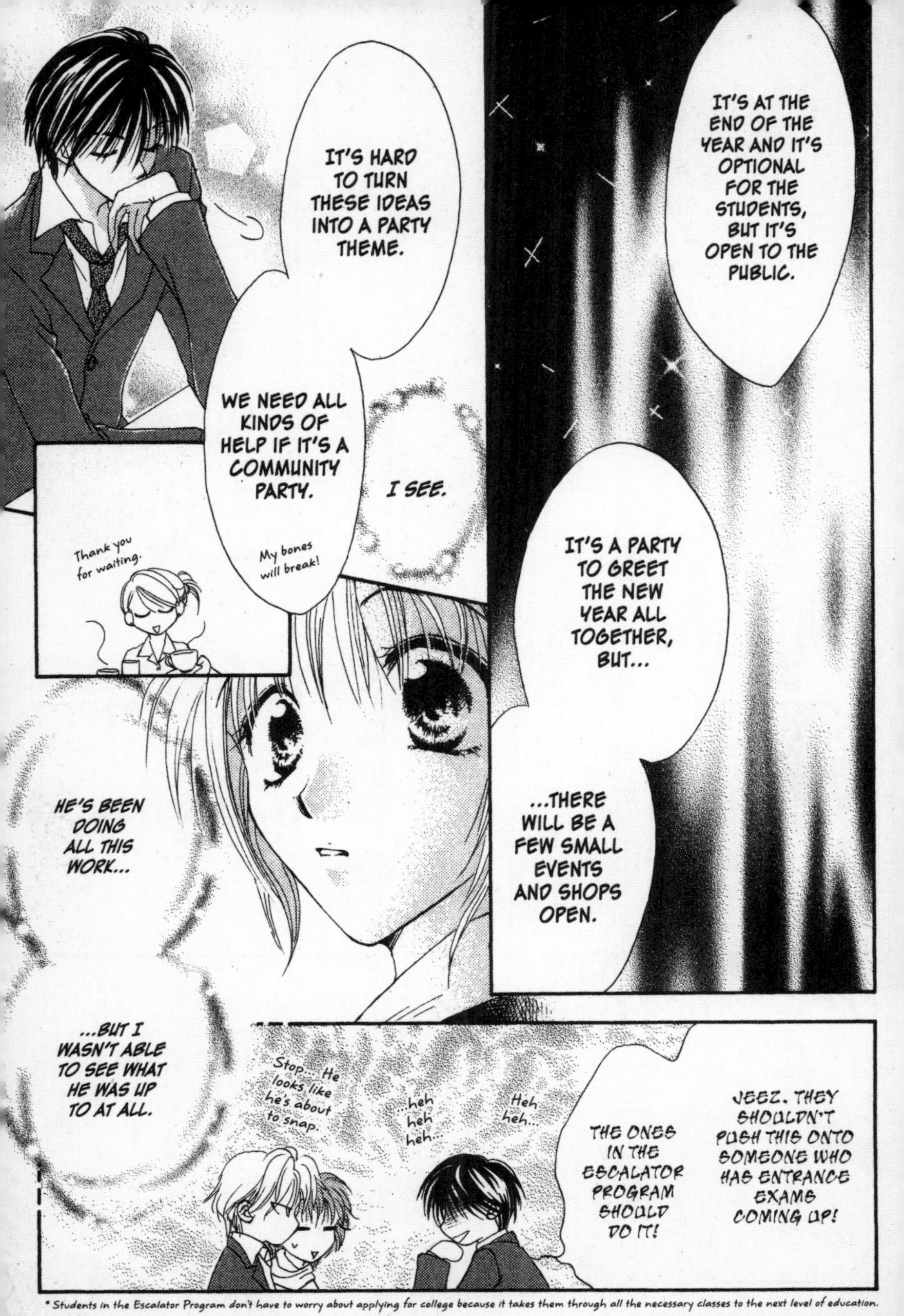
IT'S AT THE END OF THE YEAR AND IT'S OPTIONAL FOR THE STUDENTS, BUT IT'S OPEN TO THE PUBLIC.
IT'S A PARTY TO GREET THE NEW YEAR ALL TOGETHER, BUT...
...THERE WILL BE A FEW SMALL EVENTS AND SHOPS OPEN.
IT'S HARD TO TURN THESE IDEAS INTO A PARTY THEME.
WE NEED ALL KINDS OF HELP IF IT'S A COMMUNITY PARTY.
I SEE.
My bones will break!
Thank you for waiting.
HE'S BEEN DOING ALL THIS WORK...
...BUT I WASN'T ABLE TO SEE WHAT HE WAS UP TO AT ALL.
JEEZ. THEY SHOULDN'T PUSH THIS ONTO SOMEONE WHO HAS ENTRANCE EXAMS COMING UP!
THE ONES IN THE ESCALATOR PROGRAM SHOULD DO IT!
Heh heh...
...heh heh heh...
Stop... He looks like he's about to snap.

* Students in the Escalator Program don't have to worry about applying for college because it takes them through all the necessary classes to the next level of education.

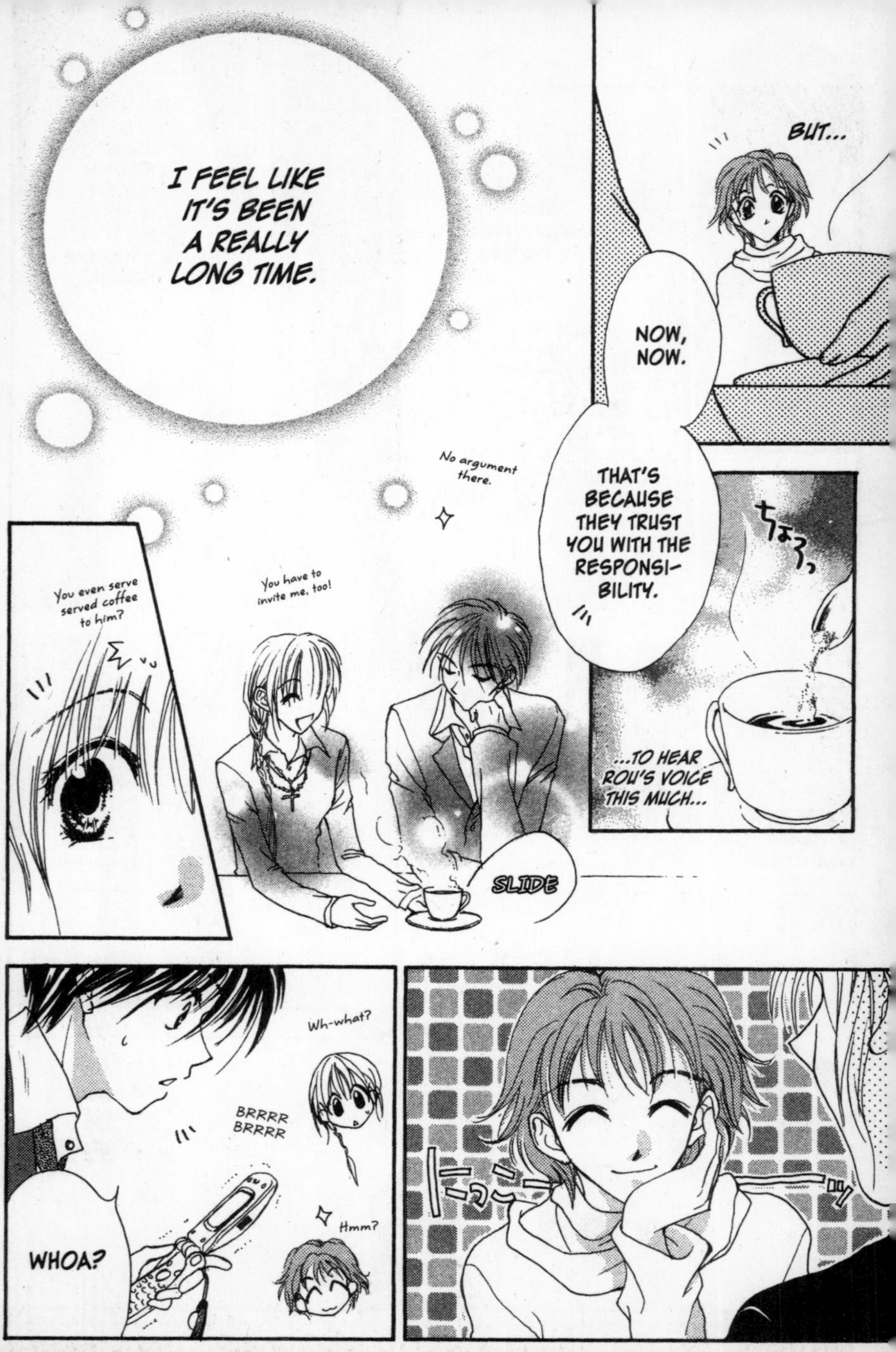
BUT...
NOW, NOW.
THAT'S BECAUSE THEY TRUST YOU WITH THE RESPONSI-BILITY.
...TO HEAR ROU'S VOICE THIS MUCH...
I FEEL LIKE IT'S BEEN A REALLY LONG TIME.
SLIDE
No argument there.
You have to invite me, too!
You even serve served coffee to him?
Wh-what?
BRRRR BRRRR
Hmm?
WHOA?

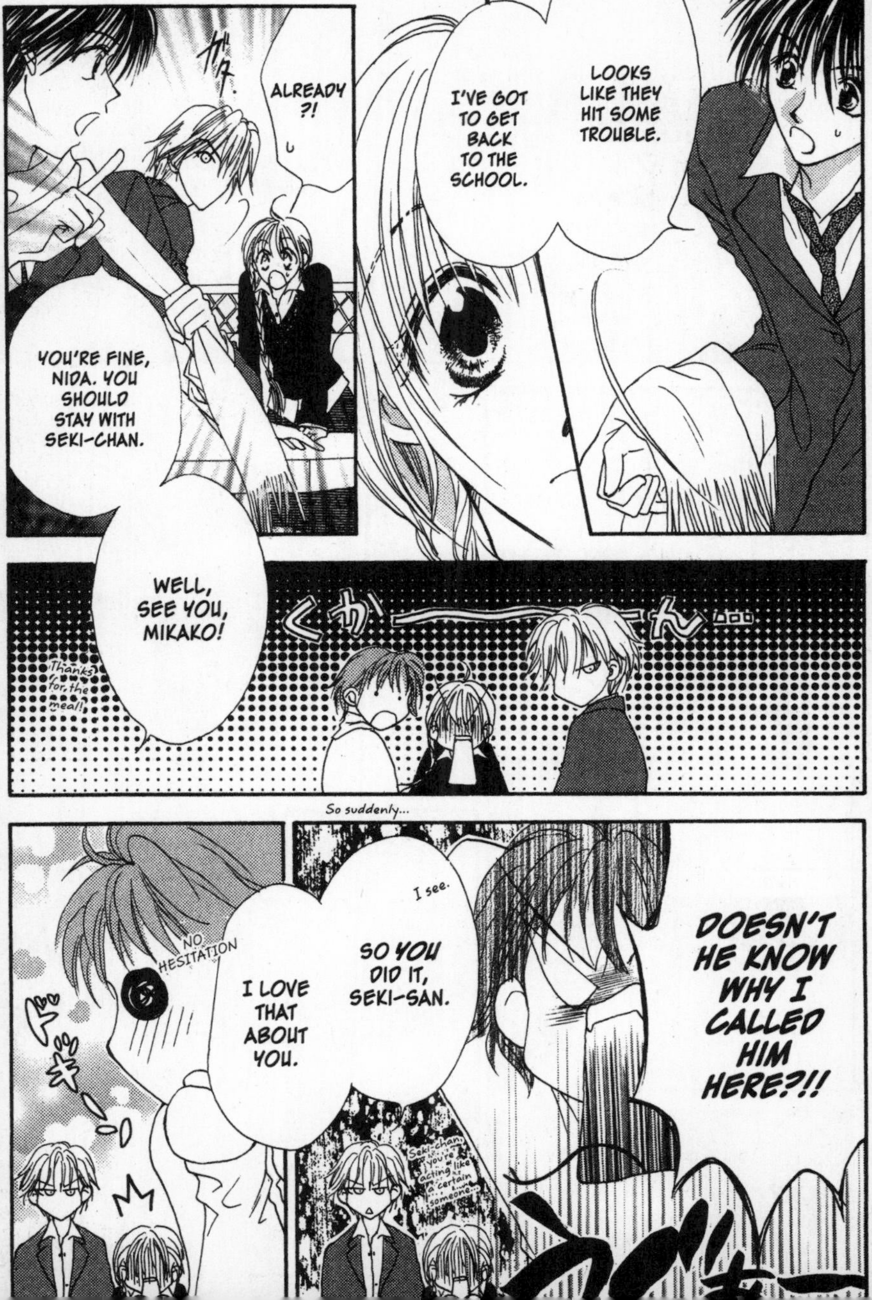
LOOKS LIKE THEY HIT SOME TROUBLE.
I'VE GOT TO GET BACK TO THE SCHOOL.
ALREADY ?!
YOU'RE FINE, NIDA. YOU SHOULD STAY WITH SEKI-CHAN.
WELL, SEE YOU, MIKAKO!
Thanks for the meal!!
くわーーーん…
So suddenly...
DOESN'T HE KNOW WHY I CALLED HIM HERE?!!
I see.
SO YOU DID IT, SEKI-SAN.
Seki-chan, you're acting like a certain someone...
I LOVE THAT ABOUT YOU.
NO HESITATION

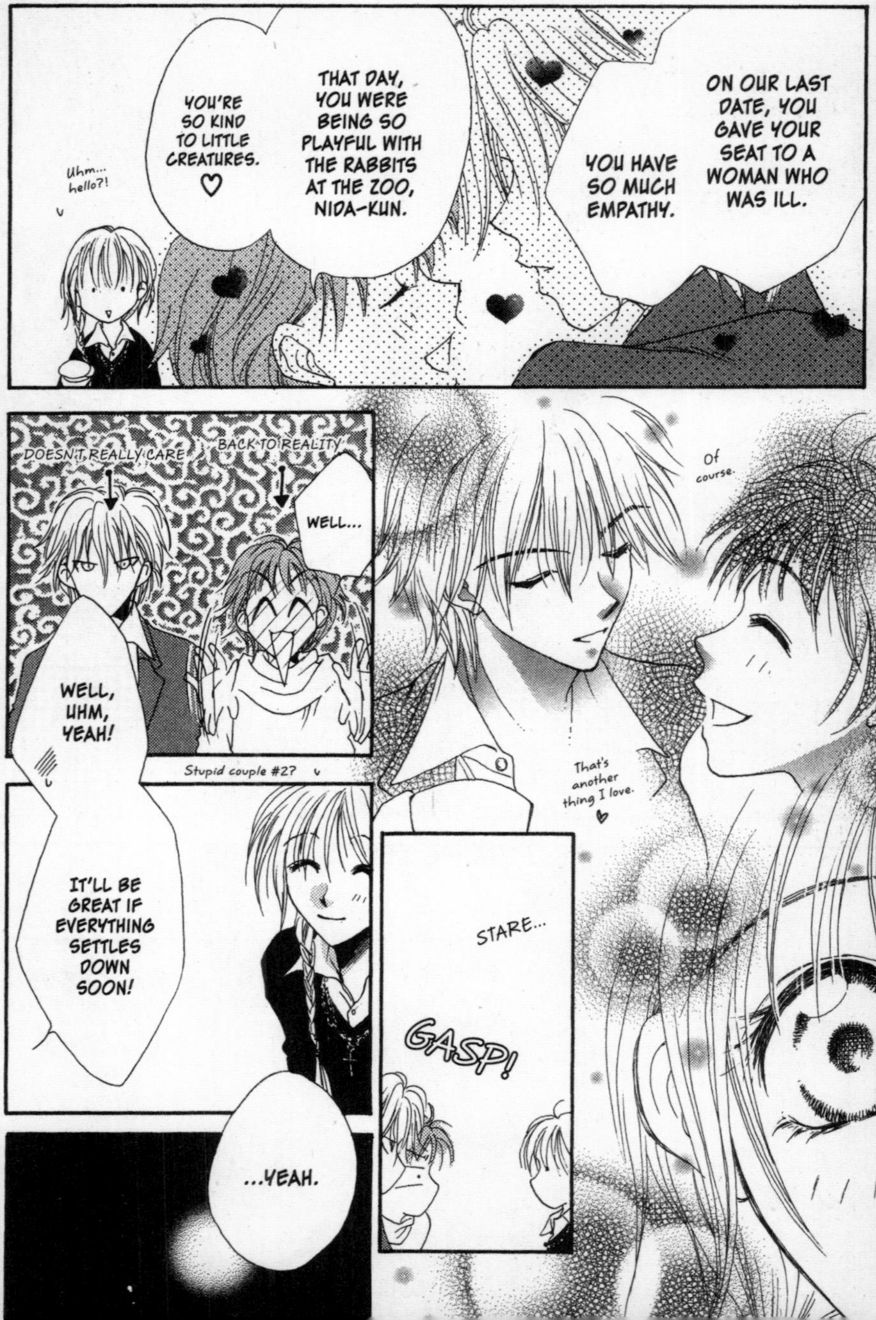
ON OUR LAST DATE, YOU GAVE YOUR SEAT TO A WOMAN WHO WAS ILL.
YOU HAVE SO MUCH EMPATHY.
THAT DAY, YOU WERE BEING SO PLAYFUL WITH THE RABBITS AT THE ZOO, NIDA-KUN.
YOU'RE SO KIND TO LITTLE CREATURES. ♡
Uhm... hello?!
Of course.
That's another thing I love. ♡
BACK TO REALITY
DOESN'T REALLY CARE
WELL...
WELL, UHM, YEAH!
Stupid couple #2?
IT'LL BE GREAT IF EVERYTHING SETTLES DOWN SOON!
STARE...
GASP!
...YEAH.

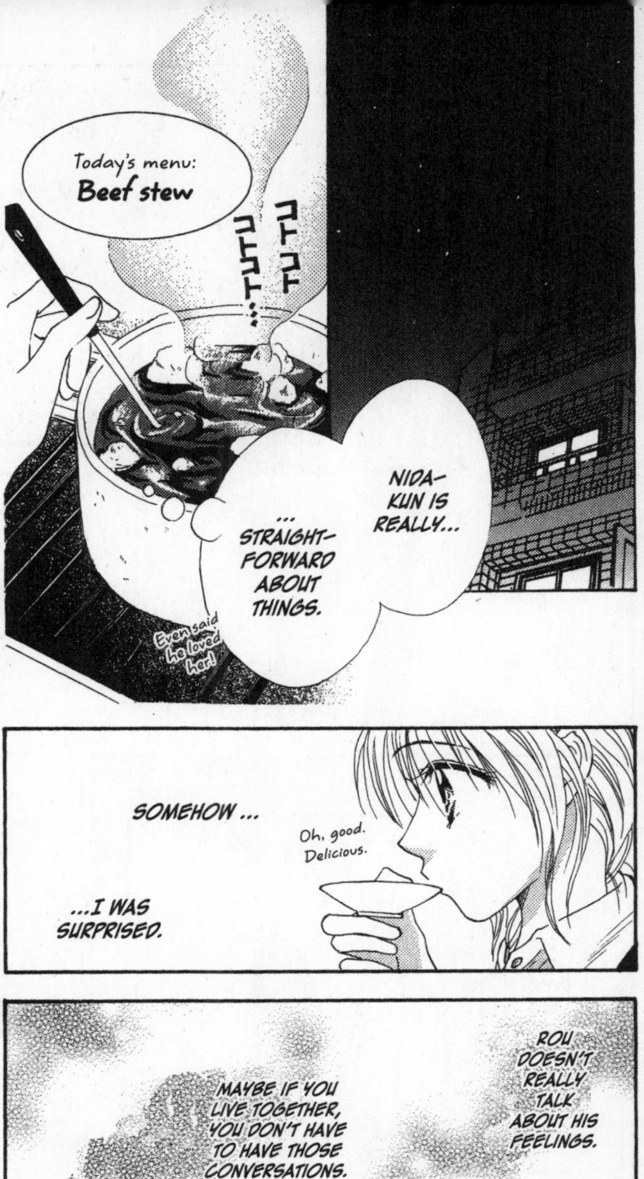
Today's menu:
Beef stew
TUTU TUTU
NIDA-KUN IS REALLY...
...STRAIGHT-FORWARD ABOUT THINGS.
Even said he loved her!
Oh, good. Delicious.
SOMEHOW...
...I WAS SURPRISED.
ROU DOESN'T REALLY TALK ABOUT HIS FEELINGS.
MAYBE IF YOU LIVE TOGETHER, YOU DON'T HAVE TO HAVE THOSE CONVERSATIONS.
WE DON'T NEED WORDS TO SHOW HOW WE FEEL.

2

CASE OF MANDARIN ORANGES

It has nothing to do with anything, but after writing the first quarter page, I said in Eyeball Geezer's voice, "Hey. Ki-rou!" Apparently, I sounded so much like Eyeball Geezer that I made my sister double over with laughter. I'm not sure how I feel about that.

So..."Case of Mandarin Oranges." I was enjoying my bento box as I was very relieved about finishing the script for Chapter 9, when there was a knock on the door. And it was my mom, with some mandarin oranges for dessert.

HOWEVER...

We had 10 mandarin oranges for three people. So we lined them up in pairs, and...

...THEY WERE ALL UPSIDE DOWN!!

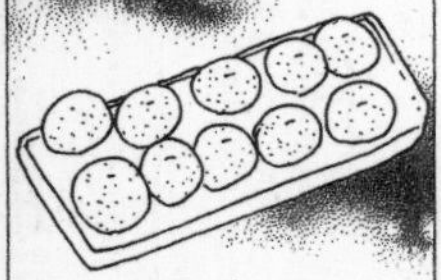

Wa ha ha ha ha ha!

Why are they all upside down?!

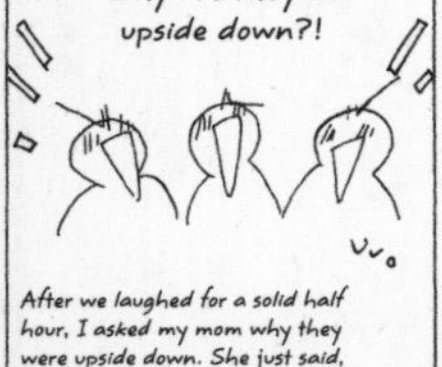

After we laughed for a solid half hour, I asked my mom why they were upside down. She just said, "Huh? Well, it seemed right."

...oh, mom...

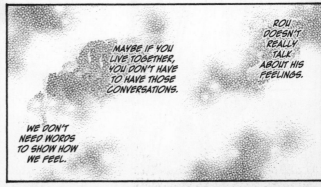

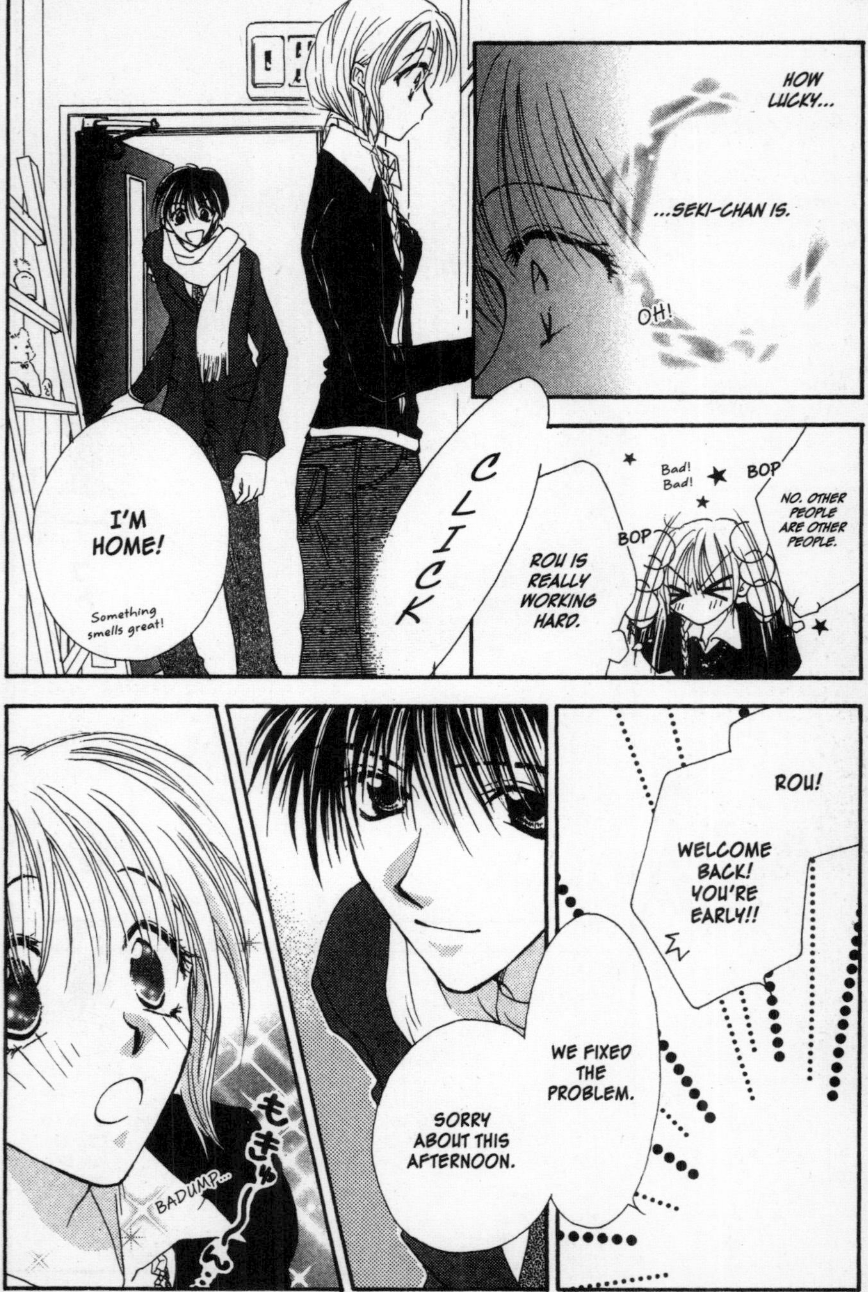
HOW LUCKY...
...SEKI-CHAN IS.
OH!
Bad! Bad!
BOP
NO. OTHER PEOPLE ARE OTHER PEOPLE.
ROU IS REALLY WORKING HARD.
BOP
CLICK
I'M HOME!
Something smells great!
ROU!
WELCOME BACK! YOU'RE EARLY!!
WE FIXED THE PROBLEM.
SORRY ABOUT THIS AFTERNOON.
BADUMP...

Stupid.

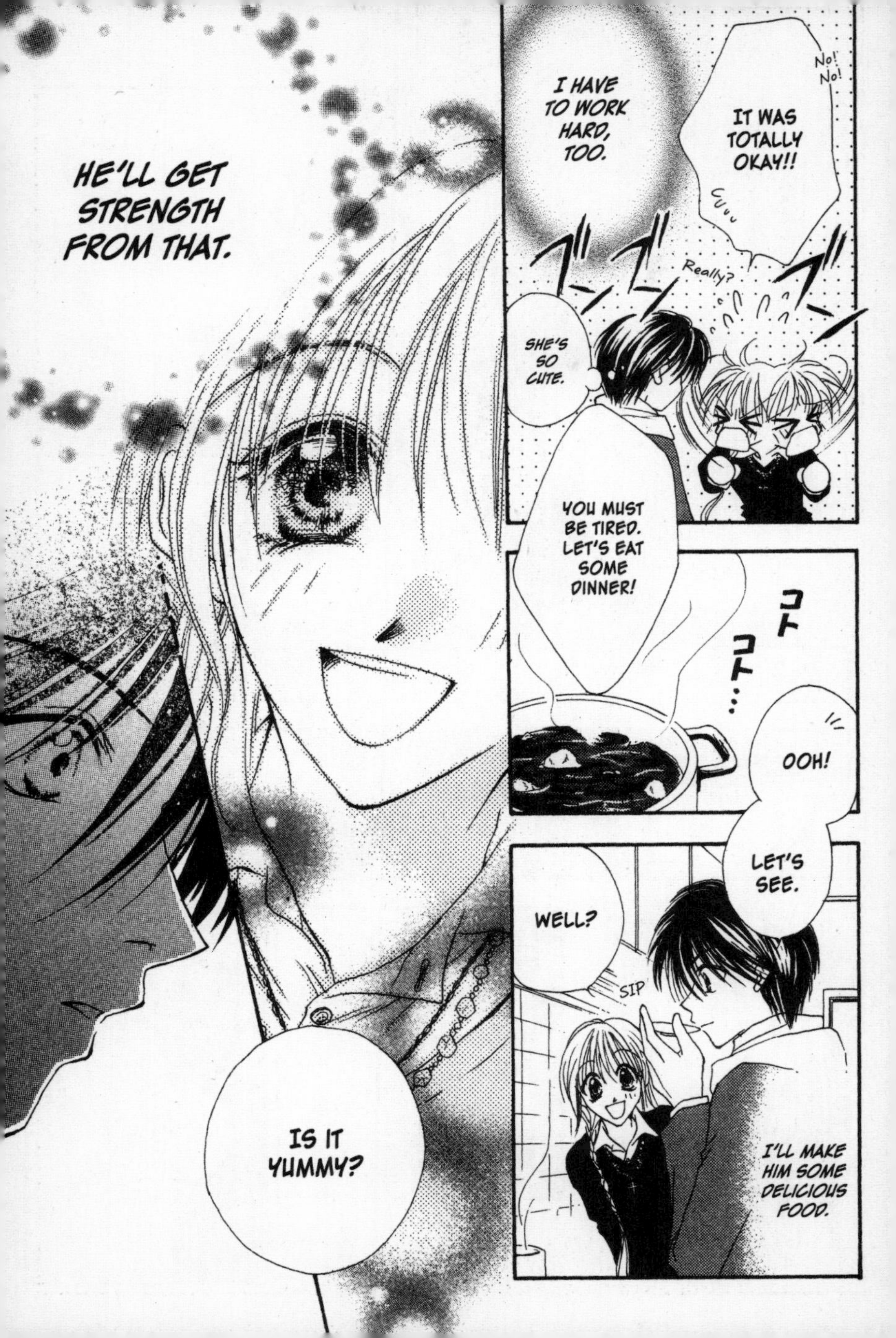
No! No!
IT WAS TOTALLY OKAY!!
I HAVE TO WORK HARD, TOO.
Really?
SHE'S SO CUTE.
YOU MUST BE TIRED. LET'S EAT SOME DINNER!
コト コト…
OOH!
LET'S SEE.
WELL?
SIP
I'LL MAKE HIM SOME DELICIOUS FOOD.
HE'LL GET STRENGTH FROM THAT.
IS IT YUMMY?

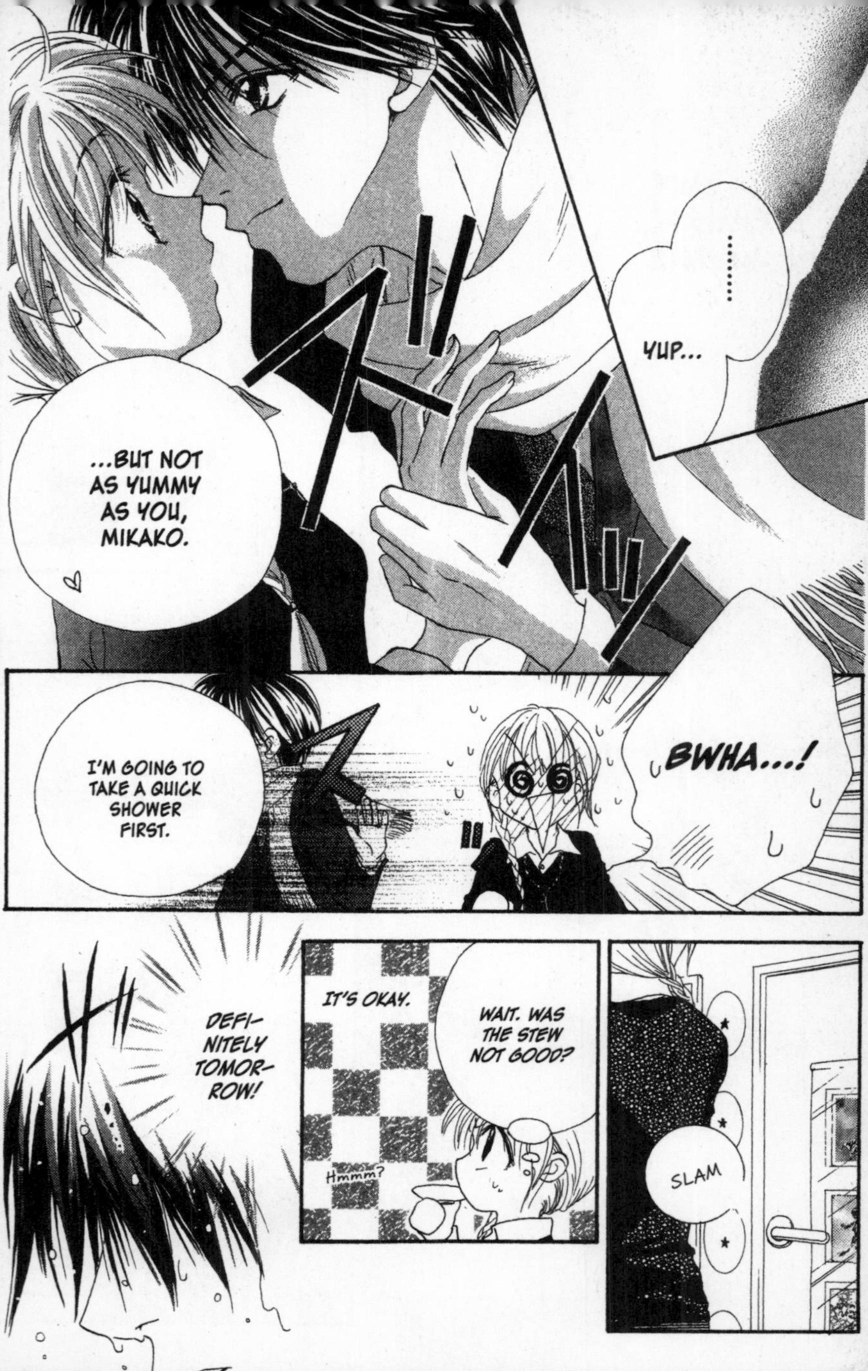
......
YUP...
...BUT NOT AS YUMMY AS YOU, MIKAKO.
BWHA...!
I'M GOING TO TAKE A QUICK SHOWER FIRST.
SLAM
WAIT. WAS THE STEW NOT GOOD?
IT'S OKAY.
Hmmm?
DEFI-NITELY TOMOR-ROW!

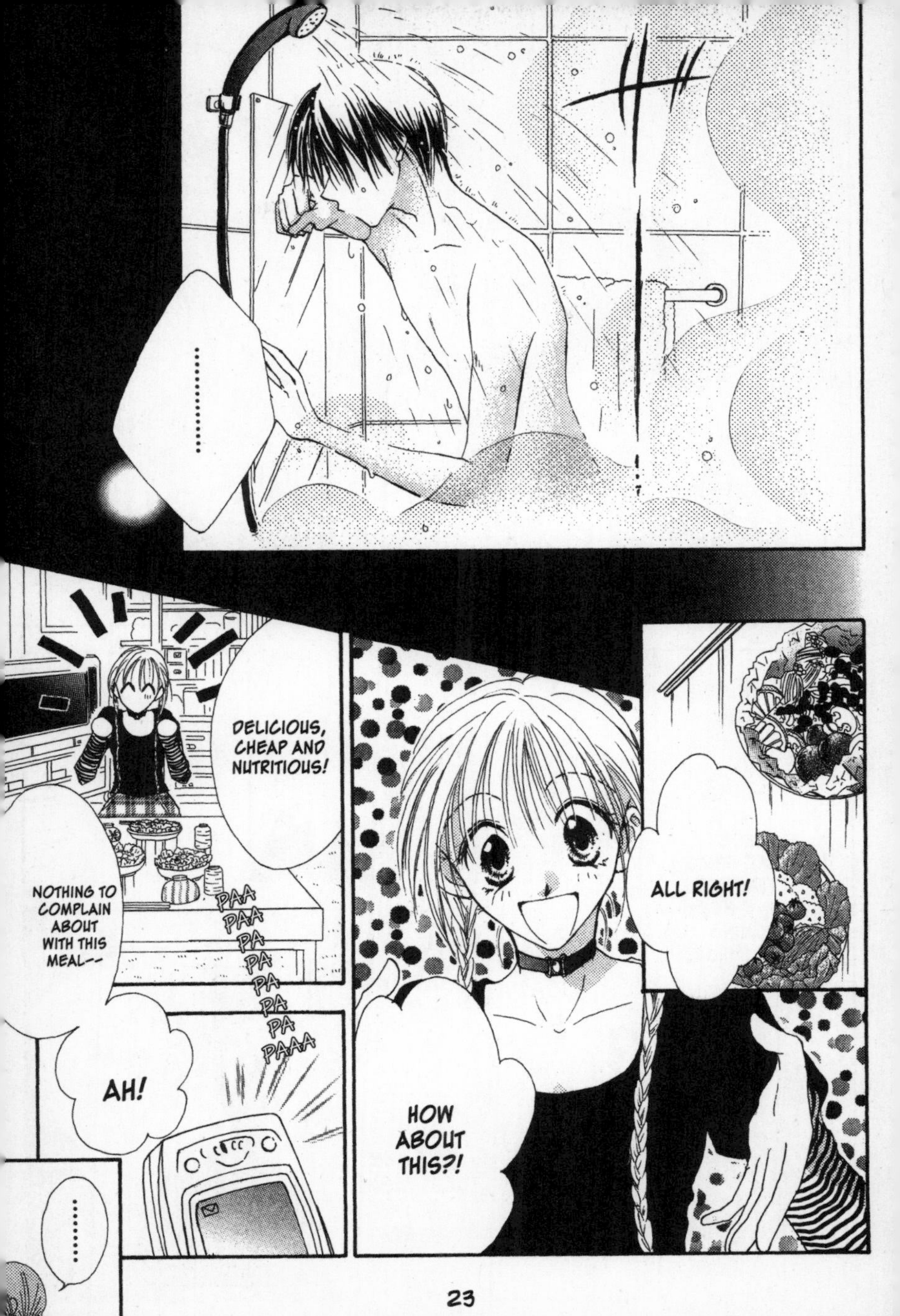
....
ALL RIGHT!
HOW ABOUT THIS?!
DELICIOUS, CHEAP AND NUTRITIOUS!
NOTHING TO COMPLAIN ABOUT WITH THIS MEAL--
PAA PAA PA PA PA PA PA PAAA
AH!
....

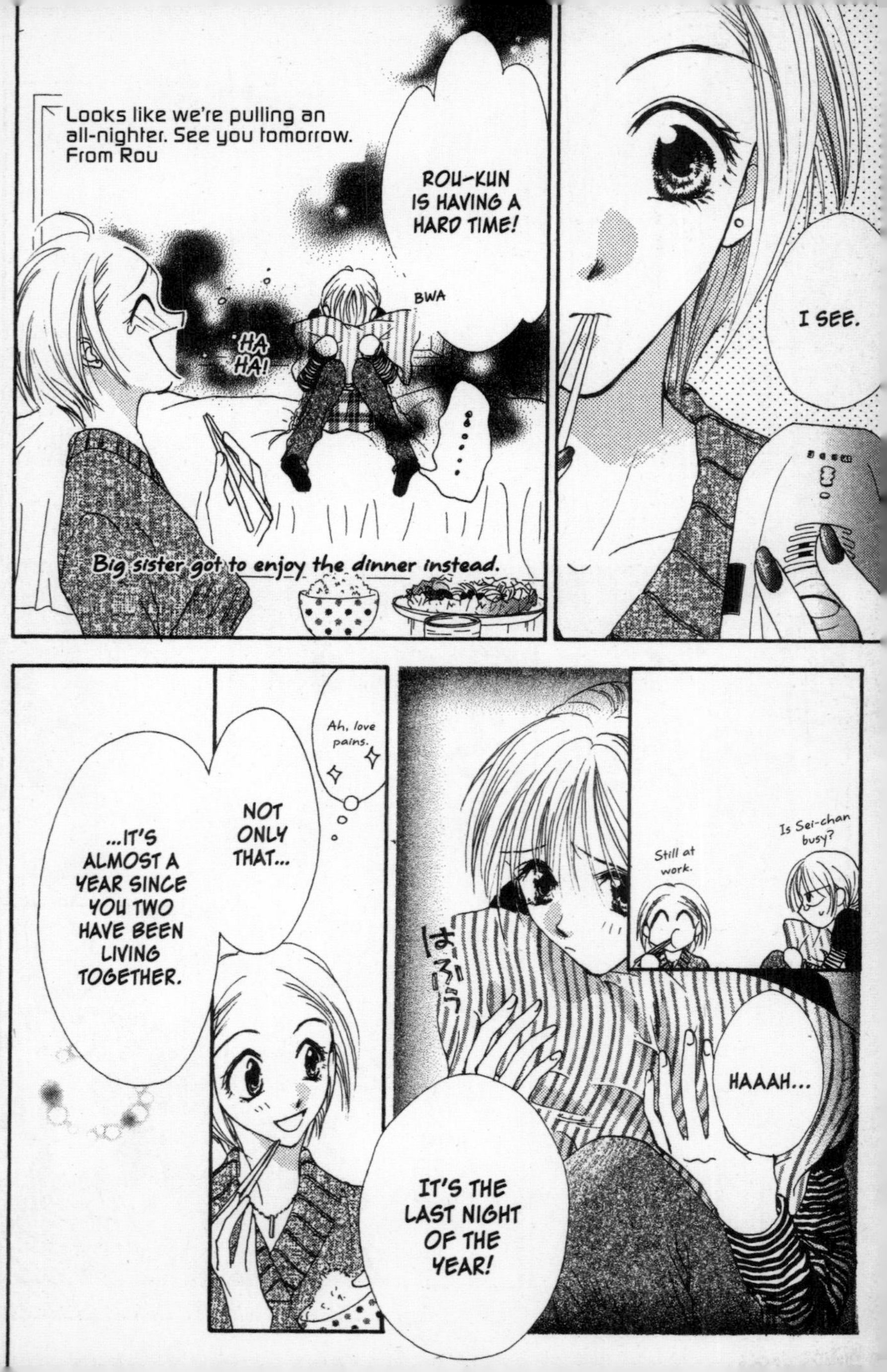
I SEE.
ROU-KUN IS HAVING A HARD TIME!
Looks like we're pulling an all-nighter. See you tomorrow. From Rou
BWA
......
HA HA!
Big sister got to enjoy the dinner instead.
Is Sei-chan busy?
Still at work.
はふぅ
HAAAH...
IT'S THE LAST NIGHT OF THE YEAR!
Ah, love pains.
NOT ONLY THAT...
...IT'S ALMOST A YEAR SINCE YOU TWO HAVE BEEN LIVING TOGETHER.

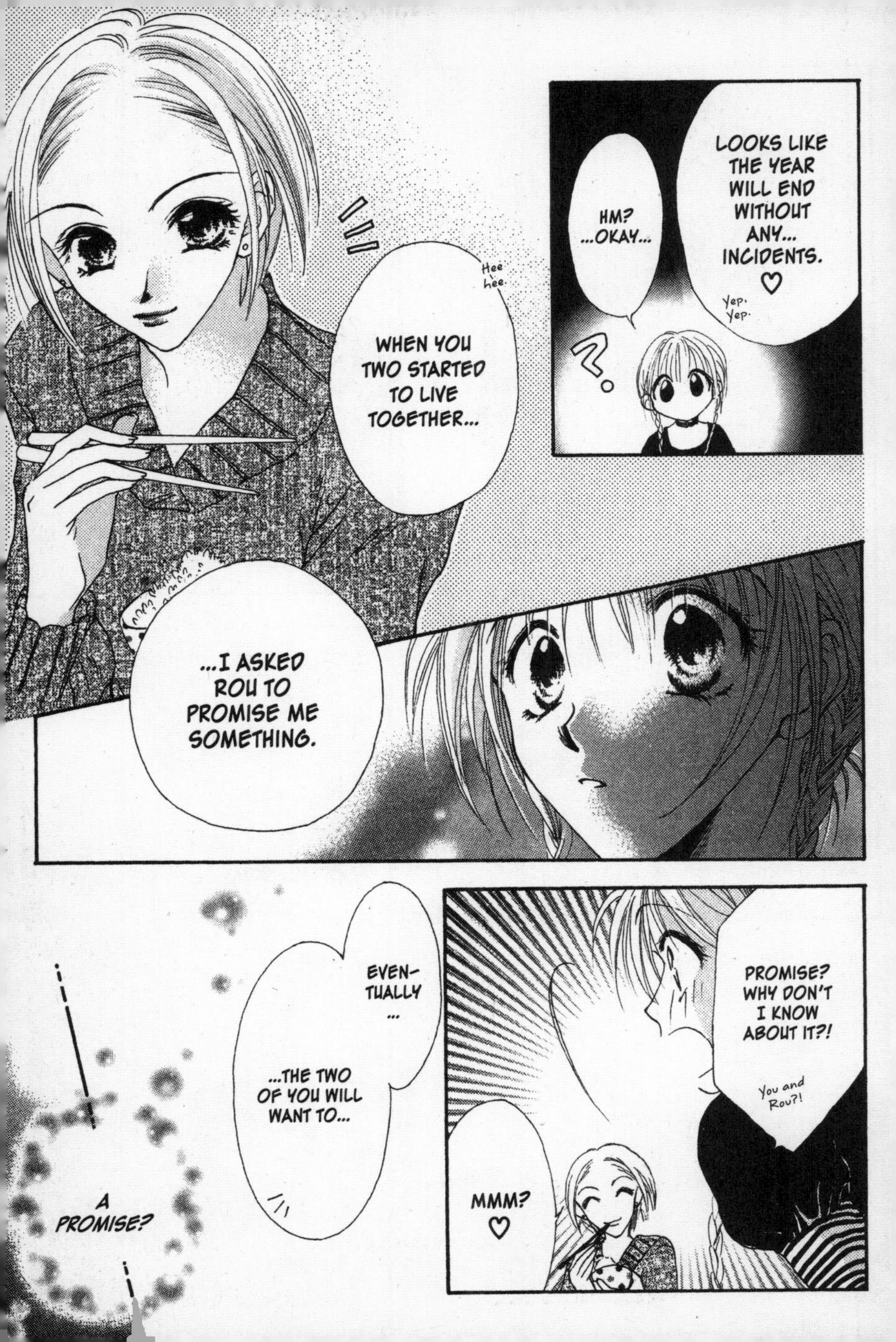
LOOKS LIKE THE YEAR WILL END WITHOUT ANY... INCIDENTS. ♡
Yep, Yep.
HM? ...OKAY...
?
Hee hee.
WHEN YOU TWO STARTED TO LIVE TOGETHER...
...I ASKED ROU TO PROMISE ME SOMETHING.
PROMISE? WHY DON'T I KNOW ABOUT IT?!
You and Rou?!
MMM? ♡
EVEN-TUALLY ...
...THE TWO OF YOU WILL WANT TO...
A PROMISE?

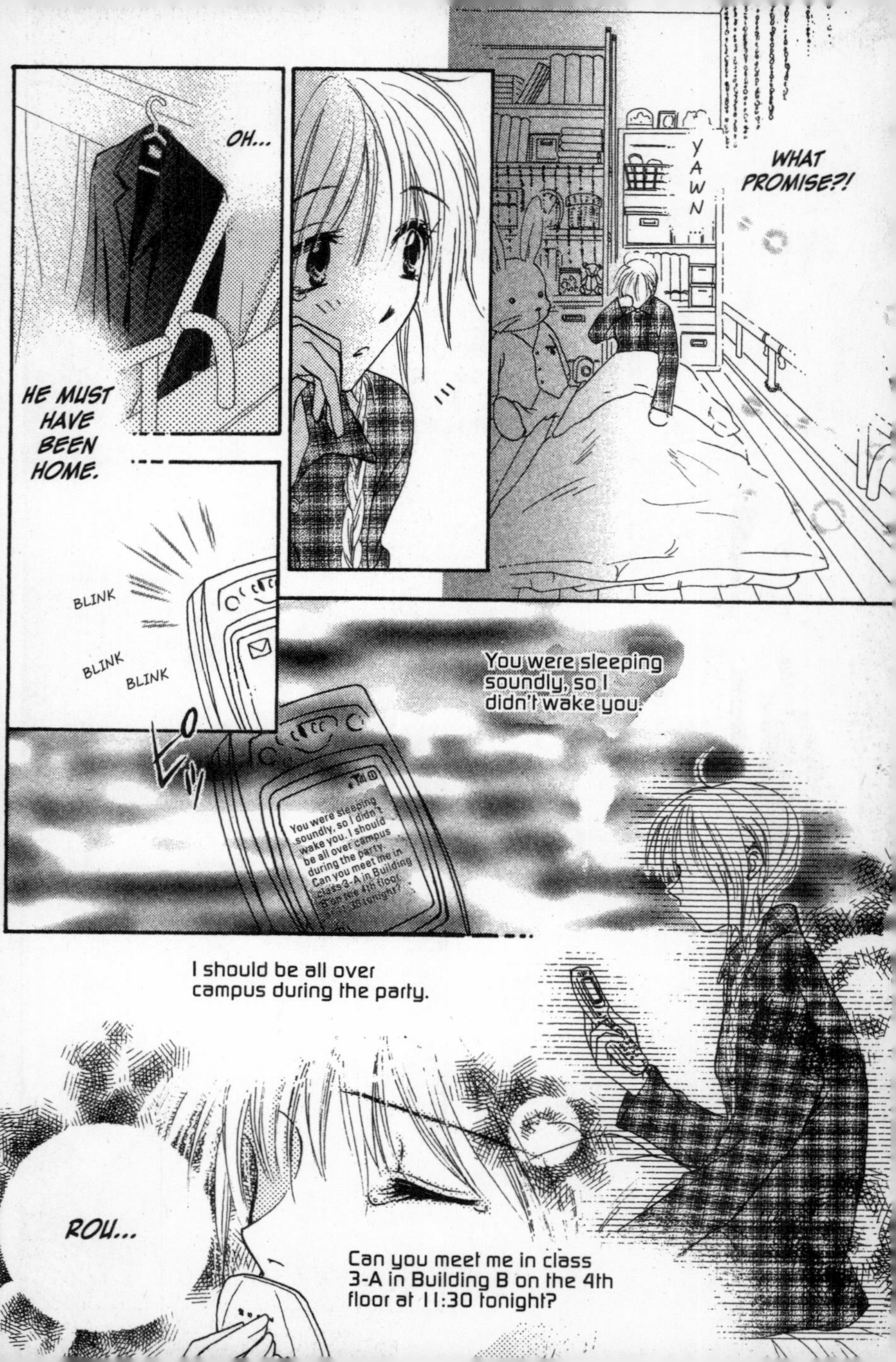
WHAT PROMISE?!
YAWN...
OH...
HE MUST HAVE BEEN HOME.
BLINK
BLINK
BLINK
You were sleeping soundly, so I didn't wake you.
You were sleeping soundly, so I didn't wake you. I should be all over campus during the party. Can you meet me in class 3-A in Building
I should be all over campus during the party.
Can you meet me in class 3-A in Building B on the 4th floor at 11:30 tonight?
ROU...

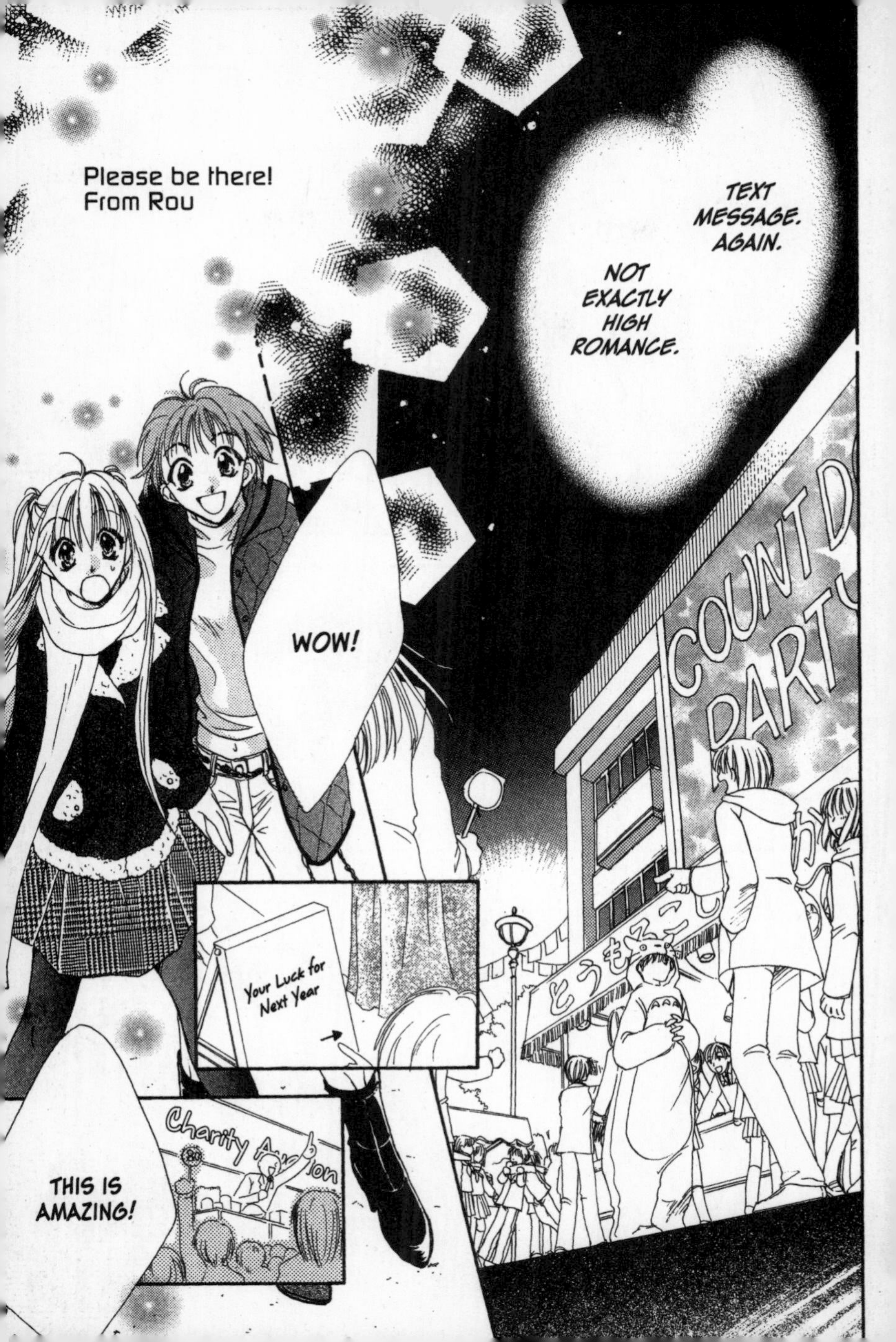
TEXT MESSAGE. AGAIN.
NOT EXACTLY HIGH ROMANCE.
Please be there!
From Rou
WOW!
Your Luck for Next Year
THIS IS AMAZING!

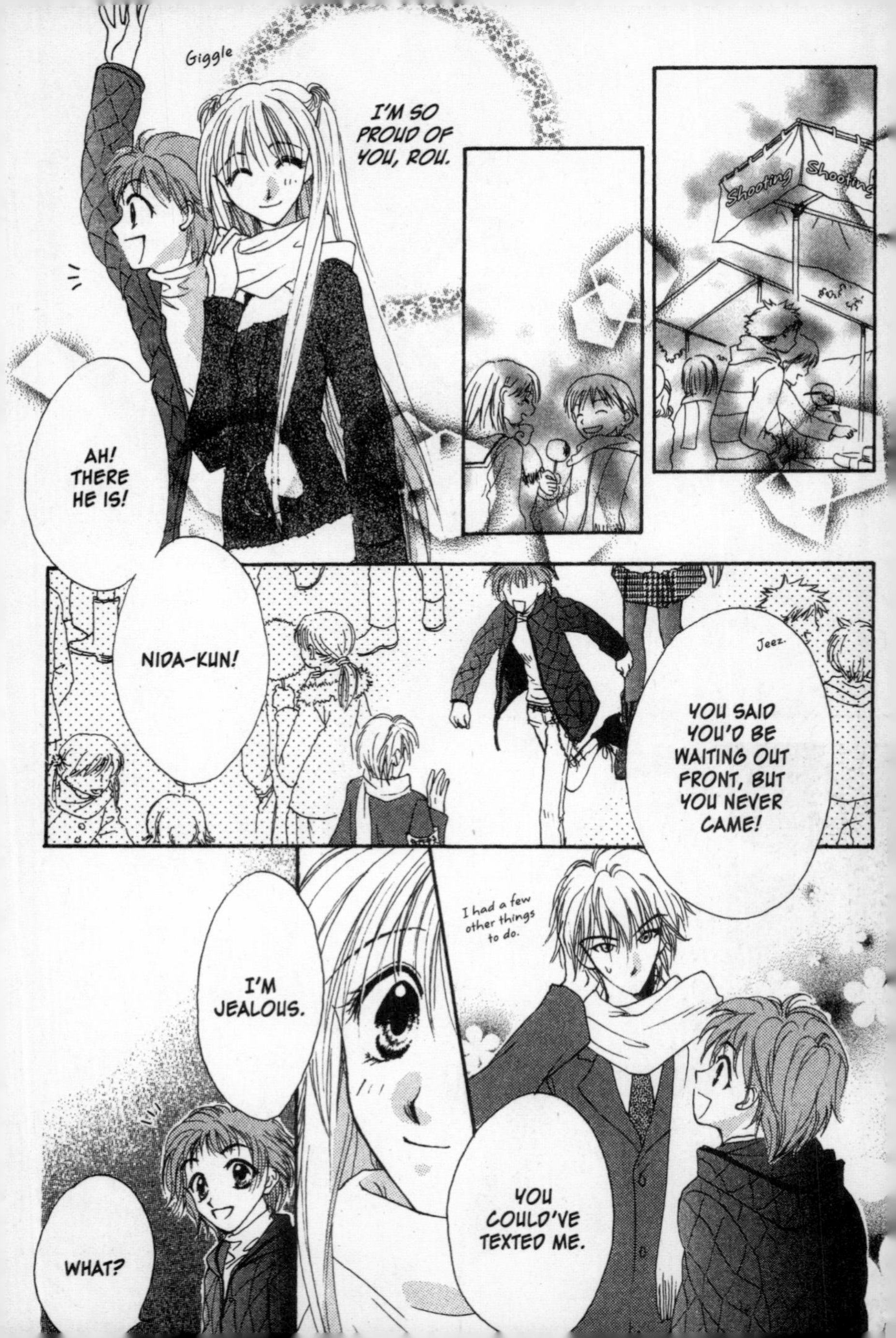
Shooting Shooting
I'M SO PROUD OF YOU, ROU.
Giggle
AH! THERE HE IS!
NIDA-KUN!
Jeez.
YOU SAID YOU'D BE WAITING OUT FRONT, BUT YOU NEVER CAME!
I had a few other things to do.
YOU COULD'VE TEXTED ME.
I'M JEALOUS.
WHAT?

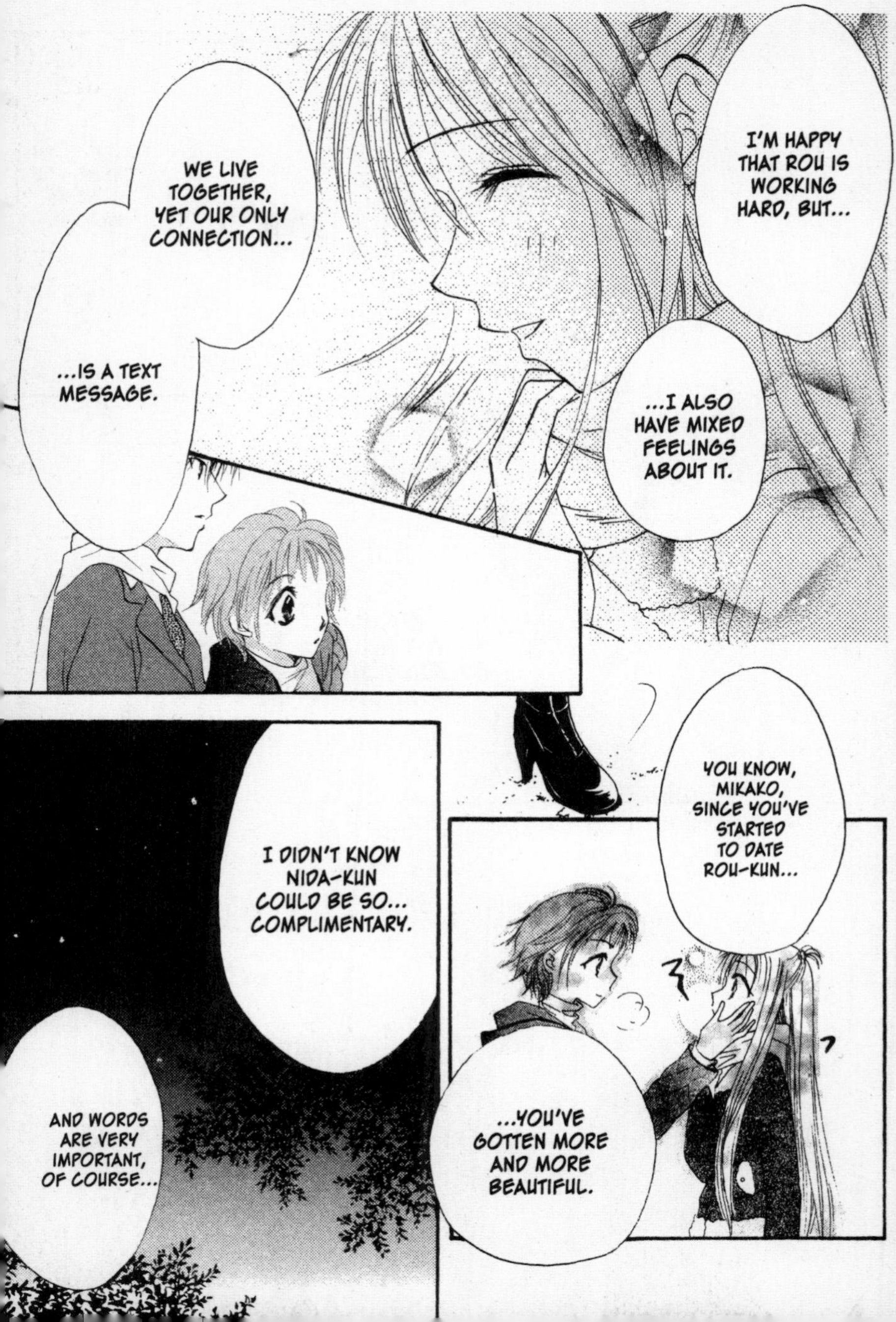
I'M HAPPY THAT ROU IS WORKING HARD, BUT...
...I ALSO HAVE MIXED FEELINGS ABOUT IT.
WE LIVE TOGETHER, YET OUR ONLY CONNECTION...
...IS A TEXT MESSAGE.
YOU KNOW, MIKAKO, SINCE YOU'VE STARTED TO DATE ROU-KUN...
...YOU'VE GOTTEN MORE AND MORE BEAUTIFUL.
I DIDN'T KNOW NIDA-KUN COULD BE SO... COMPLIMENTARY.
AND WORDS ARE VERY IMPORTANT, OF COURSE...

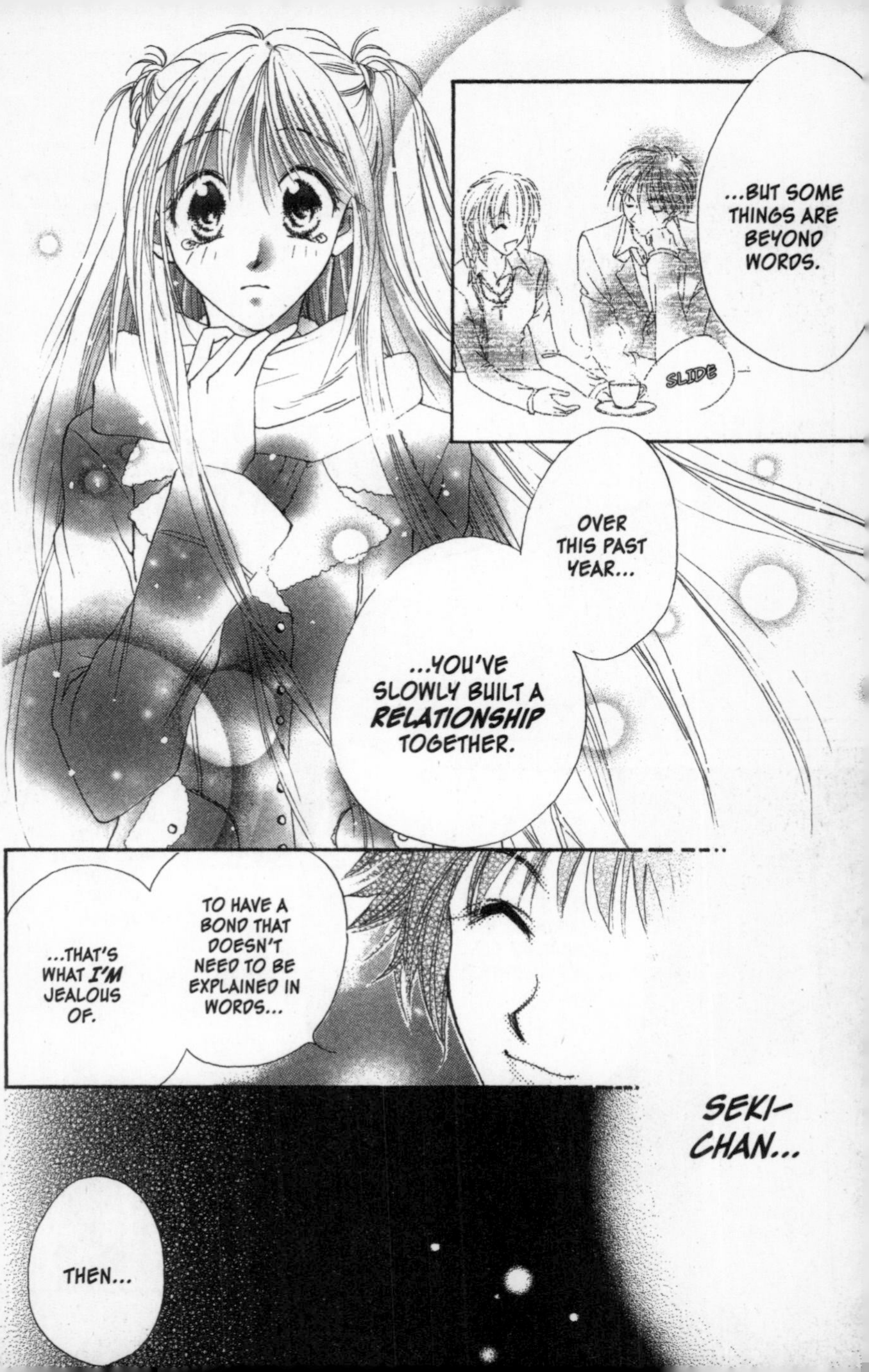
...BUT SOME THINGS ARE BEYOND WORDS.
SLIDE
OVER THIS PAST YEAR...
...YOU'VE SLOWLY BUILT A *RELATIONSHIP* TOGETHER.
TO HAVE A BOND THAT DOESN'T NEED TO BE EXPLAINED IN WORDS...
...THAT'S WHAT *I'M* JEALOUS OF.
SEKI-CHAN...
THEN...

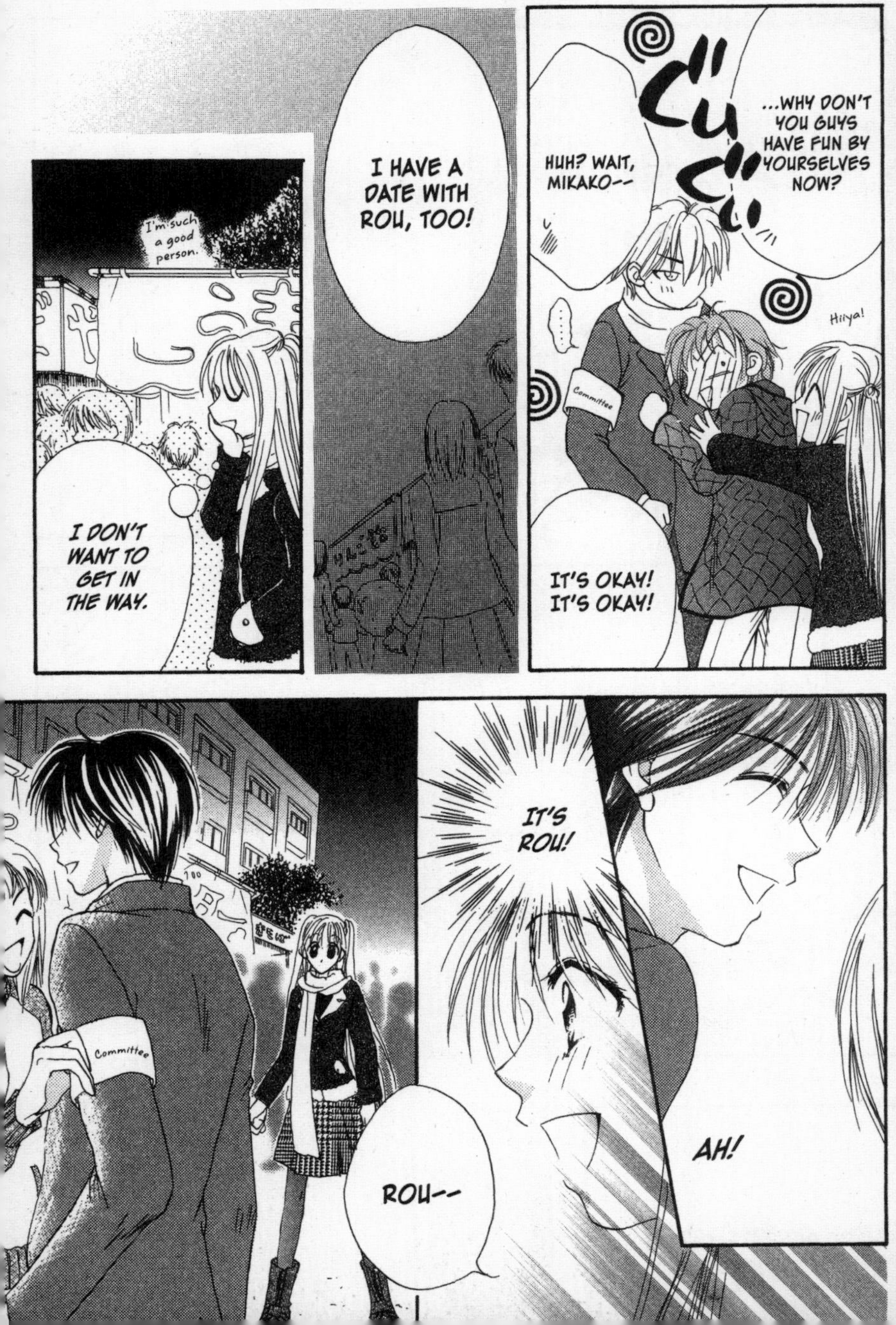
...WHY DON'T YOU GUYS HAVE FUN BY YOURSELVES NOW?
ぐいぐい
HUH? WAIT, MIKAKO--
Hiiya!
...
IT'S OKAY! IT'S OKAY!
I HAVE A DATE WITH ROU, TOO!
I'm such a good person.
I DON'T WANT TO GET IN THE WAY.
IT'S ROU!
AH!
ROU--

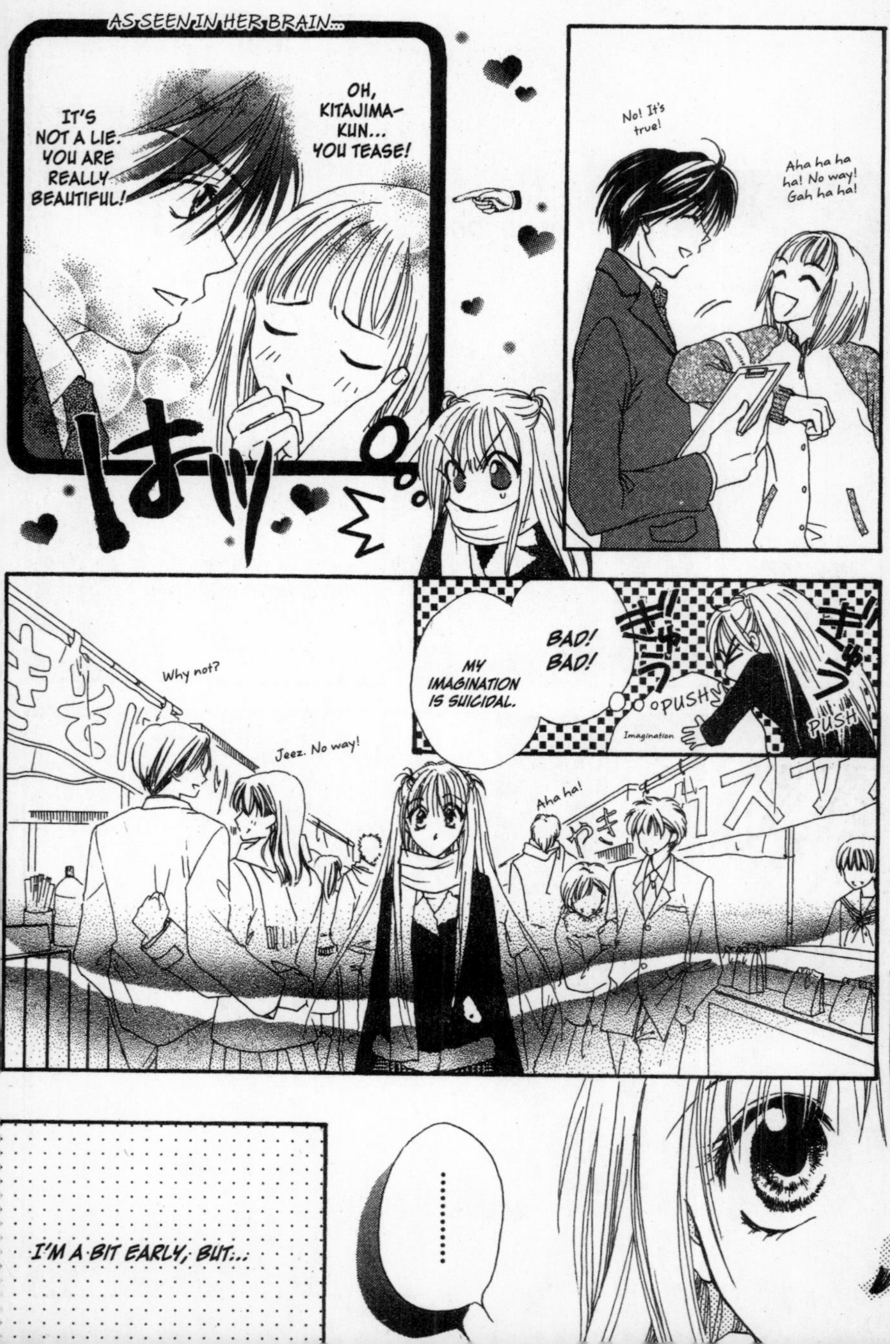
Aha ha ha ha! No way! Gah ha ha!
No! It's true!
AS SEEN IN HER BRAIN...
OH, KITAJIMA-KUN... YOU TEASE!
IT'S NOT A LIE. YOU ARE REALLY BEAUTIFUL!
はッ
ぎゅう
ぎゅう
PUSH
PUSH
Imagination
BAD! BAD!
MY IMAGINATION IS SUICIDAL.
Aha ha!
Jeez. No way!
Why not?
......
I'M A BIT EARLY, BUT...

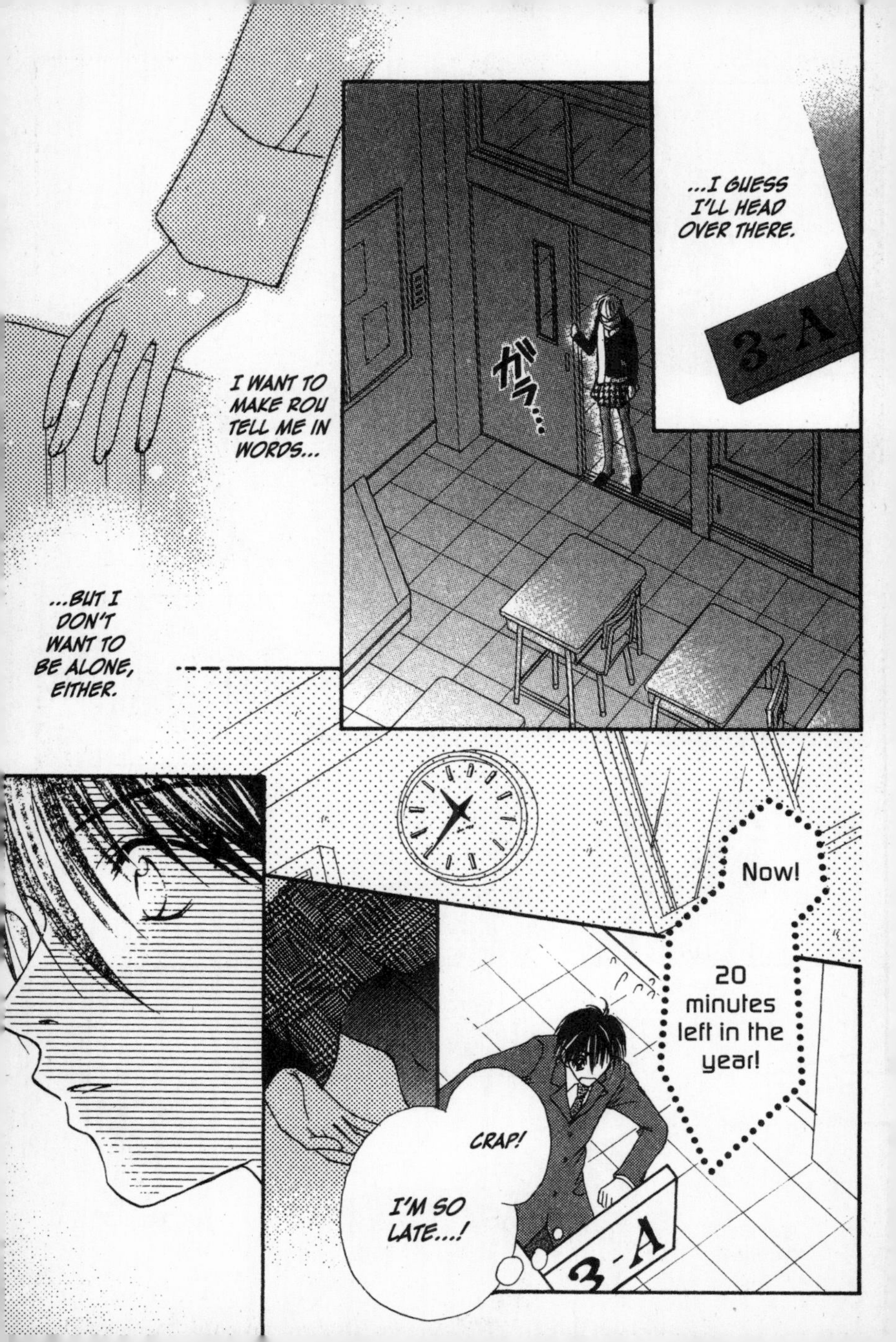

...I GUESS I'LL HEAD OVER THERE.
3-A
ガラ...
I WANT TO MAKE ROU TELL ME IN WORDS...
...BUT I DON'T WANT TO BE ALONE, EITHER.
Now!
20 minutes left in the year!
CRAP!
I'M SO LATE...!
3-A

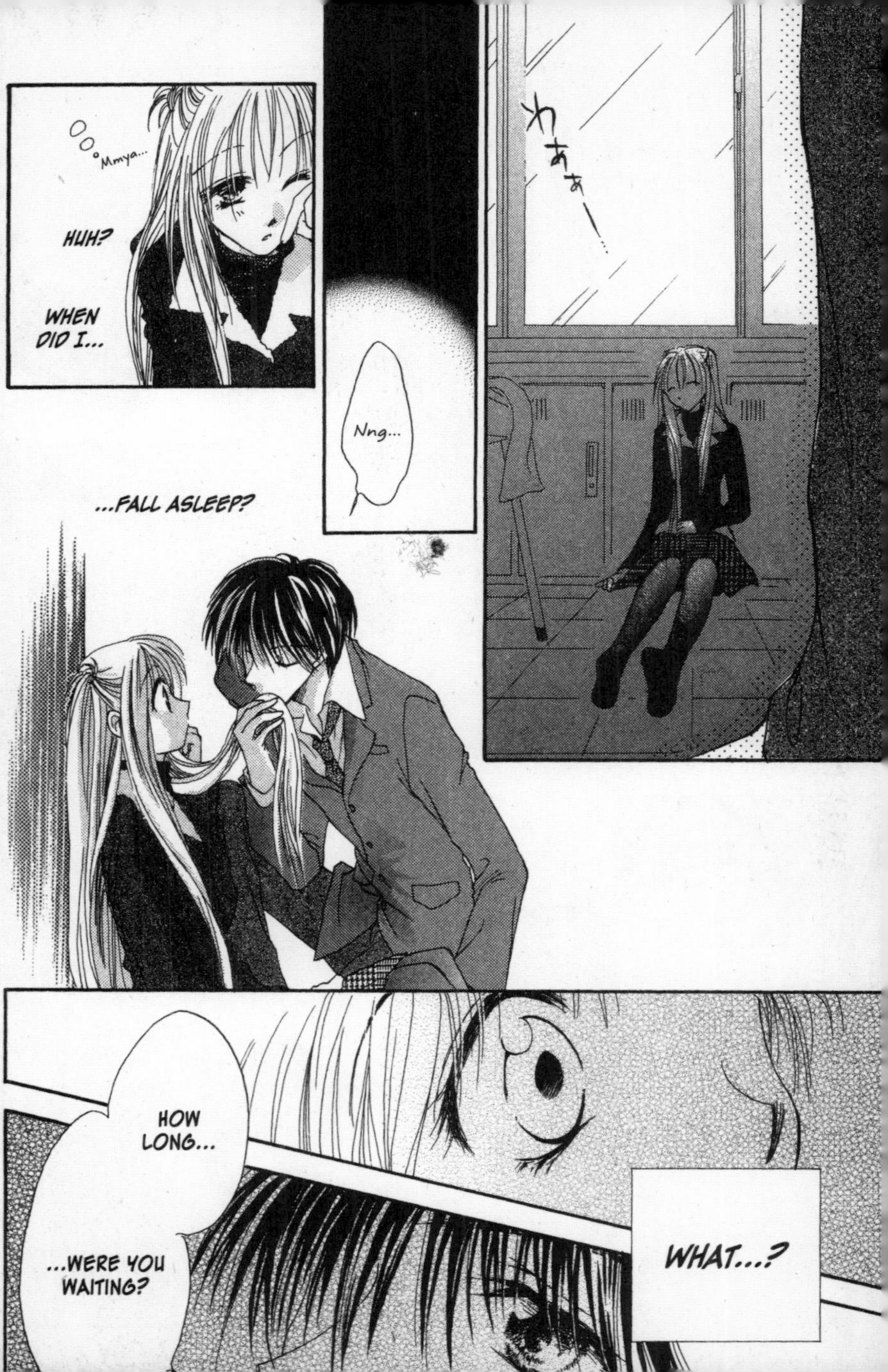
わぁぁー…
Nng...
Mmya...
HUH?
WHEN DID I...
...FALL ASLEEP?
WHAT...?
HOW LONG...
...WERE YOU WAITING?

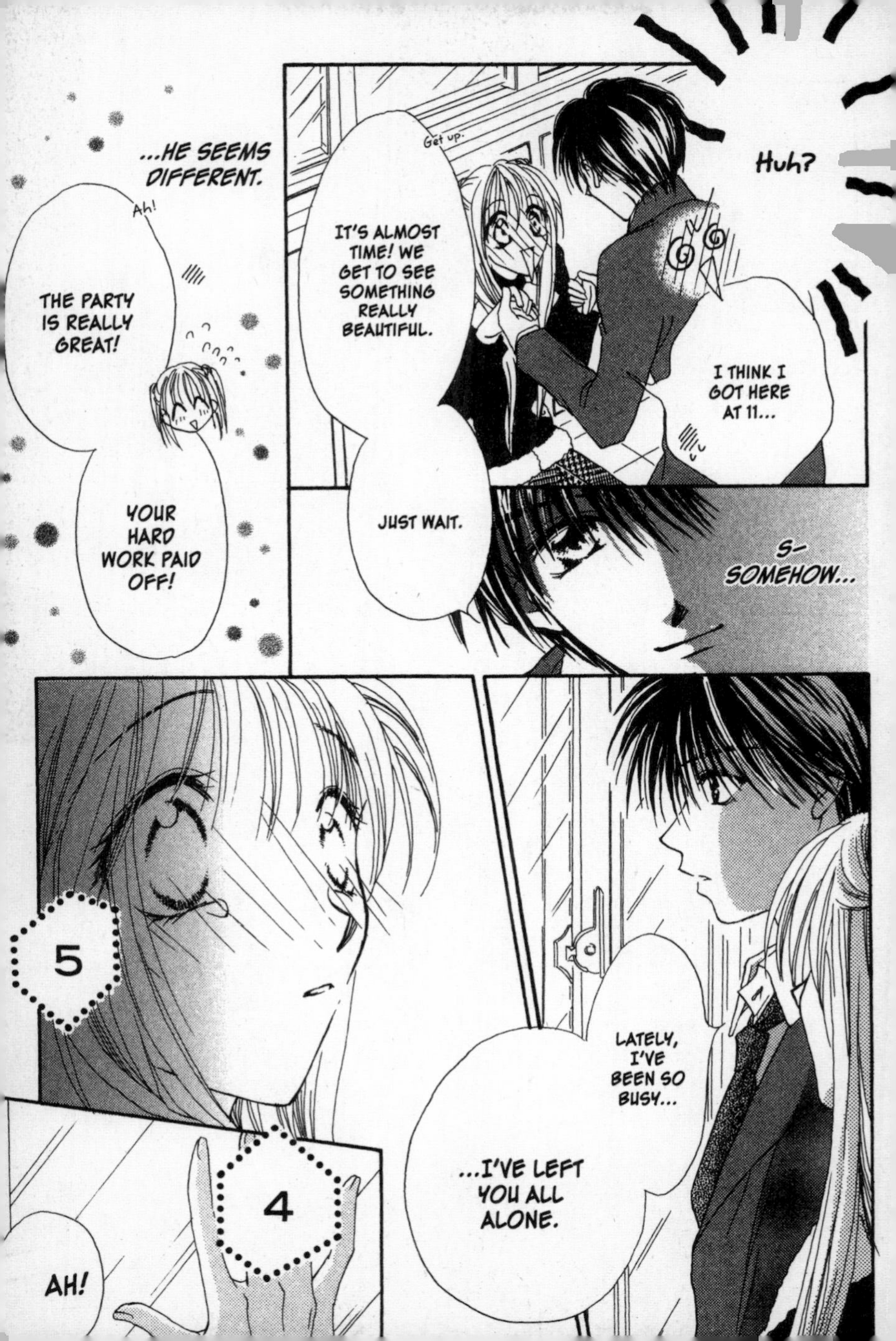
Huh?
I THINK I GOT HERE AT 11...
Get up.
IT'S ALMOST TIME! WE GET TO SEE SOMETHING REALLY BEAUTIFUL.
S-SOMEHOW...
JUST WAIT.
...HE SEEMS DIFFERENT.
Ah!
THE PARTY IS REALLY GREAT!
YOUR HARD WORK PAID OFF!
LATELY, I'VE BEEN SO BUSY...
...I'VE LEFT YOU ALL ALONE.
5
4
AH!

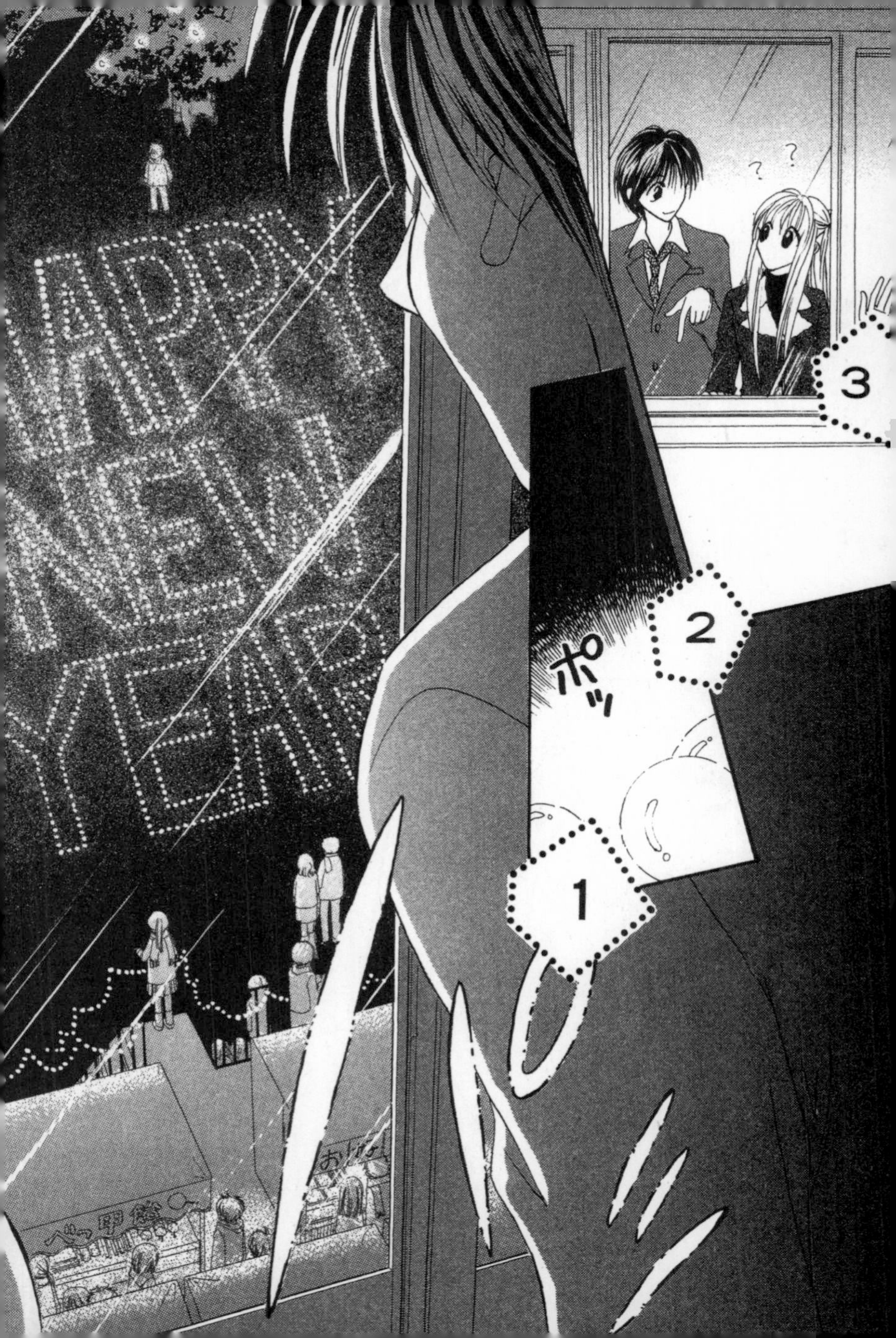
? ?
3
2
ポッ
1
APPY NEW YEAR

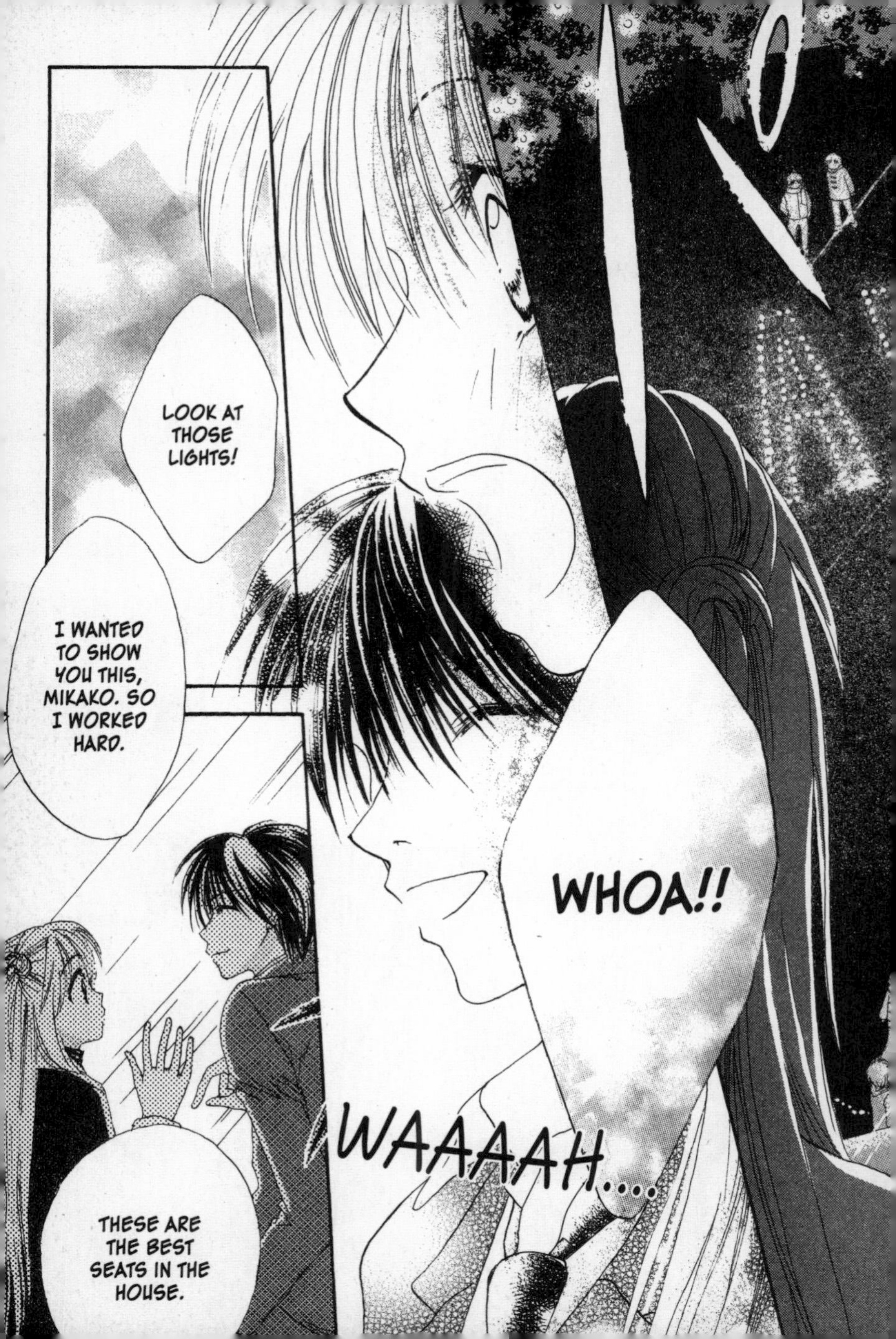
WHOA!!
WAAAAH....
LOOK AT THOSE LIGHTS!
I WANTED TO SHOW YOU THIS, MIKAKO. SO I WORKED HARD.
THESE ARE THE BEST SEATS IN THE HOUSE.

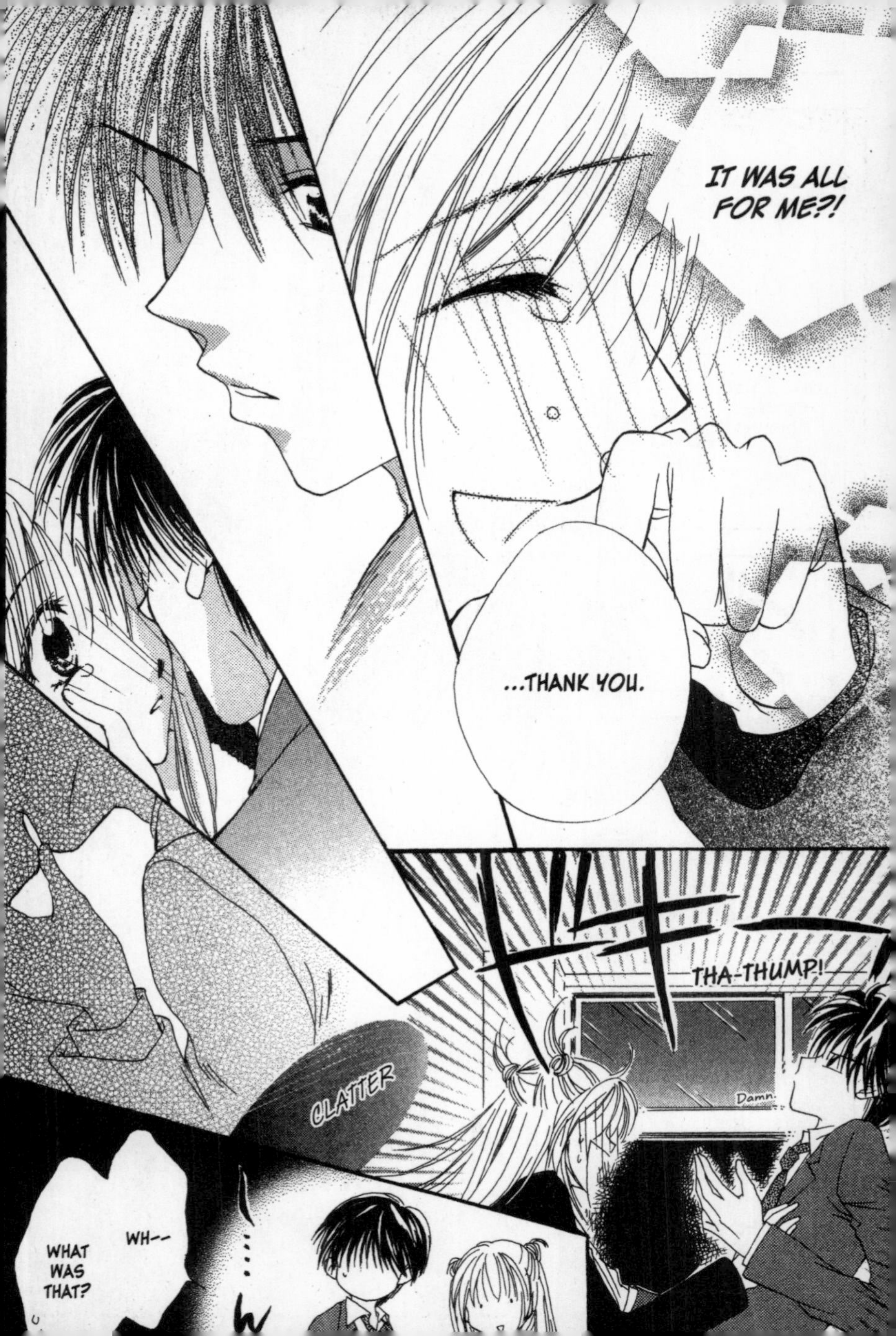
IT WAS ALL FOR ME?!
...THANK YOU.
THA-THUMP!
Damn.
CLATTER
...
WH--
WHAT WAS THAT?

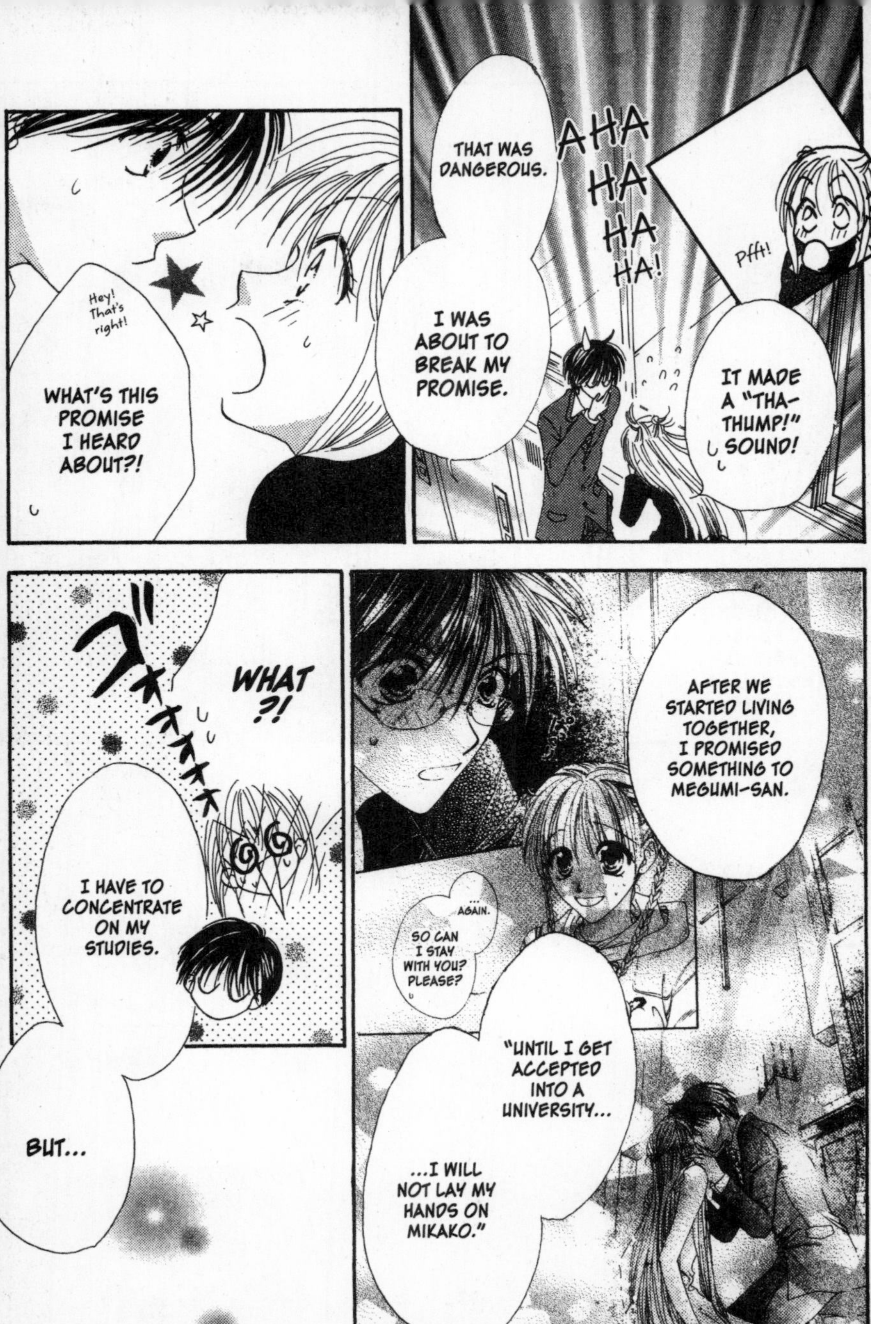
Pfft!
AHA HA HA HA!
THAT WAS DANGEROUS.
I WAS ABOUT TO BREAK MY PROMISE.
IT MADE A "THA-THUMP!" SOUND!
Hey! That's right!
WHAT'S THIS PROMISE I HEARD ABOUT?!
AFTER WE STARTED LIVING TOGETHER, I PROMISED SOMETHING TO MEGUMI-SAN.
...AGAIN.
SO CAN I STAY WITH YOU? PLEASE?
"UNTIL I GET ACCEPTED INTO A UNIVERSITY...
...I WILL NOT LAY MY HANDS ON MIKAKO."
WHAT?!
I HAVE TO CONCENTRATE ON MY STUDIES.
BUT...

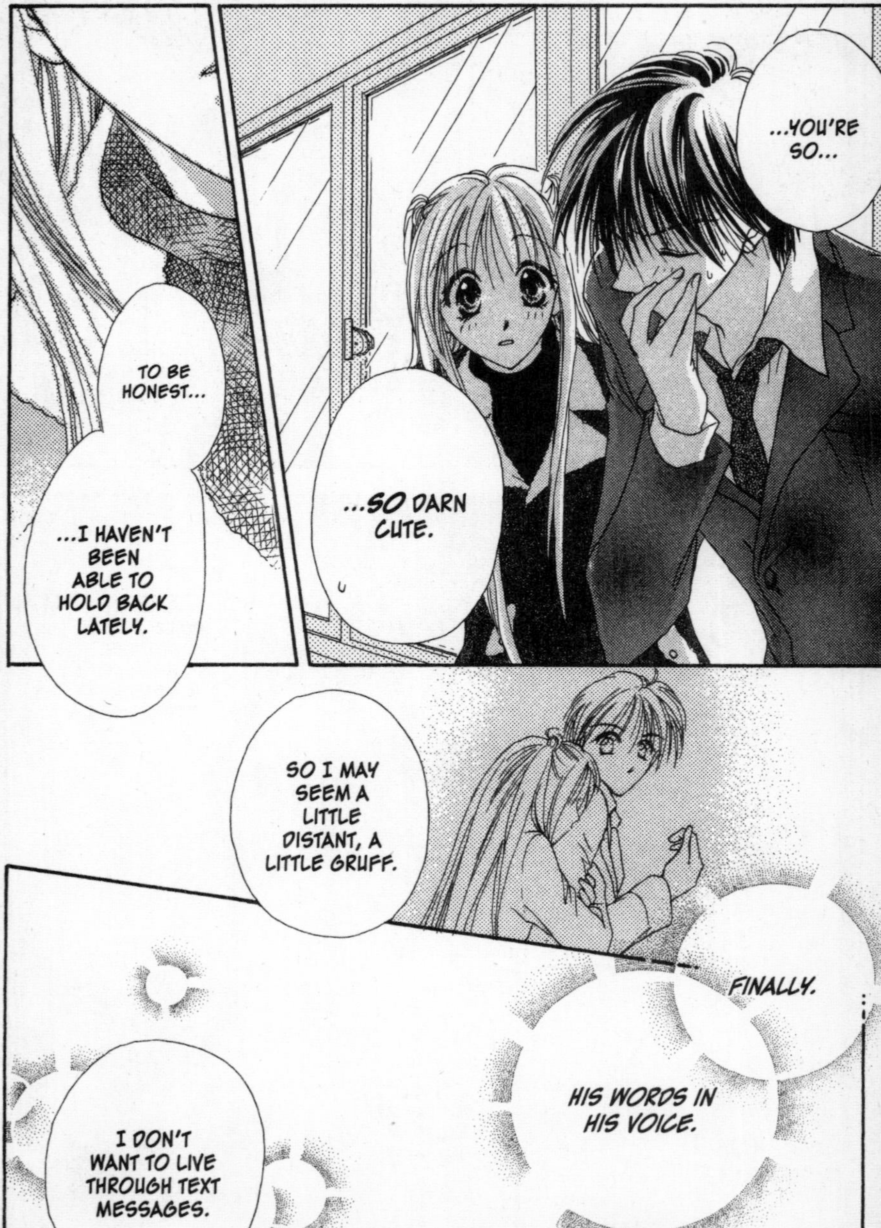
...YOU'RE SO...
...SO DARN CUTE.
TO BE HONEST...
...I HAVEN'T BEEN ABLE TO HOLD BACK LATELY.
SO I MAY SEEM A LITTLE DISTANT, A LITTLE GRUFF.
FINALLY.
HIS WORDS IN HIS VOICE.
I DON'T WANT TO LIVE THROUGH TEXT MESSAGES.

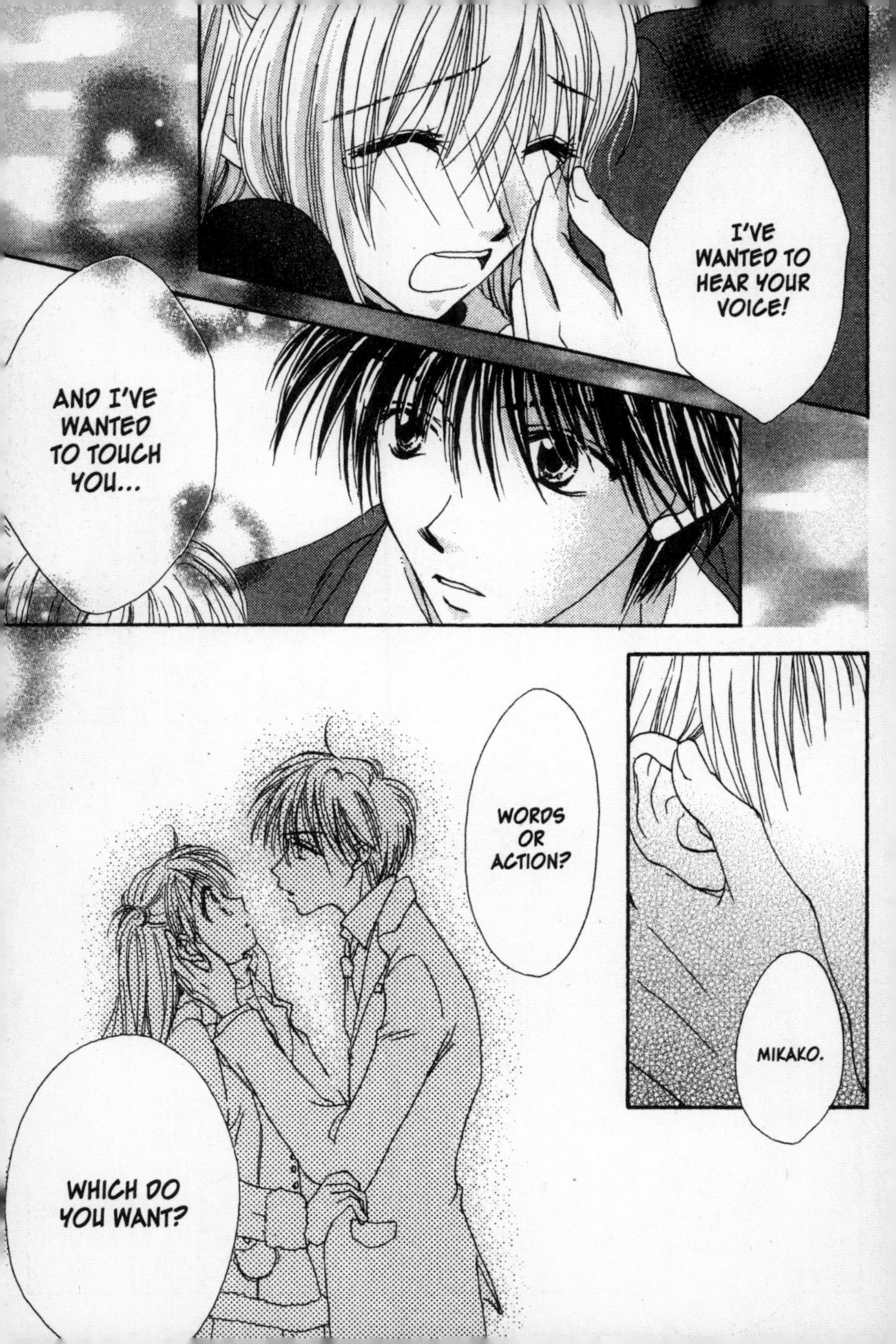
I'VE WANTED TO HEAR YOUR VOICE!
AND I'VE WANTED TO TOUCH YOU...
MIKAKO.
WORDS OR ACTION?
WHICH DO YOU WANT?

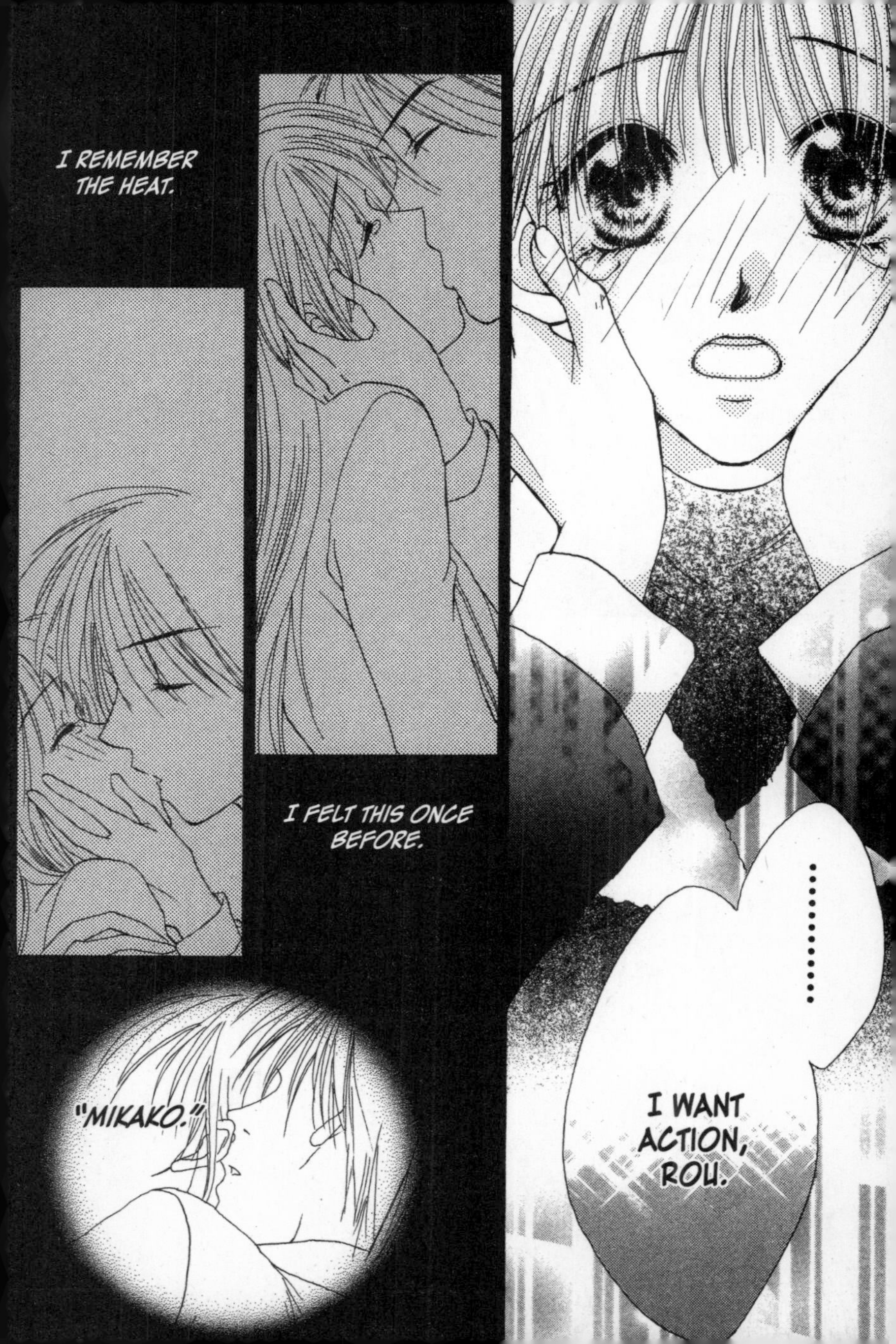

I REMEMBER THE HEAT.
I FELT THIS ONCE BEFORE.
"MIKAKO."
......
I WANT ACTION, ROU.

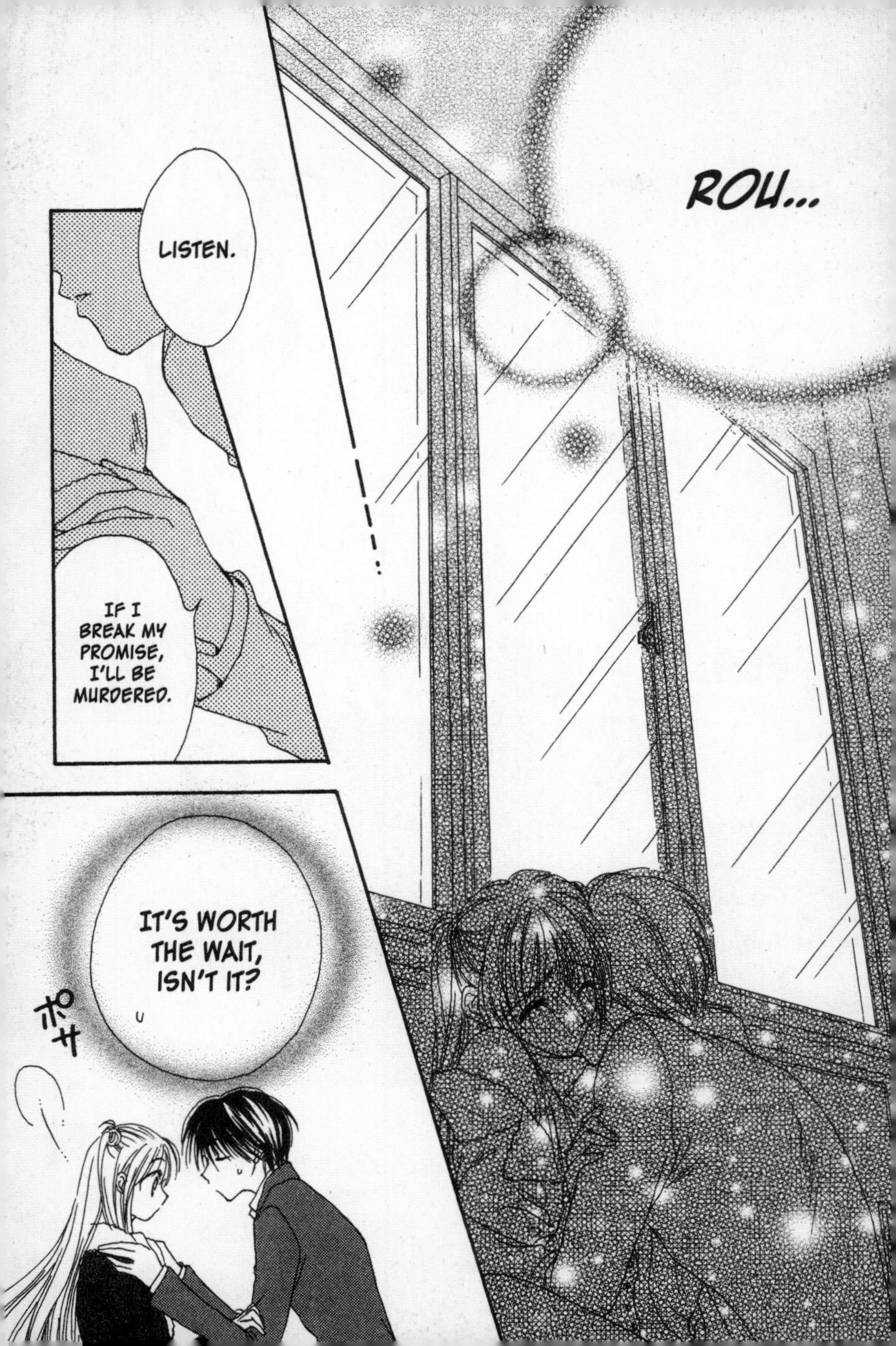
ROU...
LISTEN.
IF I BREAK MY PROMISE, I'LL BE MURDERED.
IT'S WORTH THE WAIT, ISN'T IT?
ポサ

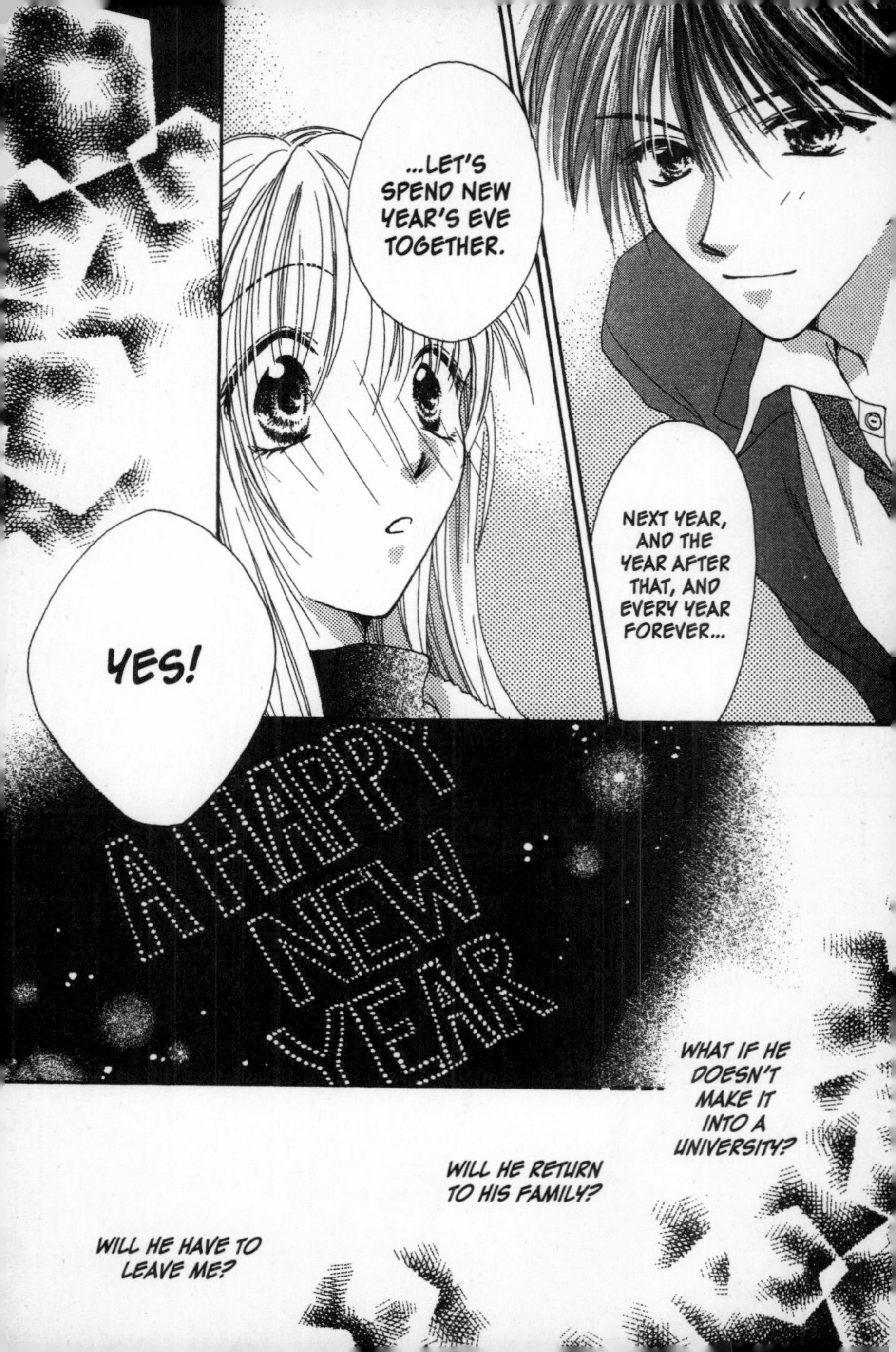
...LET'S SPEND NEW YEAR'S EVE TOGETHER.
NEXT YEAR, AND THE YEAR AFTER THAT, AND EVERY YEAR FOREVER...
YES!
A HAPPY NEW YEAR
WHAT IF HE DOESN'T MAKE IT INTO A UNIVERSITY?
WILL HE RETURN TO HIS FAMILY?
WILL HE HAVE TO LEAVE ME?

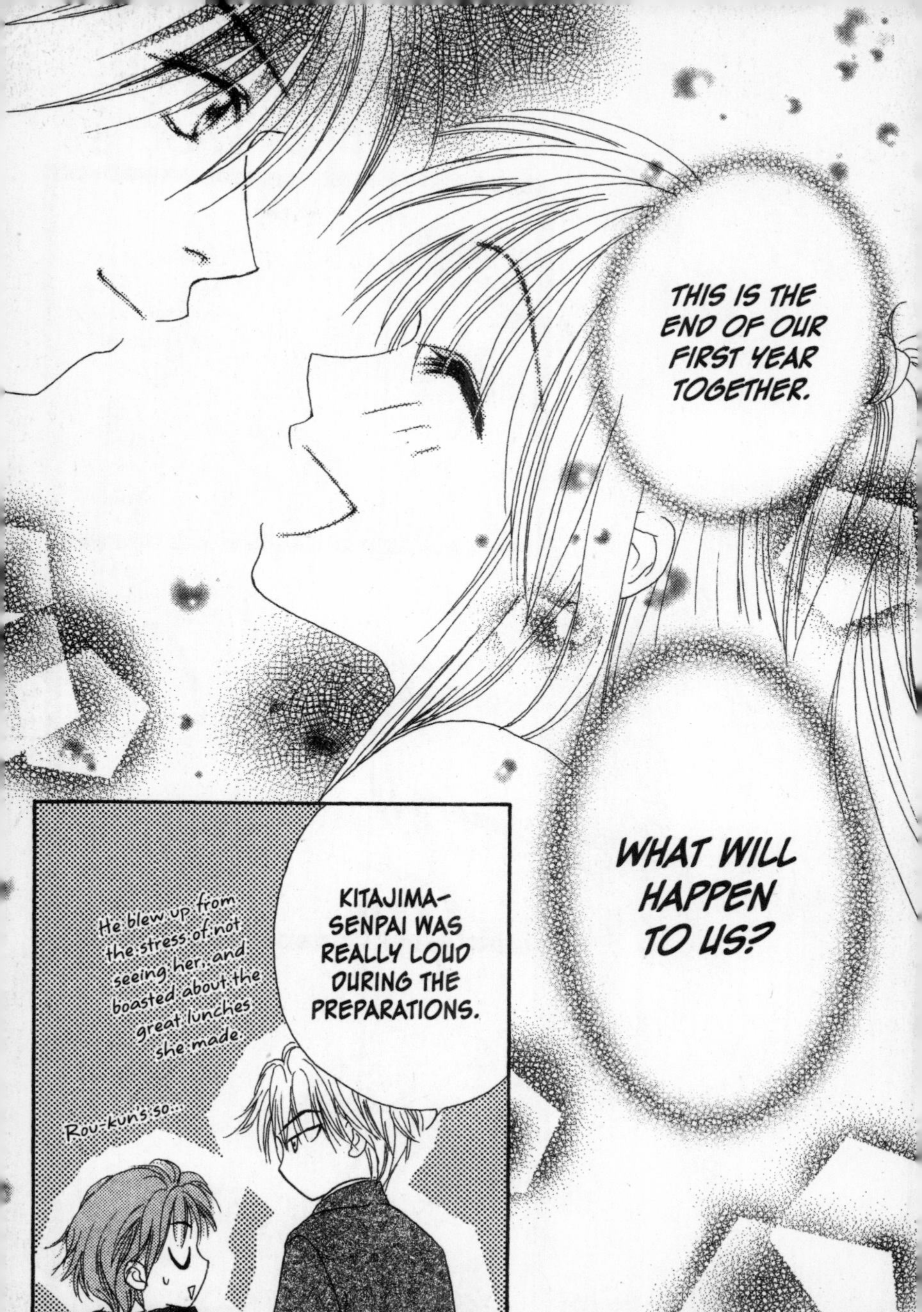
THIS IS THE END OF OUR FIRST YEAR TOGETHER.
WHAT WILL HAPPEN TO US?
KITAJIMA-SENPAI WAS REALLY LOUD DURING THE PREPARATIONS.
He blew up from the stress of not seeing her, and boasted about the great lunches she made.
Rou-kun's so...

MISSILE HAPPY! Chapter 9 / END

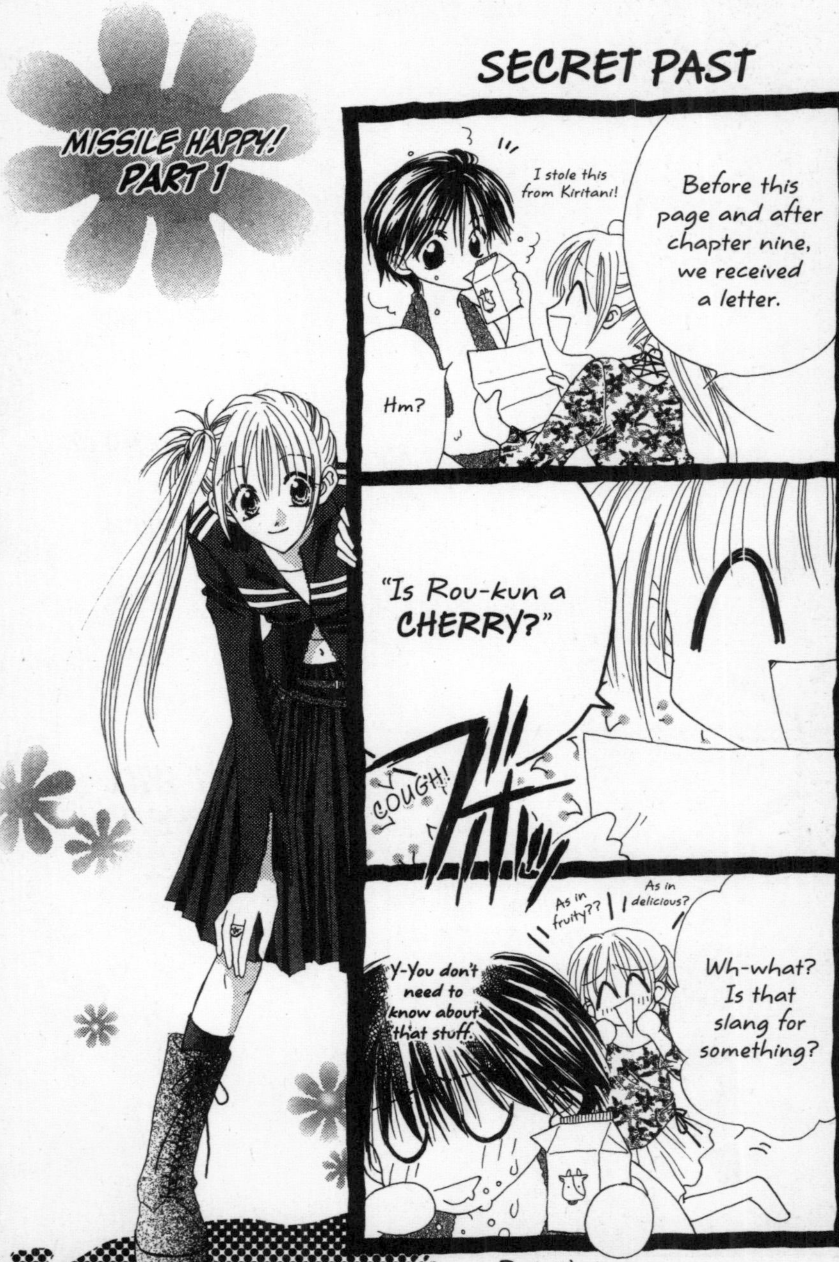
MISSILE HAPPY! PART 1
SECRET PAST
Before this page and after chapter nine, we received a letter.
I stole this from Kiritani!
Hm?
"Is Rou-kun a CHERRY?"
COUGH!
Wh-what? Is that slang for something?
As in delicious?
As in fruity??
Y-You don't need to know about that stuff.
But it's true.

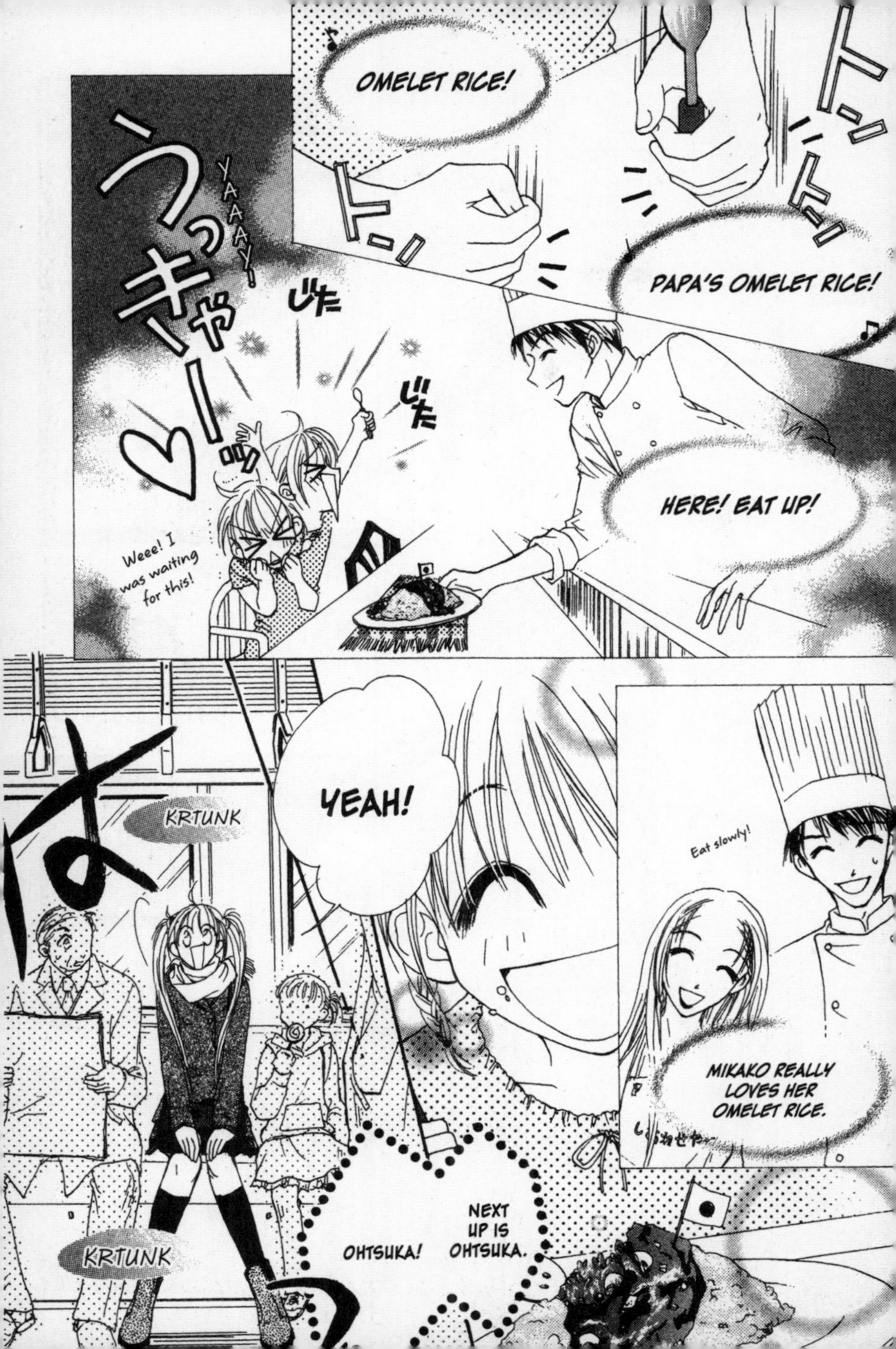
OMELET RICE!
PAPA'S OMELET RICE!
HERE! EAT UP!
YAAAAY!
Weee! I was waiting for this!
Eat slowly!
MIKAKO REALLY LOVES HER OMELET RICE.
YEAH!
NEXT UP IS OHTSUKA.
OHTSUKA!
KRTUNK
KRTUNK

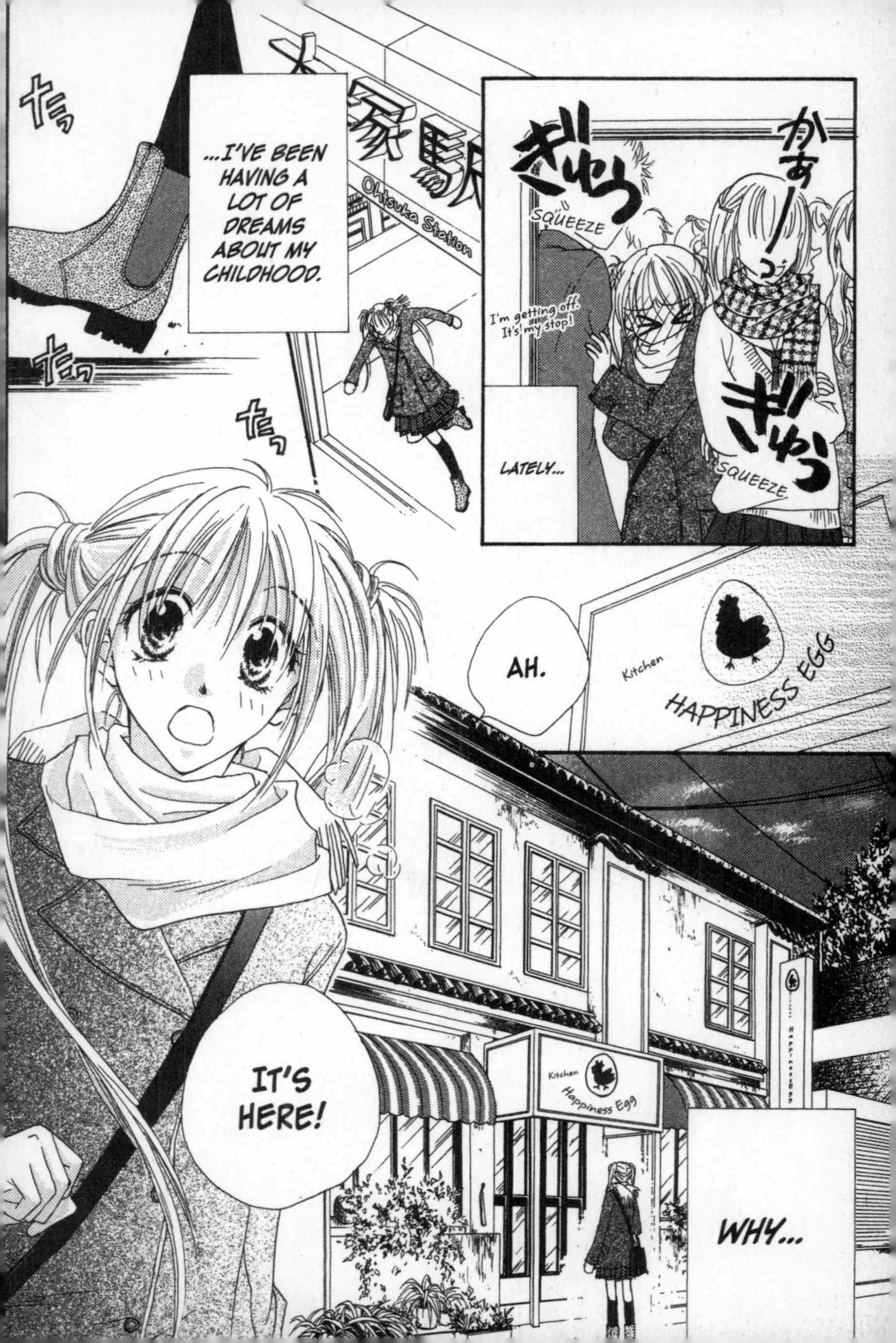
ぎゅう
SQUEEZE
I'm getting off. It's my stop!
ぎゅう
SQUEEZE
LATELY...
...I'VE BEEN HAVING A LOT OF DREAMS ABOUT MY CHILDHOOD.
Ohtsuka Station
たっ
たっ
たっ
AH.
Kitchen
HAPPINESS EGG
Kitchen
Happiness Egg
IT'S HERE!
WHY...

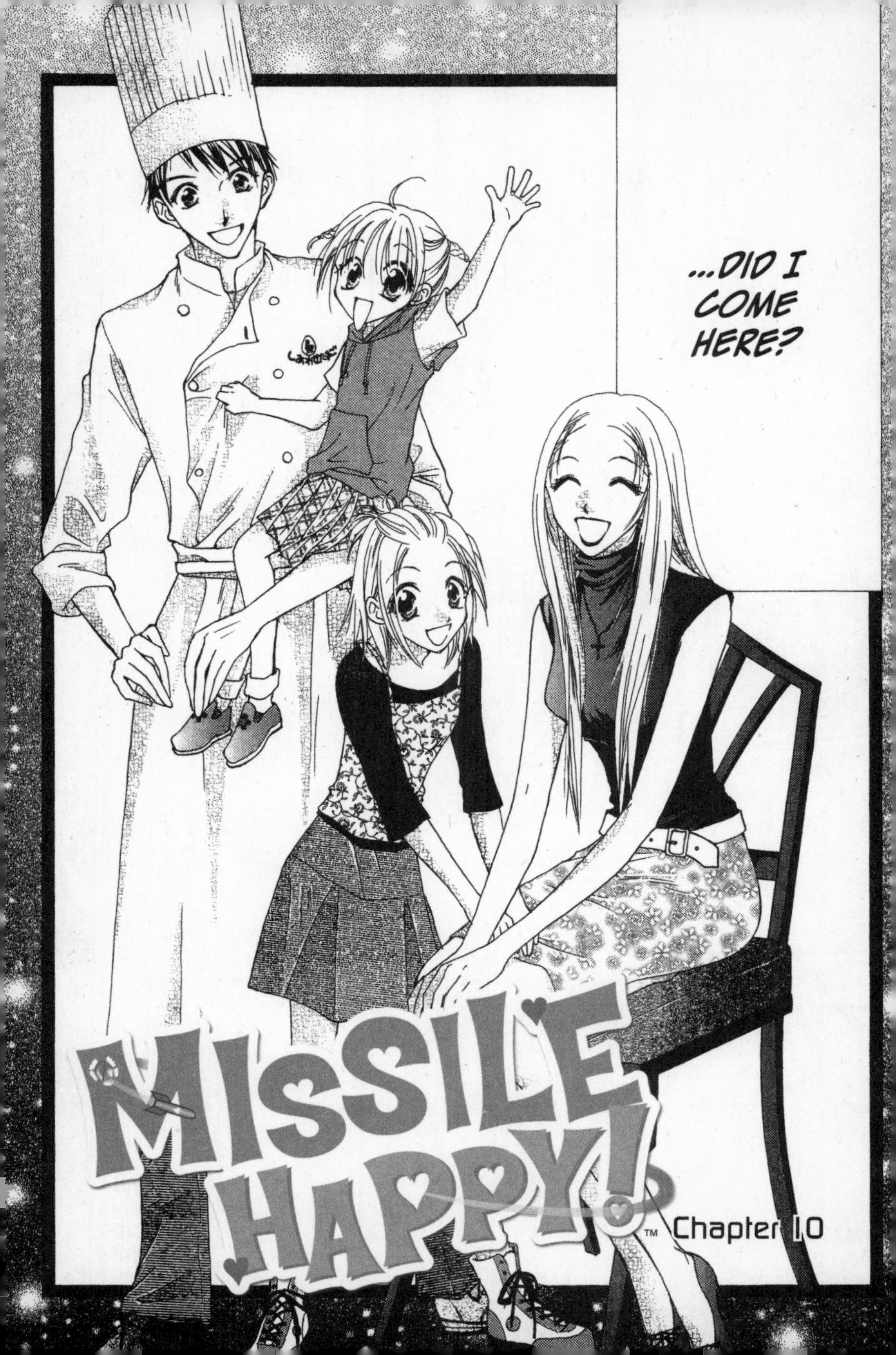
...DID I COME HERE?
MISSILE HAPPY!™
Chapter 10

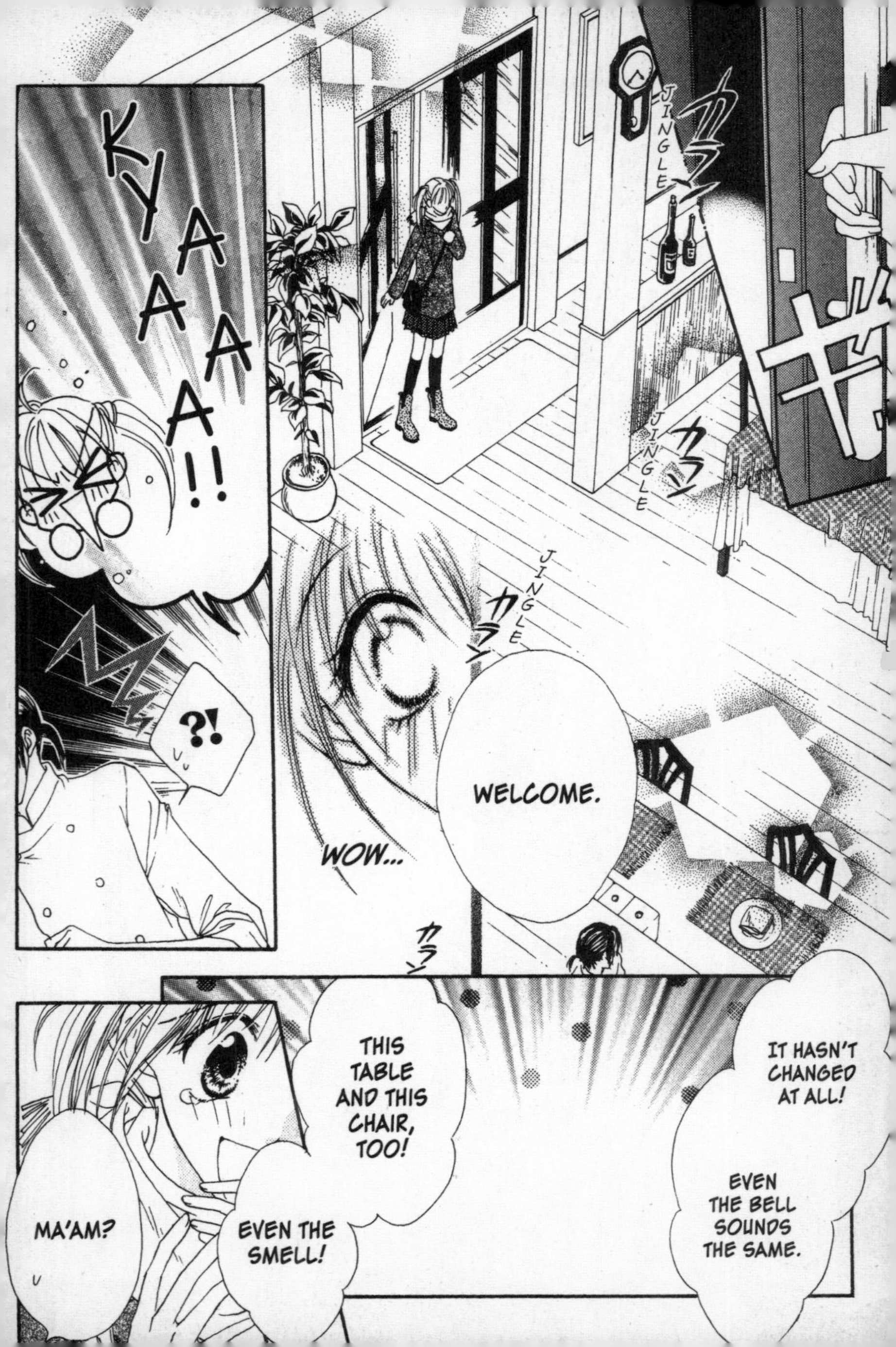
ギッ
カラン
JINGLE
カラン
JINGLE
カラン
JINGLE
WELCOME.
WOW...
カラン
KYAAAA!!
?!
IT HASN'T CHANGED AT ALL!
EVEN THE BELL SOUNDS THE SAME.
THIS TABLE AND THIS CHAIR, TOO!
EVEN THE SMELL!
MA'AM?

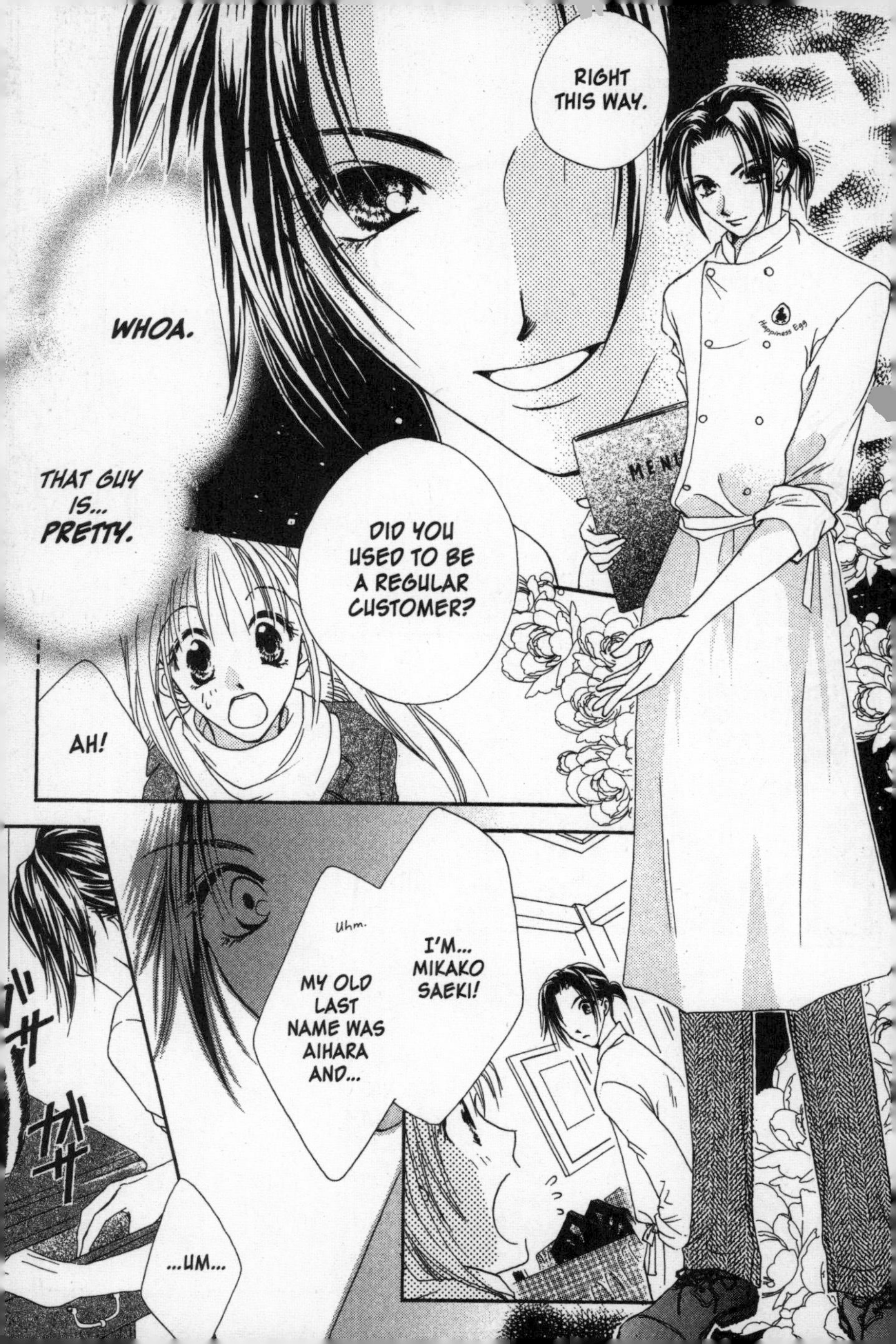
RIGHT THIS WAY.
WHOA.
THAT GUY IS... PRETTY.
DID YOU USED TO BE A REGULAR CUSTOMER?
AH!
Happiness Egg
I'M... MIKAKO SAEKI!
Uhm.
MY OLD LAST NAME WAS AIHARA AND...
...UM...

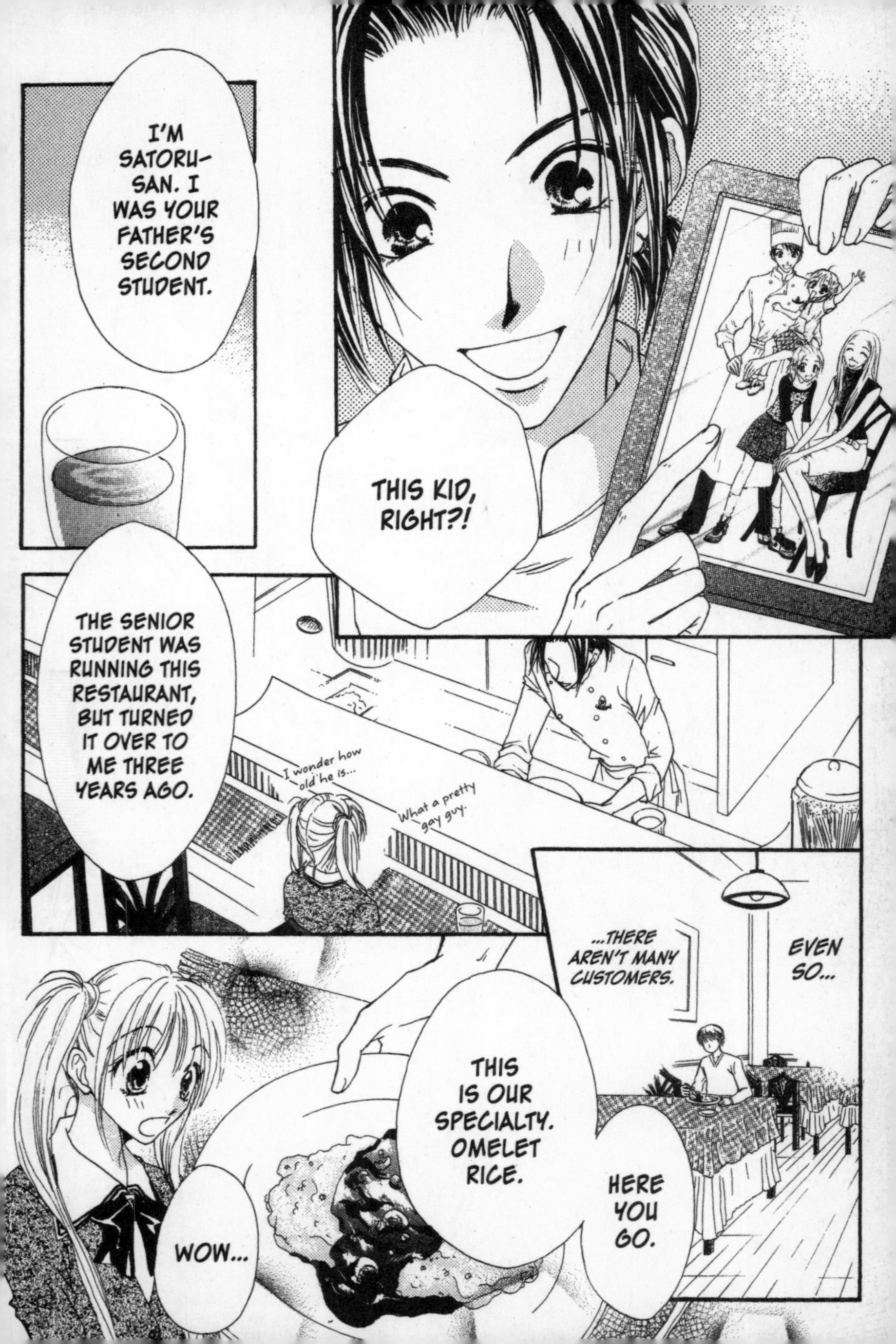
THIS KID, RIGHT?!
I'M SATORU-SAN. I WAS YOUR FATHER'S SECOND STUDENT.
THE SENIOR STUDENT WAS RUNNING THIS RESTAURANT, BUT TURNED IT OVER TO ME THREE YEARS AGO.
I wonder how old he is...
What a pretty gay guy.
EVEN SO...
...THERE AREN'T MANY CUSTOMERS.
HERE YOU GO.
THIS IS OUR SPECIALTY. OMELET RICE.
WOW...

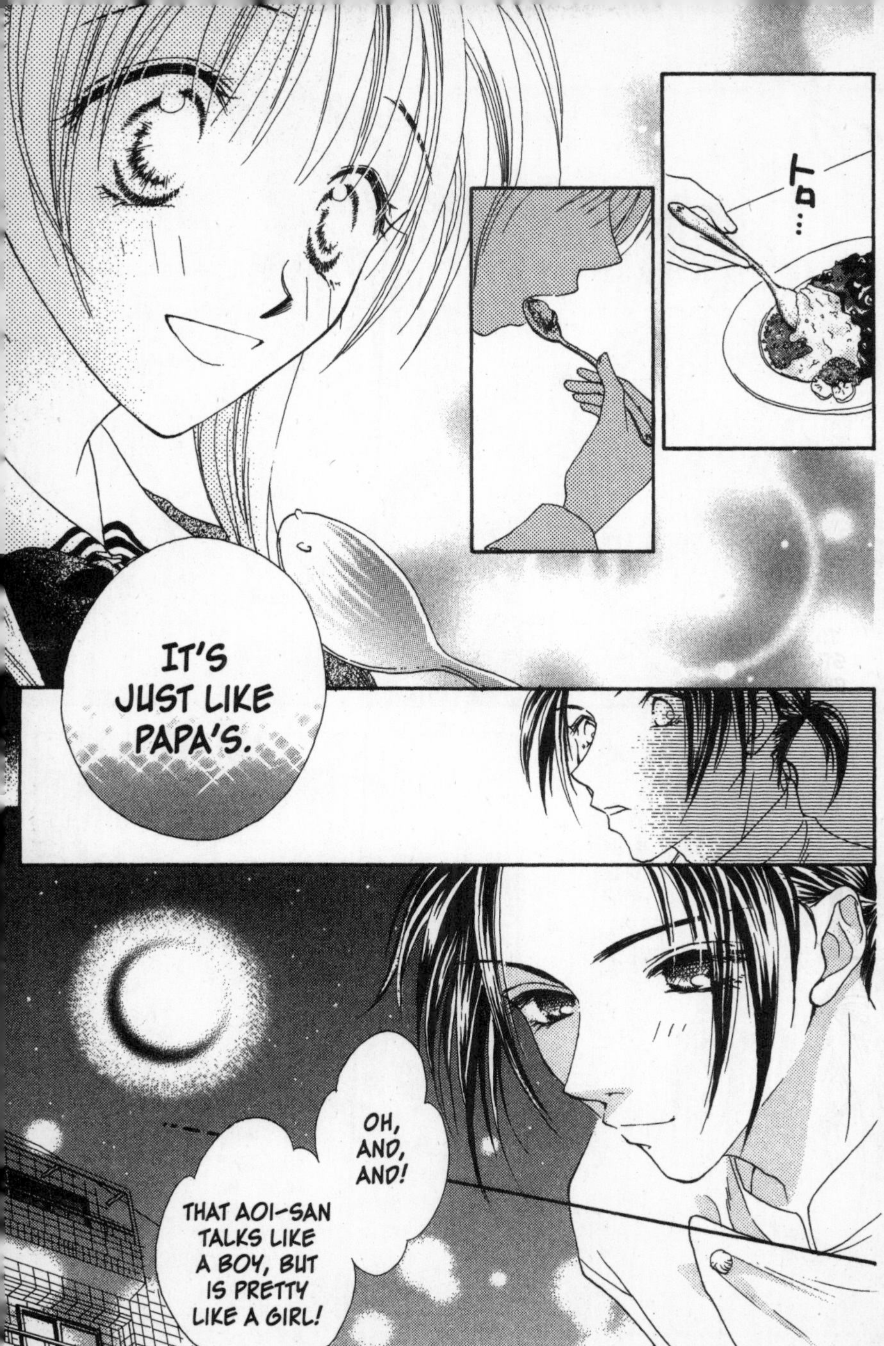
トロ…
IT'S JUST LIKE PAPA'S.
OH, AND, AND!
THAT AOI-SAN TALKS LIKE A BOY, BUT IS PRETTY LIKE A GIRL!

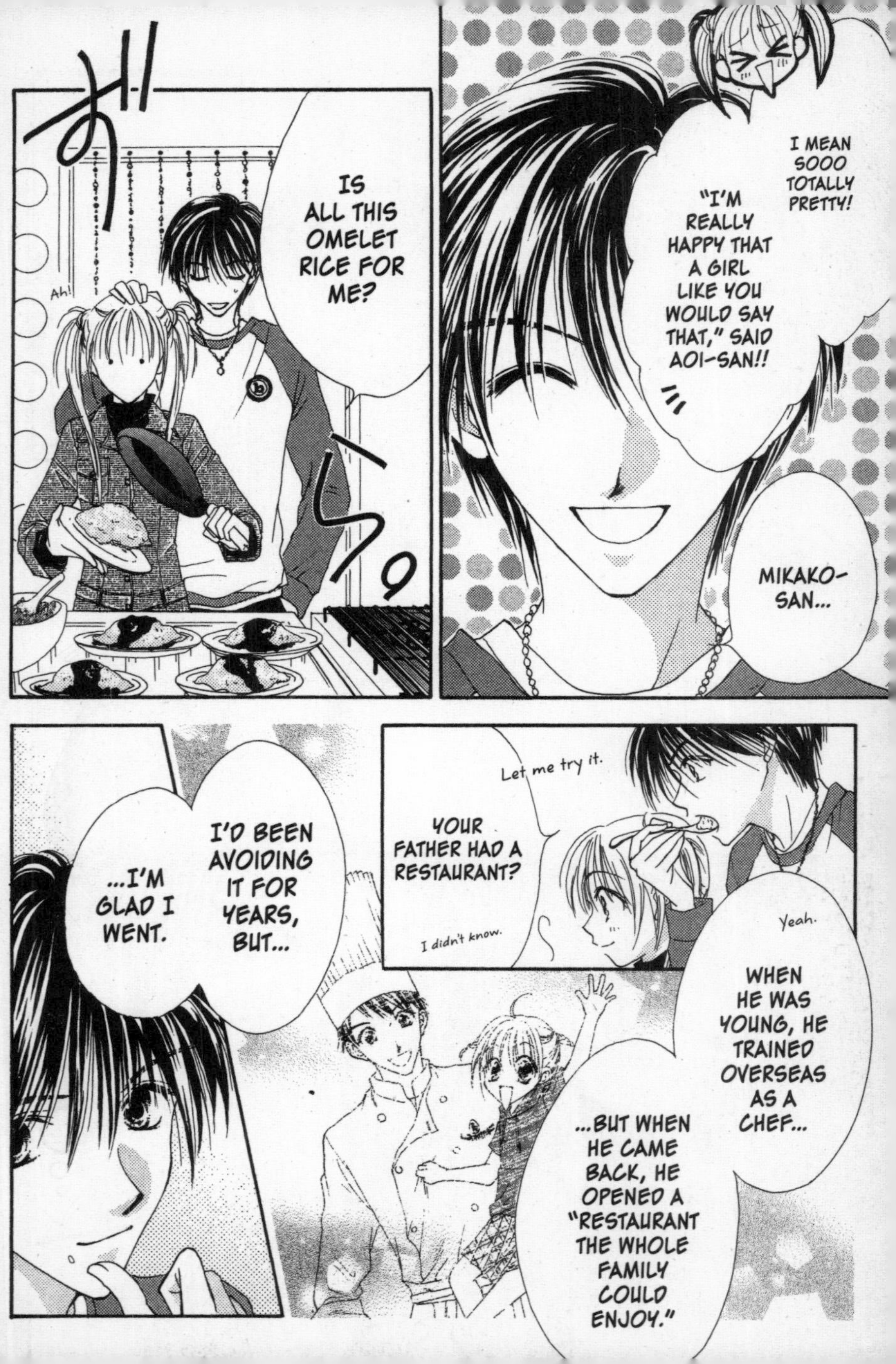
I MEAN SOOO TOTALLY PRETTY!
"I'M REALLY HAPPY THAT A GIRL LIKE YOU WOULD SAY THAT," SAID AOI-SAN!!
MIKAKO-SAN...
Ah!
IS ALL THIS OMELET RICE FOR ME?
Let me try it.
YOUR FATHER HAD A RESTAURANT?
I didn't know.
Yeah.
WHEN HE WAS YOUNG, HE TRAINED OVERSEAS AS A CHEF...
...BUT WHEN HE CAME BACK, HE OPENED A "RESTAURANT THE WHOLE FAMILY COULD ENJOY."
I'D BEEN AVOIDING IT FOR YEARS, BUT...
...I'M GLAD I WENT.

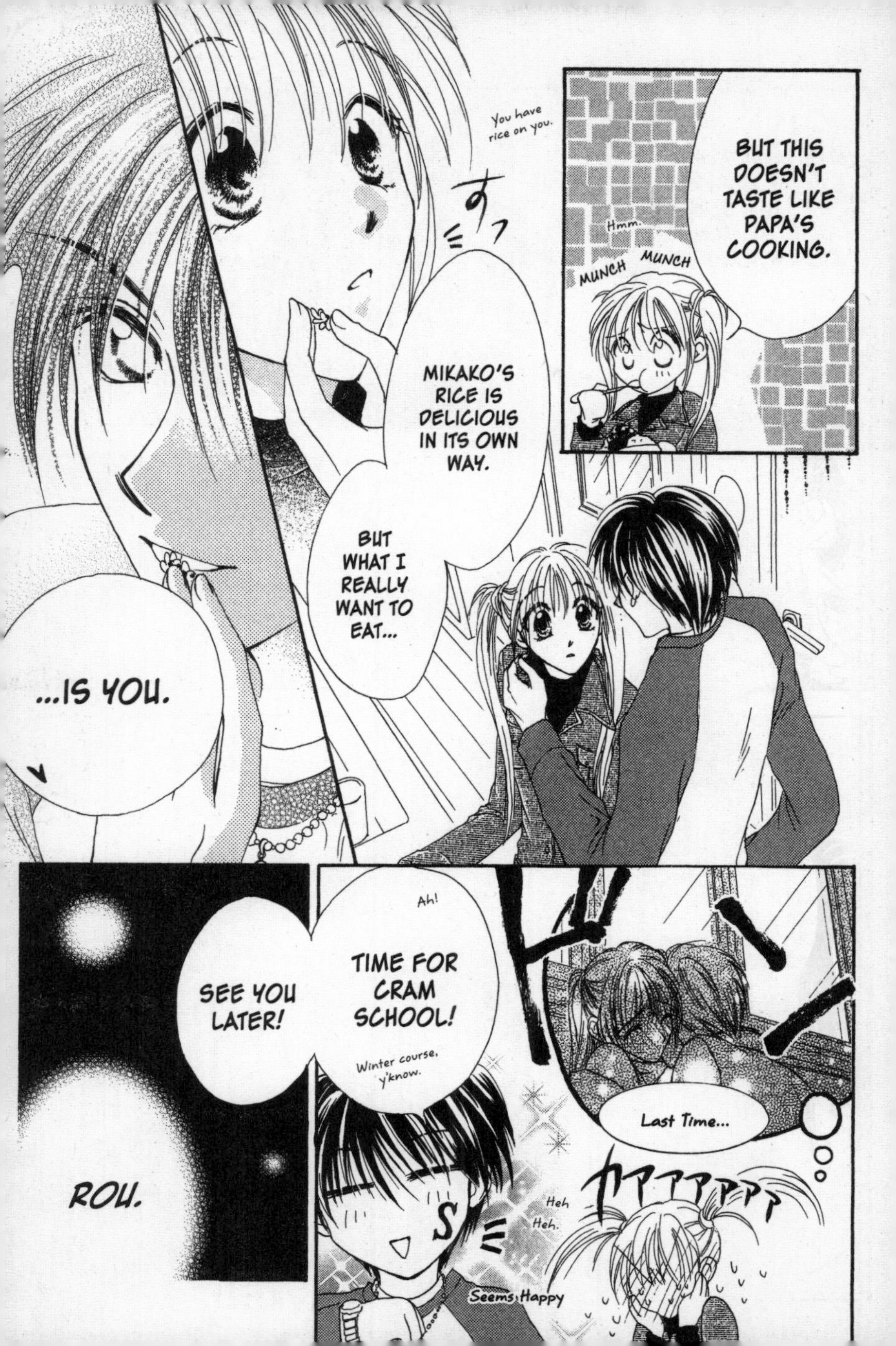
MUNCH MUNCH
Hmm.
BUT THIS DOESN'T TASTE LIKE PAPA'S COOKING.
You have rice on you.
MIKAKO'S RICE IS DELICIOUS IN ITS OWN WAY.
BUT WHAT I REALLY WANT TO EAT...
...IS YOU.
Last Time...
Ah!
TIME FOR CRAM SCHOOL!
Winter course, y'know.
SEE YOU LATER!
Heh Heh.
Seems Happy
ROU.

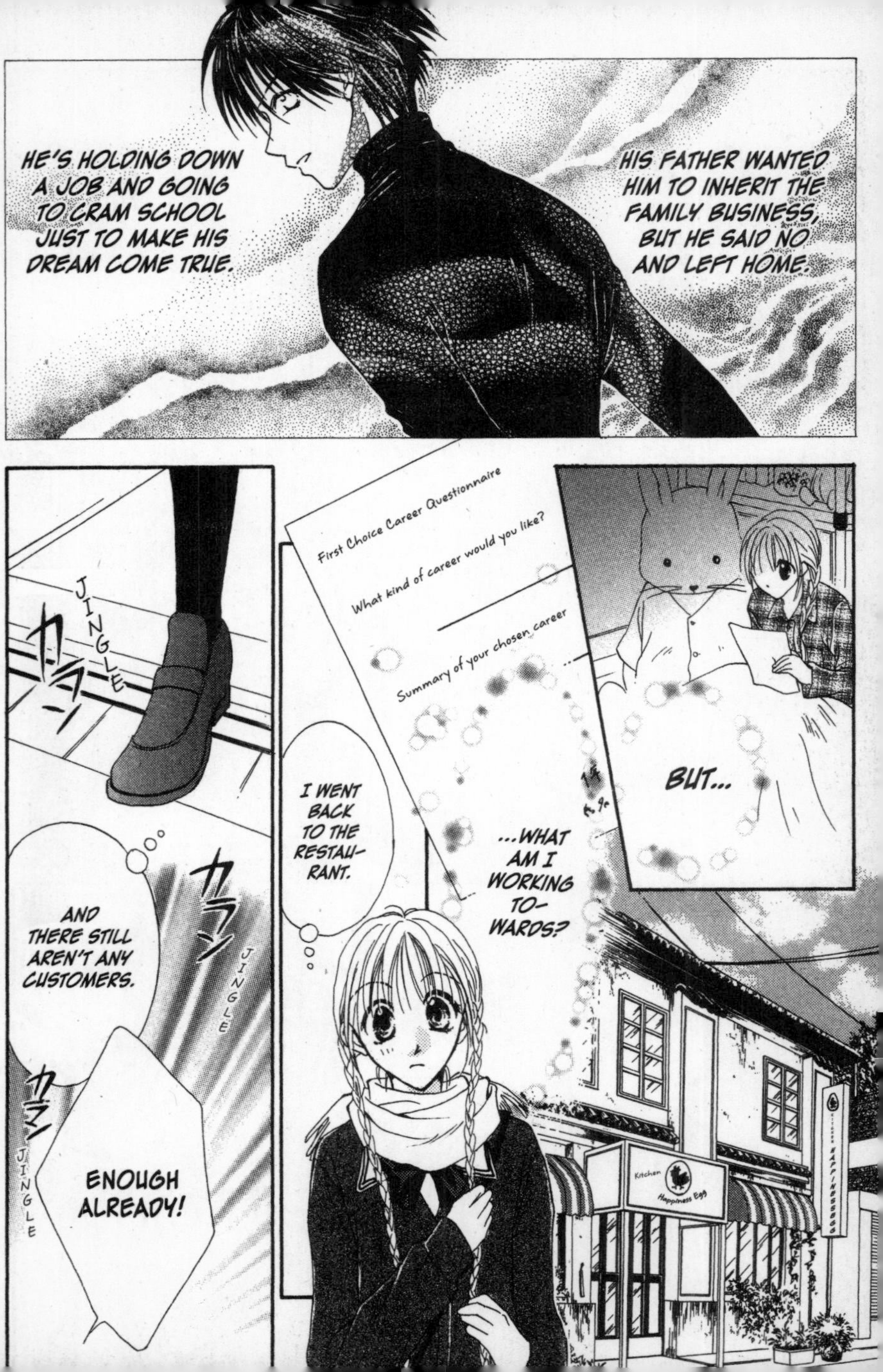
HIS FATHER WANTED HIM TO INHERIT THE FAMILY BUSINESS, BUT HE SAID NO AND LEFT HOME.
HE'S HOLDING DOWN A JOB AND GOING TO CRAM SCHOOL JUST TO MAKE HIS DREAM COME TRUE.
BUT...
First Choice Career Questionnaire
What kind of career would you like?
Summary of your chosen career
...WHAT AM I WORKING TO-WARDS?
I WENT BACK TO THE RESTAU-RANT.
Kitchen Happiness Egg
JINGLE
JINGLE
AND THERE STILL AREN'T ANY CUSTOMERS.
JINGLE
ENOUGH ALREADY!

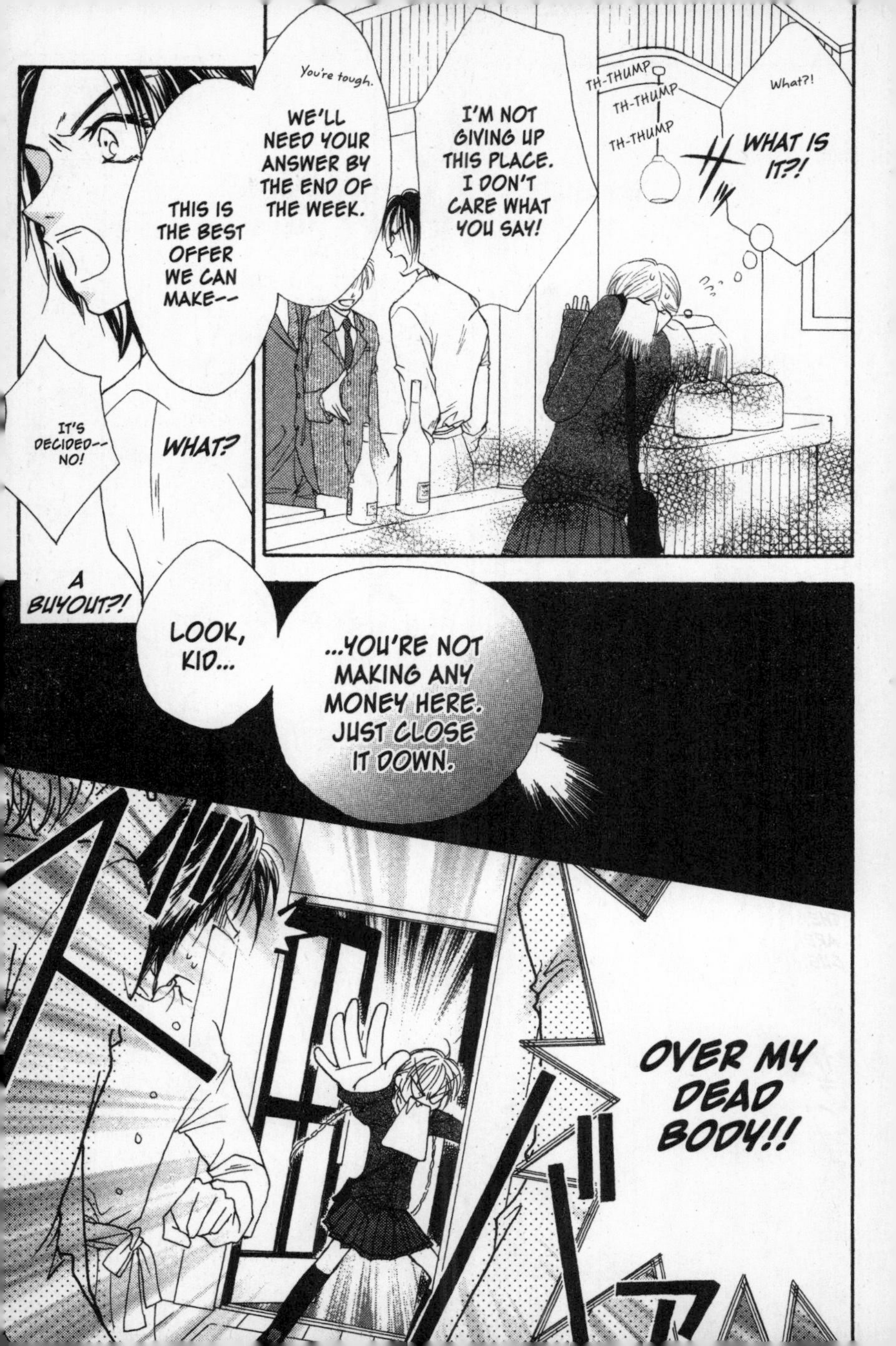
What?!
WHAT IS IT?!
TH-THUMP
TH-THUMP
TH-THUMP
I'M NOT GIVING UP THIS PLACE. I DON'T CARE WHAT YOU SAY!
You're tough.
WE'LL NEED YOUR ANSWER BY THE END OF THE WEEK.
THIS IS THE BEST OFFER WE CAN MAKE--
WHAT?
A BUYOUT?!
IT'S DECIDED-- NO!
LOOK, KID...
...YOU'RE NOT MAKING ANY MONEY HERE. JUST CLOSE IT DOWN.
OVER MY DEAD BODY!!

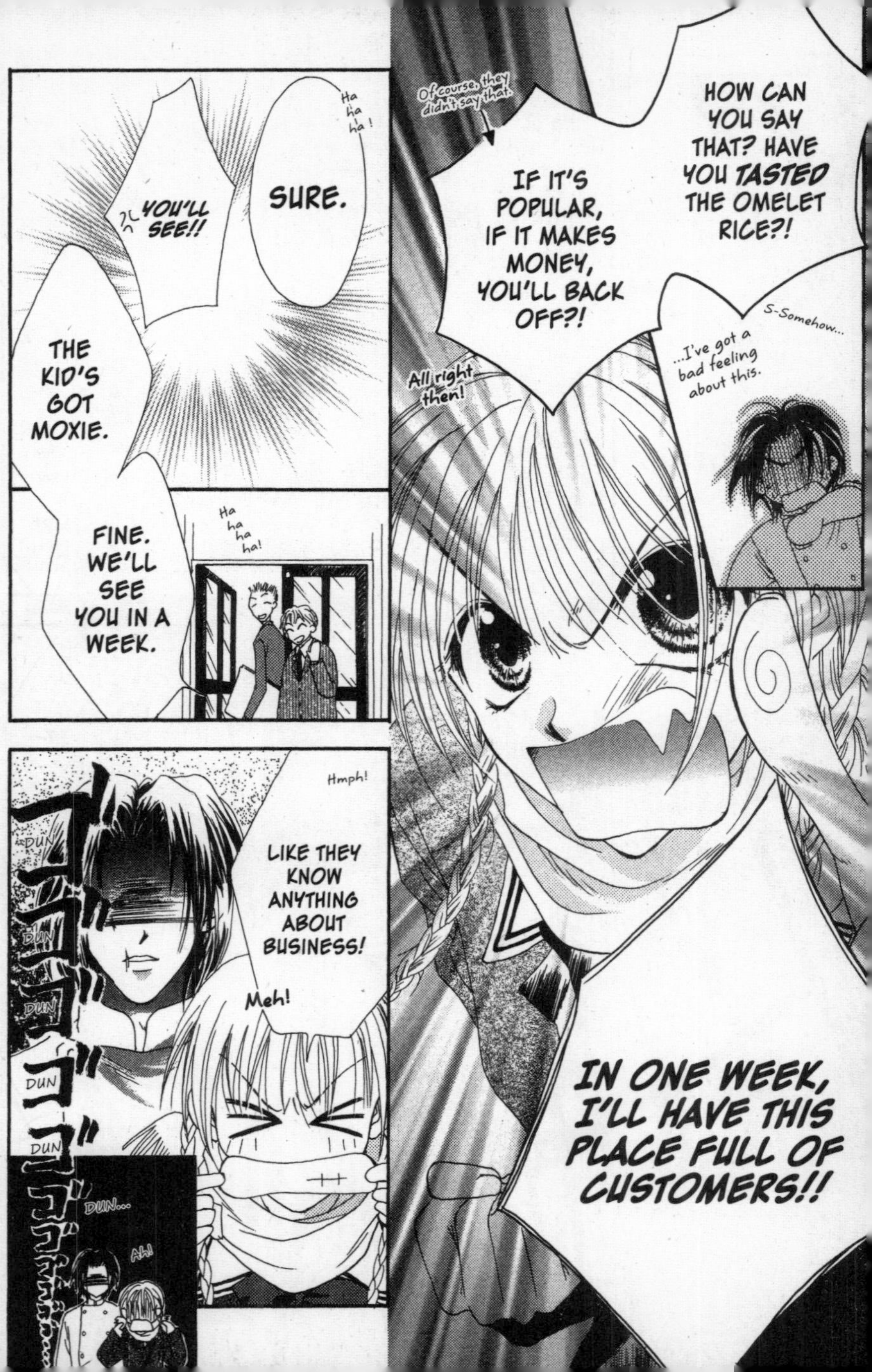
HOW CAN YOU SAY THAT? HAVE YOU TASTED THE OMELET RICE?!
Of course, they didn't say that.
IF IT'S POPULAR, IF IT MAKES MONEY, YOU'LL BACK OFF?!
S-Somehow...
...I've got a bad feeling about this.
All right then!
IN ONE WEEK, I'LL HAVE THIS PLACE FULL OF CUSTOMERS!!
Ha ha ha!
SURE.
YOU'LL SEE!!
THE KID'S GOT MOXIE.
Ha ha ha ha!
FINE. WE'LL SEE YOU IN A WEEK.
Hmph!
LIKE THEY KNOW ANYTHING ABOUT BUSINESS!
Meh!
DUN
DUN
DUN
DUN
DUN
DUN...
Ah!

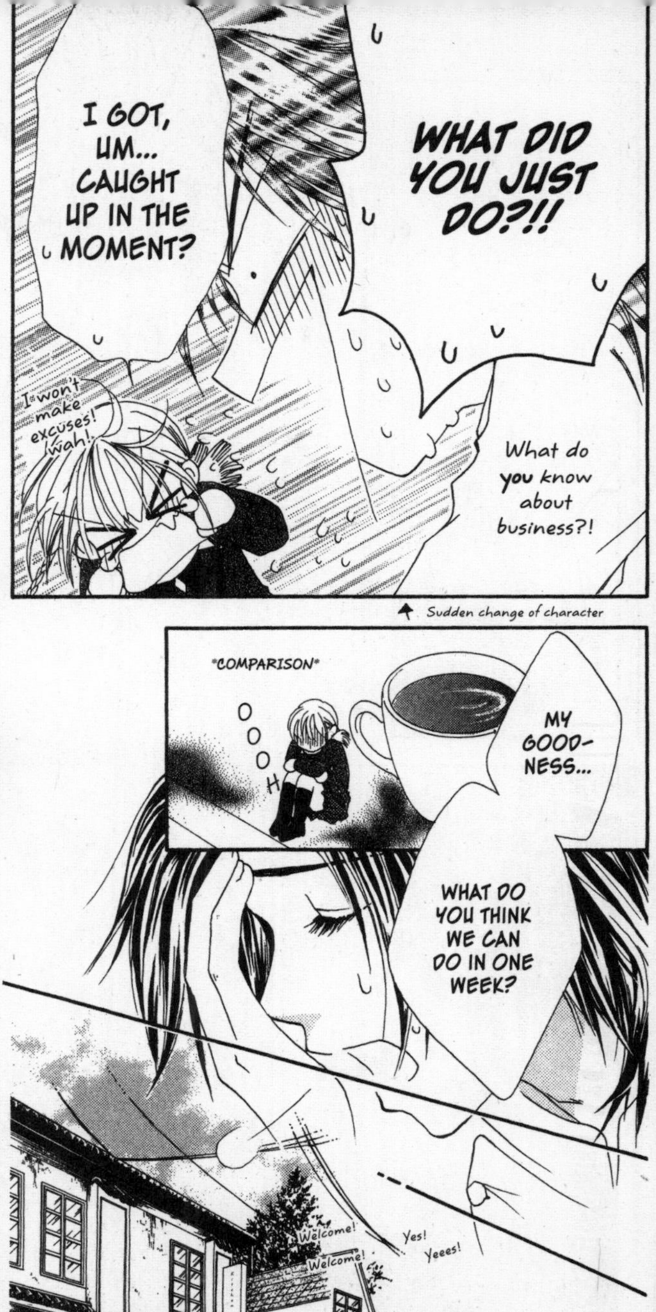
WHAT DID YOU JUST DO?!!
I GOT, UM... CAUGHT UP IN THE MOMENT?
I won't make excuses! Wah!
What do you know about business?!
Sudden change of character
COMPARISON
OOOH
MY GOODNESS...
WHAT DO YOU THINK WE CAN DO IN ONE WEEK?
Yes! Yeees!
Welcome!
Welcome!
Kitchen Happiness Egg

NEW EDITOR
PART ONE

At the end of Chapter 11, in April of 2003, I changed editor. I'd been with my old editor since my first manga, but she confessed that she was leaving the business and I'd have to get a new representative. I spent an hour crying loudly on the phone to her.

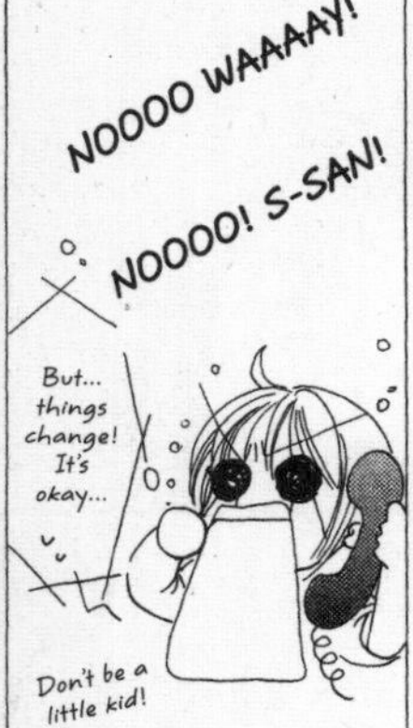
NOOOO WAAAAY!
NOOOO! S-SAN!
But... things change! It's okay...
Don't be a little kid!

She said my new editor was male, and I became even more of a Kiritani, completely unsure. The new editor is named I-San...and I'd met him before!

So I'd like to thank S-San for all she's done for me, and ask that she look favorably upon me in the future.

And please call from time to time!! Sob!!

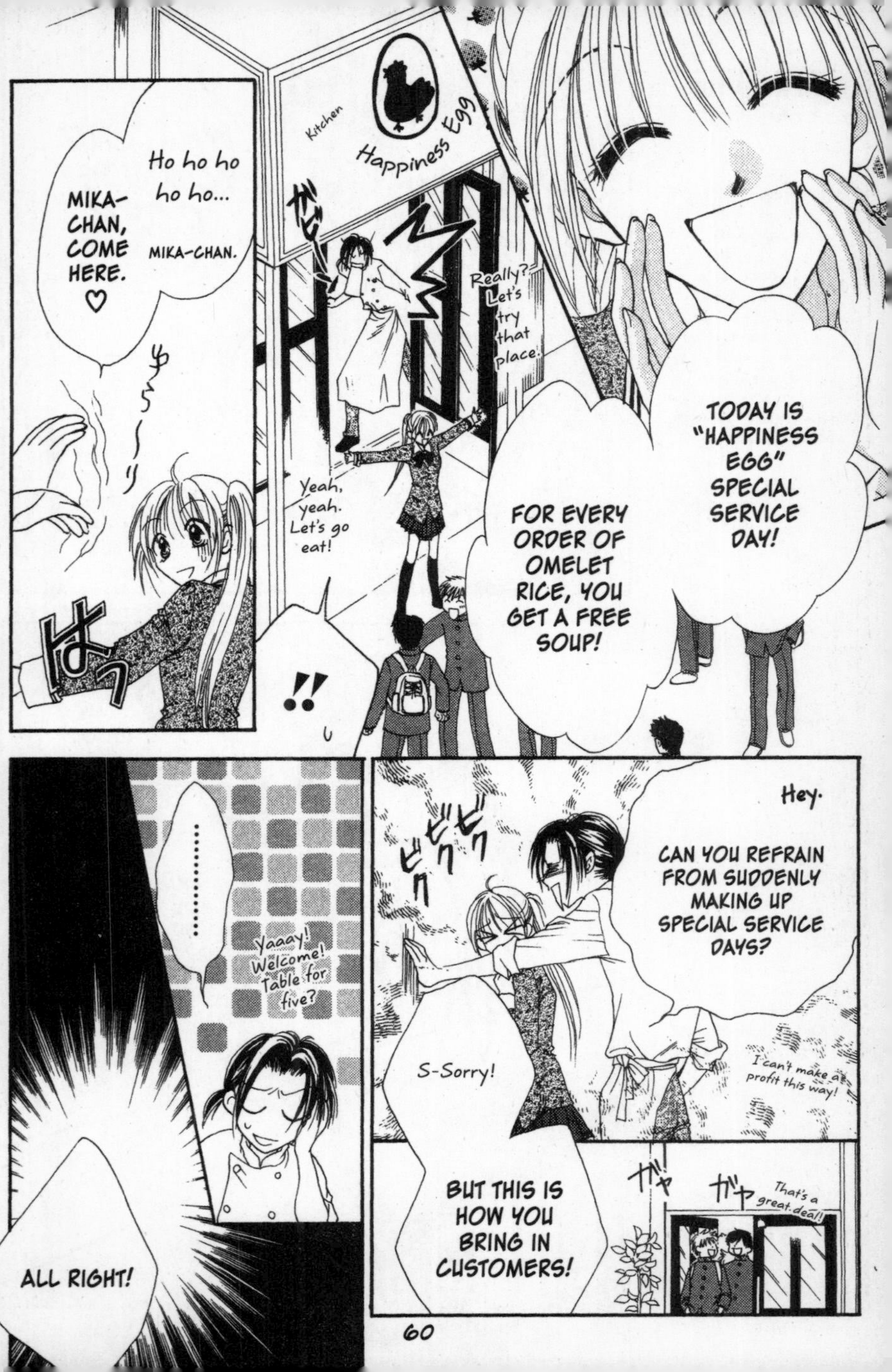
Kitchen
Happiness Egg
TODAY IS "HAPPINESS EGG" SPECIAL SERVICE DAY!
FOR EVERY ORDER OF OMELET RICE, YOU GET A FREE SOUP!
Really? Let's try that place!
Yeah, yeah. Let's go eat!
!!
Ho ho ho ho ho... MIKA-CHAN.
MIKA-CHAN, COME HERE. ♡
Hey. CAN YOU REFRAIN FROM SUDDENLY MAKING UP SPECIAL SERVICE DAYS?
I can't make a profit this way!
S-Sorry!
That's a great deal!
BUT THIS IS HOW YOU BRING IN CUSTOMERS!
......
Yaaay! Welcome! Table for five?
ALL RIGHT!

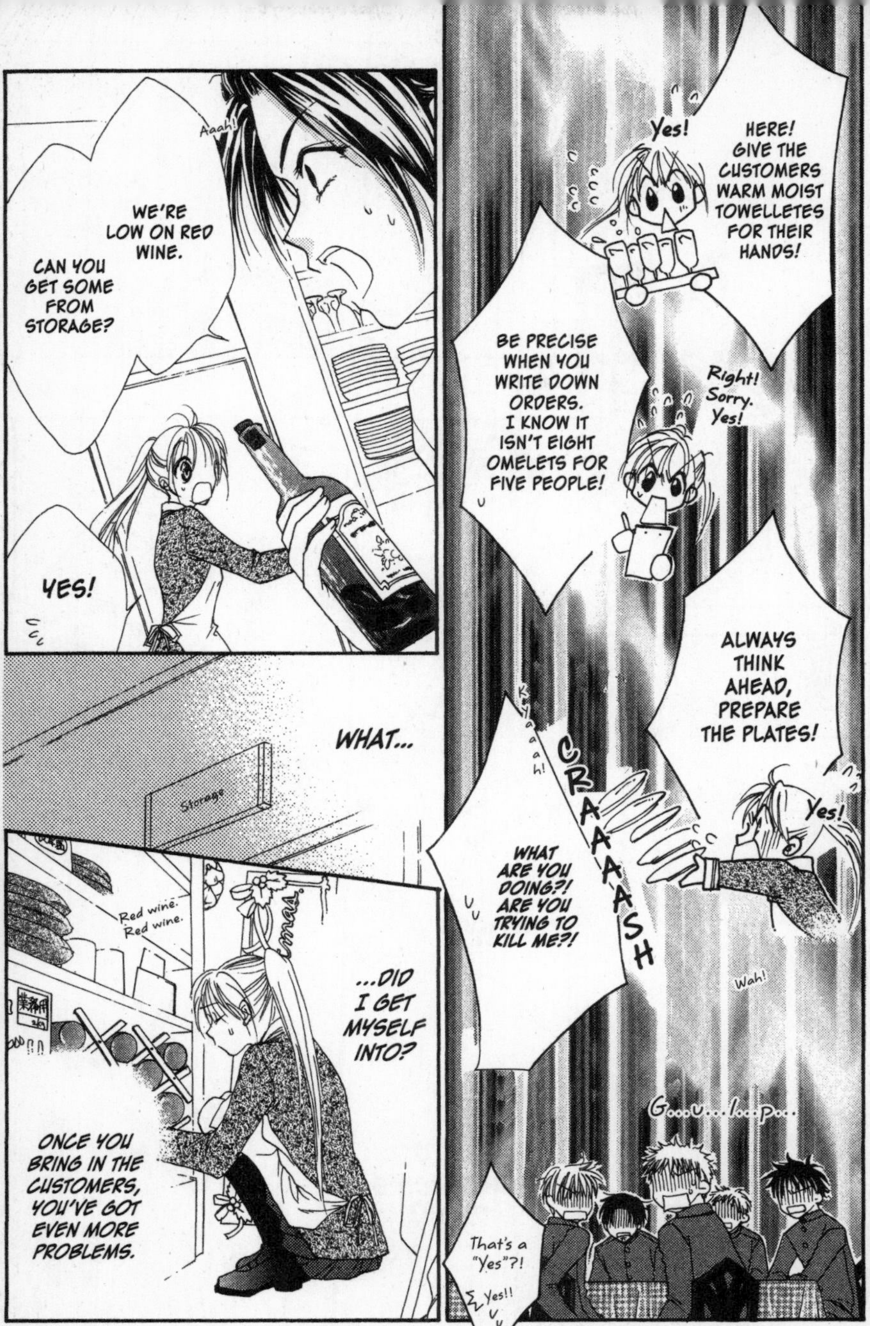

HERE! GIVE THE CUSTOMERS WARM MOIST TOWELLETES FOR THEIR HANDS!
Yes!
BE PRECISE WHEN YOU WRITE DOWN ORDERS. I KNOW IT ISN'T EIGHT OMELETS FOR FIVE PEOPLE!
Right! Sorry. Yes!
ALWAYS THINK AHEAD, PREPARE THE PLATES!
Yes!
Kyaaaah!
CRAAAASH
WHAT ARE YOU DOING?! ARE YOU TRYING TO KILL ME?!
Wah!
G...u...l...p...
That's a "Yes"?!
Yes!!
Aaah!
WE'RE LOW ON RED WINE.
CAN YOU GET SOME FROM STORAGE?
YES!
WHAT...
Storage
...DID I GET MYSELF INTO?
Red wine. Red wine.
ONCE YOU BRING IN THE CUSTOMERS, YOU'VE GOT EVEN MORE PROBLEMS.

Students continue to hold their breath.

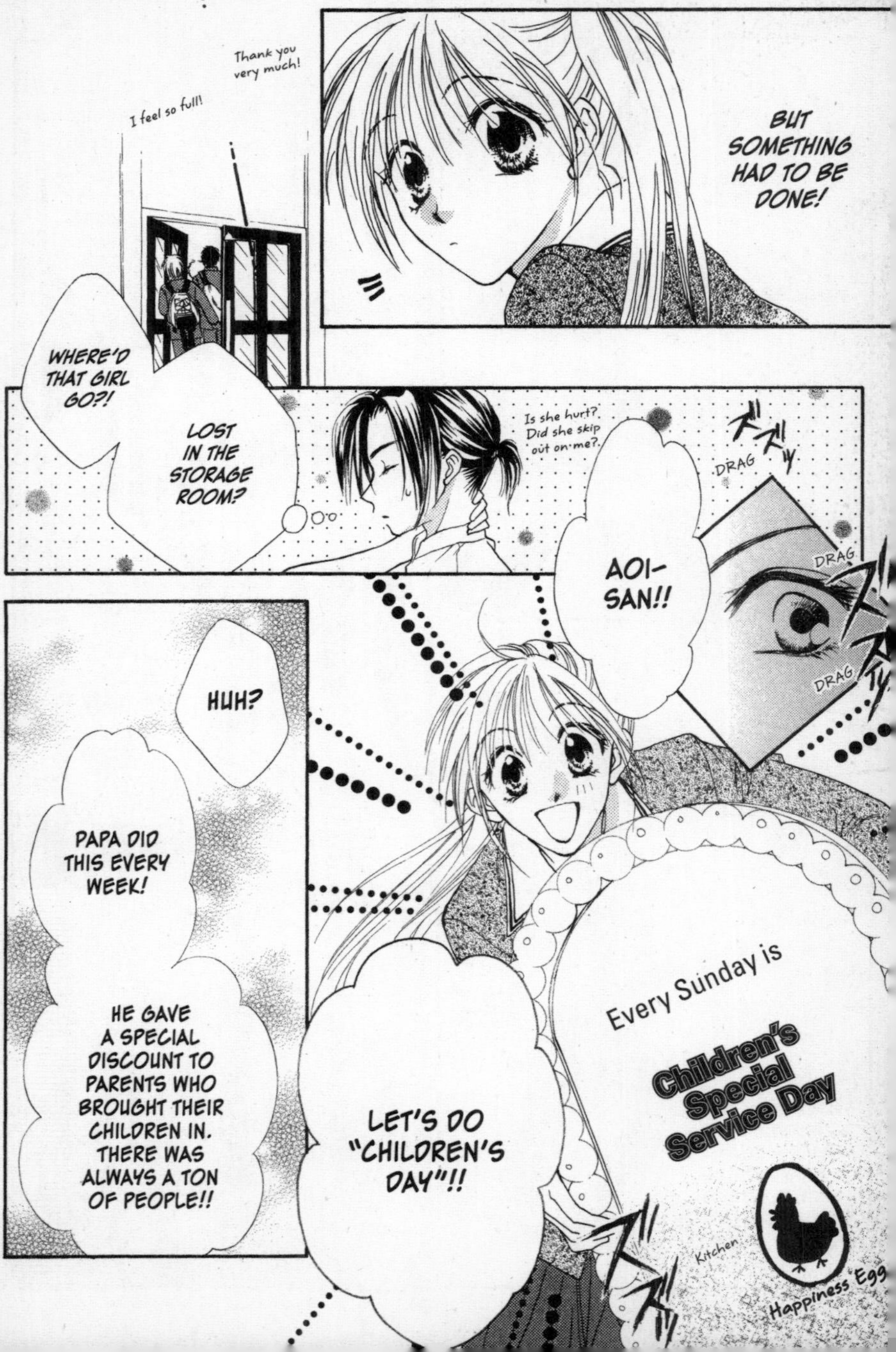
BUT SOMETHING HAD TO BE DONE!
Thank you very much!
I feel so full!
WHERE'D THAT GIRL GO?!
LOST IN THE STORAGE ROOM?
Is she hurt? Did she skip out on me?
DRAG
DRAG
DRAG
AOI-SAN!!
Every Sunday is
Children's Special Service Day
Happiness Egg
Kitchen
LET'S DO "CHILDREN'S DAY"!!
HUH?
PAPA DID THIS EVERY WEEK!
HE GAVE A SPECIAL DISCOUNT TO PARENTS WHO BROUGHT THEIR CHILDREN IN. THERE WAS ALWAYS A TON OF PEOPLE!!

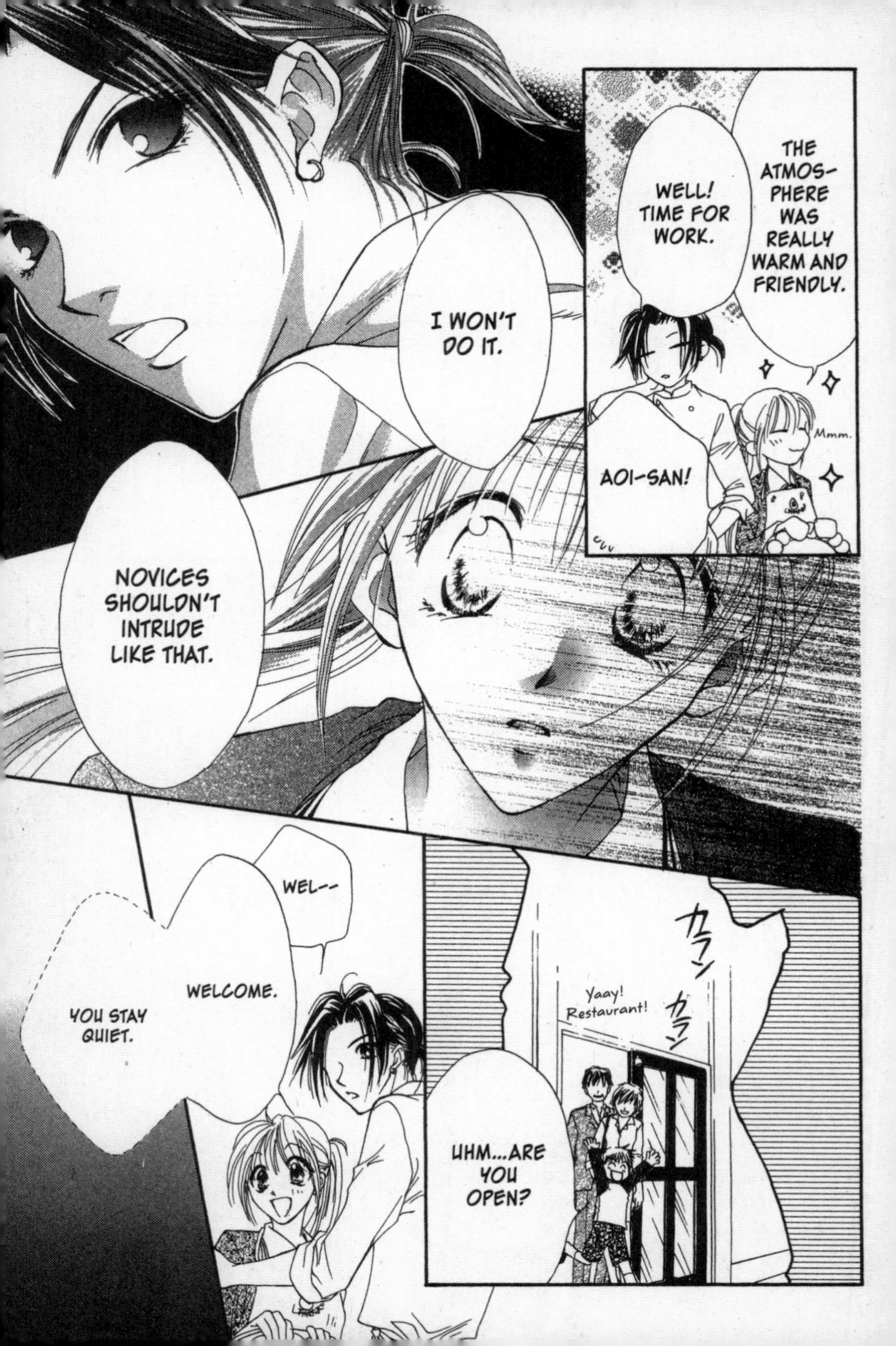
THE ATMOSPHERE WAS REALLY WARM AND FRIENDLY.
WELL! TIME FOR WORK.
Mmm.
AOI-SAN!
I WON'T DO IT.
NOVICES SHOULDN'T INTRUDE LIKE THAT.
カラン
カラン
Yaay! Restaurant!
UHM...ARE YOU OPEN?
WEL--
WELCOME.
YOU STAY QUIET.

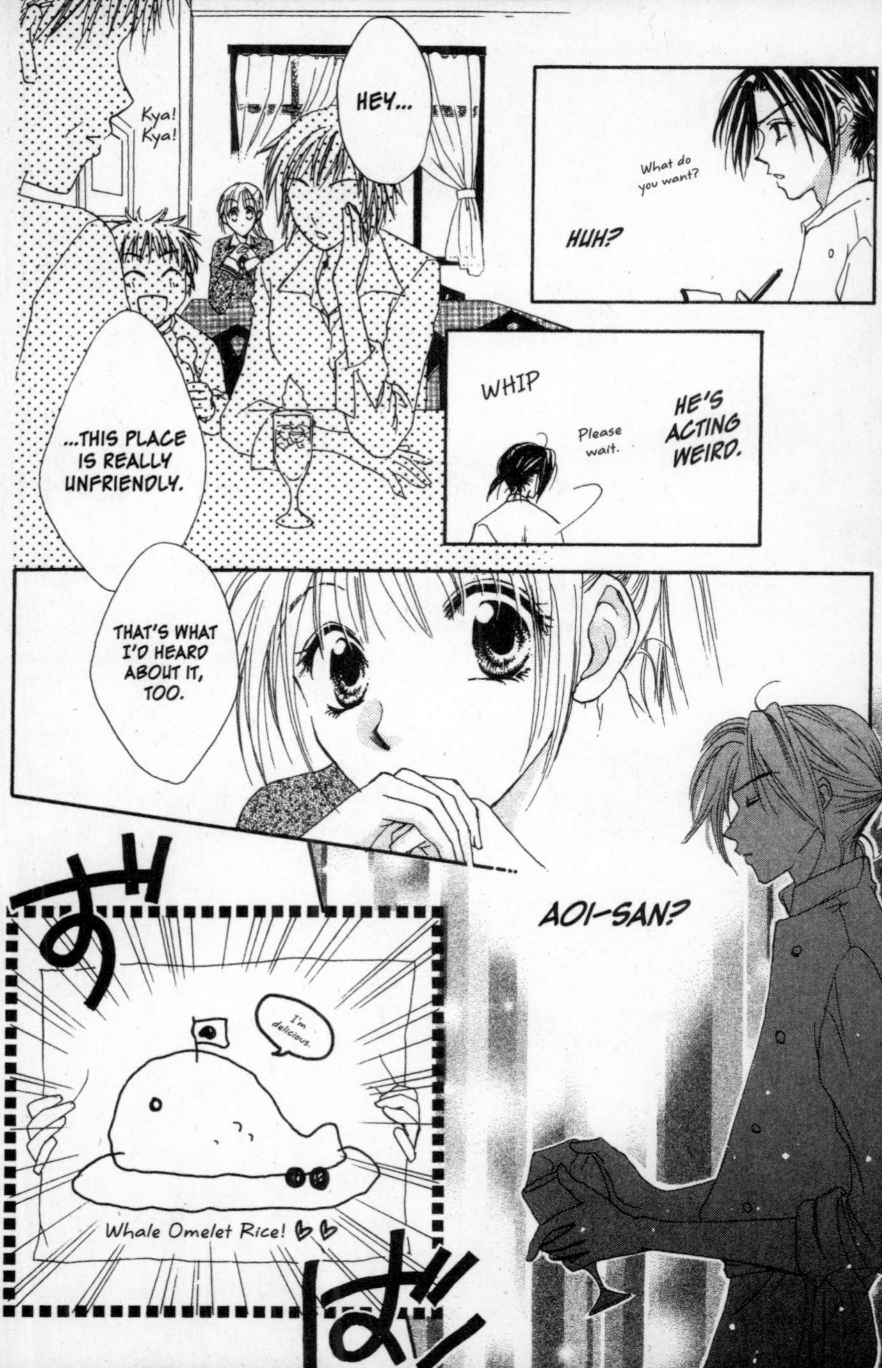

What do you want?
HUH?
WHIP
HE'S ACTING WEIRD.
Please wait.
HEY...
Kya! Kya!
...THIS PLACE IS REALLY UNFRIENDLY.
THAT'S WHAT I'D HEARD ABOUT IT, TOO.
AOI-SAN?
I'm delicious.
Whale Omelet Rice!

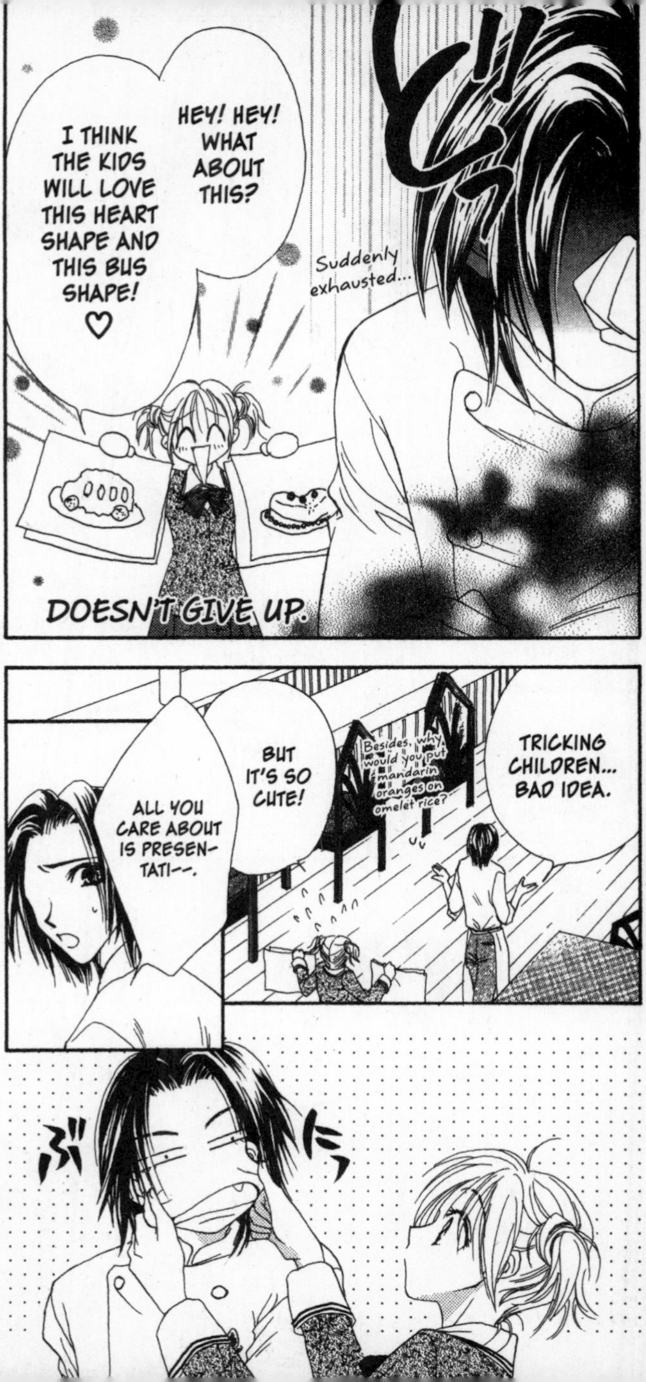
Suddenly exhausted...
HEY! HEY! WHAT ABOUT THIS?
I THINK THE KIDS WILL LOVE THIS HEART SHAPE AND THIS BUS SHAPE! ♡
DOESN'T GIVE UP.
TRICKING CHILDREN... BAD IDEA.
Besides, why would you put mandarin oranges on omelet rice?
BUT IT'S SO CUTE!
ALL YOU CARE ABOUT IS PRESEN-TATI--.

NEW EDITOR PART TWO

In May 2003, I had lunch with my old editor and my new editor (I called it the "Three-person interview"). We had a great Chinese meal and then went to a bar that usually caters to businessmen. I had a great time, but when two editors get together they tend to form an alliance to pick on the writer. Since this little Kiritani is so useless, I got lectured a lot and even received a few "warnings." I guess I got what I deserved. I tried to drink as much sake as possible to take the sting out of it. (I didn't end up drinking enough, though.)

I found out that my new editor, I-san, is the same age as my older brother. When I told him that, he said, "You should think of me as your second older brother from now on." I thought that was a little creepy.

I-san! After this job is done, please take me out to all the delicious restaurants you were talking about. This non-gourmet Kiritani loves to be impressed.

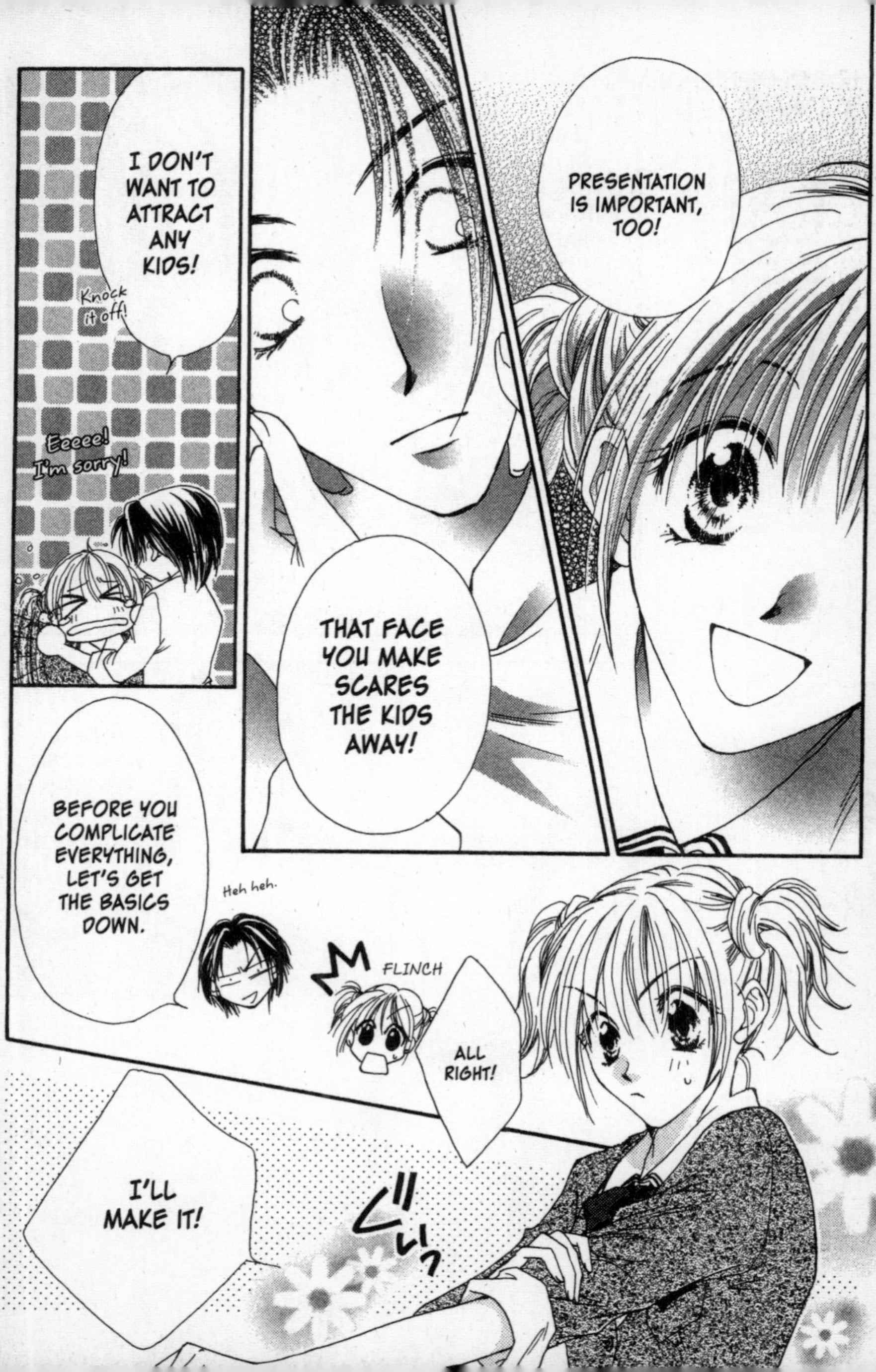
PRESENTATION IS IMPORTANT, TOO!
THAT FACE YOU MAKE SCARES THE KIDS AWAY!
I DON'T WANT TO ATTRACT ANY KIDS!
Knock it off!
Eeeee! I'm sorry!
BEFORE YOU COMPLICATE EVERYTHING, LET'S GET THE BASICS DOWN.
Heh heh.
FLINCH
ALL RIGHT!
I'LL MAKE IT!

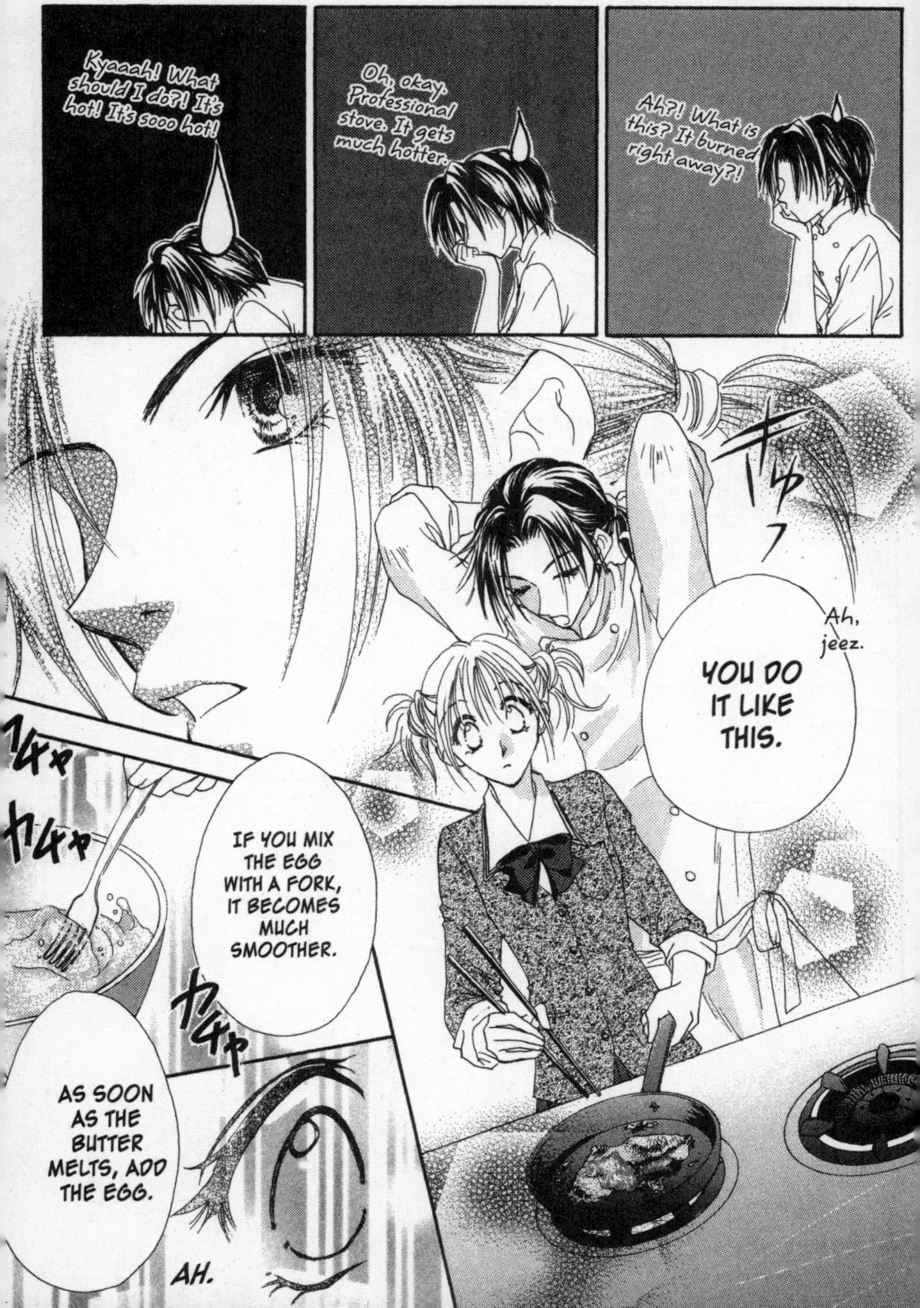
Ah?! What is this? It burned right away?!
Oh, okay. Professional stove. It gets much hotter.
Kyaaah! What should I do?! It's hot! It's sooo hot!
Ah, jeez.
YOU DO IT LIKE THIS.
IF YOU MIX THE EGG WITH A FORK, IT BECOMES MUCH SMOOTHER.
AS SOON AS THE BUTTER MELTS, ADD THE EGG.
AH.

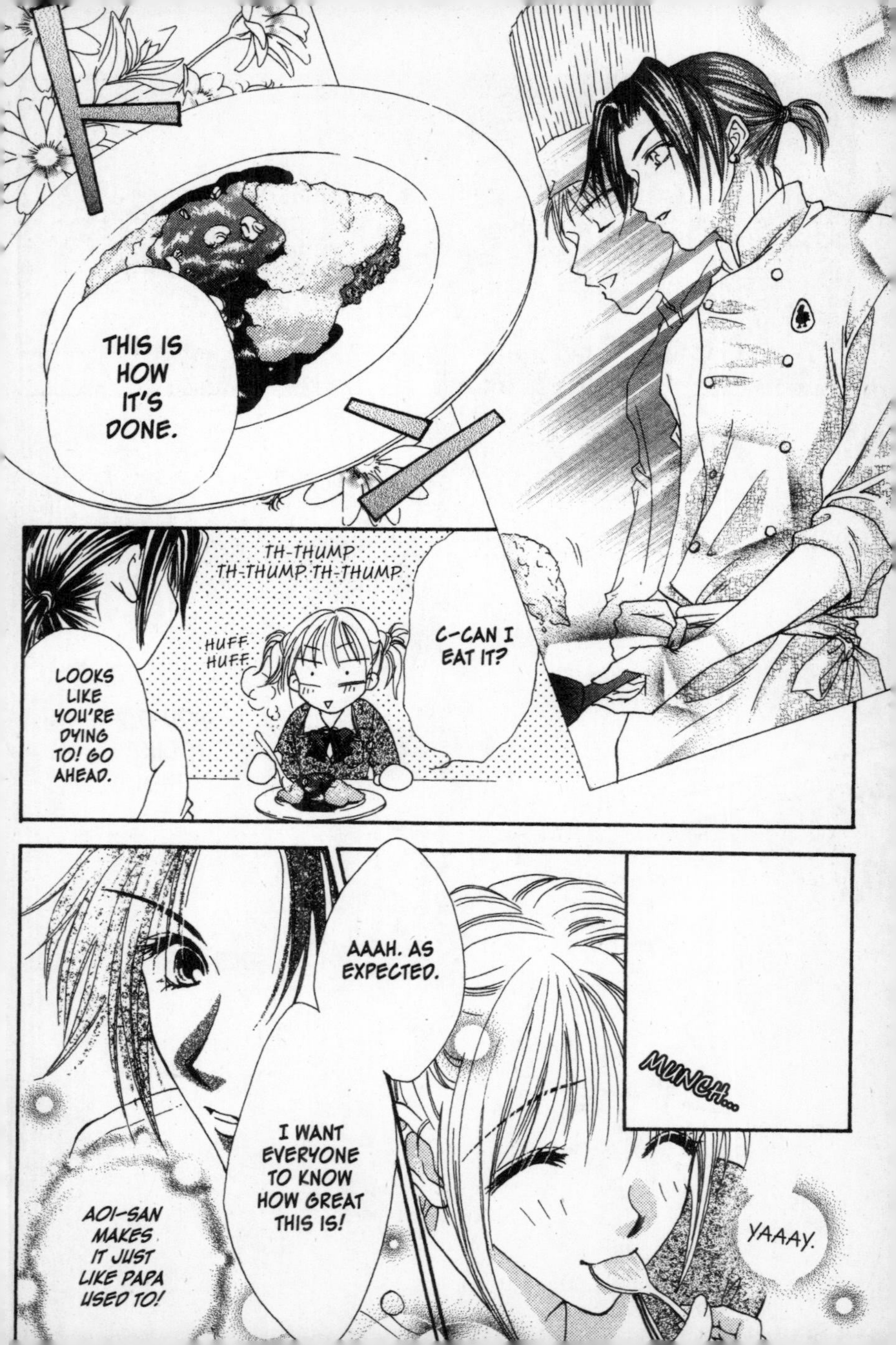
THIS IS HOW IT'S DONE.
C-CAN I EAT IT?
TH-THUMP TH-THUMP TH-THUMP
HUFF HUFF
LOOKS LIKE YOU'RE DYING TO! GO AHEAD.
MUNCH...
YAAAY.
AAAH. AS EXPECTED.
I WANT EVERYONE TO KNOW HOW GREAT THIS IS!
AOI-SAN MAKES IT JUST LIKE PAPA USED TO!

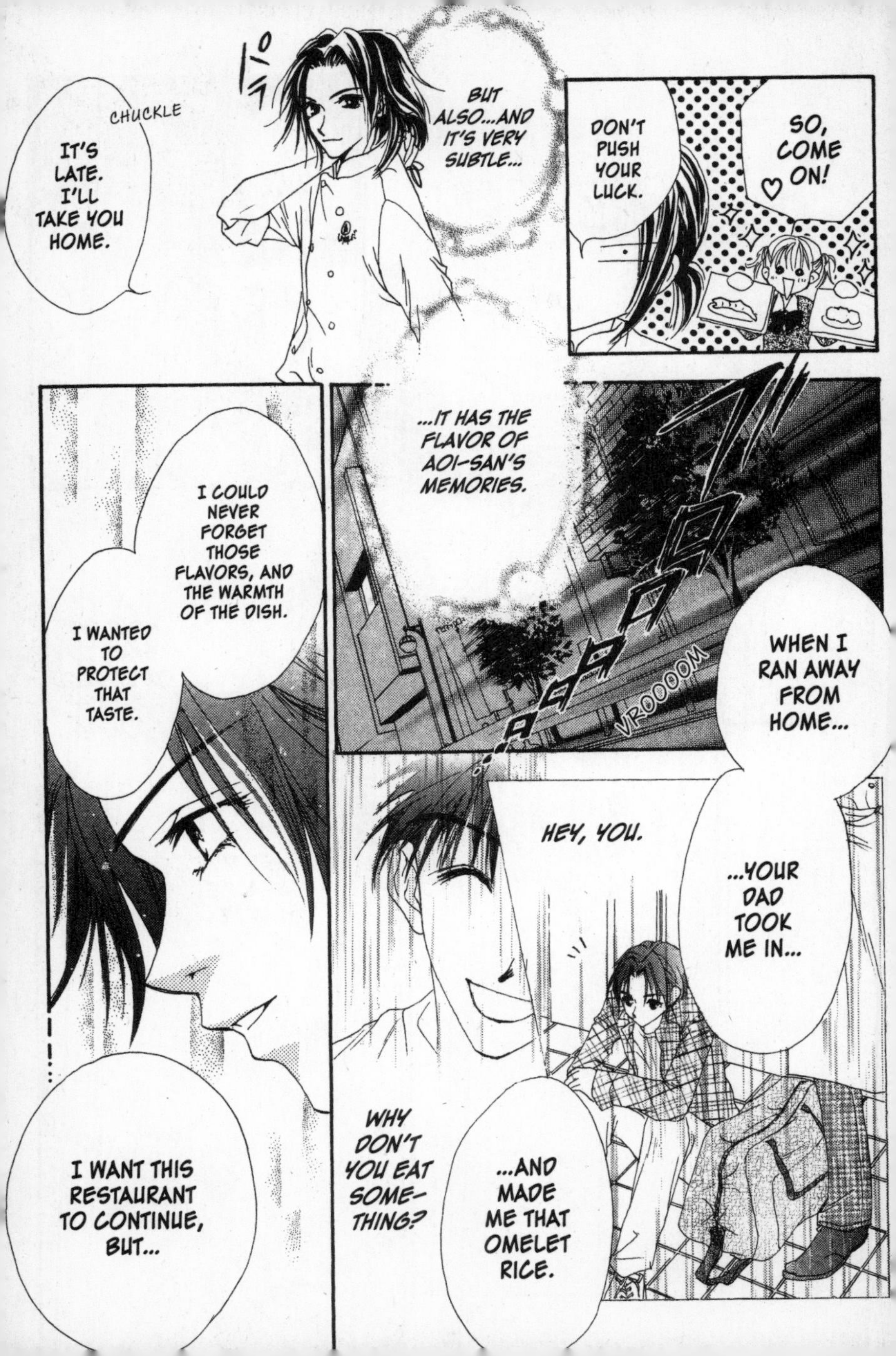
SO, COME ON!
DON'T PUSH YOUR LUCK.
BUT ALSO...AND IT'S VERY SUBTLE...
CHUCKLE
IT'S LATE. I'LL TAKE YOU HOME.
...IT HAS THE FLAVOR OF AOI-SAN'S MEMORIES.
VROOOOM
WHEN I RAN AWAY FROM HOME...
...YOUR DAD TOOK ME IN...
HEY, YOU.
WHY DON'T YOU EAT SOME-THING?
...AND MADE ME THAT OMELET RICE.
I COULD NEVER FORGET THOSE FLAVORS, AND THE WARMTH OF THE DISH.
I WANTED TO PROTECT THAT TASTE.
I WANT THIS RESTAURANT TO CONTINUE, BUT...

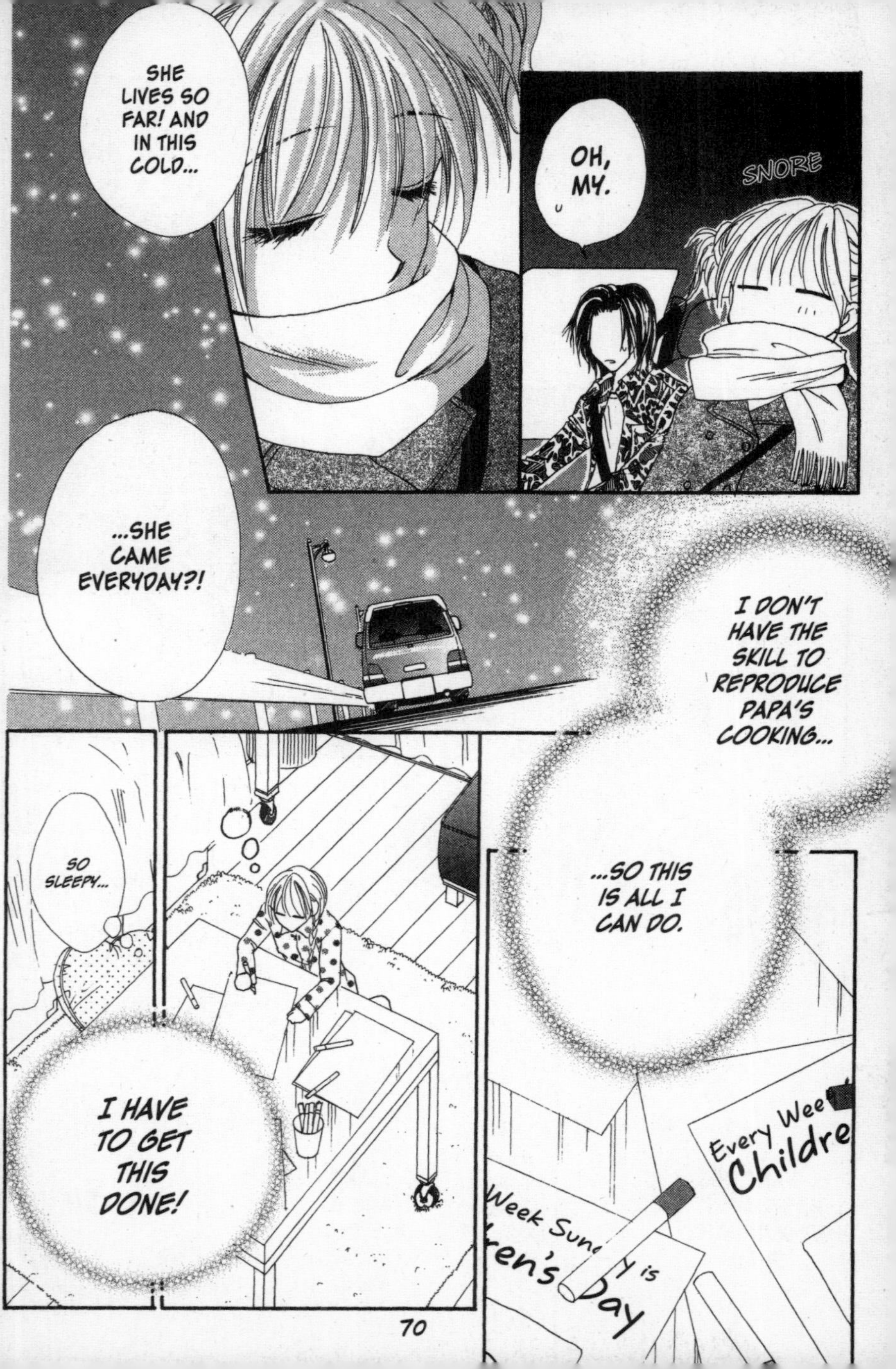
OH, MY.
SNORE
SHE LIVES SO FAR! AND IN THIS COLD...
...SHE CAME EVERYDAY?!
I DON'T HAVE THE SKILL TO REPRODUCE PAPA'S COOKING...
...SO THIS IS ALL I CAN DO.
Every Wee Childre
Week Sun y is ren's Day
SO SLEEPY...
I HAVE TO GET THIS DONE!

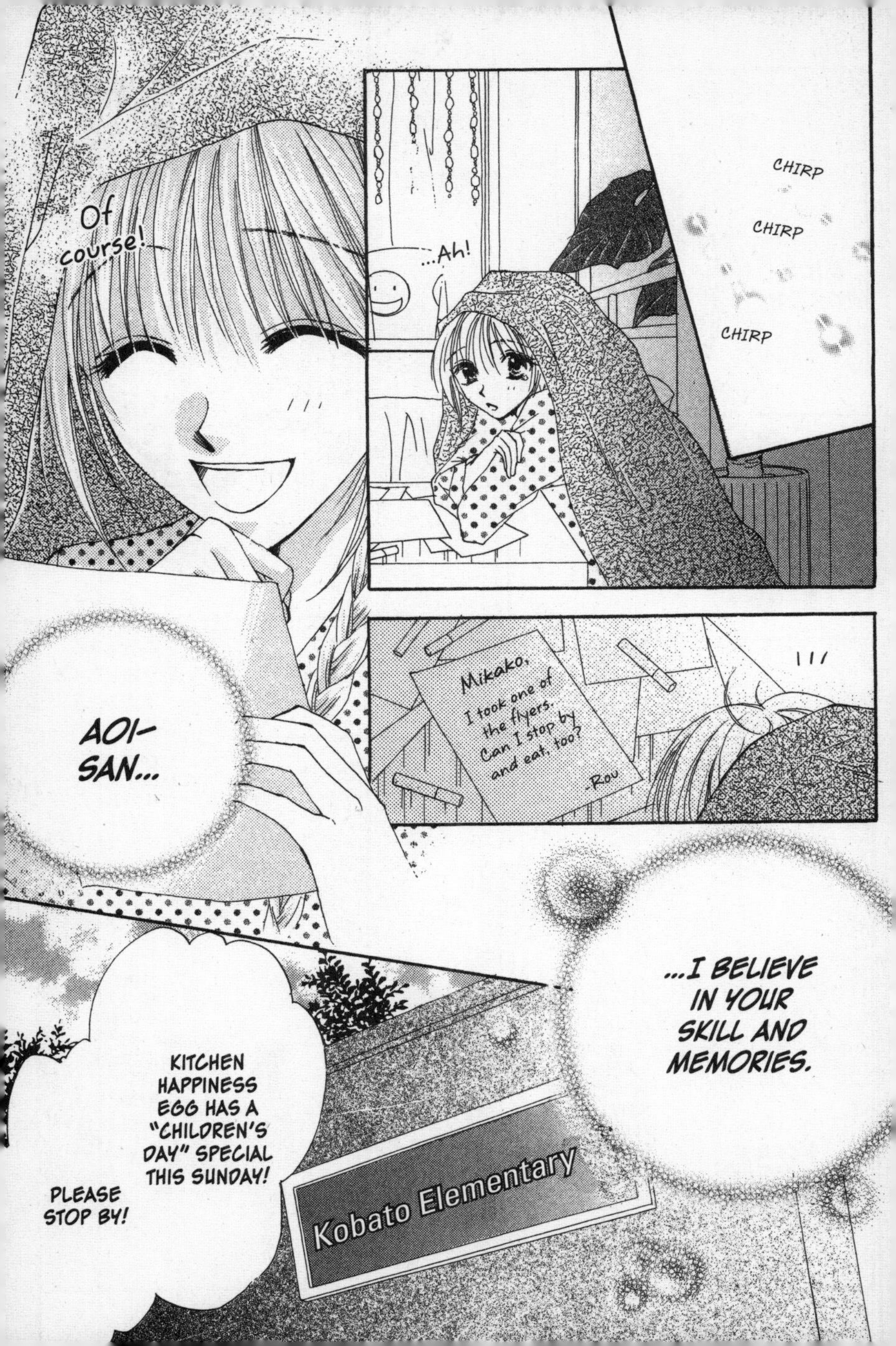

CHIRP
CHIRP
CHIRP
...Ah!
Mikako,
I took one of the flyers. Can I stop by and eat, too?
-Rou
Of course!
AOI-SAN...
...I BELIEVE IN YOUR SKILL AND MEMORIES.
Kobato Elementary
KITCHEN HAPPINESS EGG HAS A "CHILDREN'S DAY" SPECIAL THIS SUNDAY!
PLEASE STOP BY!

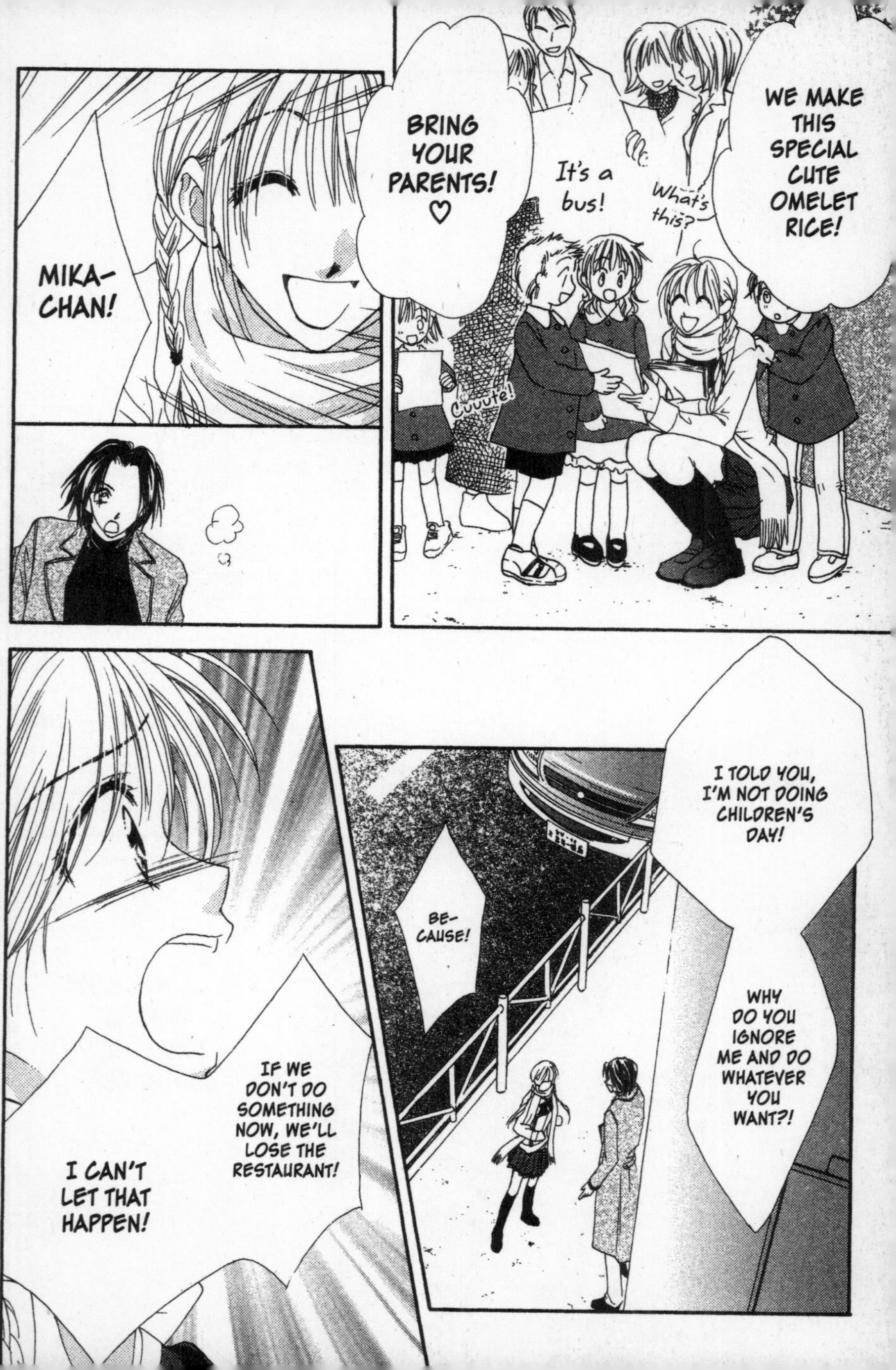
WE MAKE THIS SPECIAL CUTE OMELET RICE!
What's this?
It's a bus!
BRING YOUR PARENTS! ♡
Cuuute!
MIKA-CHAN!
I TOLD YOU, I'M NOT DOING CHILDREN'S DAY!
WHY DO YOU IGNORE ME AND DO WHATEVER YOU WANT?!
BE-CAUSE!
IF WE DON'T DO SOMETHING NOW, WE'LL LOSE THE RESTAURANT!
I CAN'T LET THAT HAPPEN!

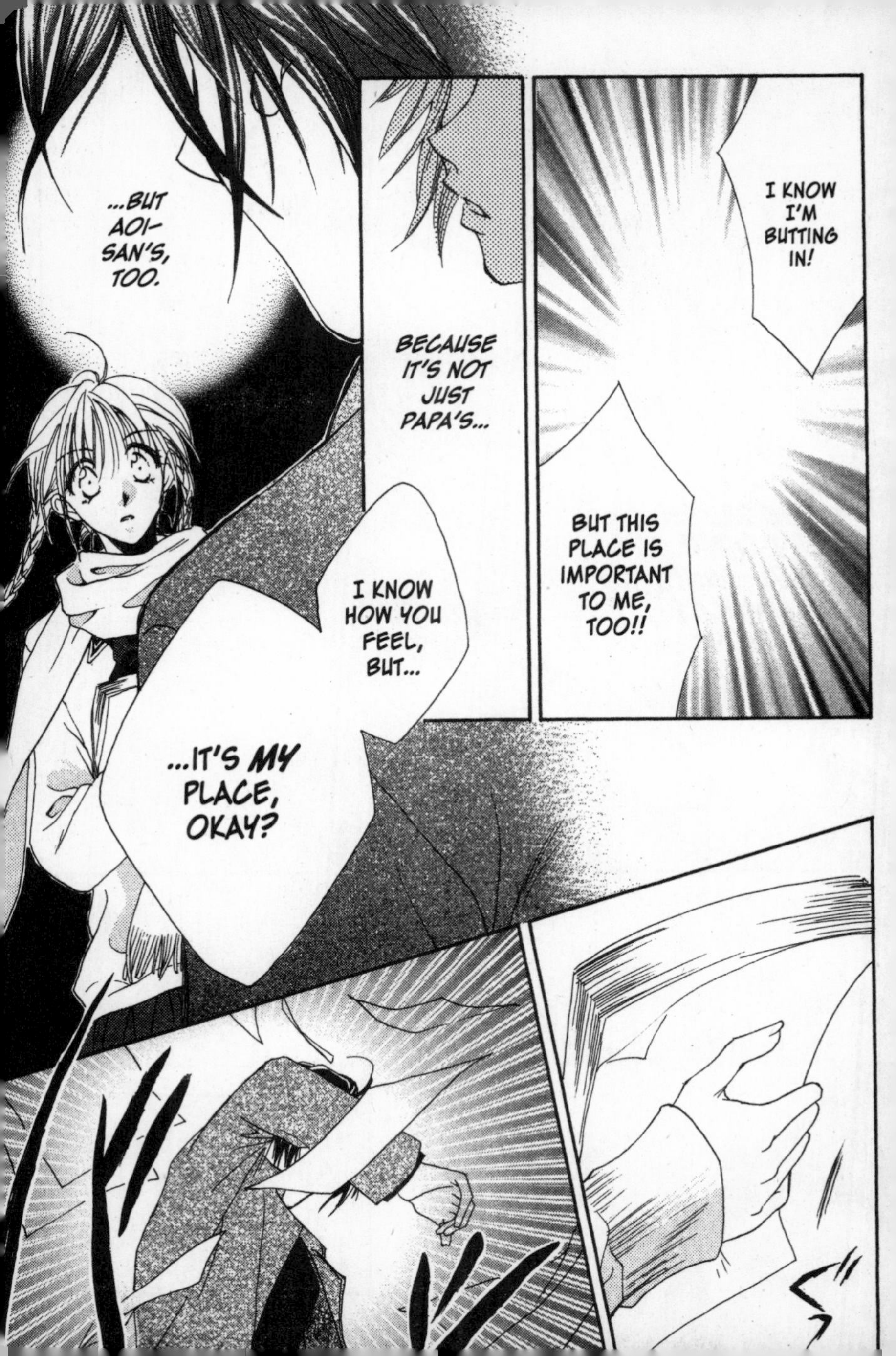
I KNOW I'M BUTTING IN!
BUT THIS PLACE IS IMPORTANT TO ME, TOO!!
BECAUSE IT'S NOT JUST PAPA'S...
...BUT AOI-SAN'S, TOO.
I KNOW HOW YOU FEEL, BUT...
...IT'S *MY* PLACE, OKAY?

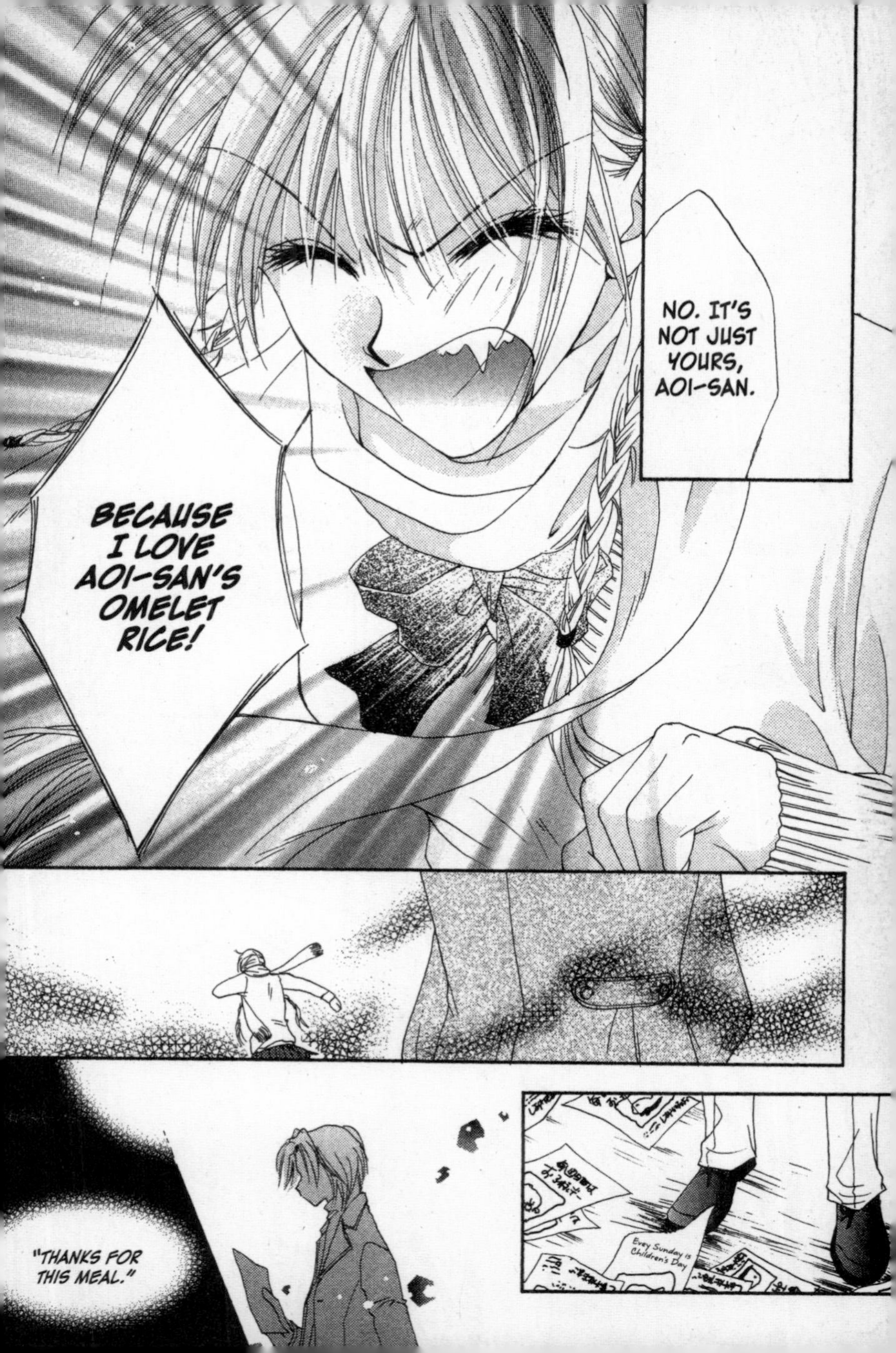
NO. IT'S NOT JUST YOURS, AOI-SAN.
BECAUSE I LOVE AOI-SAN'S OMELET RICE!
Evey Sunday is Children's Day
"THANKS FOR THIS MEAL."

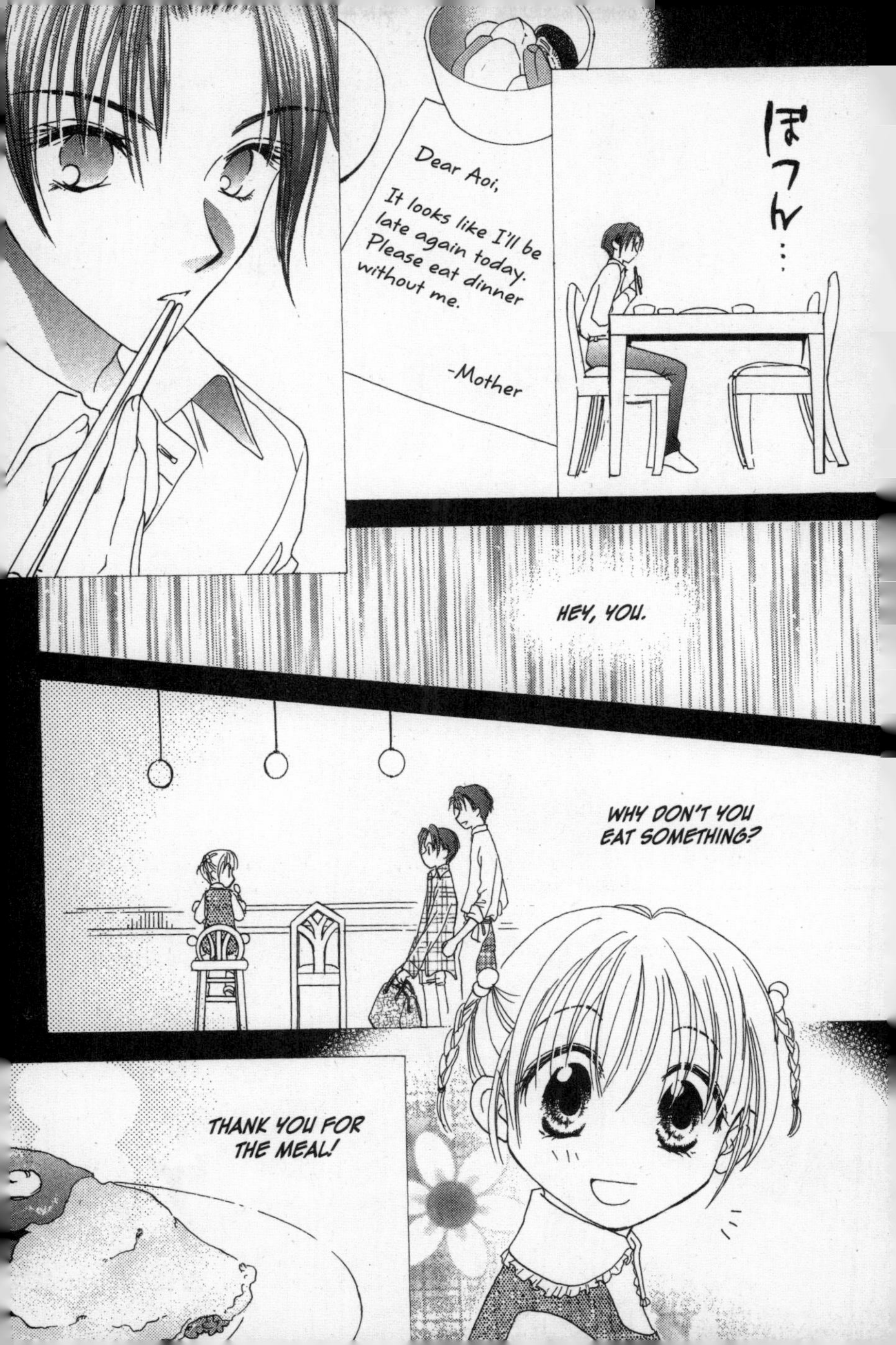
ぽつん…
Dear Aoi,
It looks like I'll be late again today. Please eat dinner without me.
-Mother
HEY, YOU.
WHY DON'T YOU EAT SOMETHING?
THANK YOU FOR THE MEAL!

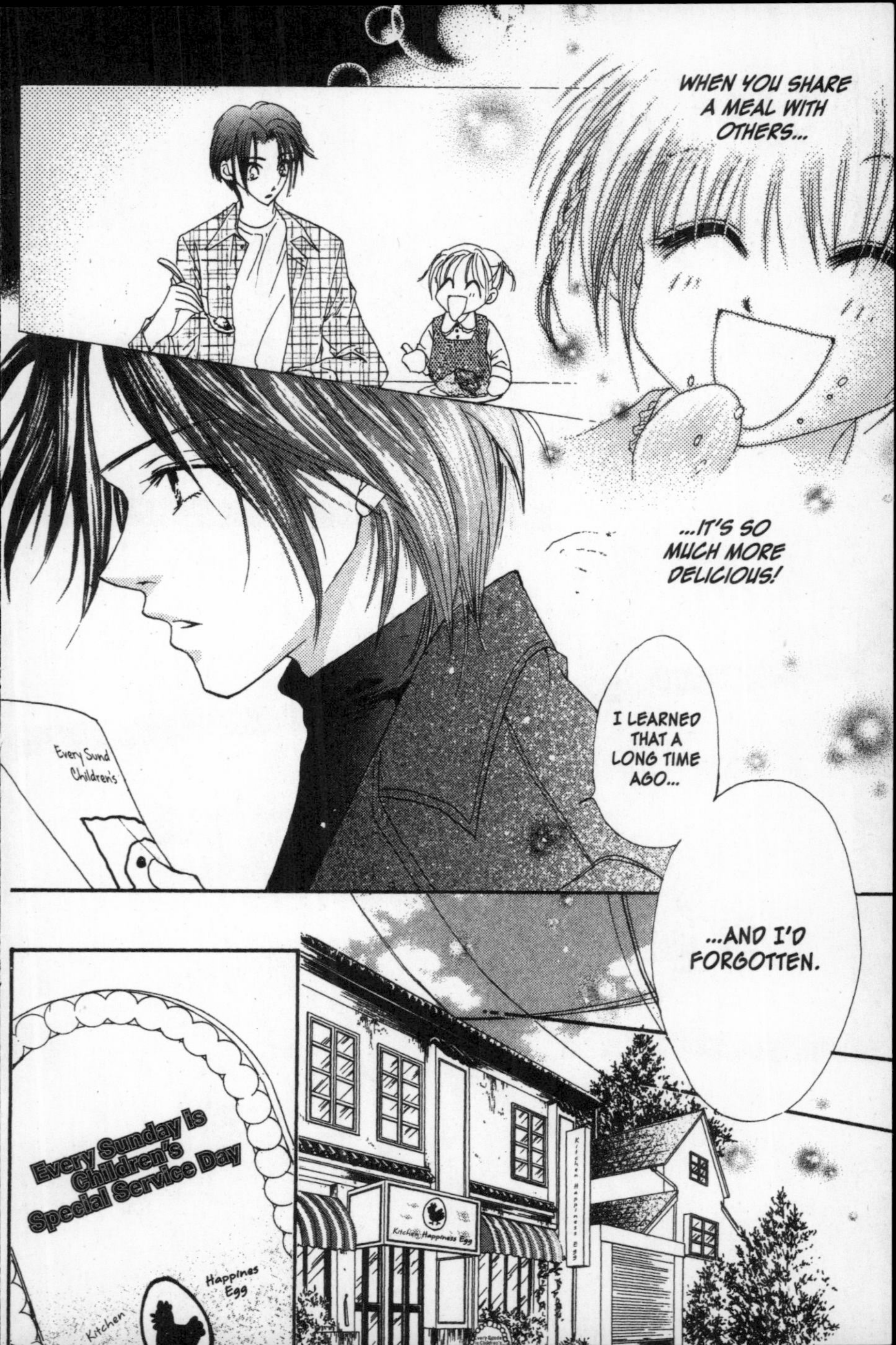
WHEN YOU SHARE A MEAL WITH OTHERS...
...IT'S SO MUCH MORE DELICIOUS!
Every Sund Children's
I LEARNED THAT A LONG TIME AGO...
...AND I'D FORGOTTEN.
Kitchen Happiness Egg
Kitchen Happiness Egg
Every Sunday is Children's Special Service Day
Happines Egg
Kitchen

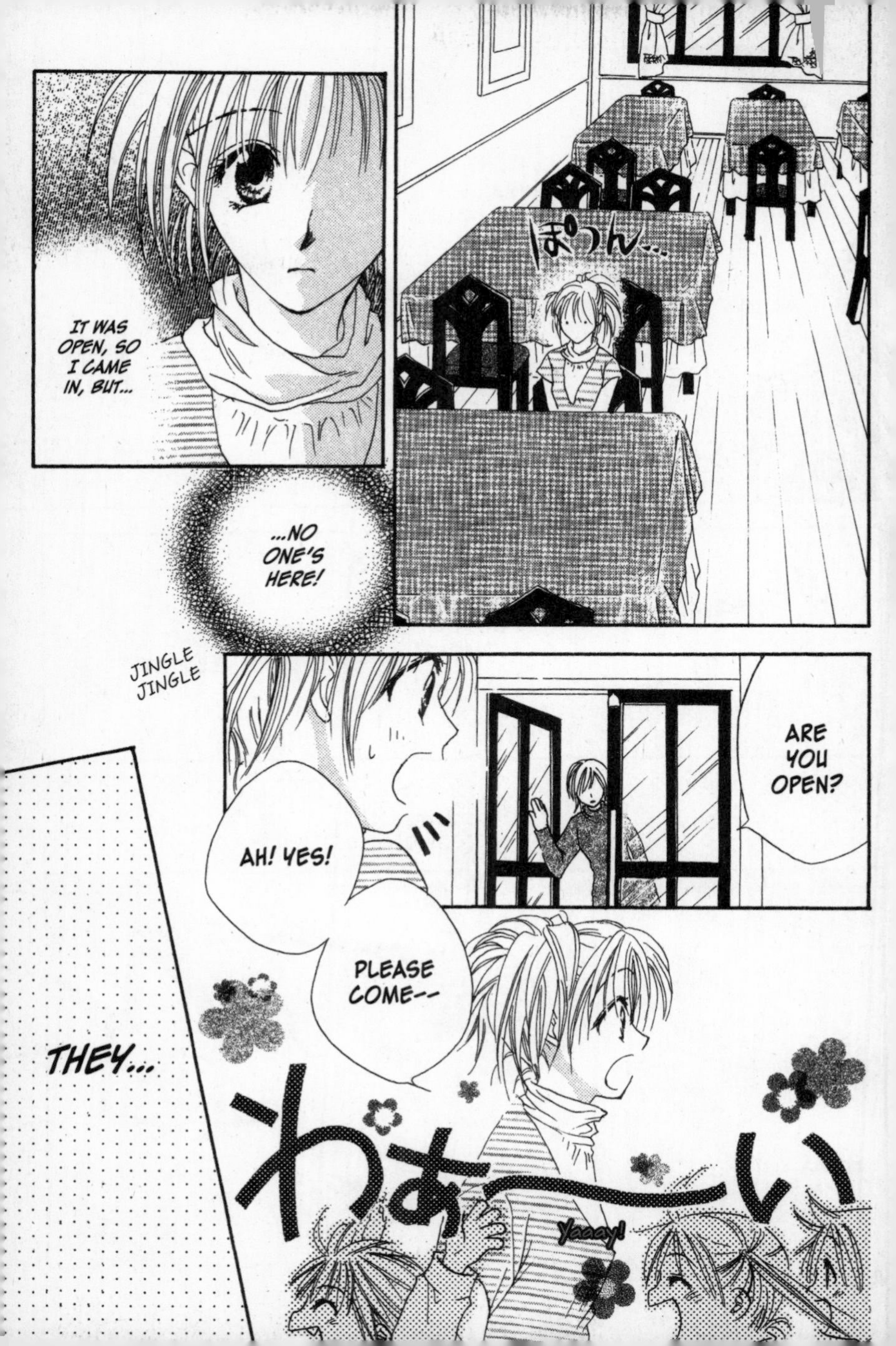
ぽつん...
IT WAS OPEN, SO I CAME IN, BUT...
...NO ONE'S HERE!
JINGLE JINGLE
ARE YOU OPEN?
AH! YES!
PLEASE COME--
わぁーい
Yaaay!
THEY...

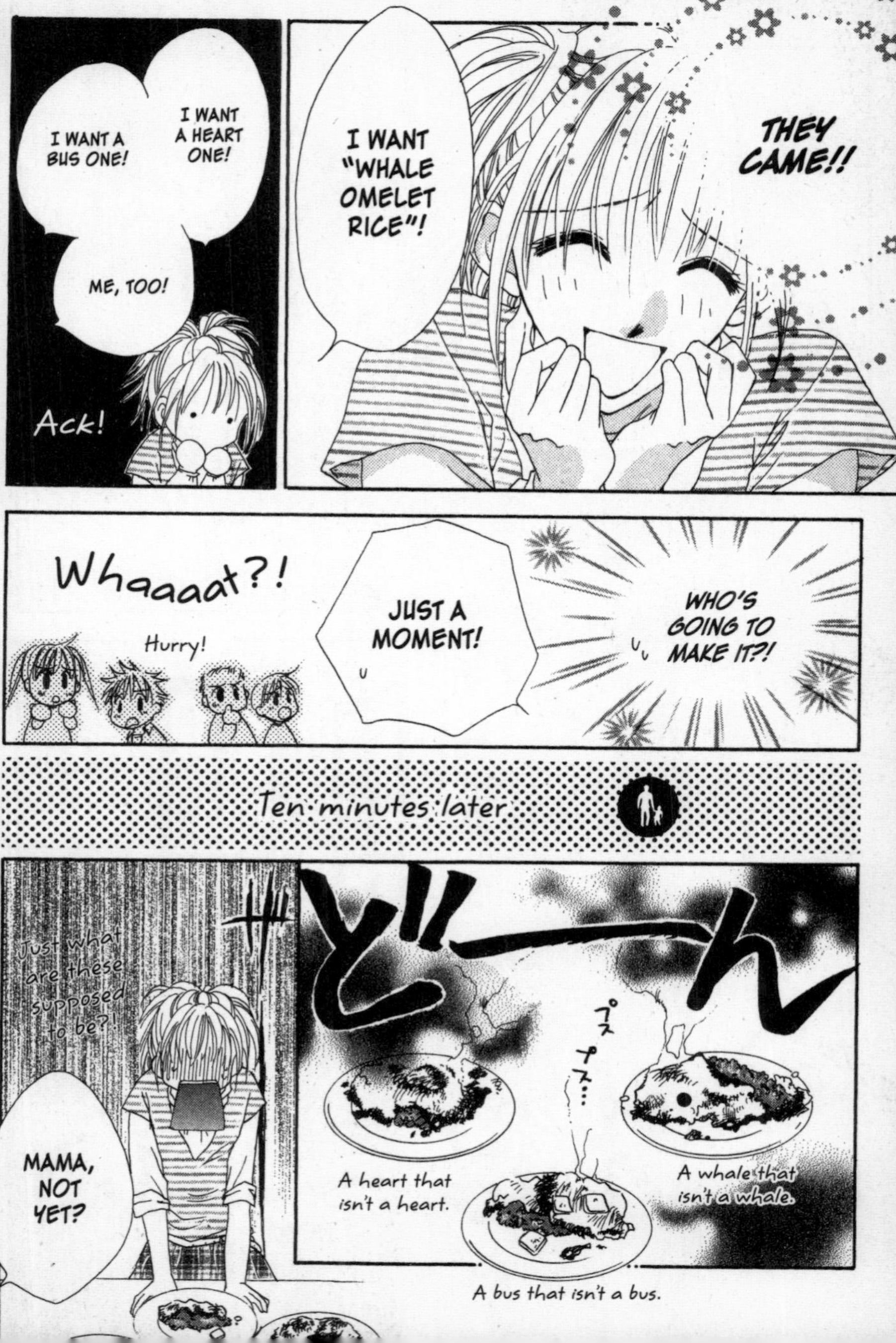
THEY CAME!!
I WANT "WHALE OMELET RICE"!
I WANT A HEART ONE!
I WANT A BUS ONE!
ME, TOO!
Ack!
WHO'S GOING TO MAKE IT?!
JUST A MOMENT!
Hurry!
Whaaaat?!
Ten minutes later
どーん
ぷす ぷす…
A whale that isn't a whale.
A heart that isn't a heart.
A bus that isn't a bus.
Just what are these supposed to be?!
MAMA, NOT YET?

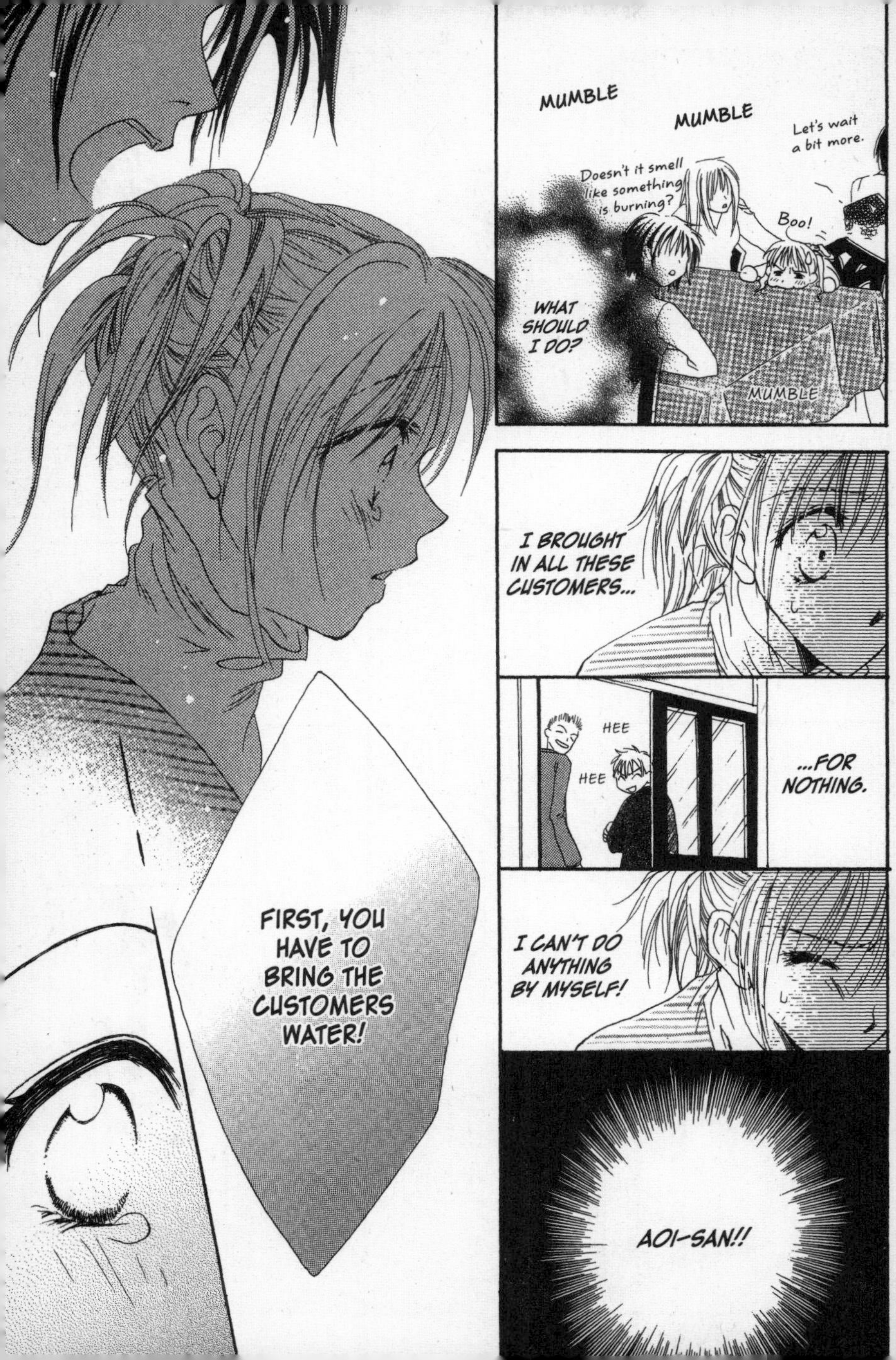
Let's wait a bit more.
MUMBLE
MUMBLE
Doesn't it smell like something is burning?
Boo!
WHAT SHOULD I DO?
MUMBLE
I BROUGHT IN ALL THESE CUSTOMERS...
...FOR NOTHING.
HEE
HEE
I CAN'T DO ANYTHING BY MYSELF!
AOI-SAN!!
FIRST, YOU HAVE TO BRING THE CUSTOMERS WATER!

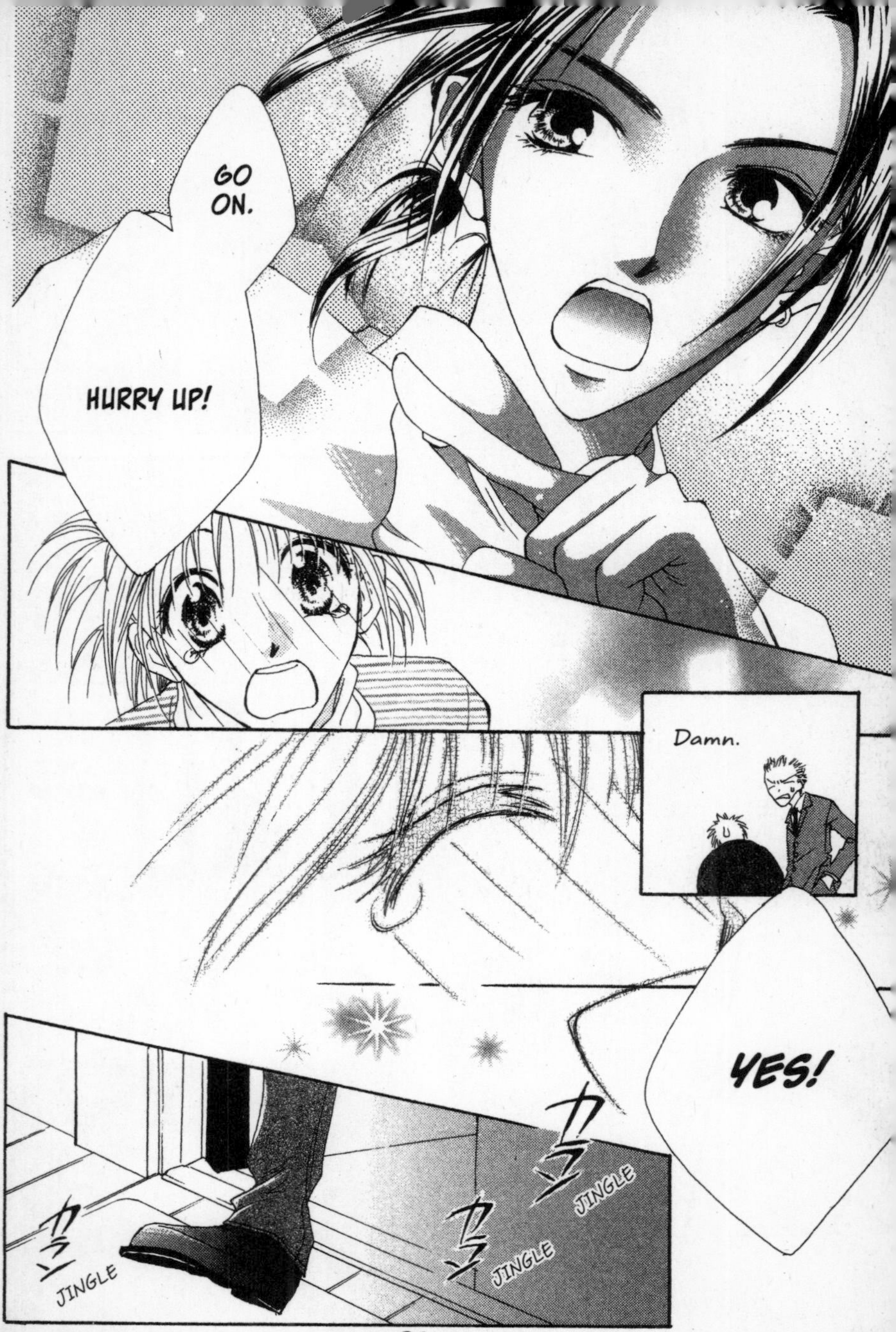
GO ON.
HURRY UP!
Damn.
YES!
カラン
JINGLE
カラン
JINGLE
カラン
JINGLE

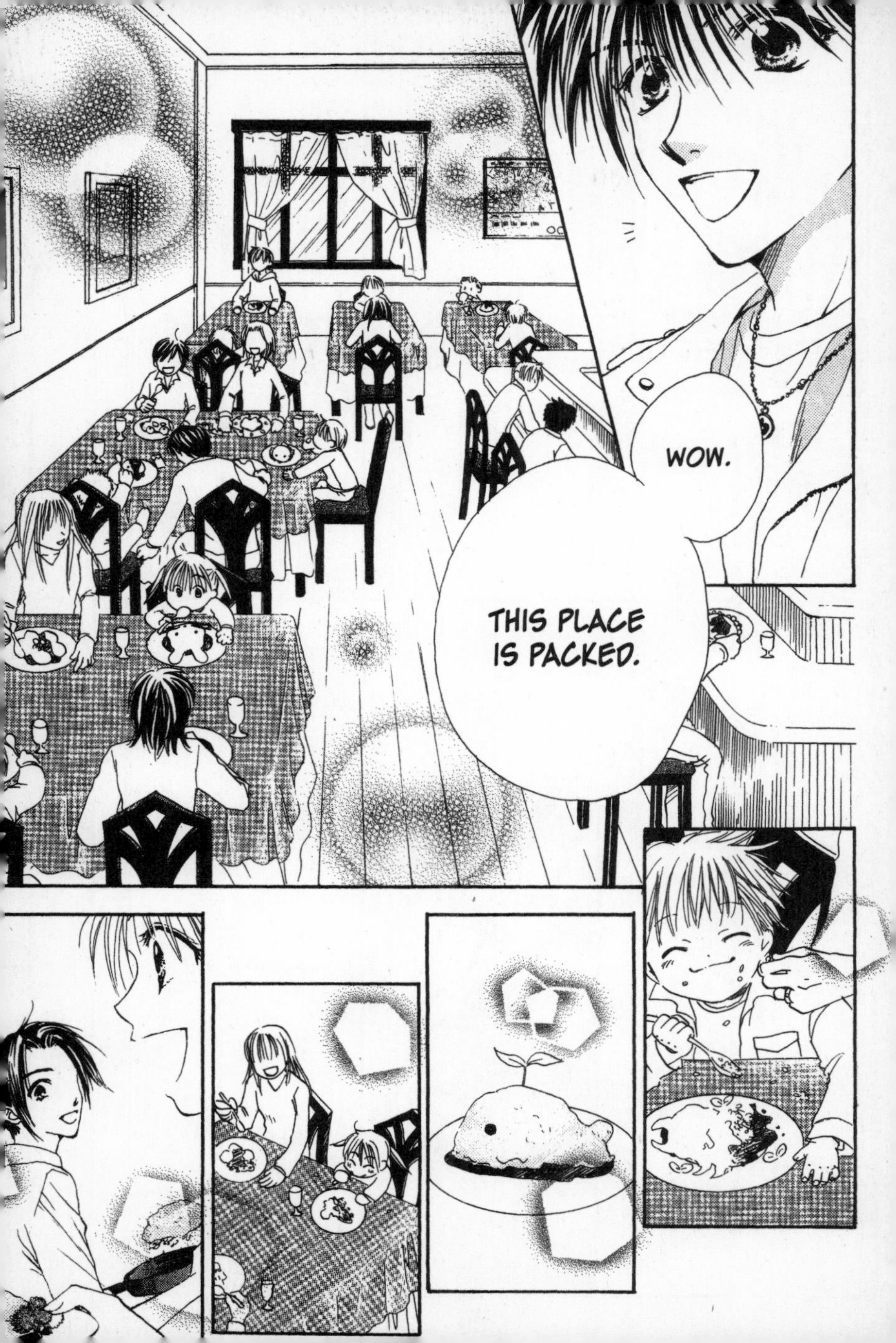
WOW.
THIS PLACE IS PACKED.

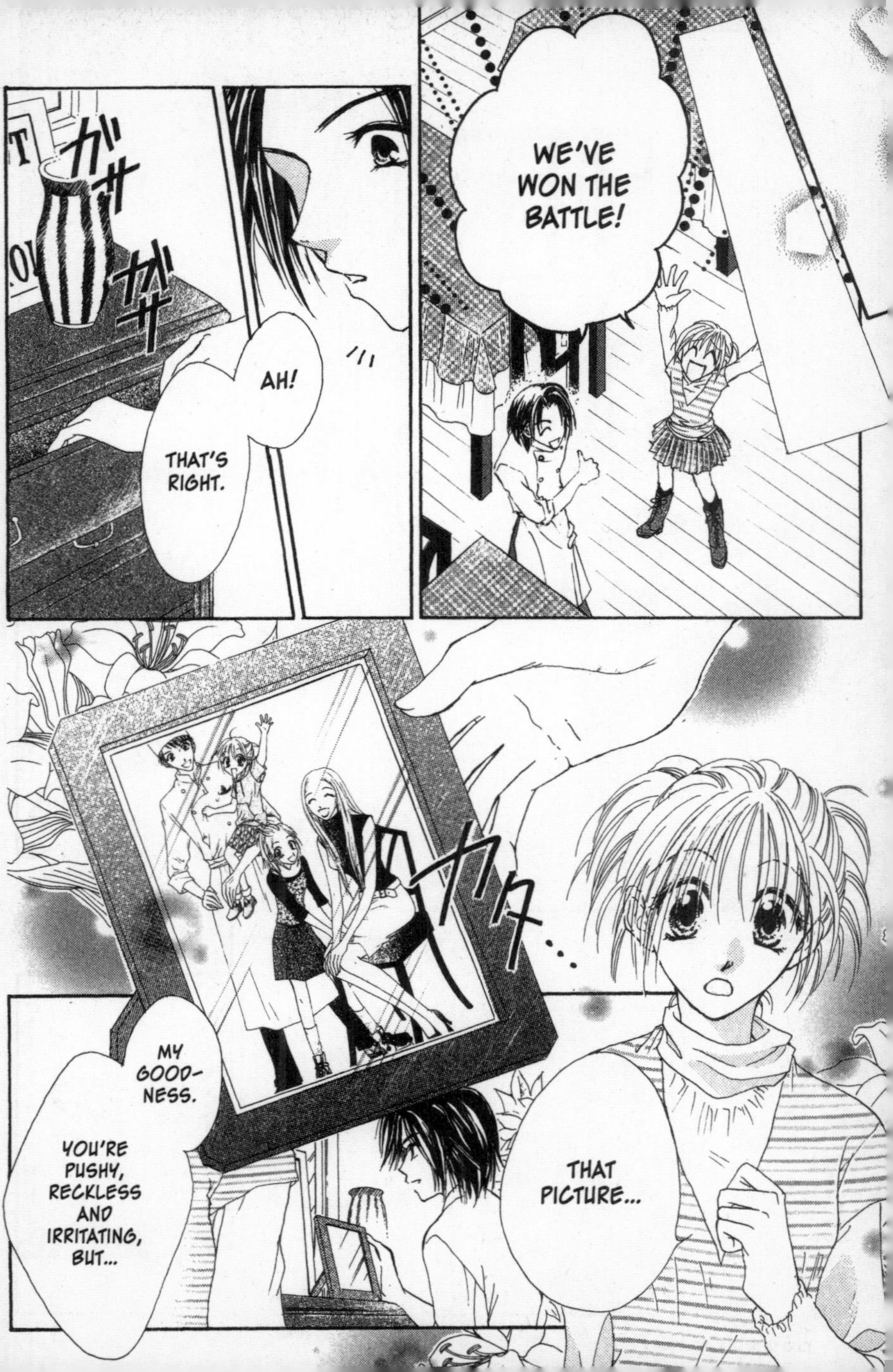
WE'VE WON THE BATTLE!
ガサ
ガサ
AH!
THAT'S RIGHT.
カタ…
THAT PICTURE...
MY GOODNESS.
YOU'RE PUSHY, RECKLESS AND IRRITATING, BUT...

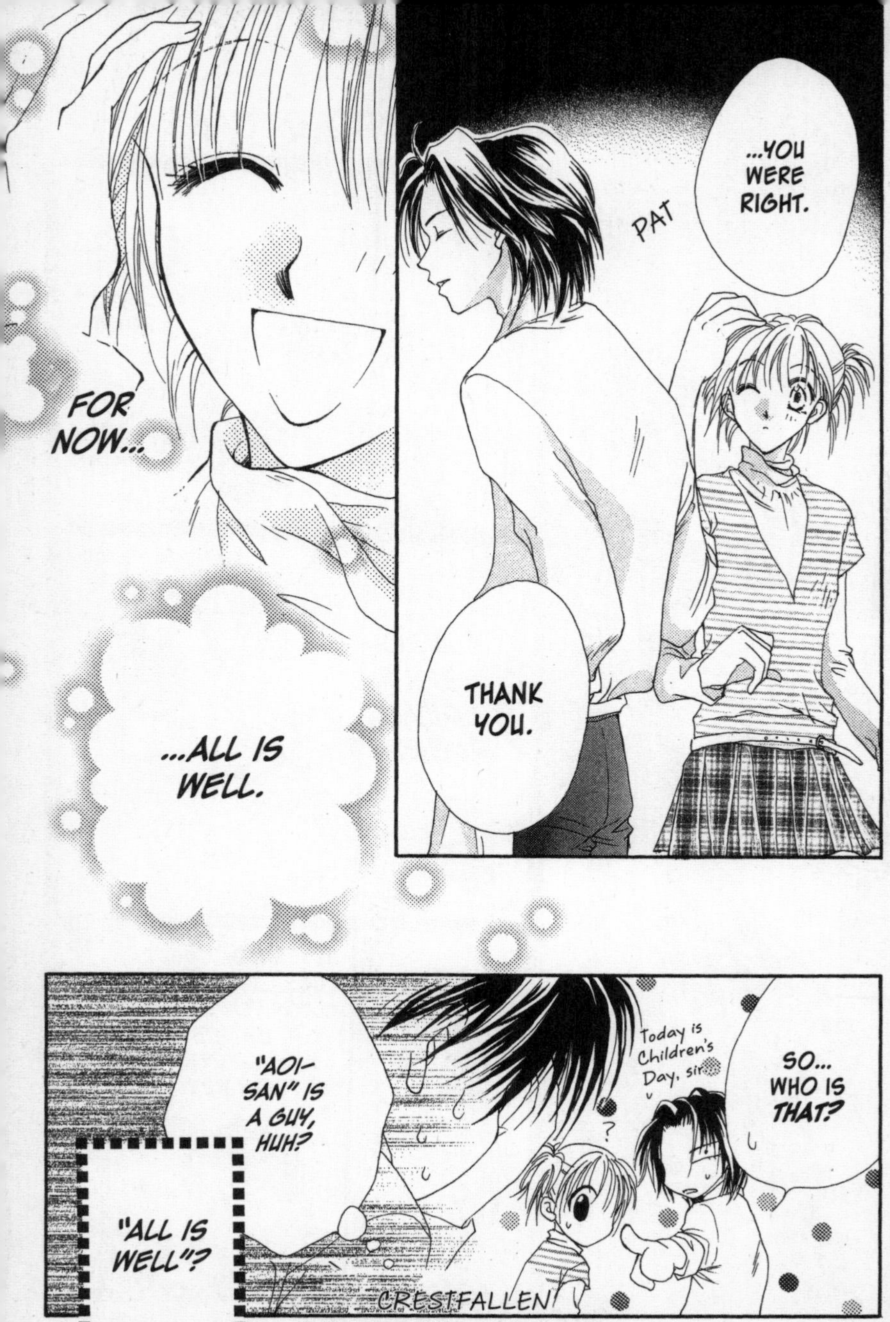
...YOU WERE RIGHT.
PAT
THANK YOU.
FOR NOW...
...ALL IS WELL.
SO... WHO IS THAT?
Today is Children's Day, sir.
"AOI-SAN" IS A GUY, HUH?
CRESTFALLEN
"ALL IS WELL"?

MISSILE HAPPY! Chapter 10 / END

A CERTAIN CASE

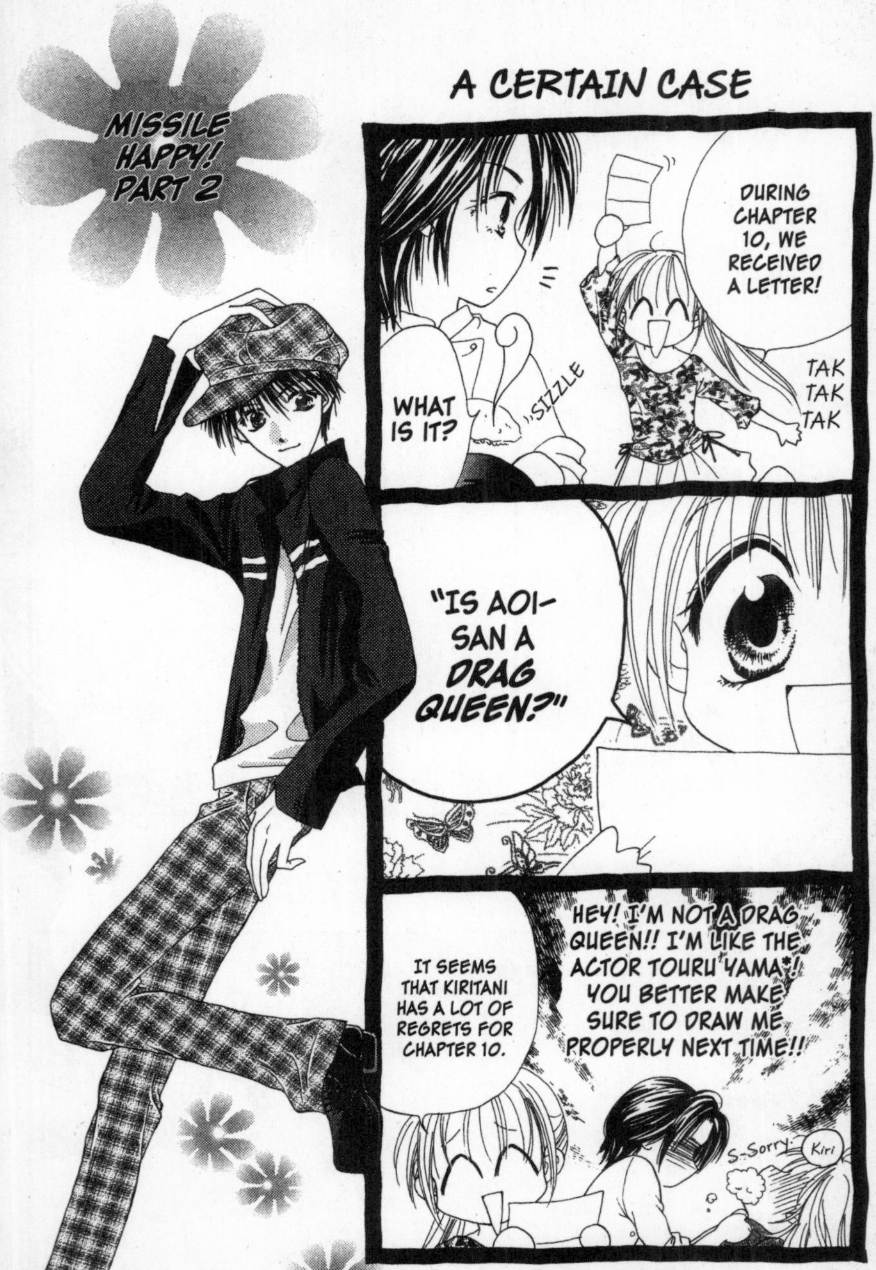
MISSILE HAPPY! PART 2
DURING CHAPTER 10, WE RECEIVED A LETTER!
TAK TAK TAK
WHAT IS IT?
SIZZLE
"IS AOI-SAN A DRAG QUEEN?"
HEY! I'M NOT A DRAG QUEEN!! I'M LIKE THE ACTOR TOURU YAMA*! YOU BETTER MAKE SURE TO DRAW ME PROPERLY NEXT TIME!!
IT SEEMS THAT KIRITANI HAS A LOT OF REGRETS FOR CHAPTER 10.
Kiri
S-Sorry.

I apologize. I apologize!

* He's a horror manga creator, actor and singer. Also very pretty.

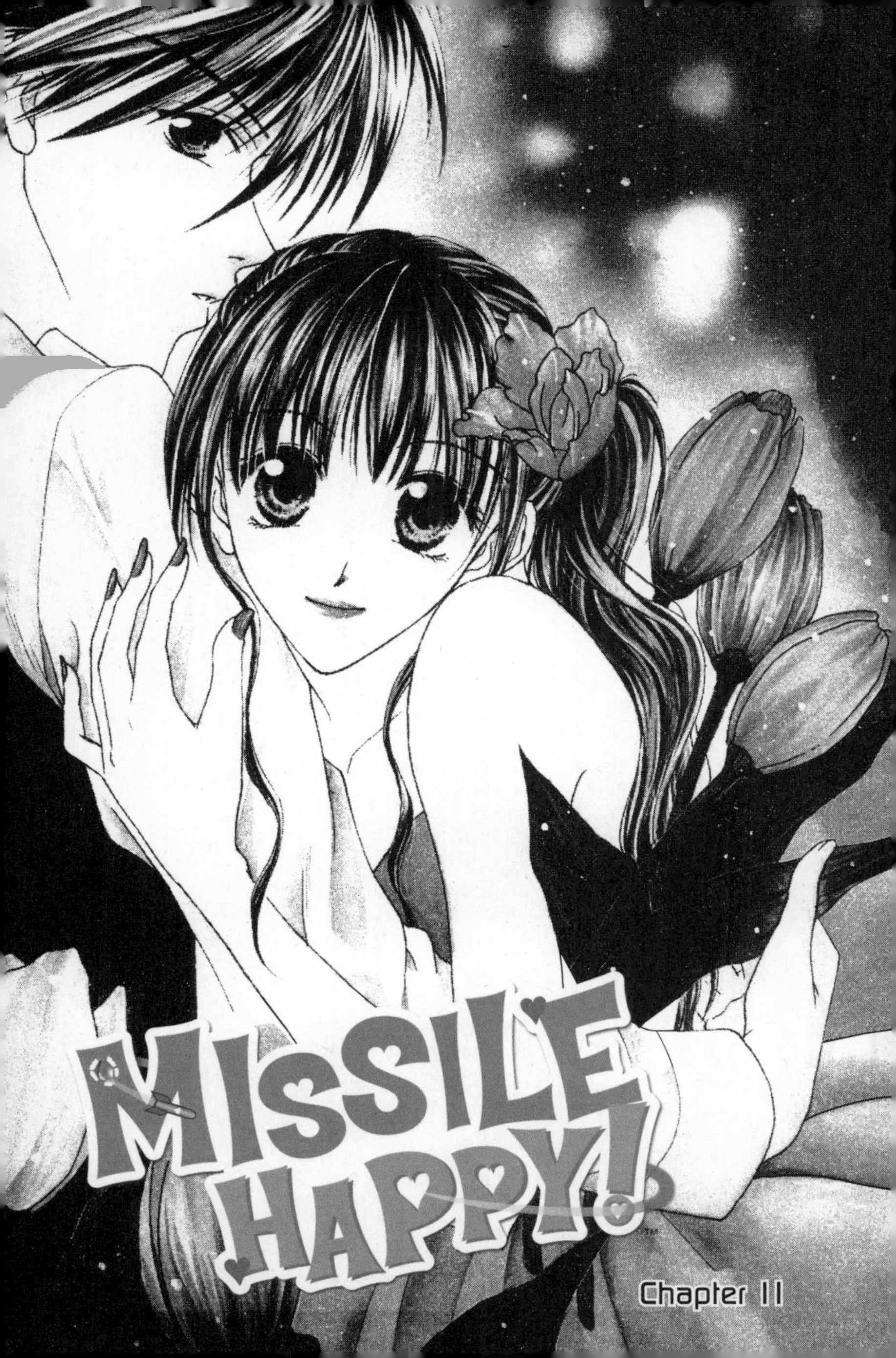
MISSILE HAPPY!™
Chapter 11

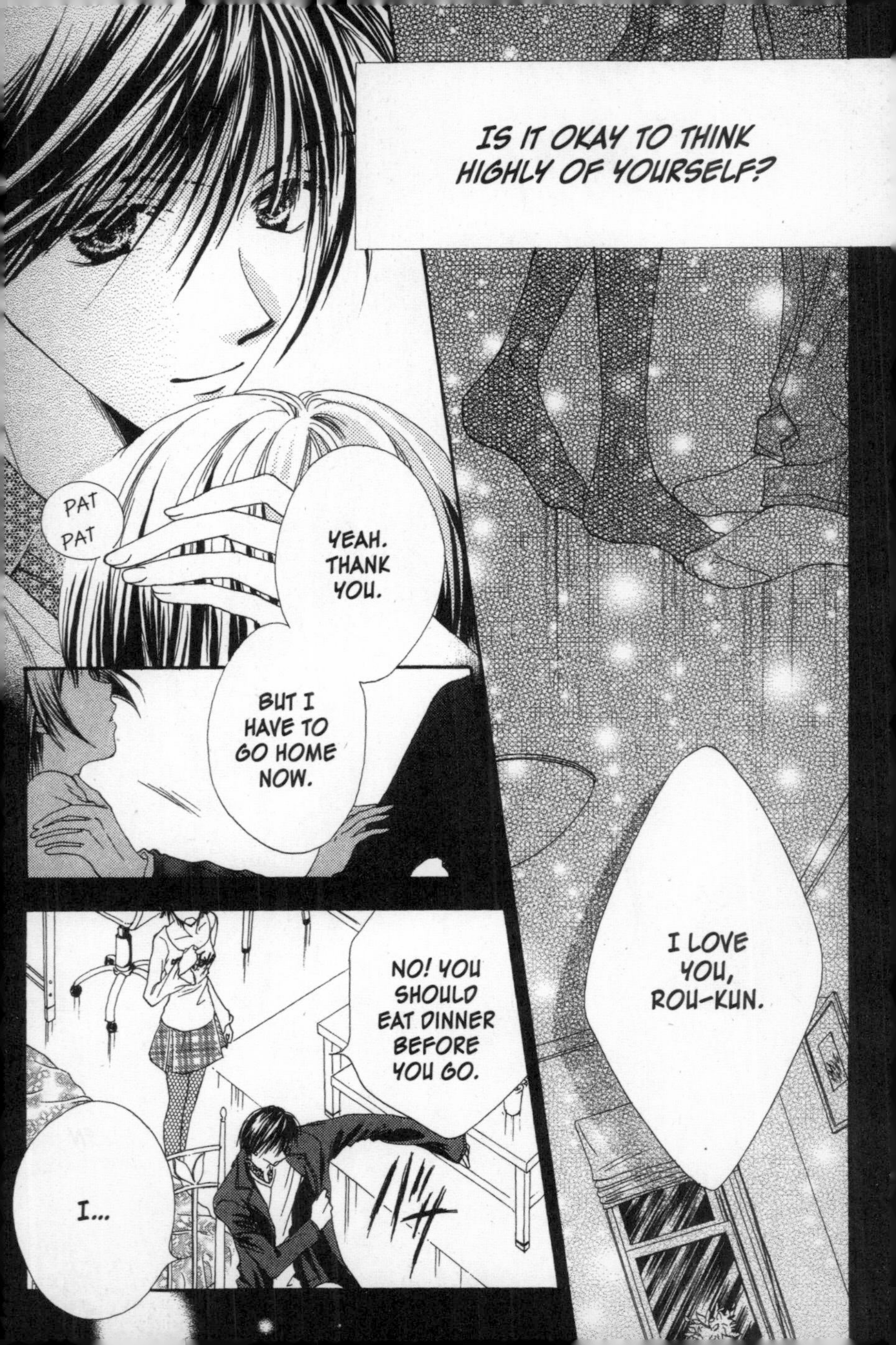
IS IT OKAY TO THINK HIGHLY OF YOURSELF?
I LOVE YOU, ROU-KUN.
YEAH. THANK YOU.
PAT PAT
BUT I HAVE TO GO HOME NOW.
NO! YOU SHOULD EAT DINNER BEFORE YOU GO.
I...

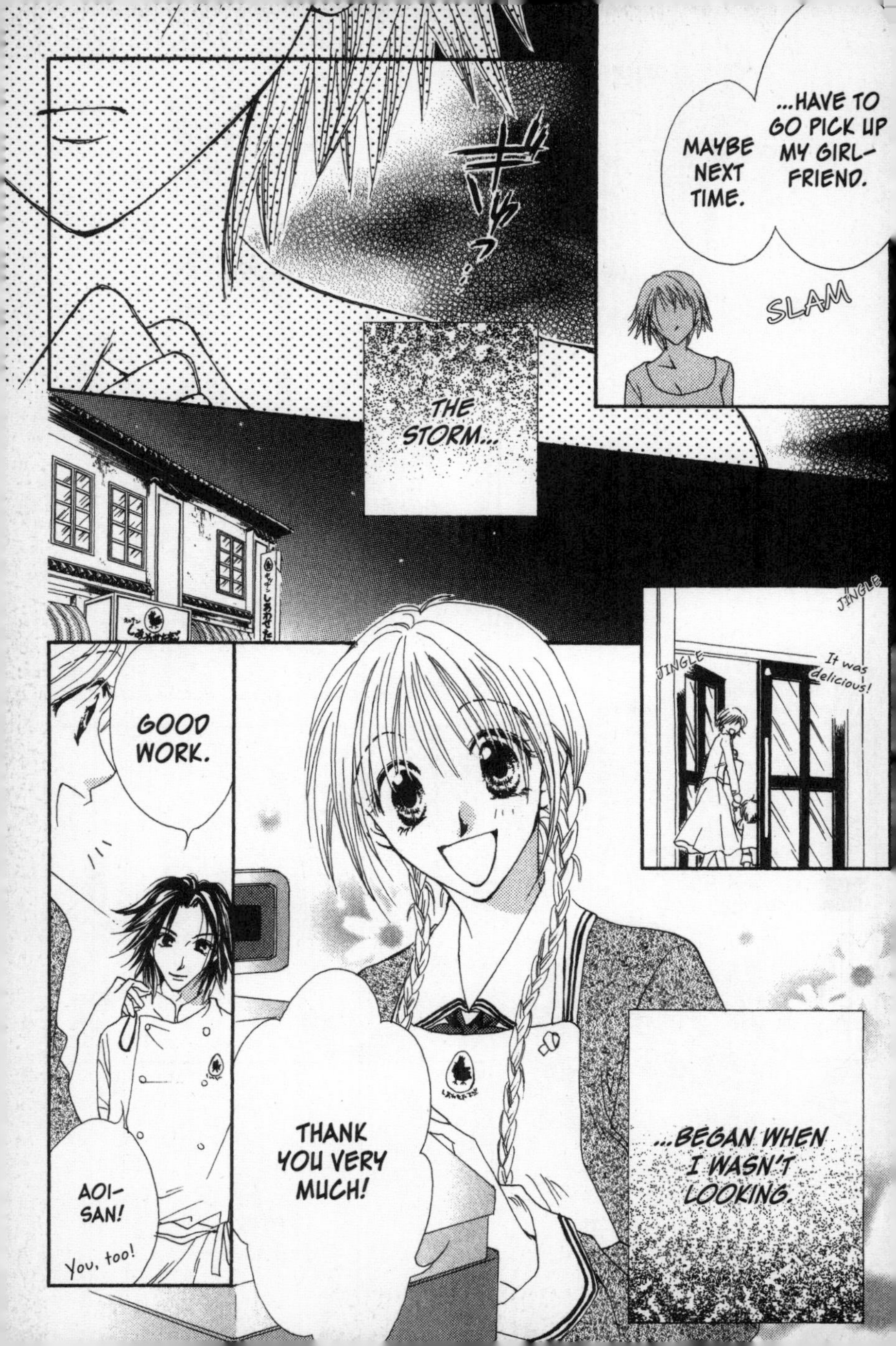
MAYBE NEXT TIME. ...HAVE TO GO PICK UP MY GIRL-FRIEND.
SLAM
THE STORM...
JINGLE
It was delicious!
JINGLE
...BEGAN WHEN I WASN'T LOOKING.
GOOD WORK.
THANK YOU VERY MUCH!
AOI-SAN!
You, too!

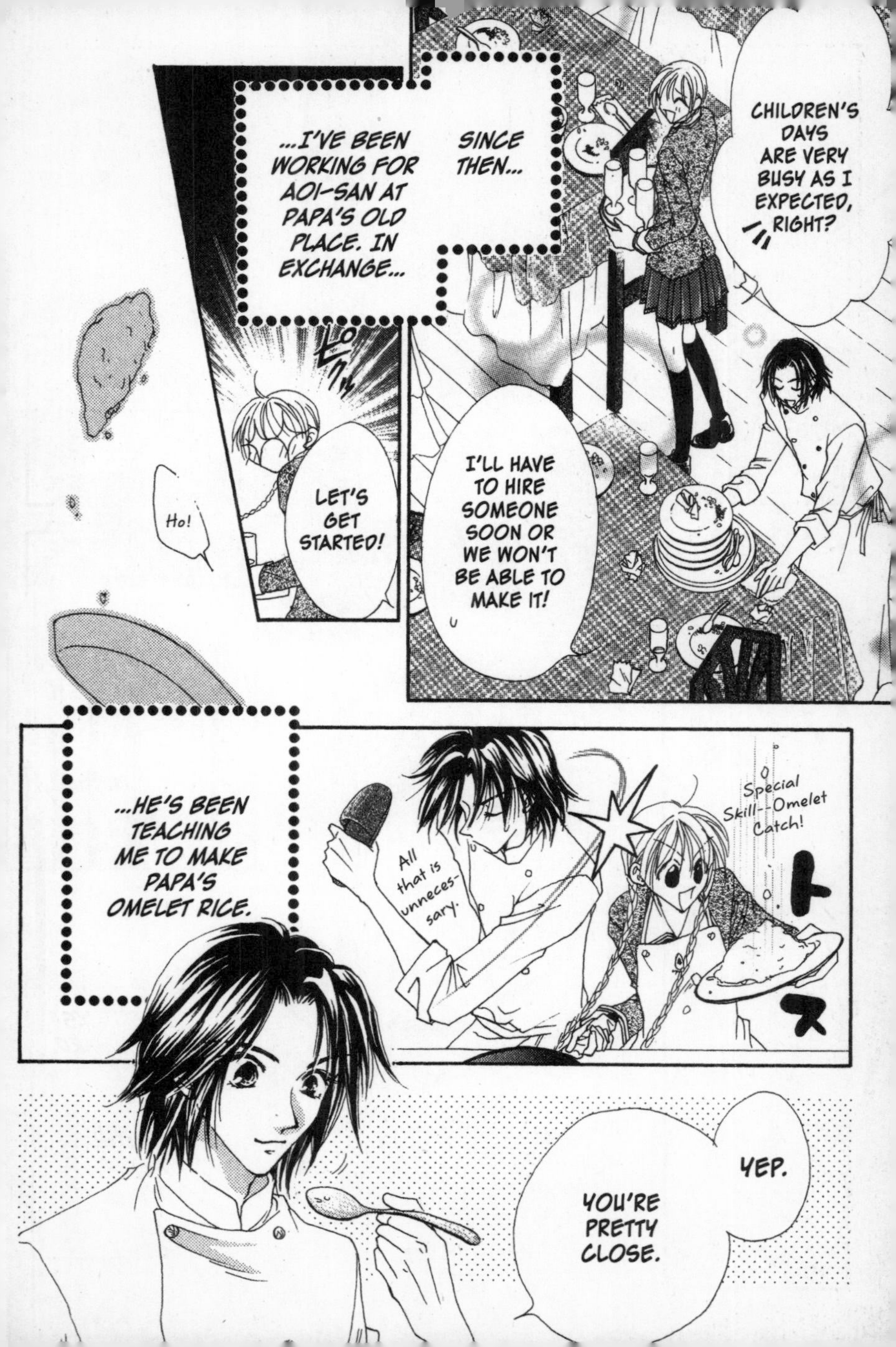
CHILDREN'S DAYS ARE VERY BUSY AS I EXPECTED, RIGHT?
I'LL HAVE TO HIRE SOMEONE SOON OR WE WON'T BE ABLE TO MAKE IT!
SINCE THEN...
...I'VE BEEN WORKING FOR AOI-SAN AT PAPA'S OLD PLACE. IN EXCHANGE...
LET'S GET STARTED!
Ho!
Special Skill--Omelet Catch!
ト
ス
All that is unneces-sary.
...HE'S BEEN TEACHING ME TO MAKE PAPA'S OMELET RICE.
YEP.
YOU'RE PRETTY CLOSE.

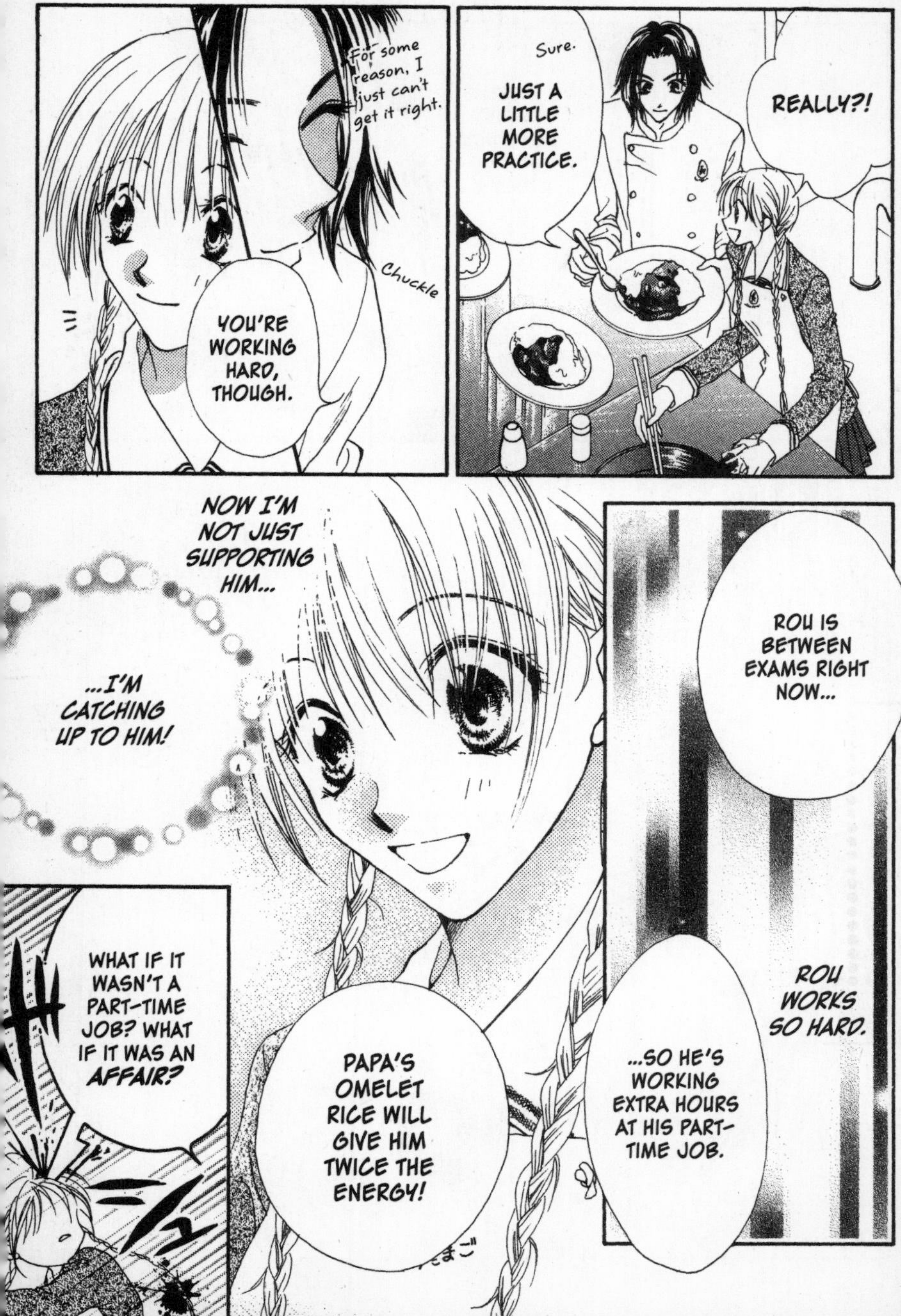
REALLY?!
Sure.
JUST A LITTLE MORE PRACTICE.
For some reason, I just can't get it right.
Chuckle
YOU'RE WORKING HARD, THOUGH.
ROU IS BETWEEN EXAMS RIGHT NOW...
ROU WORKS SO HARD.
...SO HE'S WORKING EXTRA HOURS AT HIS PART-TIME JOB.
NOW I'M NOT JUST SUPPORTING HIM...
...I'M CATCHING UP TO HIM!
PAPA'S OMELET RICE WILL GIVE HIM TWICE THE ENERGY!
WHAT IF IT WASN'T A PART-TIME JOB? WHAT IF IT WAS AN AFFAIR?

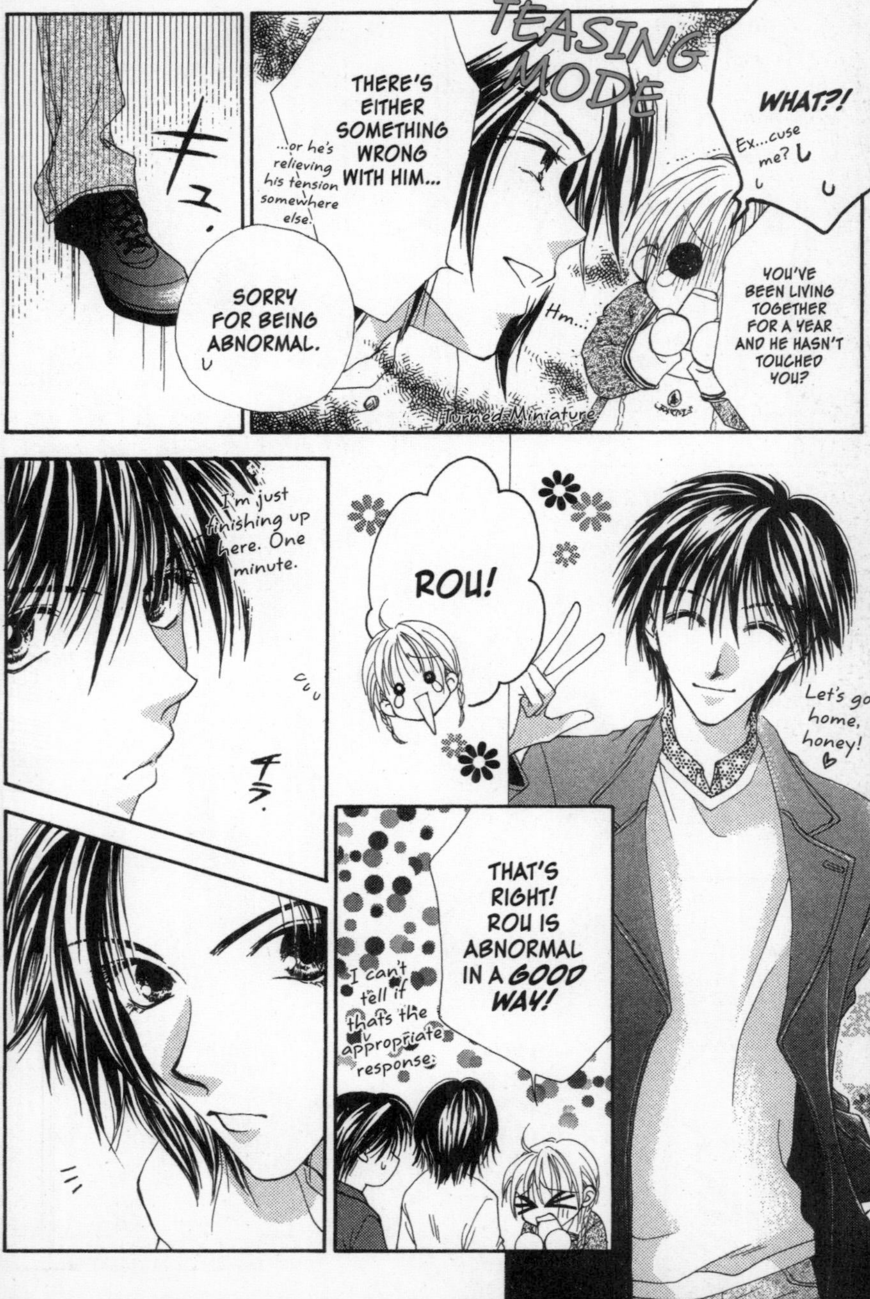
TEASING MODE
WHAT?!
Ex...cuse me?
YOU'VE BEEN LIVING TOGETHER FOR A YEAR AND HE HASN'T TOUCHED YOU?
Hm...
THERE'S EITHER SOMETHING WRONG WITH HIM...
...or he's relieving his tension somewhere else.
Turned Miniature
SORRY FOR BEING ABNORMAL.
キュ.
Let's go home, honey!
ROU!
I'm just finishing up here. One minute.
チラ.
THAT'S RIGHT! ROU IS ABNORMAL IN A GOOD WAY!
I can't tell if thats the appropriate response.

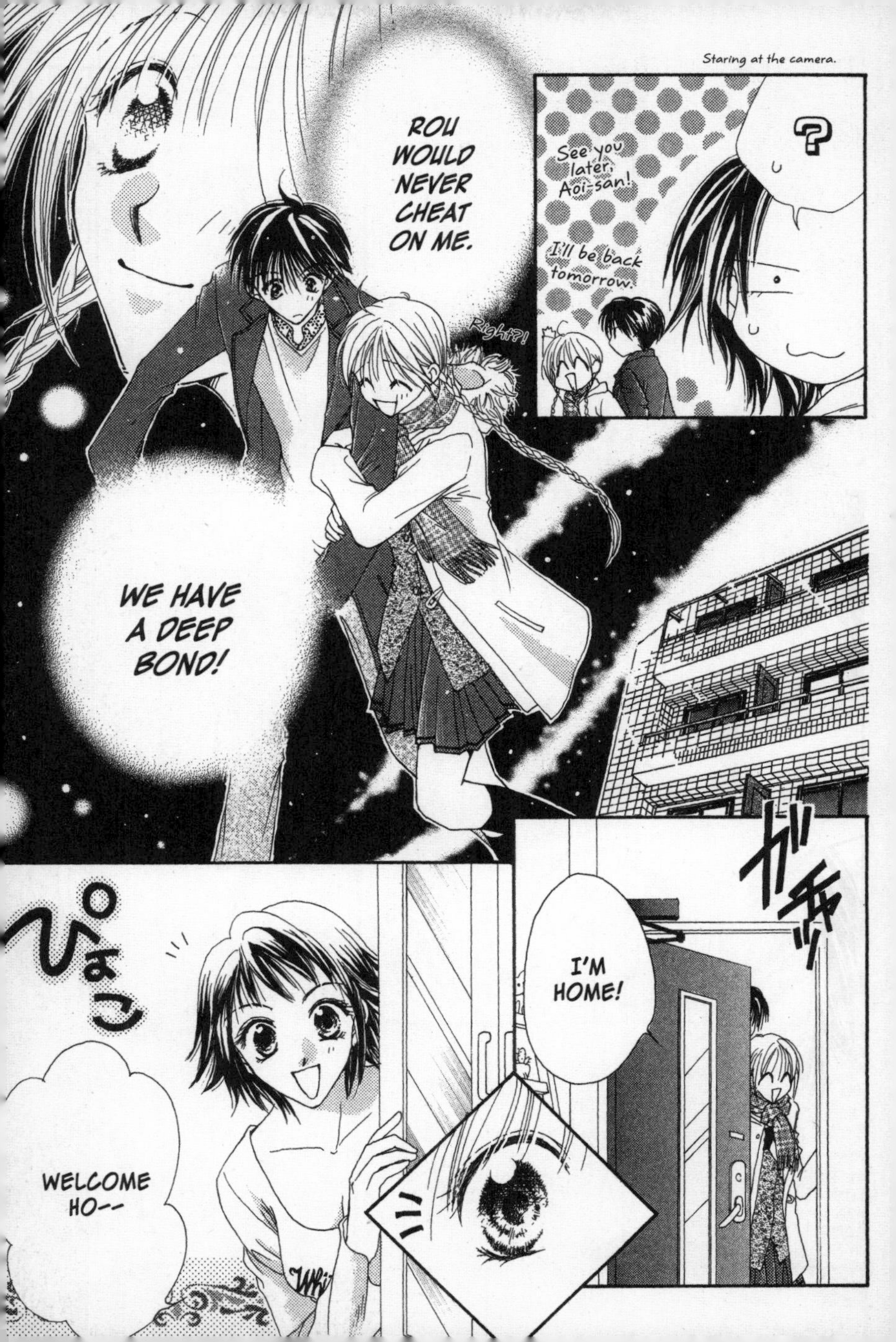
Staring at the camera.
?
See you later, Aoi-san!
I'll be back tomorrow.
ROU WOULD NEVER CHEAT ON ME.
Right?!
WE HAVE A DEEP BOND!
ガチャッ
I'M HOME!
ぴょこ
WELCOME HO--

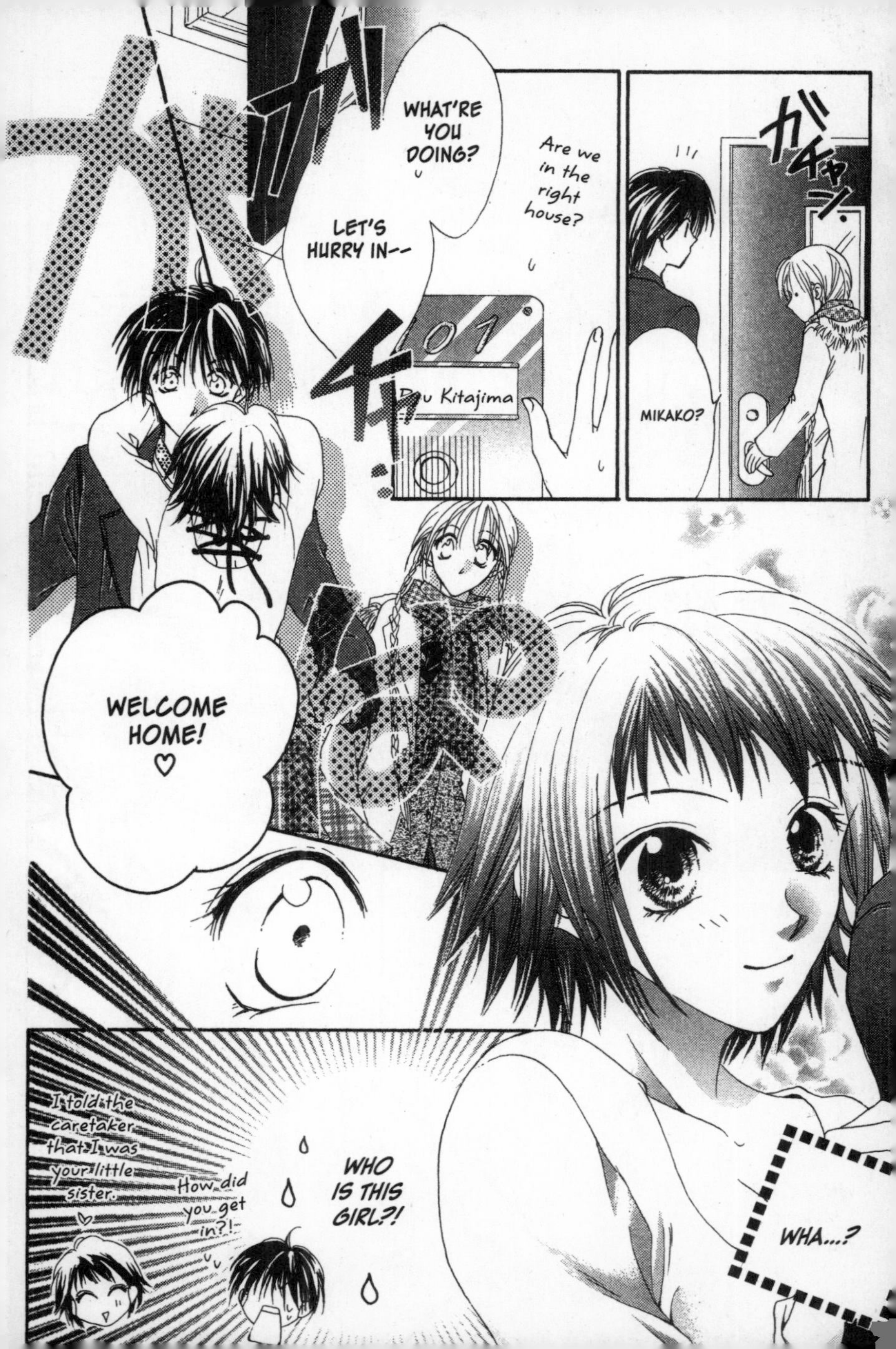

ガチャン
MIKAKO?
Are we in the right house?
101
Kitajima
WHAT'RE YOU DOING?
LET'S HURRY IN--
WELCOME HOME! ♡
WHA...?
WHO IS THIS GIRL?!
How did you get in?!
I told the caretaker that I was your little sister. ♡

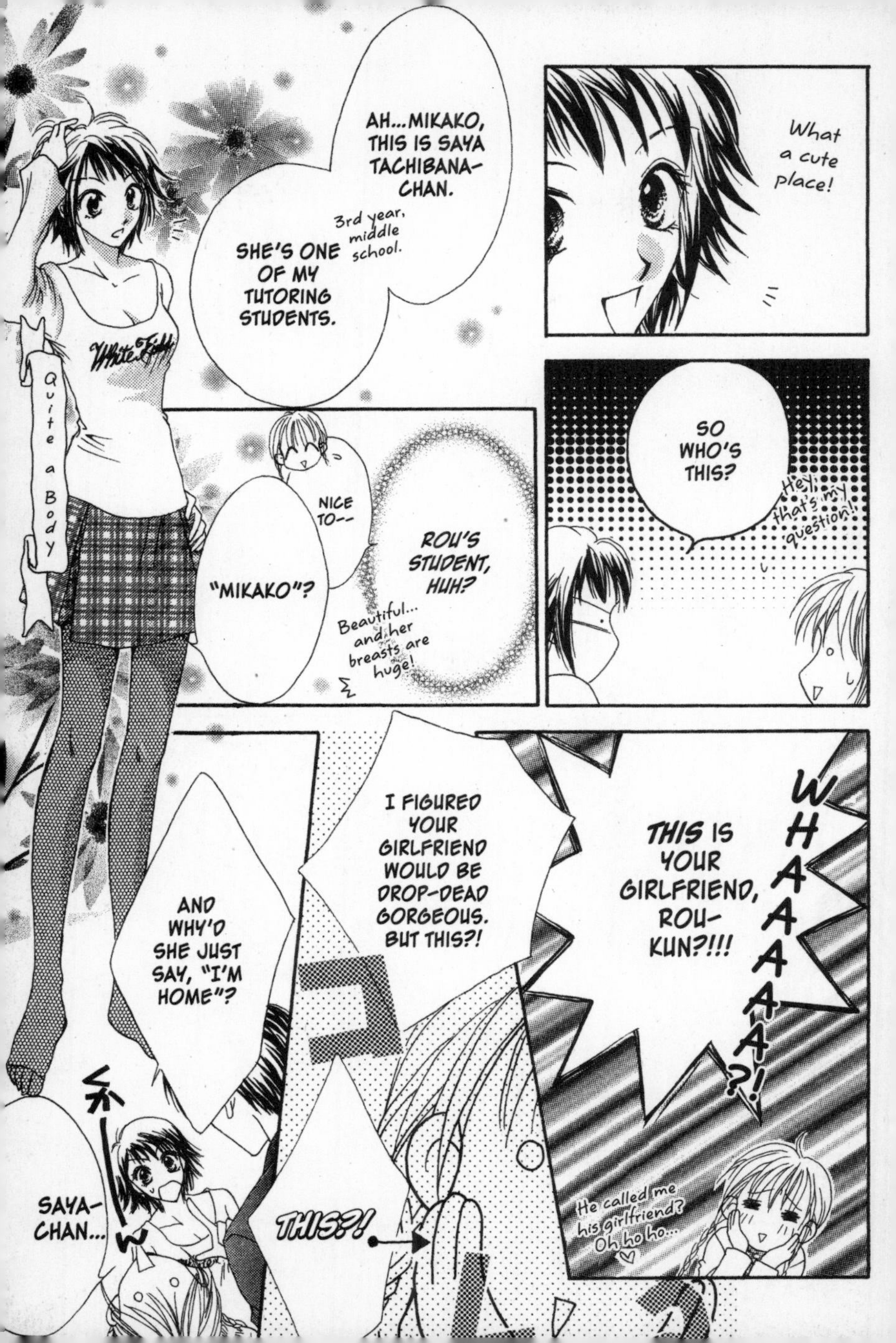

What a cute place!
AH...MIKAKO, THIS IS SAYA TACHIBANA-CHAN.
SHE'S ONE OF MY TUTORING STUDENTS.
3rd year, middle school.
SO WHO'S THIS?
Hey, that's my question!
ROU'S STUDENT, HUH?
Beautiful... and her breasts are huge!
NICE TO--
"MIKAKO"?
Quite a Body
WHAAAAAAA?!
THIS IS YOUR GIRLFRIEND, ROU-KUN?!!!
He called me his girlfriend? Oh ho ho...
I FIGURED YOUR GIRLFRIEND WOULD BE DROP-DEAD GORGEOUS. BUT THIS?!
THIS?!
AND WHY'D SHE JUST SAY, "I'M HOME"?
SAYA-CHAN...

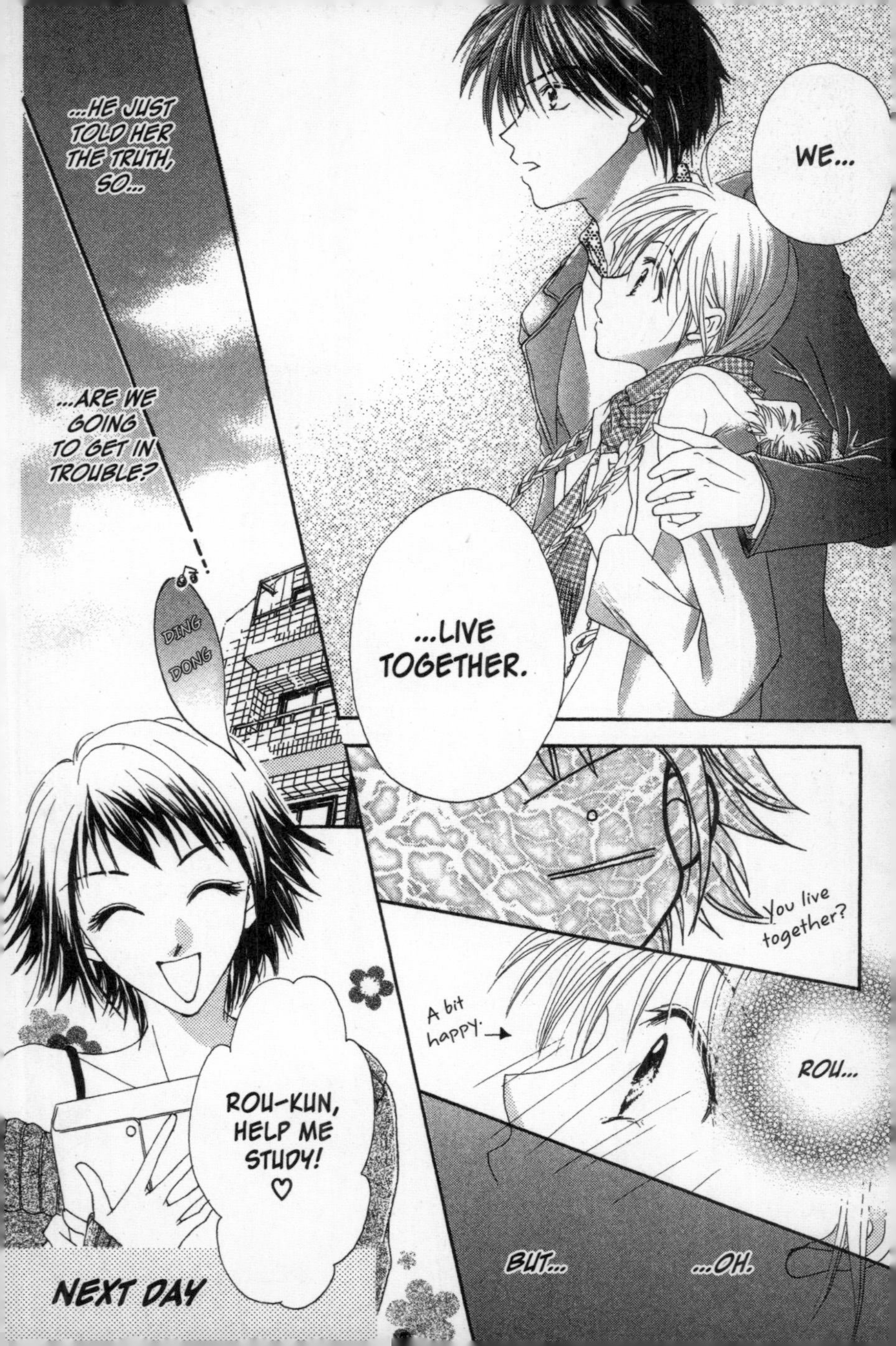
WE...
...LIVE TOGETHER.
You live together?
ROU...
A bit happy.
...OH.
BUT...
...HE JUST TOLD HER THE TRUTH, SO...
...ARE WE GOING TO GET IN TROUBLE?
DING DONG
ROU-KUN, HELP ME STUDY! ♡
NEXT DAY

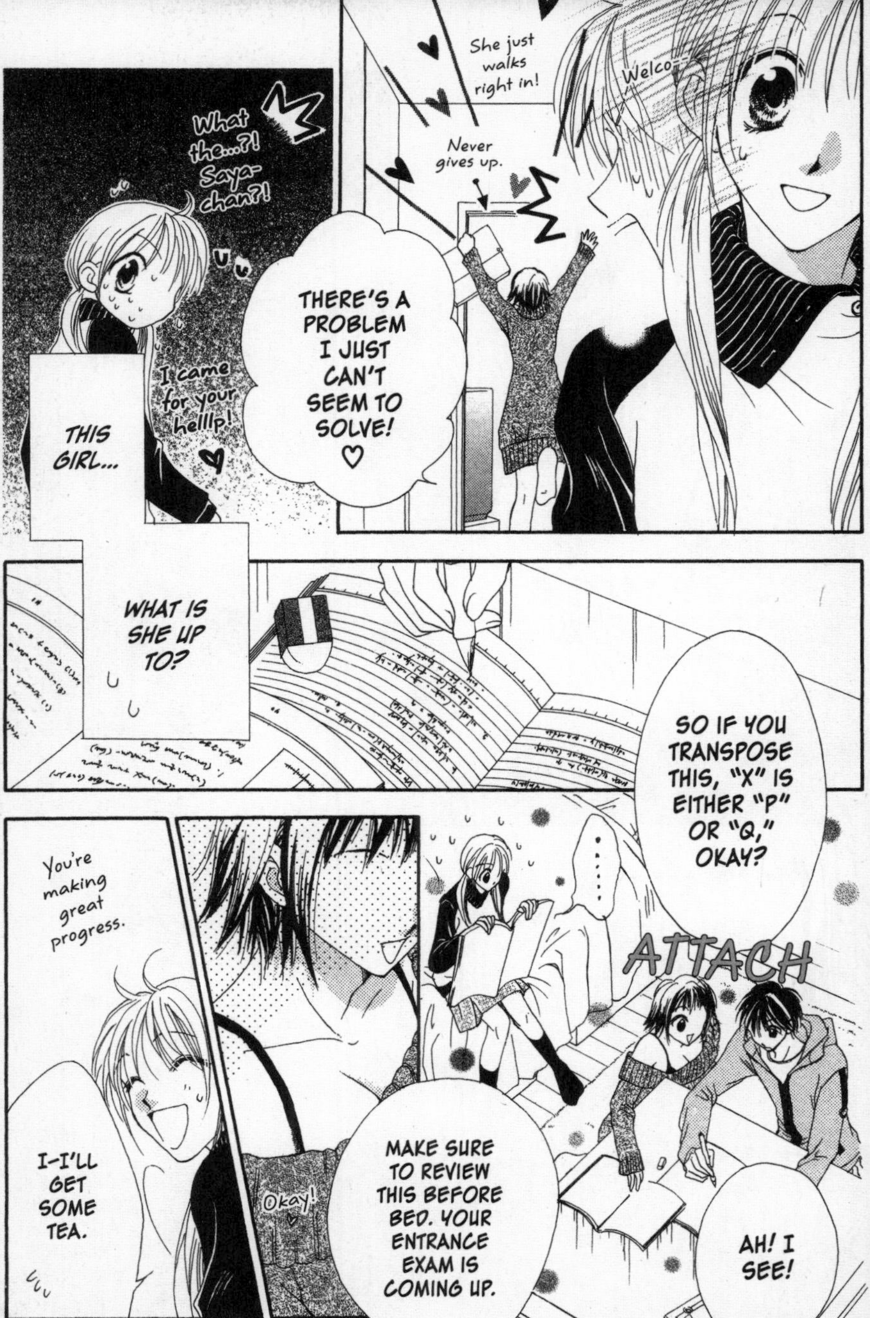
Welco—
She just walks right in!
Never gives up.
THERE'S A PROBLEM I JUST CAN'T SEEM TO SOLVE! ♡
What the...?! Saya-chan?!
I came for your helllp! ♥
THIS GIRL...
WHAT IS SHE UP TO?
SO IF YOU TRANSPOSE THIS, "X" IS EITHER "P" OR "Q," OKAY?
ATTACH
AH! I SEE!
......
MAKE SURE TO REVIEW THIS BEFORE BED. YOUR ENTRANCE EXAM IS COMING UP.
Okay! ♥
You're making great progress.
I-I'LL GET SOME TEA.

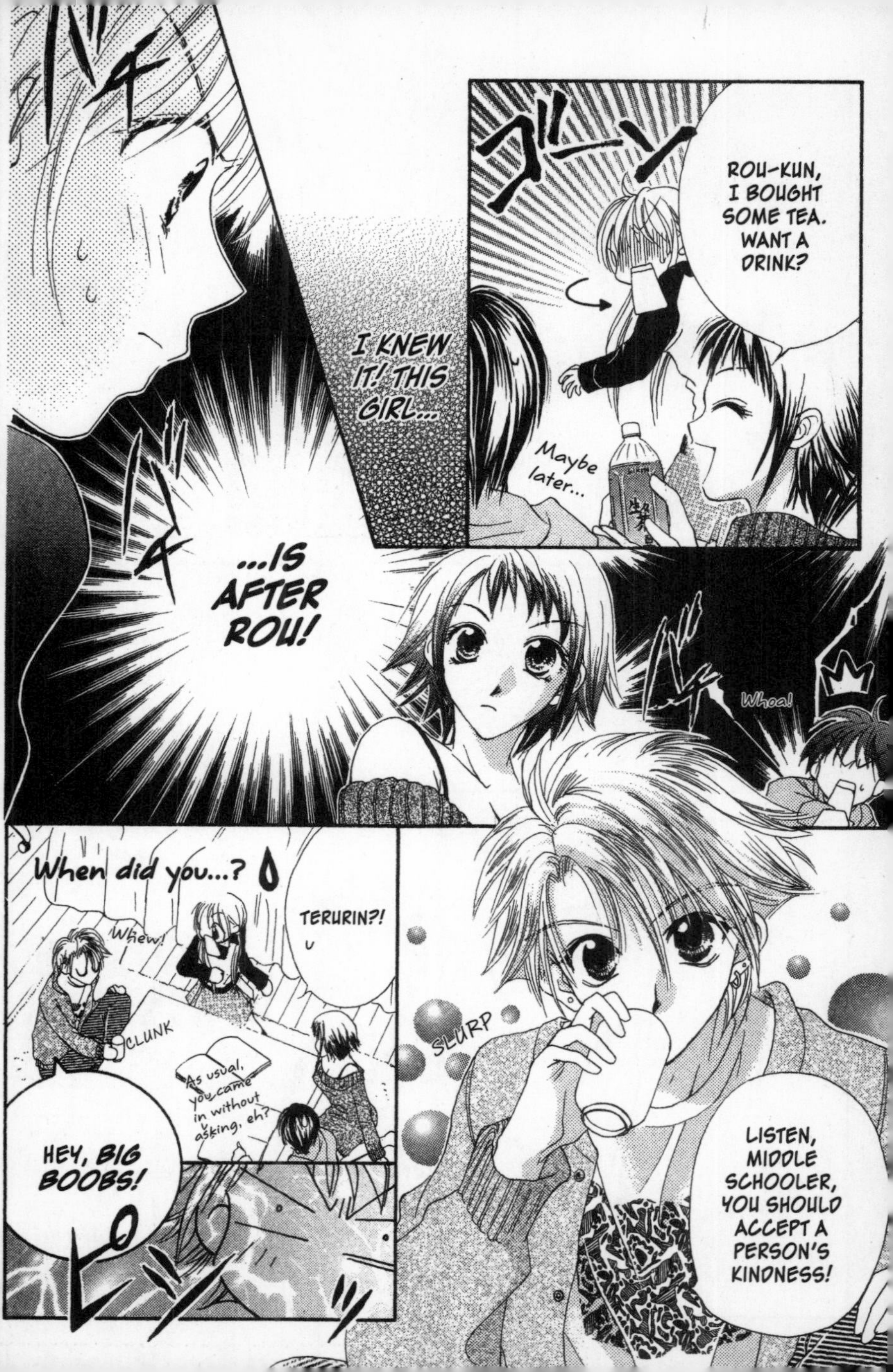

ROU-KUN, I BOUGHT SOME TEA. WANT A DRINK?
Maybe later...
Whoa!
I KNEW IT! THIS GIRL...
...IS AFTER ROU!
SLURP
LISTEN, MIDDLE SCHOOLER, YOU SHOULD ACCEPT A PERSON'S KINDNESS!
TERURIN?!
When did you...?
Whew!
CLUNK
As usual, you came in without asking, eh?
HEY, BIG BOOBS!

5

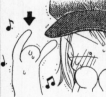

SHHH.

It's early August now. A few days ago, I went to Tokyo Disney Sea. It was the hottest day of the summer, but I walked all over the park and enjoyed every second of it. The heat kept people away, so we were able to get on every ride. I went on "The Center of the Earth" ride twice, once during the day and once at night. We were lucky, too, because we caught a jazz (or was it samba?) band during dinner. They had dancers and everything. The dancers even pulled me up to join them so Kiritani danced!

My friend can't dance, but she had to fake it anyway.

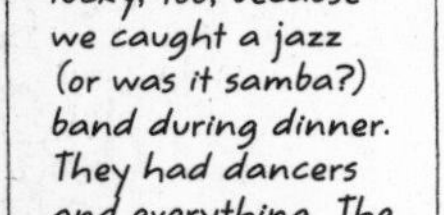

It was hilarious! We were there mainly to enjoy the rides, but I thought the passionate dancing was a pretty great scene and couldn't help taking a picture!

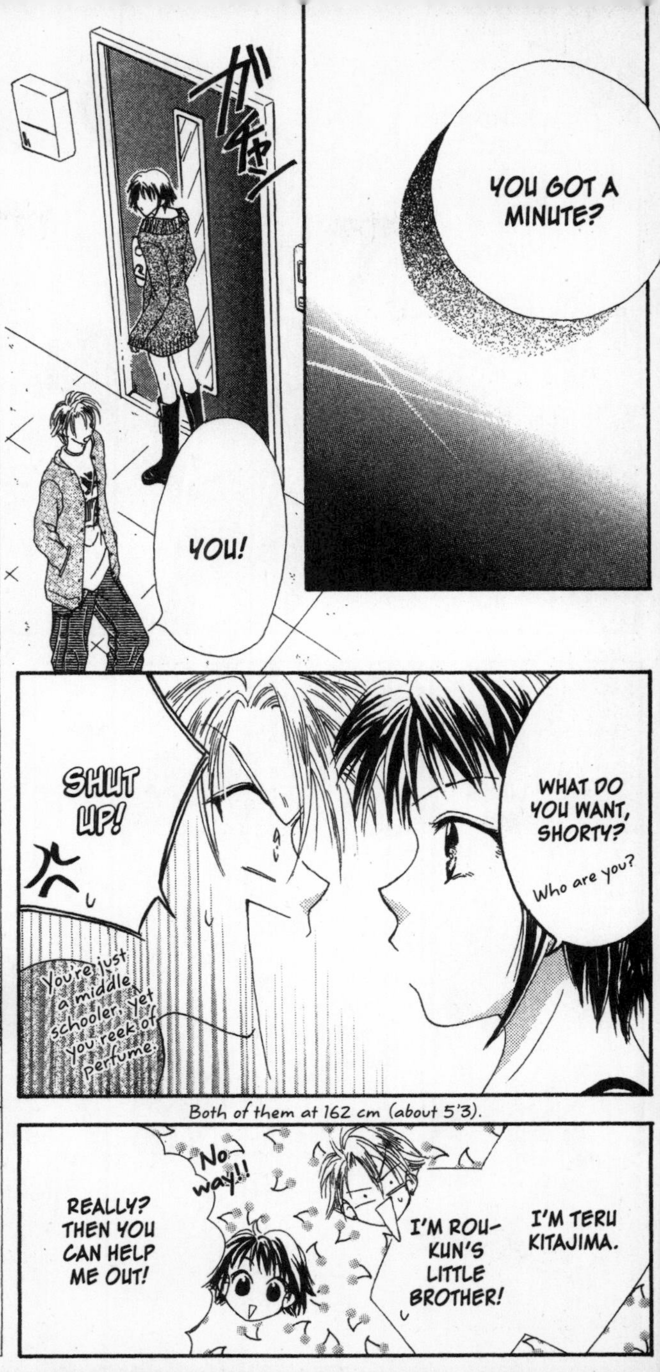
YOU GOT A MINUTE?
ガチャ
YOU!
WHAT DO YOU WANT, SHORTY?
Who are you?
SHUT UP!
You're just a middle schooler, yet you reek of perfume.
Both of them at 162 cm (about 5'3).
I'M TERU KITAJIMA.
I'M ROU-KUN'S LITTLE BROTHER!
No way!!
REALLY? THEN YOU CAN HELP ME OUT!

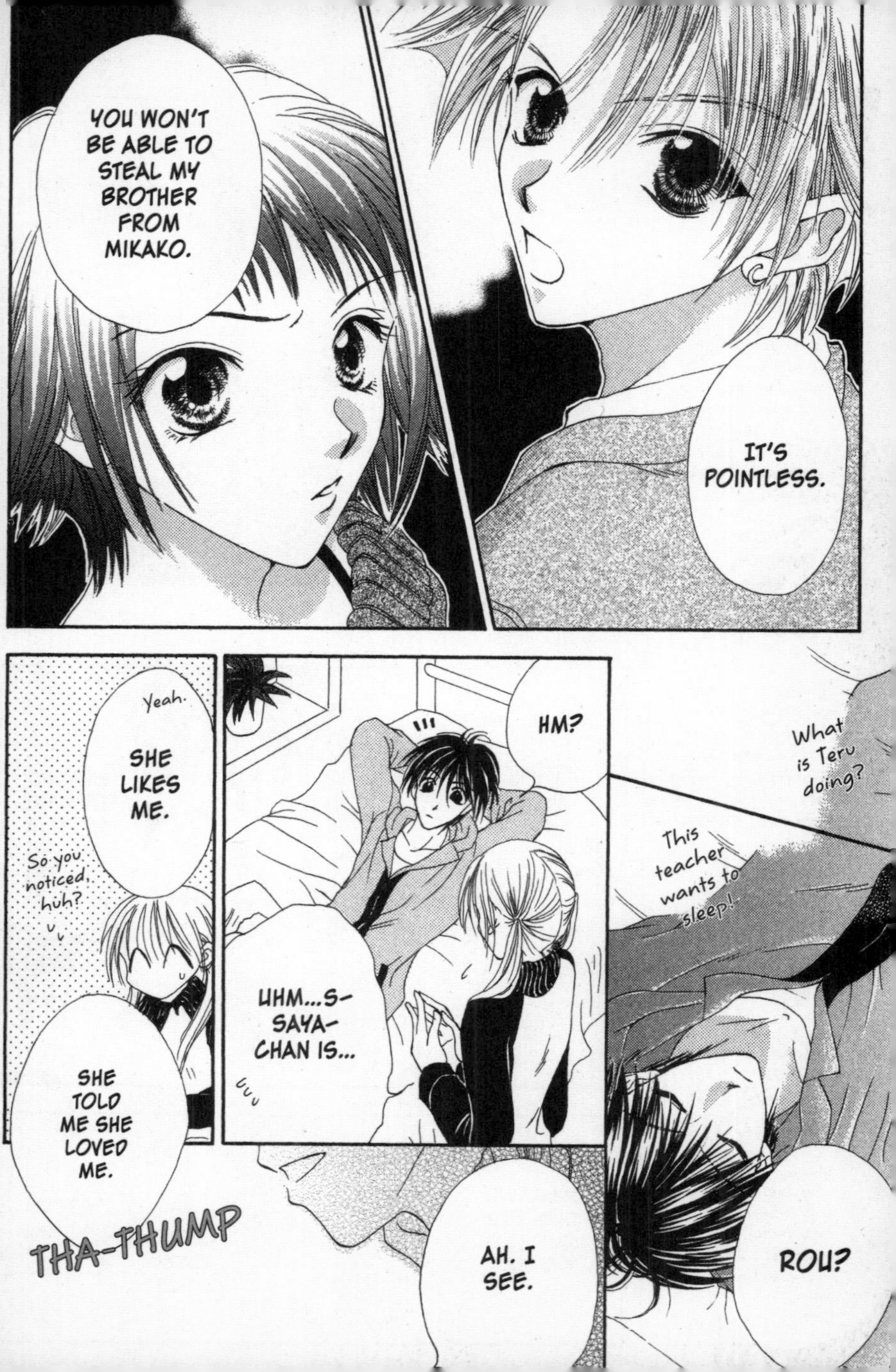
IT'S POINTLESS.
YOU WON'T BE ABLE TO STEAL MY BROTHER FROM MIKAKO.
What is Teru doing?
This teacher wants to sleep!
HM?
UHM...S-SAYA-CHAN IS...
Yeah.
SHE LIKES ME.
So you noticed, huh?
SHE TOLD ME SHE LOVED ME.
ROU?
AH. I SEE.
THA-THUMP

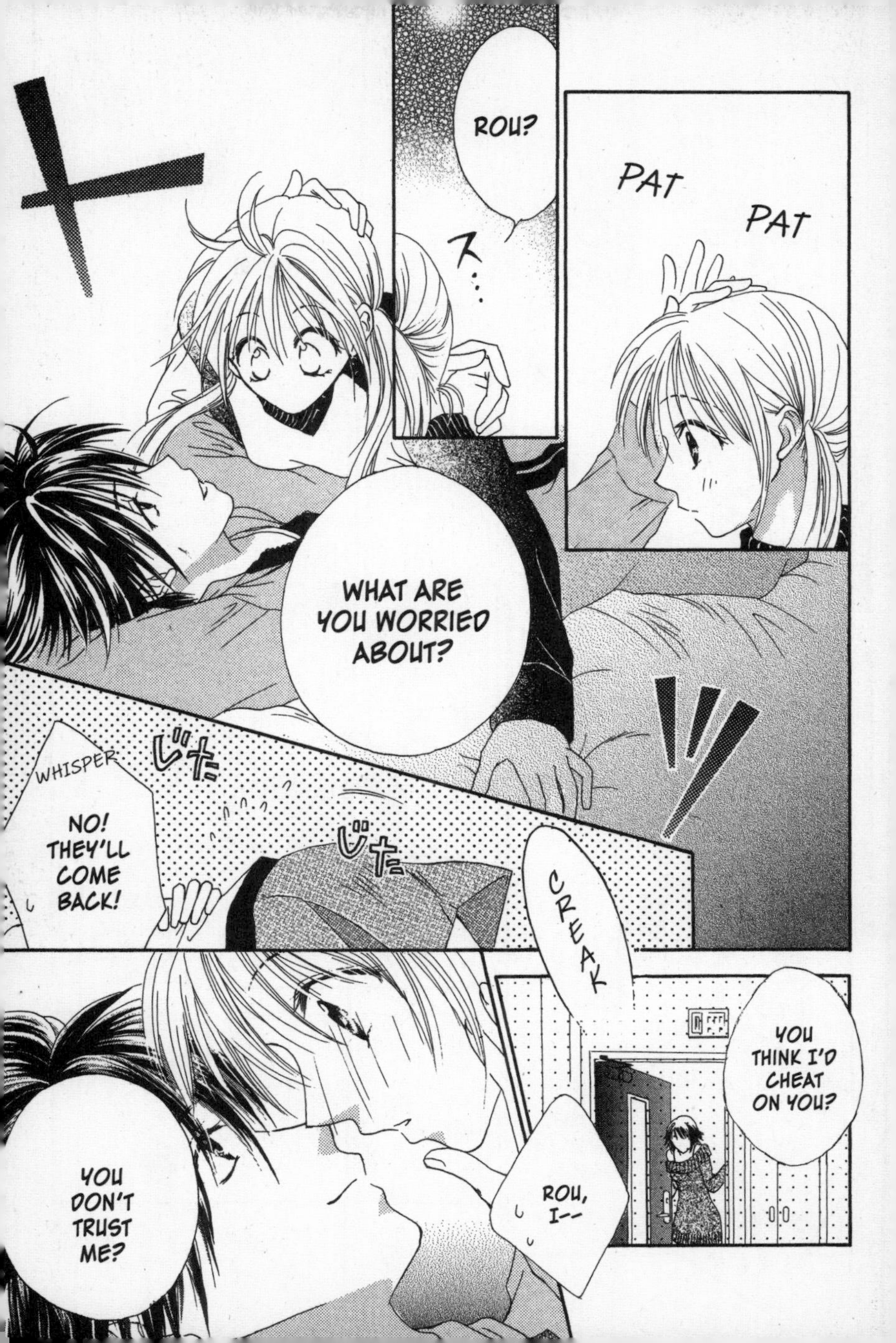
PAT
PAT
ROU?
ス…
WHAT ARE YOU WORRIED ABOUT?
CREAK
じた
じた
WHISPER
NO! THEY'LL COME BACK!
YOU THINK I'D CHEAT ON YOU?
ROU, I--
YOU DON'T TRUST ME?

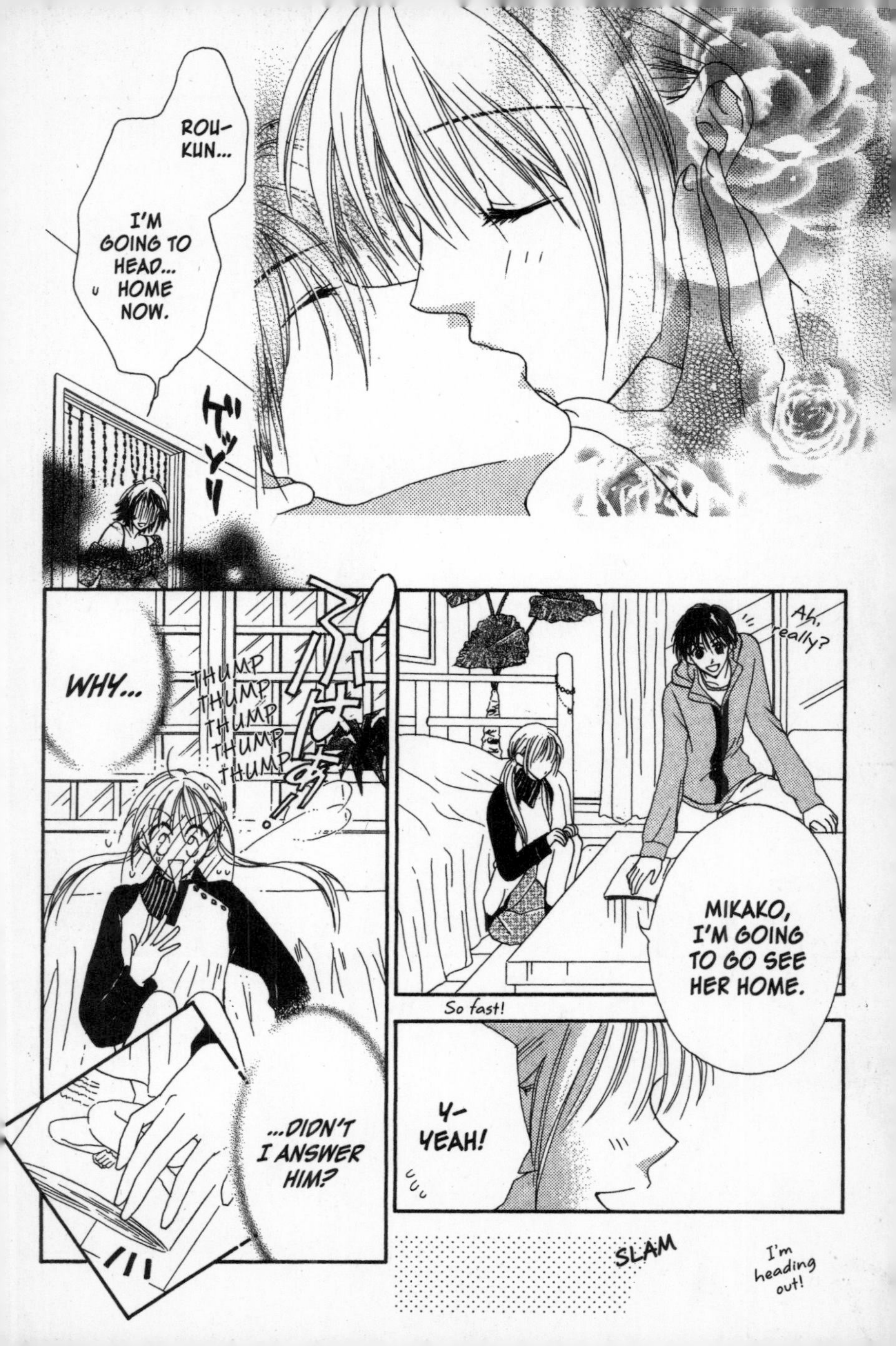
ROU-KUN...
I'M GOING TO HEAD... HOME NOW.
Ah, really?
MIKAKO, I'M GOING TO GO SEE HER HOME.
So fast!
Y-YEAH!
WHY...
THUMP THUMP THUMP THUMP THUMP
...DIDN'T I ANSWER HIM?
I'm heading out!
SLAM

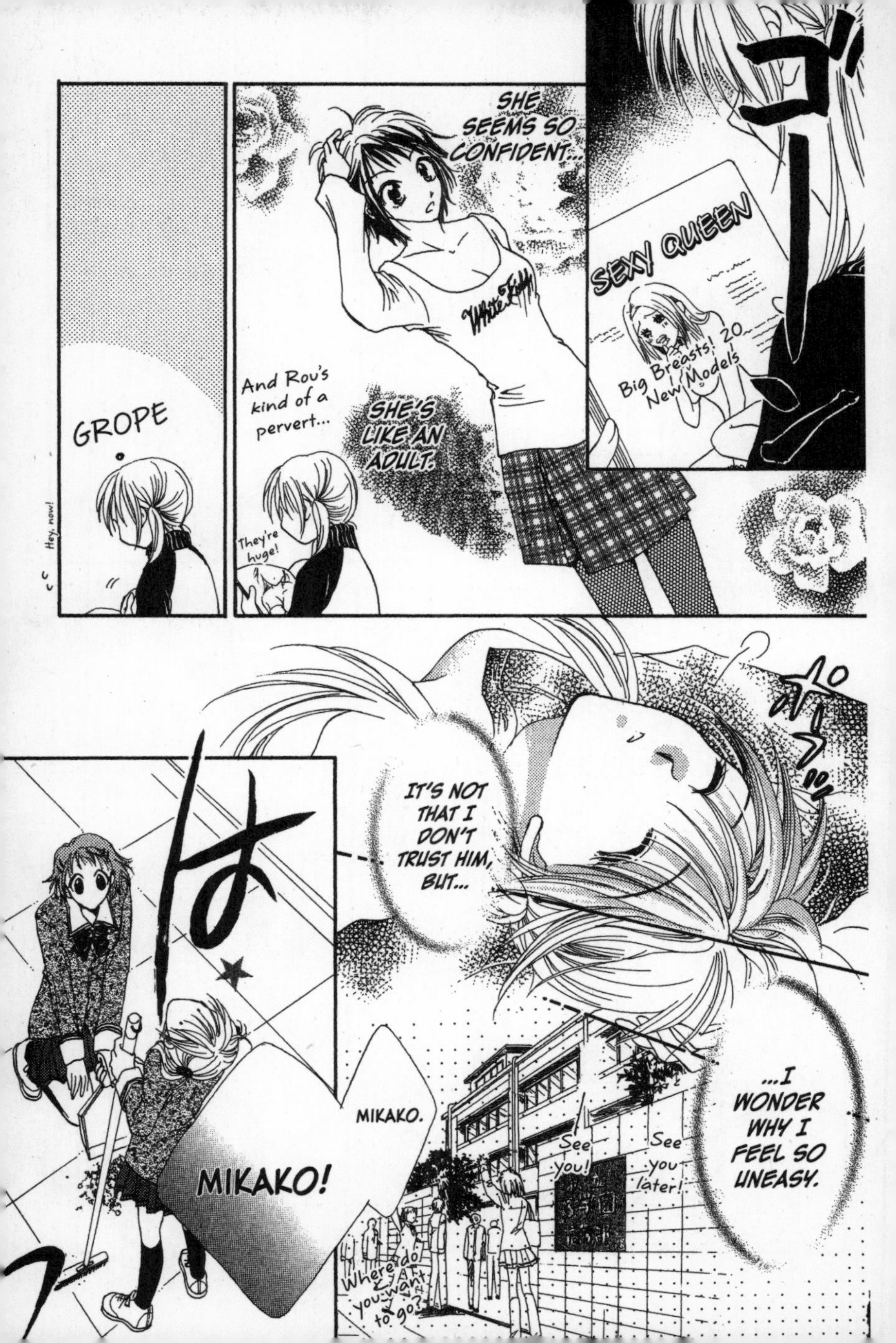
SEXY QUEEN
Big Breasts! 20 New Models!
SHE SEEMS SO CONFIDENT...
SHE'S LIKE AN ADULT.
And Rou's kind of a pervert...
They're huge!
GROPE
Hey, now!
IT'S NOT THAT I DON'T TRUST HIM, BUT...
...I WONDER WHY I FEEL SO UNEASY.
See you later!
See you!
Where do you want to go?
MIKAKO.
MIKAKO!

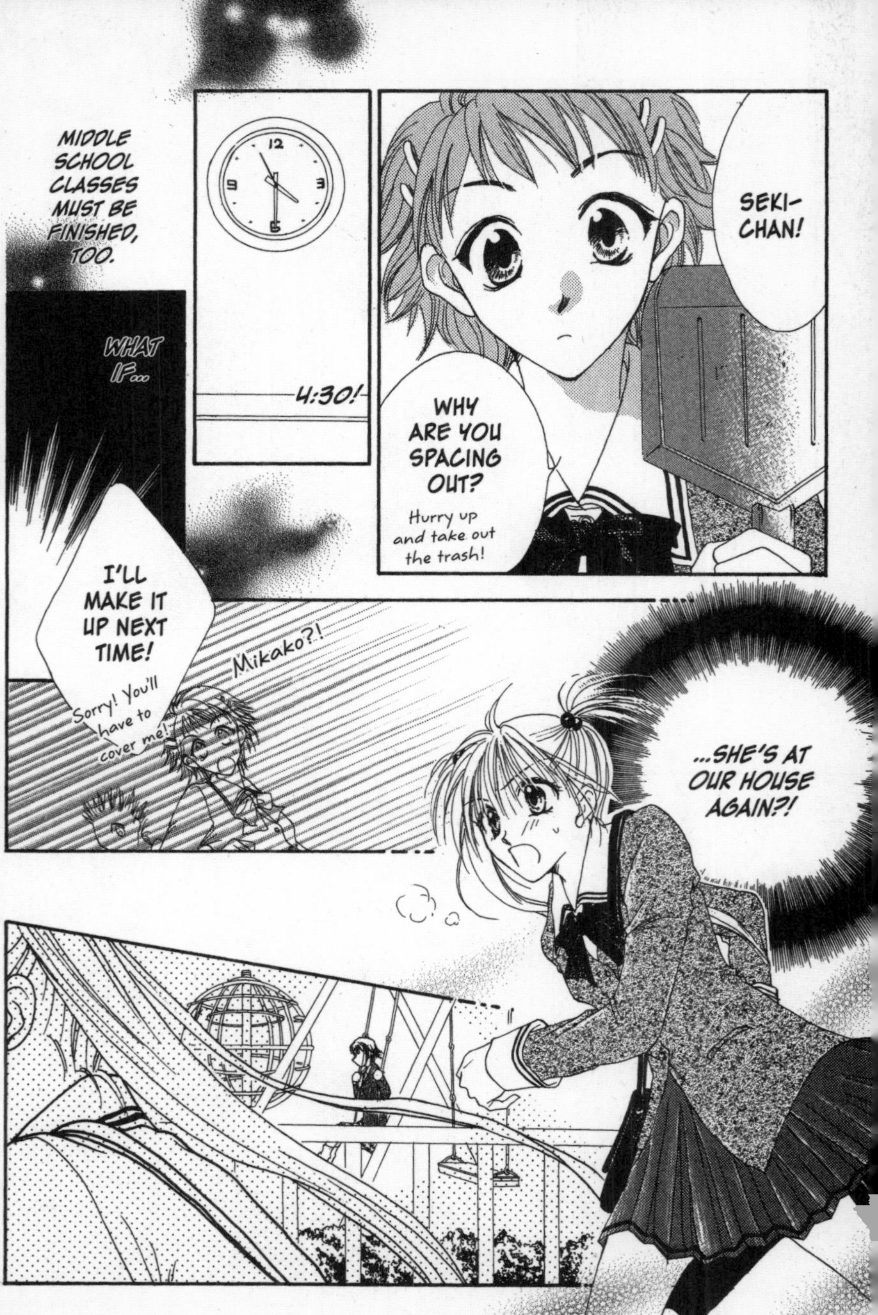
SEKI-CHAN!
WHY ARE YOU SPACING OUT?
Hurry up and take out the trash!
4:30!
MIDDLE SCHOOL CLASSES MUST BE FINISHED, TOO.
WHAT IF...
...SHE'S AT OUR HOUSE AGAIN?!
I'LL MAKE IT UP NEXT TIME!
Sorry! You'll have to cover me!
Mikako?!

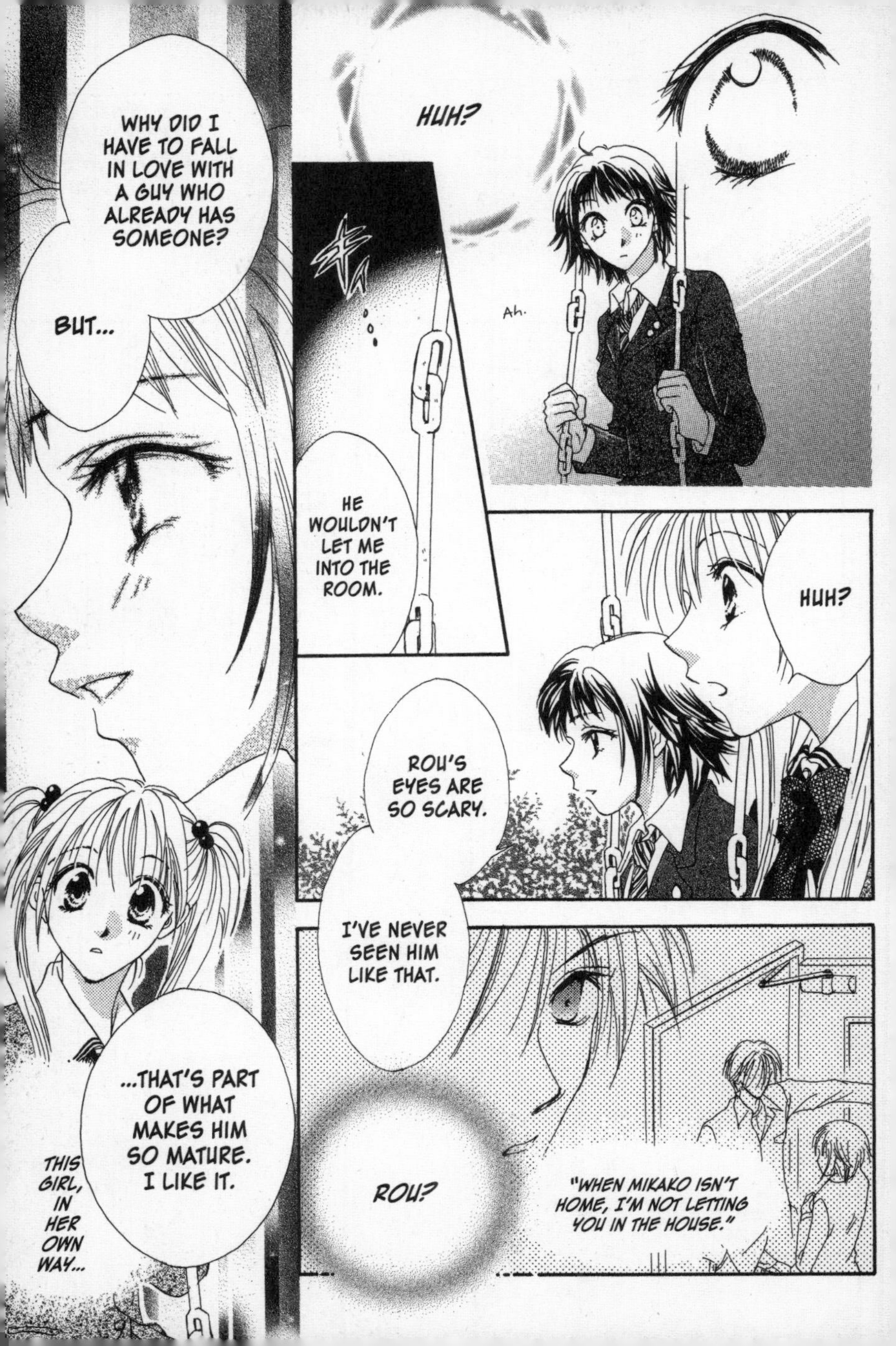
HUH?
Ah.
HE WOULDN'T LET ME INTO THE ROOM.
HUH?
ROU'S EYES ARE SO SCARY.
I'VE NEVER SEEN HIM LIKE THAT.
"WHEN MIKAKO ISN'T HOME, I'M NOT LETTING YOU IN THE HOUSE."
ROU?
WHY DID I HAVE TO FALL IN LOVE WITH A GUY WHO ALREADY HAS SOMEONE?
BUT...
...THAT'S PART OF WHAT MAKES HIM SO MATURE. I LIKE IT.
THIS GIRL, IN HER OWN WAY...

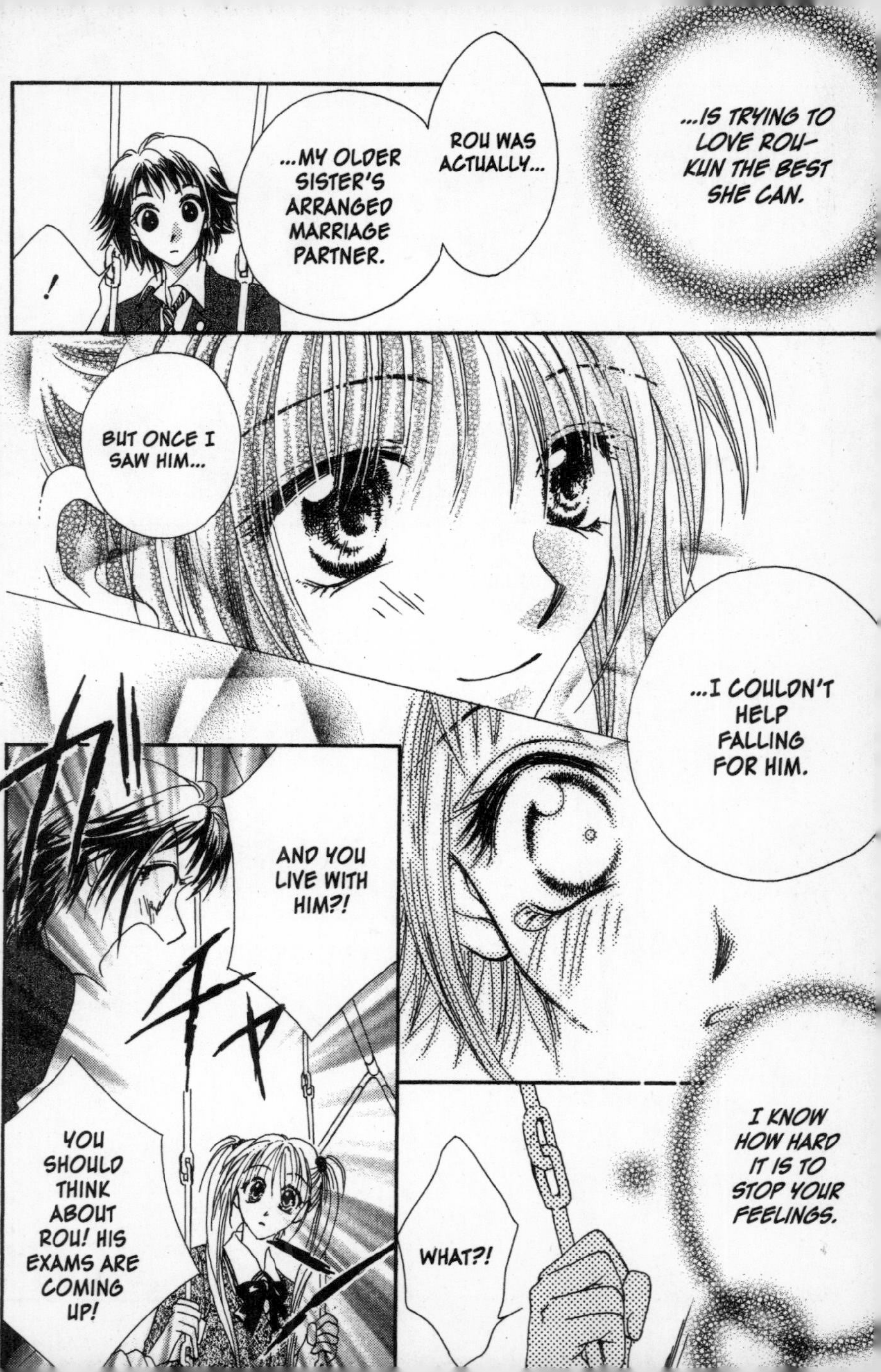
...IS TRYING TO LOVE ROU-KUN THE BEST SHE CAN.
ROU WAS ACTUALLY...
...MY OLDER SISTER'S ARRANGED MARRIAGE PARTNER.
!
BUT ONCE I SAW HIM...
...I COULDN'T HELP FALLING FOR HIM.
I KNOW HOW HARD IT IS TO STOP YOUR FEELINGS.
WHAT?!
AND YOU LIVE WITH HIM?!
YOU SHOULD THINK ABOUT ROU! HIS EXAMS ARE COMING UP!

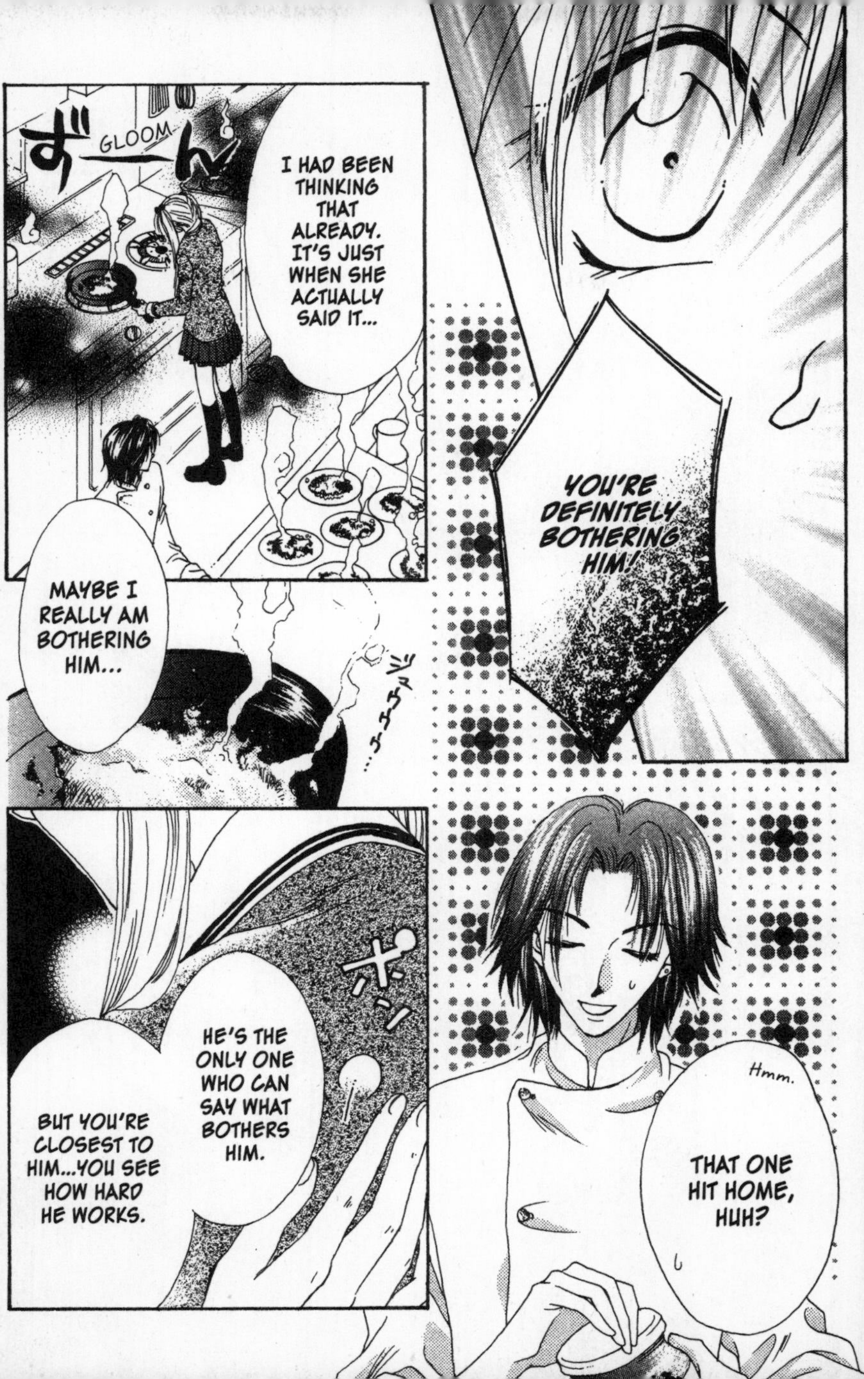
YOU'RE DEFINITELY BOTHERING HIM!
GLOOM
I HAD BEEN THINKING THAT ALREADY. IT'S JUST WHEN SHE ACTUALLY SAID IT...
MAYBE I REALLY AM BOTHERING HIM...
Hmm.
THAT ONE HIT HOME, HUH?
HE'S THE ONLY ONE WHO CAN SAY WHAT BOTHERS HIM.
BUT YOU'RE CLOSEST TO HIM...YOU SEE HOW HARD HE WORKS.

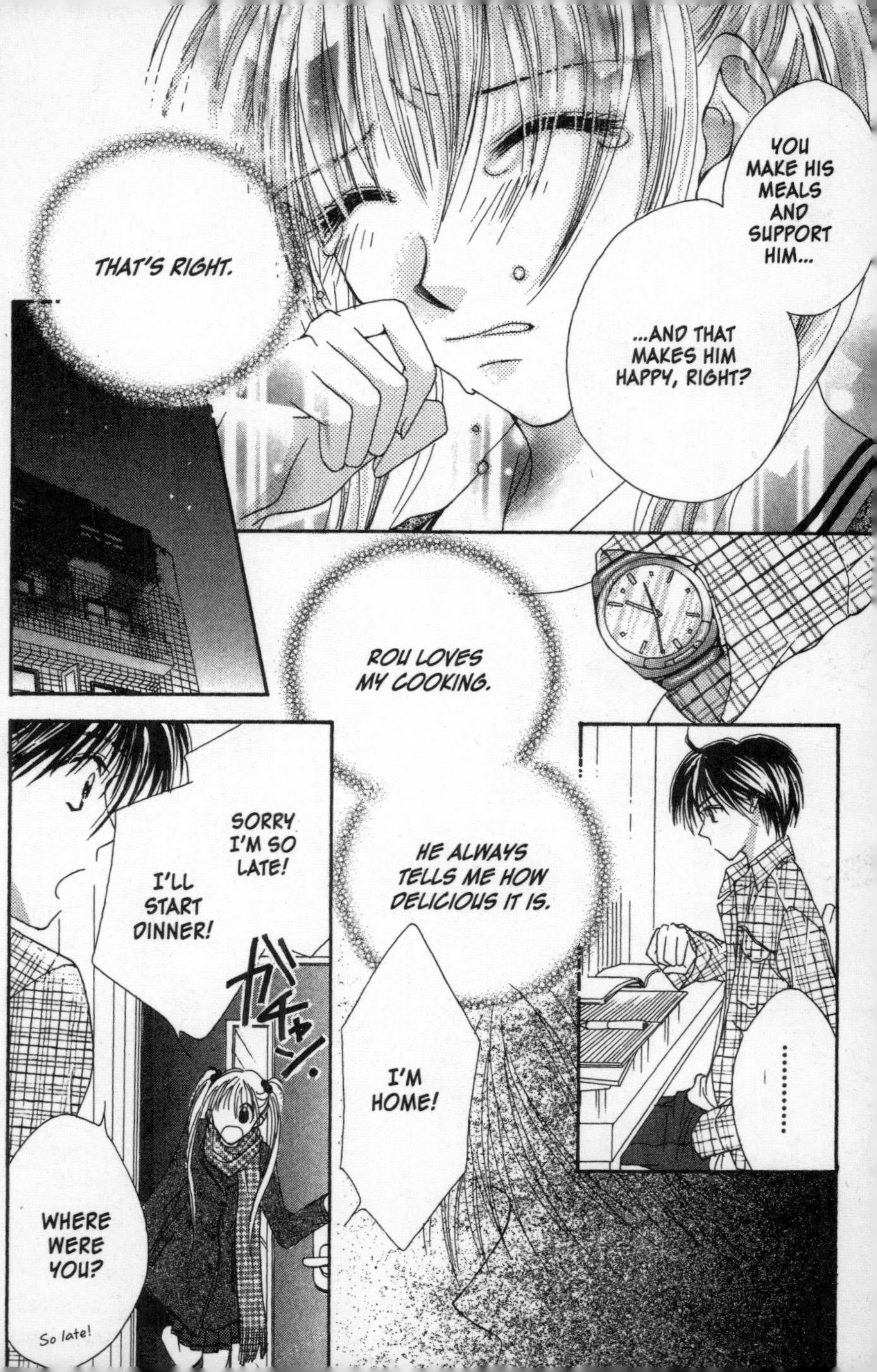
YOU MAKE HIS MEALS AND SUPPORT HIM...
...AND THAT MAKES HIM HAPPY, RIGHT?
THAT'S RIGHT.
ROU LOVES MY COOKING.
HE ALWAYS TELLS ME HOW DELICIOUS IT IS.
......
I'M HOME!
ガチャン!
SORRY I'M SO LATE!
I'LL START DINNER!
WHERE WERE YOU?
So late!

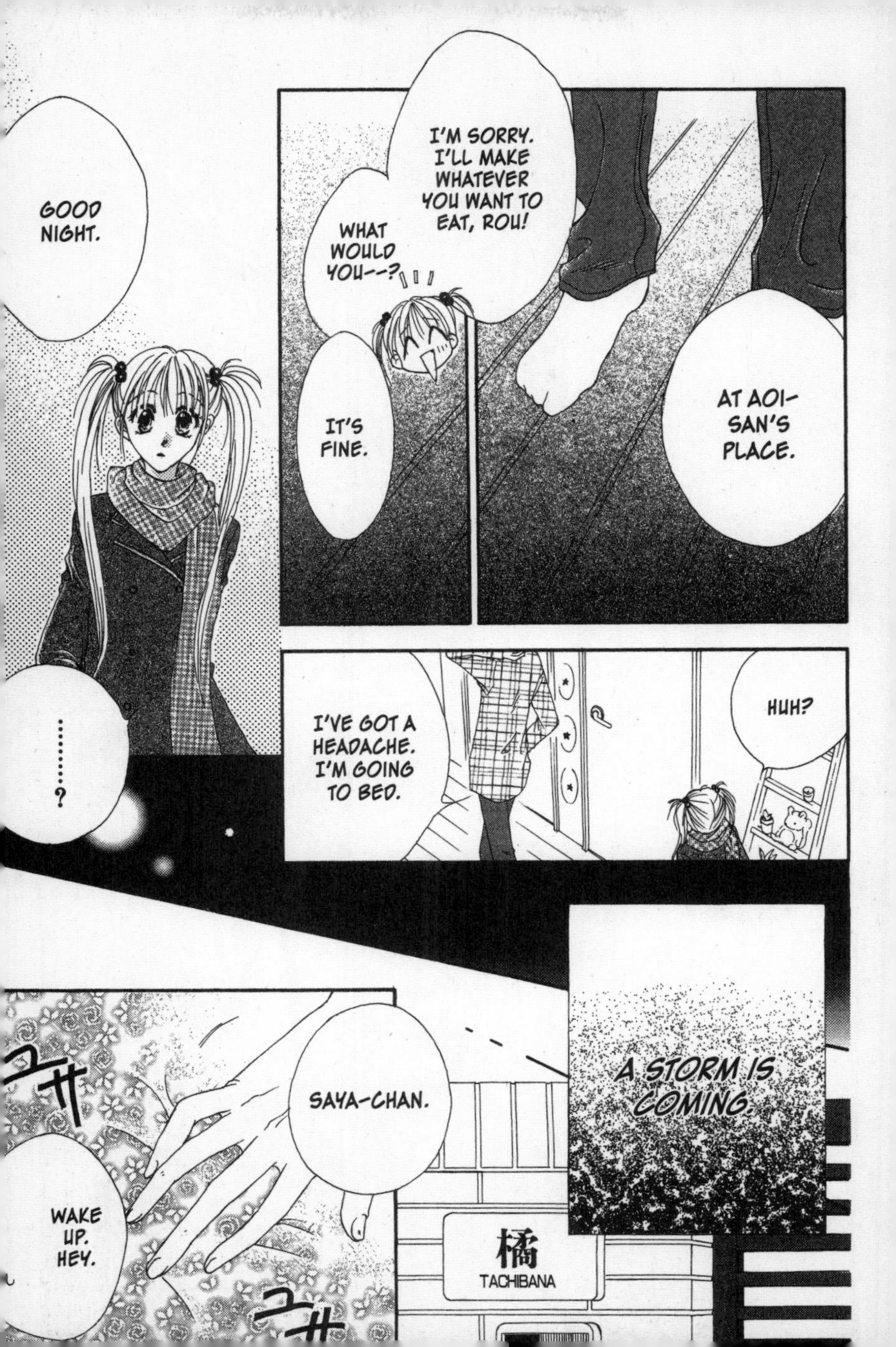
AT AOI-SAN'S PLACE.
I'M SORRY. I'LL MAKE WHATEVER YOU WANT TO EAT, ROU!
WHAT WOULD YOU--?
IT'S FINE.
HUH?
I'VE GOT A HEADACHE. I'M GOING TO BED.
GOOD NIGHT.
......?
A STORM IS COMING.
橘
TACHIBANA
SAYA-CHAN.
ユサ
WAKE UP. HEY.
ユサ

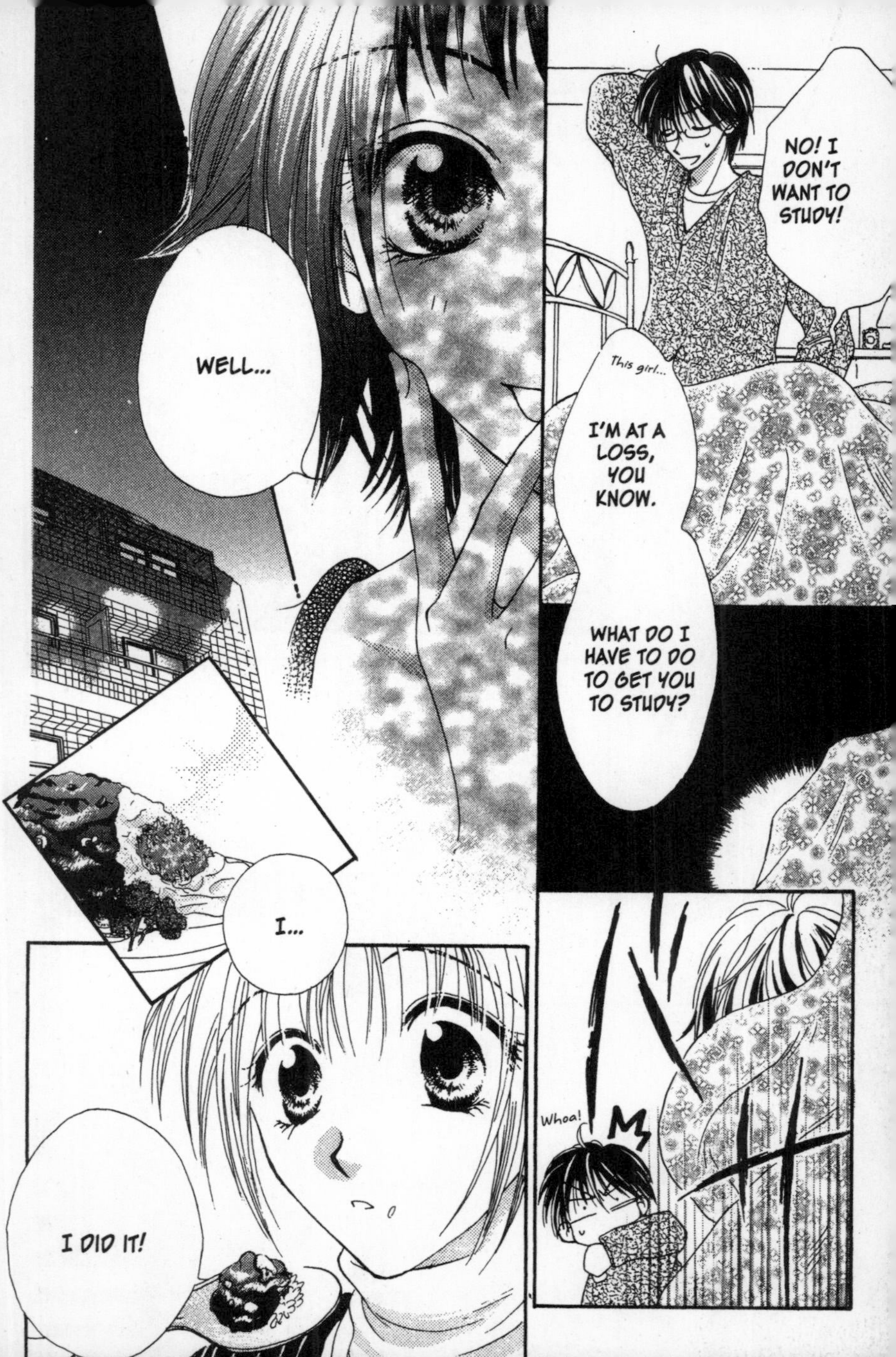
NO! I DON'T WANT TO STUDY!
This girl...
I'M AT A LOSS, YOU KNOW.
WHAT DO I HAVE TO DO TO GET YOU TO STUDY?
Whoa!
WELL...
I...
I DID IT!

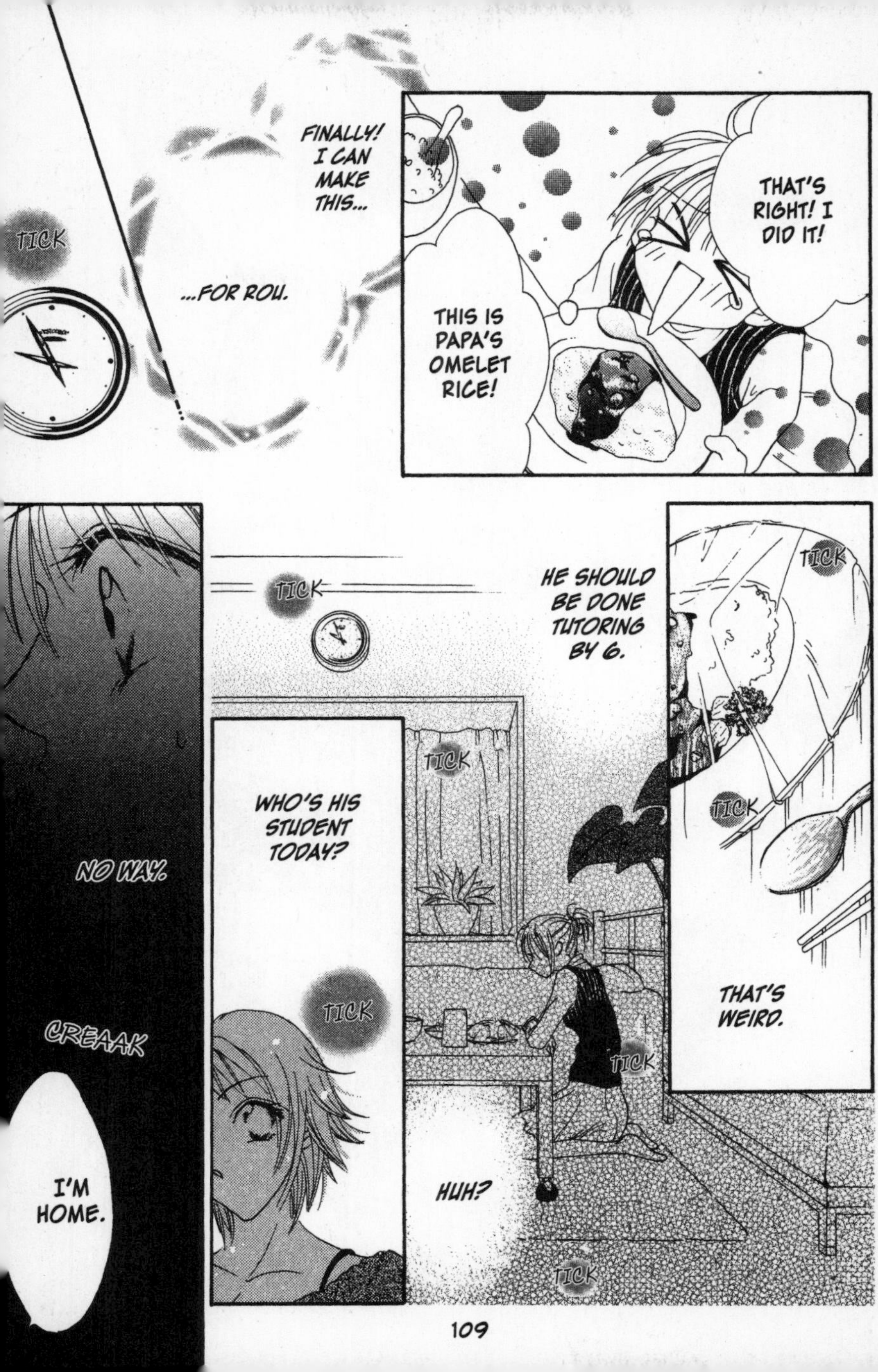
THAT'S RIGHT! I DID IT!
THIS IS PAPA'S OMELET RICE!
FINALLY! I CAN MAKE THIS...
...FOR ROU.
TICK
TICK
HE SHOULD BE DONE TUTORING BY 6.
TICK
THAT'S WEIRD.
TICK
TICK
WHO'S HIS STUDENT TODAY?
TICK
TICK
HUH?
TICK
NO WAY.
CREAAK
I'M HOME.

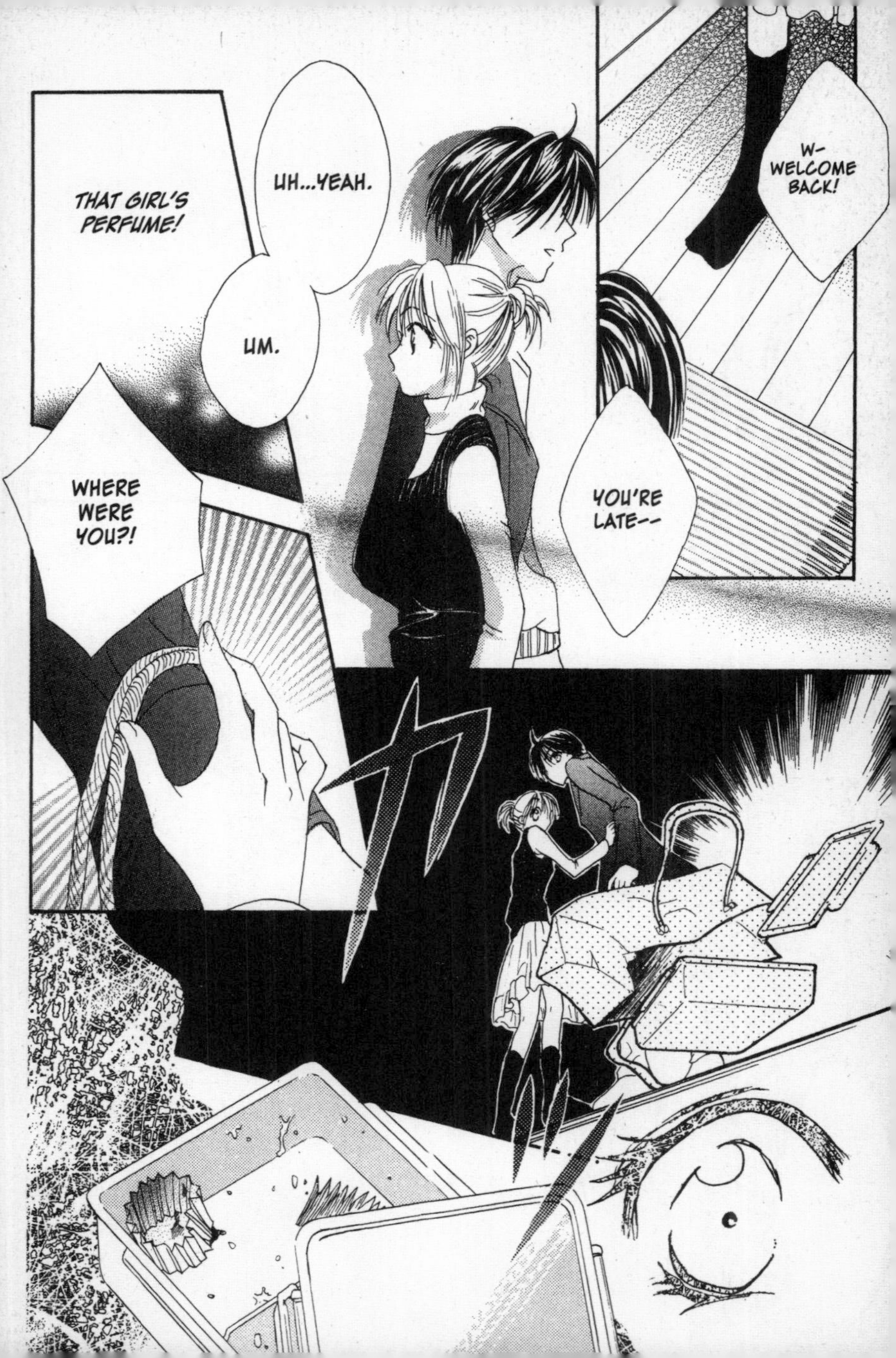
W-WELCOME BACK!
YOU'RE LATE--
UH...YEAH.
UM.
THAT GIRL'S PERFUME!
WHERE WERE YOU?!

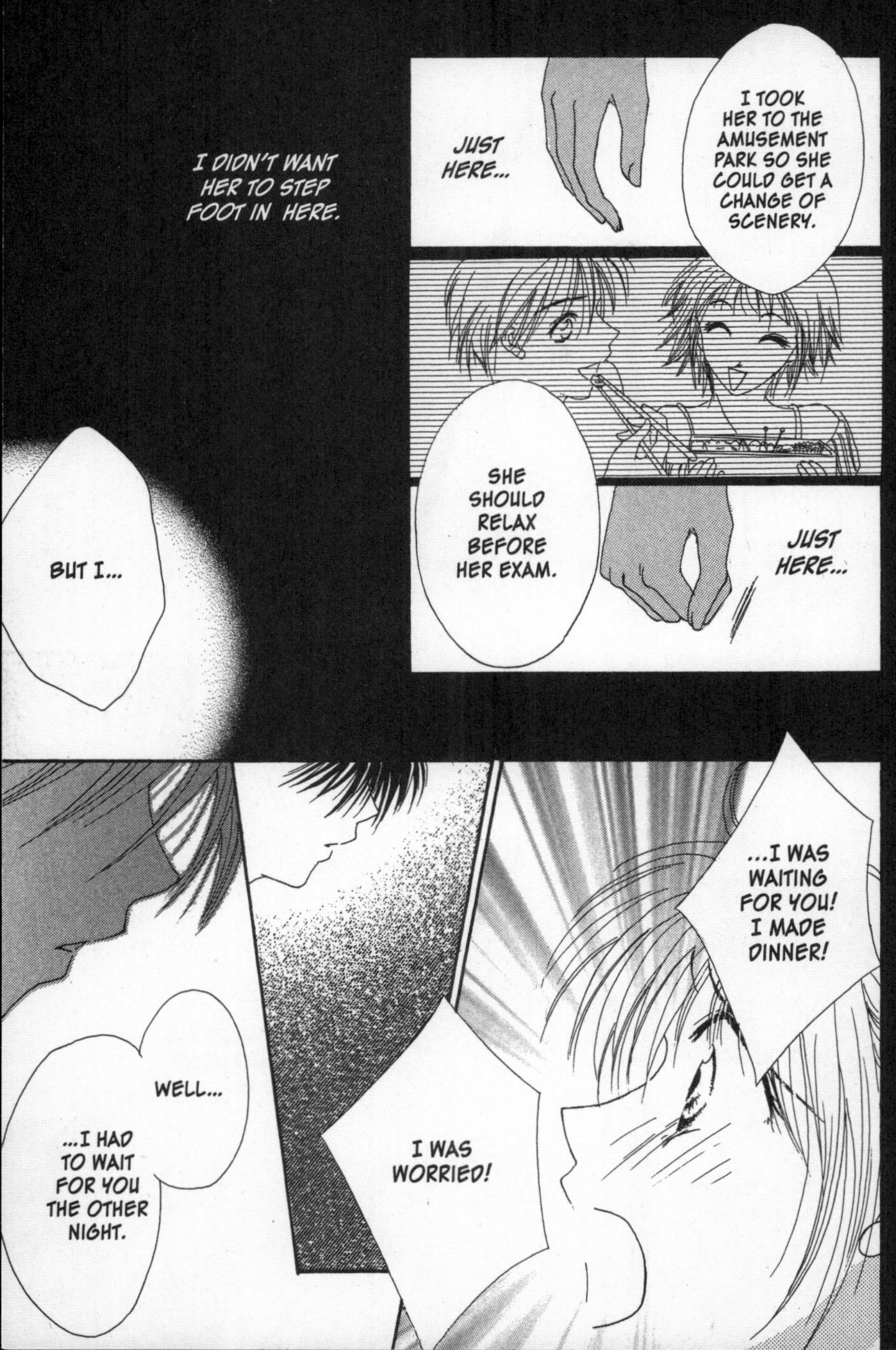
I TOOK HER TO THE AMUSEMENT PARK SO SHE COULD GET A CHANGE OF SCENERY.
JUST HERE...
SHE SHOULD RELAX BEFORE HER EXAM.
JUST HERE...
I DIDN'T WANT HER TO STEP FOOT IN HERE.
BUT I...
...I WAS WAITING FOR YOU! I MADE DINNER!
I WAS WORRIED!
WELL...
...I HAD TO WAIT FOR YOU THE OTHER NIGHT.

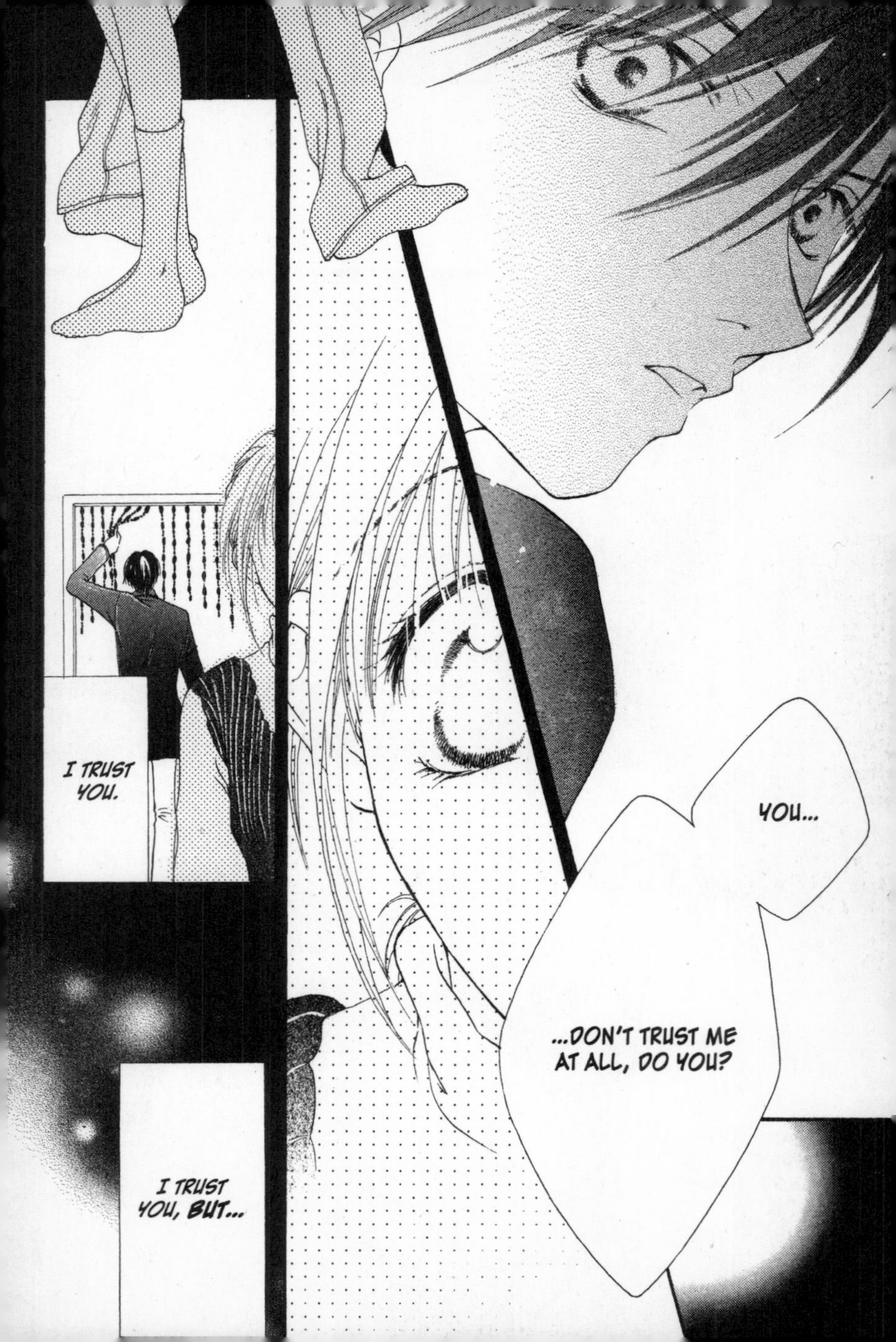
YOU...
...DON'T TRUST ME AT ALL, DO YOU?
I TRUST YOU.
I TRUST YOU, BUT...

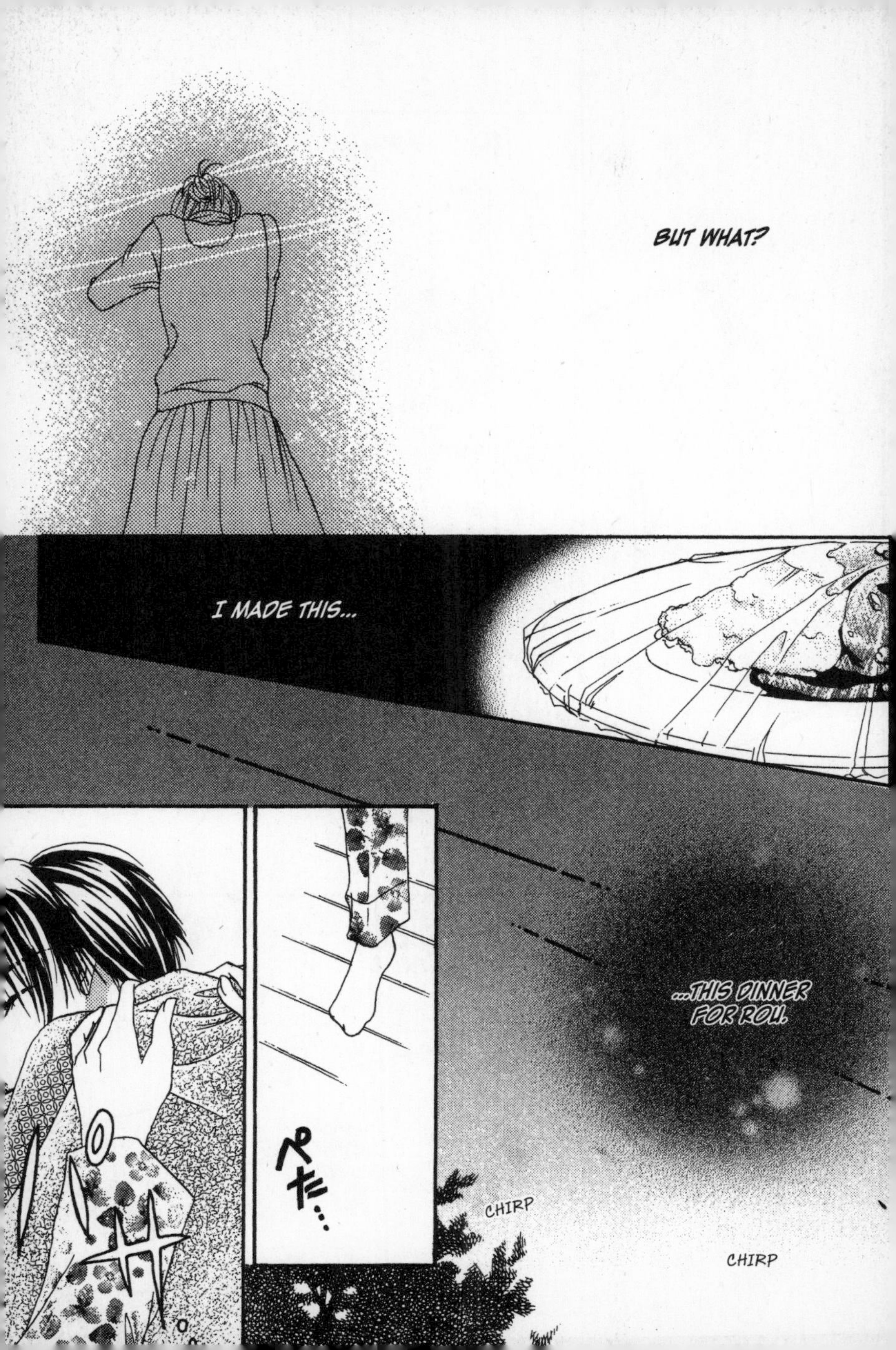
BUT WHAT?
I MADE THIS...
...THIS DINNER FOR ROU.
CHIRP
CHIRP
ぺた...

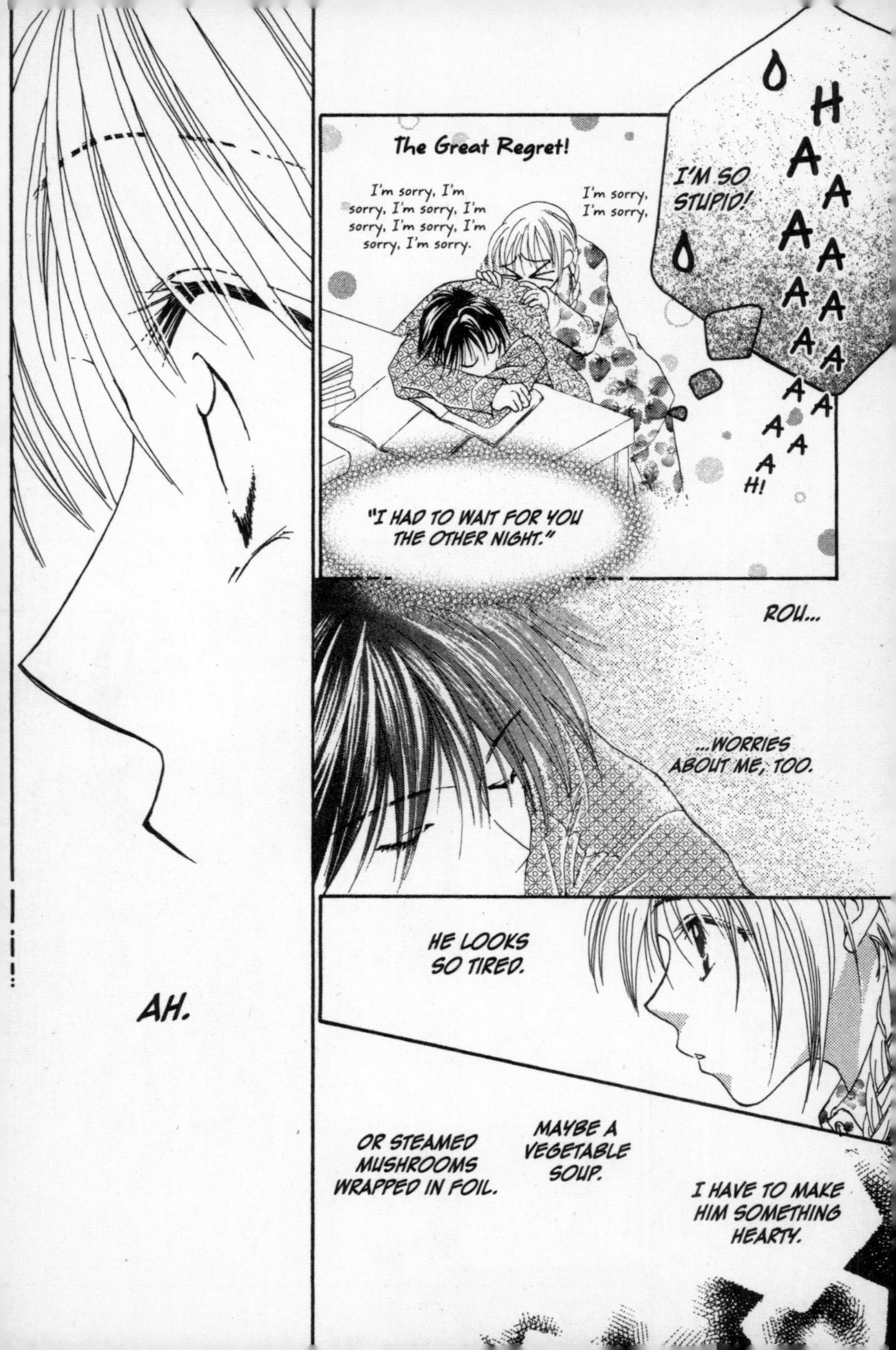
I'M SO STUPID!
OHAAAAAAAAAAAAAAAH!
The Great Regret!
I'm sorry, I'm sorry,
I'm sorry, I'm sorry, I'm sorry, I'm sorry, I'm sorry, I'm sorry, I'm sorry.
"I HAD TO WAIT FOR YOU THE OTHER NIGHT."
ROU...
...WORRIES ABOUT ME, TOO.
HE LOOKS SO TIRED.
I HAVE TO MAKE HIM SOMETHING HEARTY.
MAYBE A VEGETABLE SOUP.
OR STEAMED MUSHROOMS WRAPPED IN FOIL.
AH.

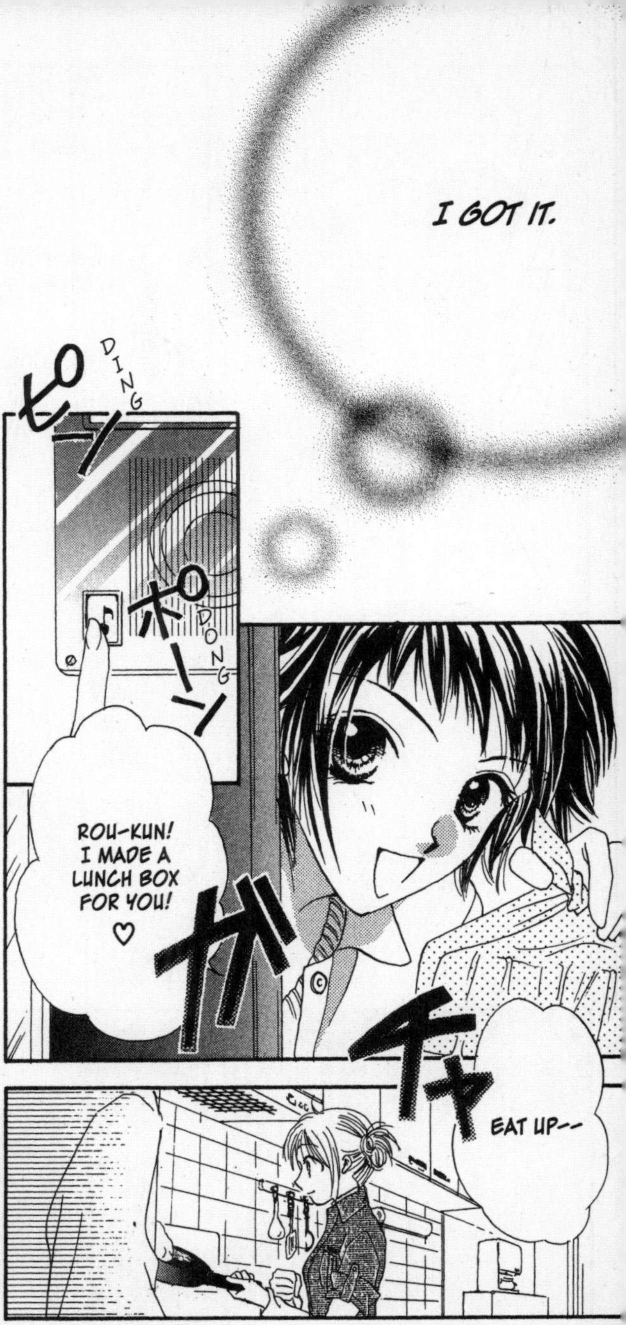
I GOT IT.
DING
DONG
ROU-KUN! I MADE A LUNCH BOX FOR YOU! ♡
ガチャ
EAT UP--

6

DIET

The day after Disney Sea, we went to play at Cosmo World on our way back from Yokohama. On the roller coaster, I, Kiritani, screamed, "I'm going to die!!!" and laughed. This year I've gone to SeaPara and Nanja Town and theme parks for three different kinds of fun. While I was at Sea, every time I took a picture on my digital camera I kept thinking, "My face looks pretty round..." And it's true. When I got home and got on my scale... I HAD GAINED THREE KILOGRAMS!! (About 6.6 lbs.)

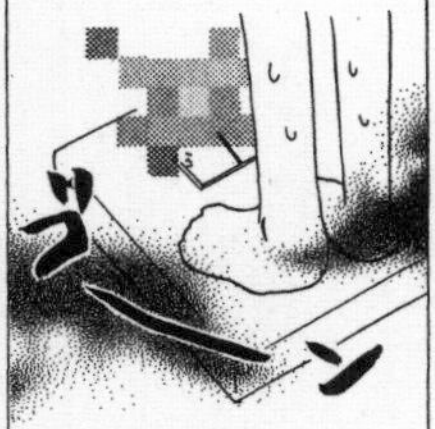

So I cut down my portions and cut out the snacks, and I got down to normal weight in three days. I guess my body's used to its usual size. My editor kept up steady e-mails of encouragement:

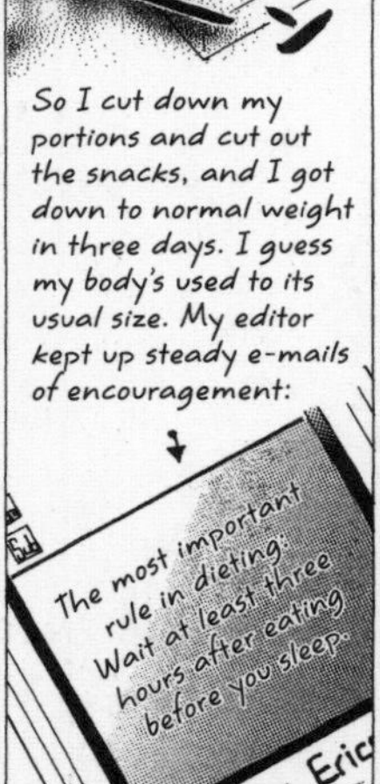
The most important rule in dieting: Wait at least three hours after eating before you sleep.

Please don't tempt me.

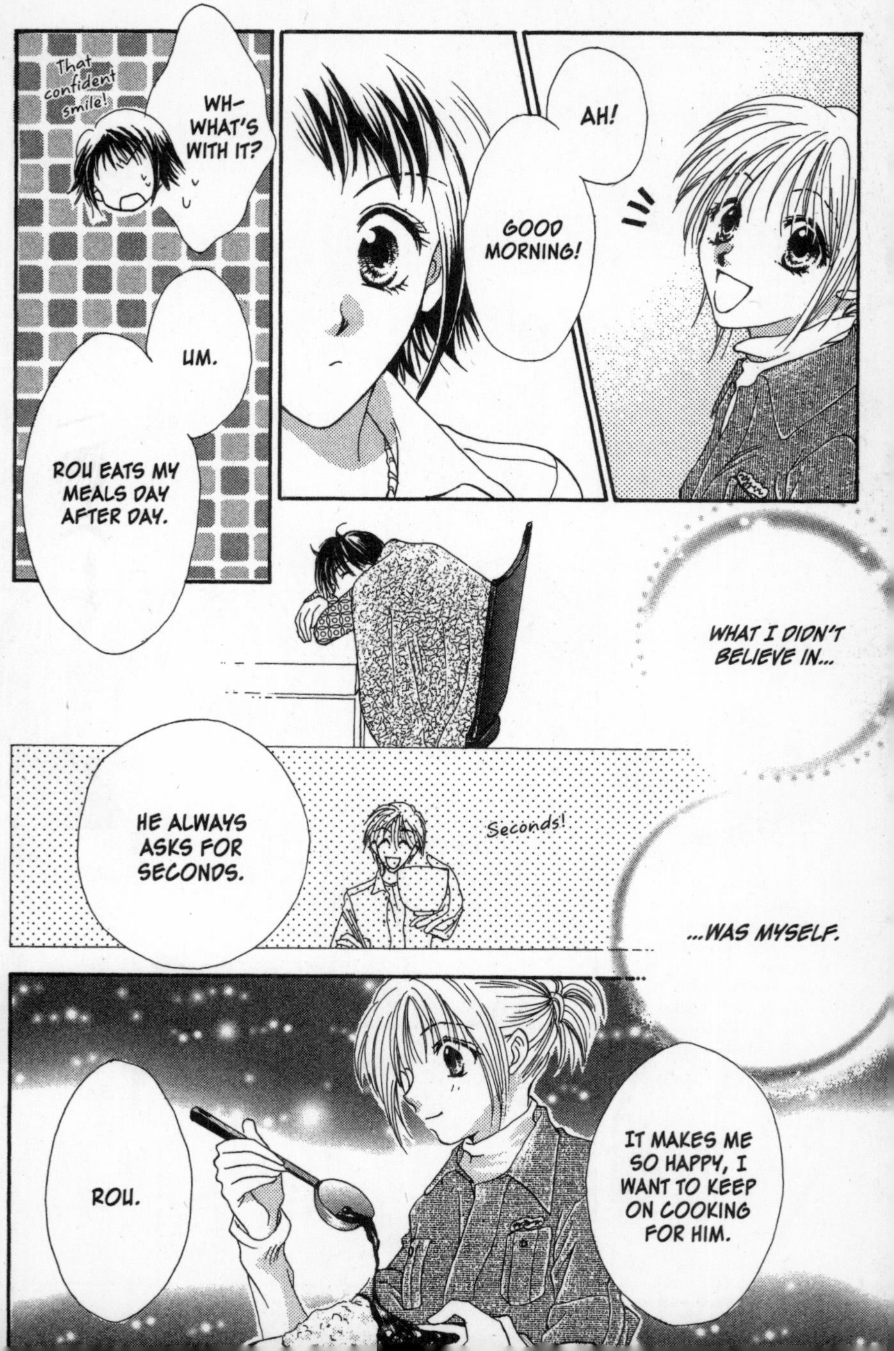
AH!
GOOD MORNING!
That confident smile!
WH-WHAT'S WITH IT?
UM.
ROU EATS MY MEALS DAY AFTER DAY.
WHAT I DIDN'T BELIEVE IN...
Seconds!
HE ALWAYS ASKS FOR SECONDS.
...WAS MYSELF.
IT MAKES ME SO HAPPY, I WANT TO KEEP ON COOKING FOR HIM.
ROU.

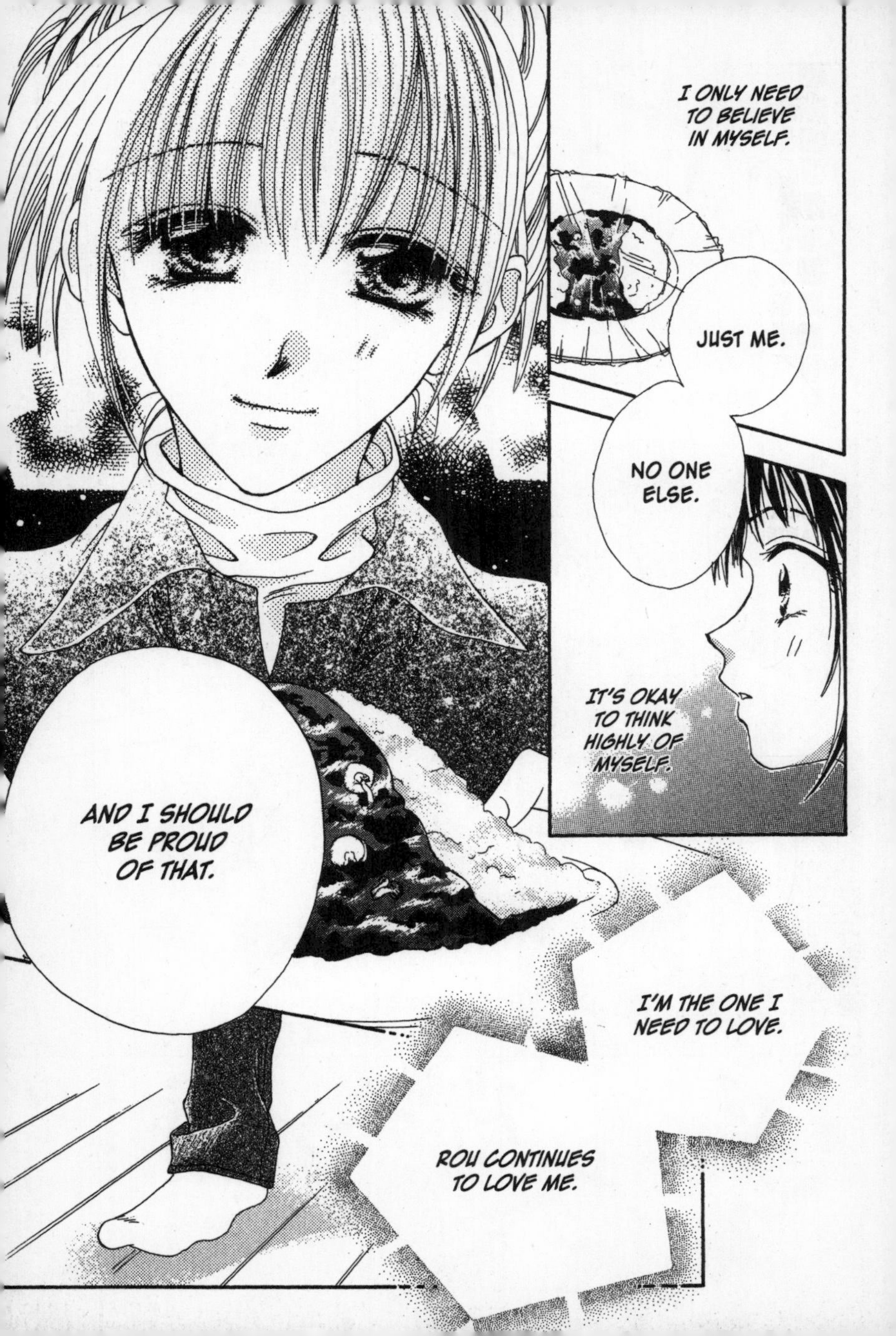
I ONLY NEED TO BELIEVE IN MYSELF.
JUST ME.
NO ONE ELSE.
IT'S OKAY TO THINK HIGHLY OF MYSELF.
AND I SHOULD BE PROUD OF THAT.
I'M THE ONE I NEED TO LOVE.
ROU CONTINUES TO LOVE ME.

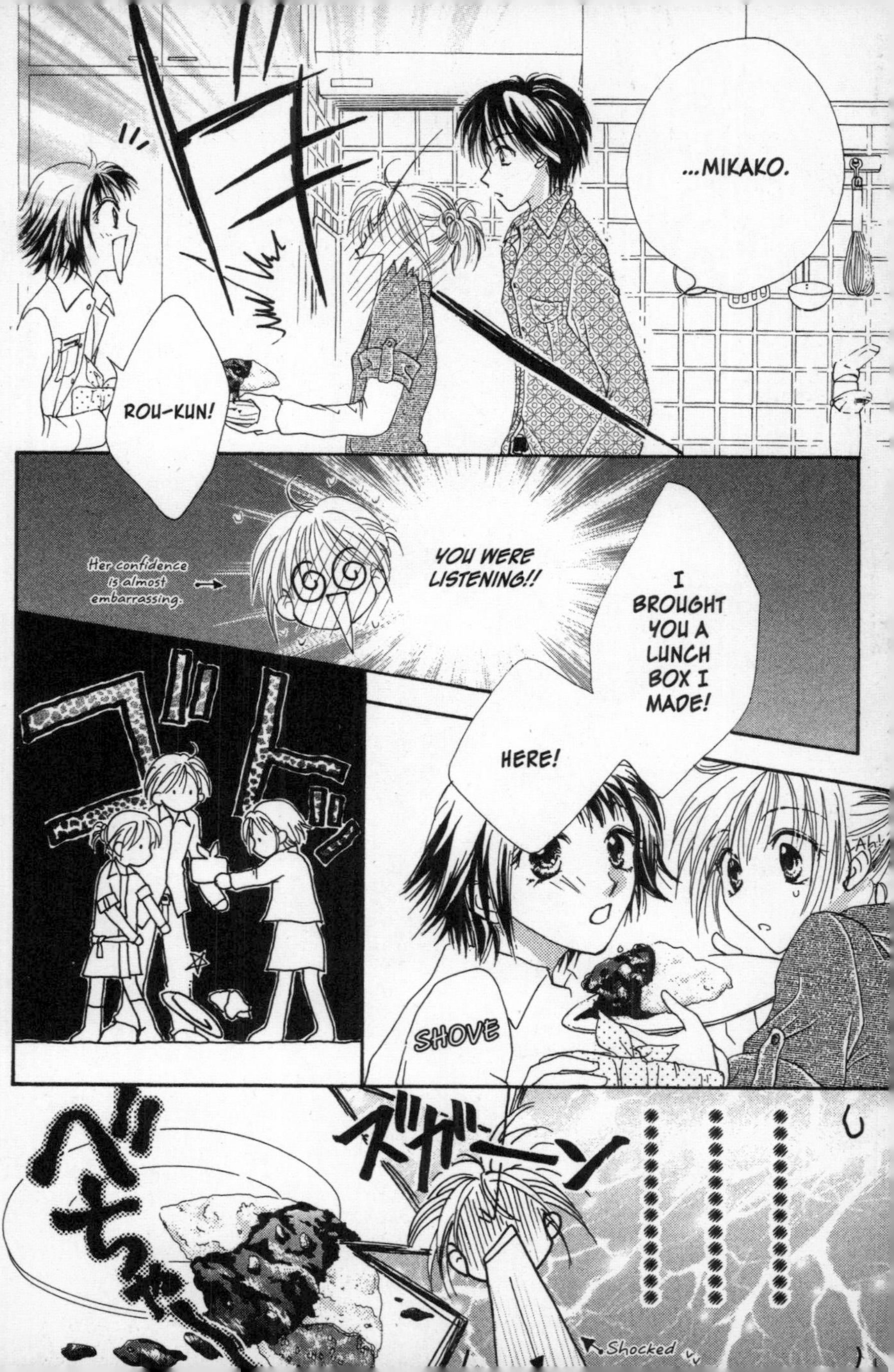
...MIKAKO.
ROU-KUN!
YOU WERE LISTENING!!
Her confidence is almost embarrassing.
I BROUGHT YOU A LUNCH BOX I MADE!
HERE!
Ah!
SHOVE
Shocked

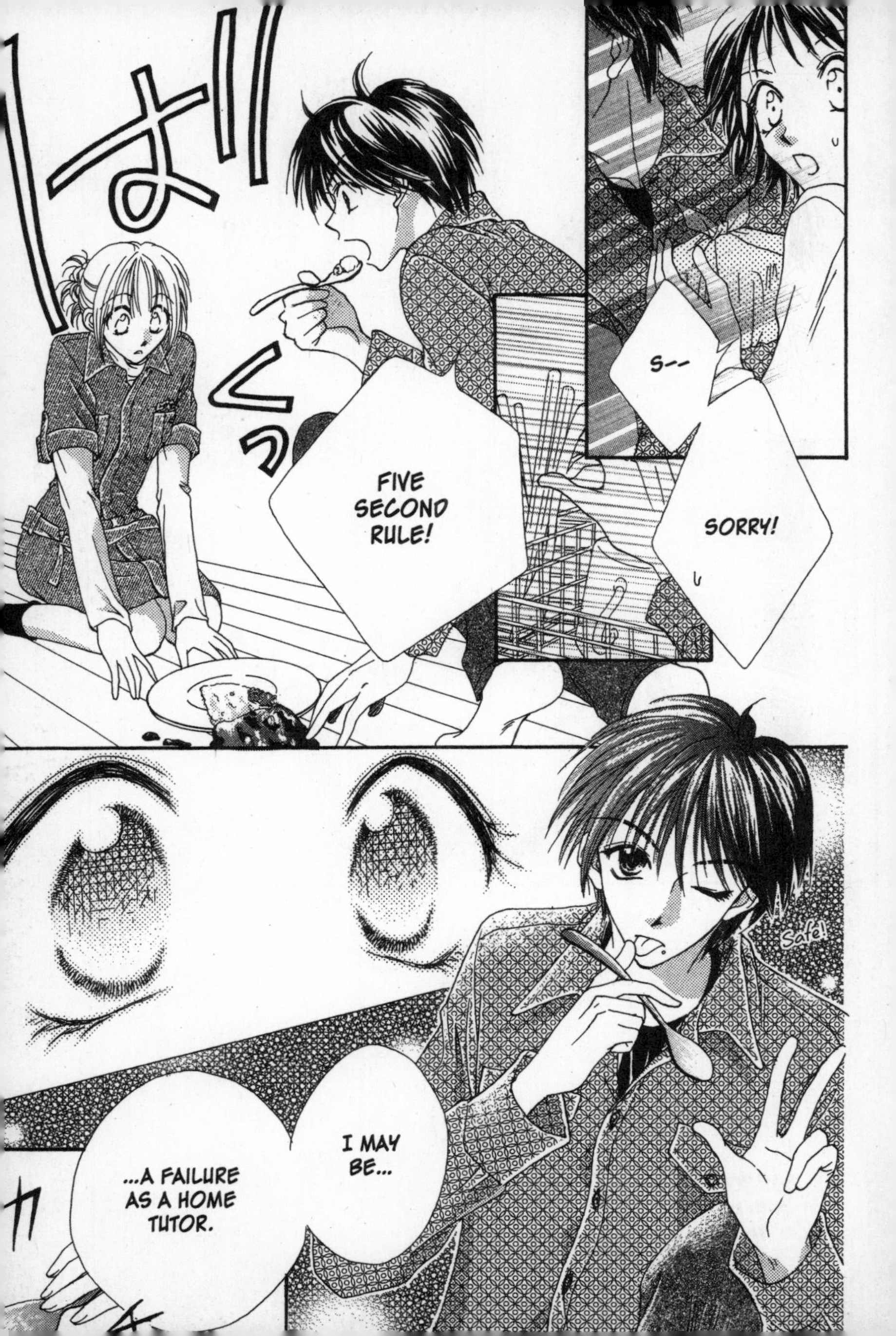
S--
SORRY!
FIVE SECOND RULE!
Safe!
I MAY BE...
...A FAILURE AS A HOME TUTOR.

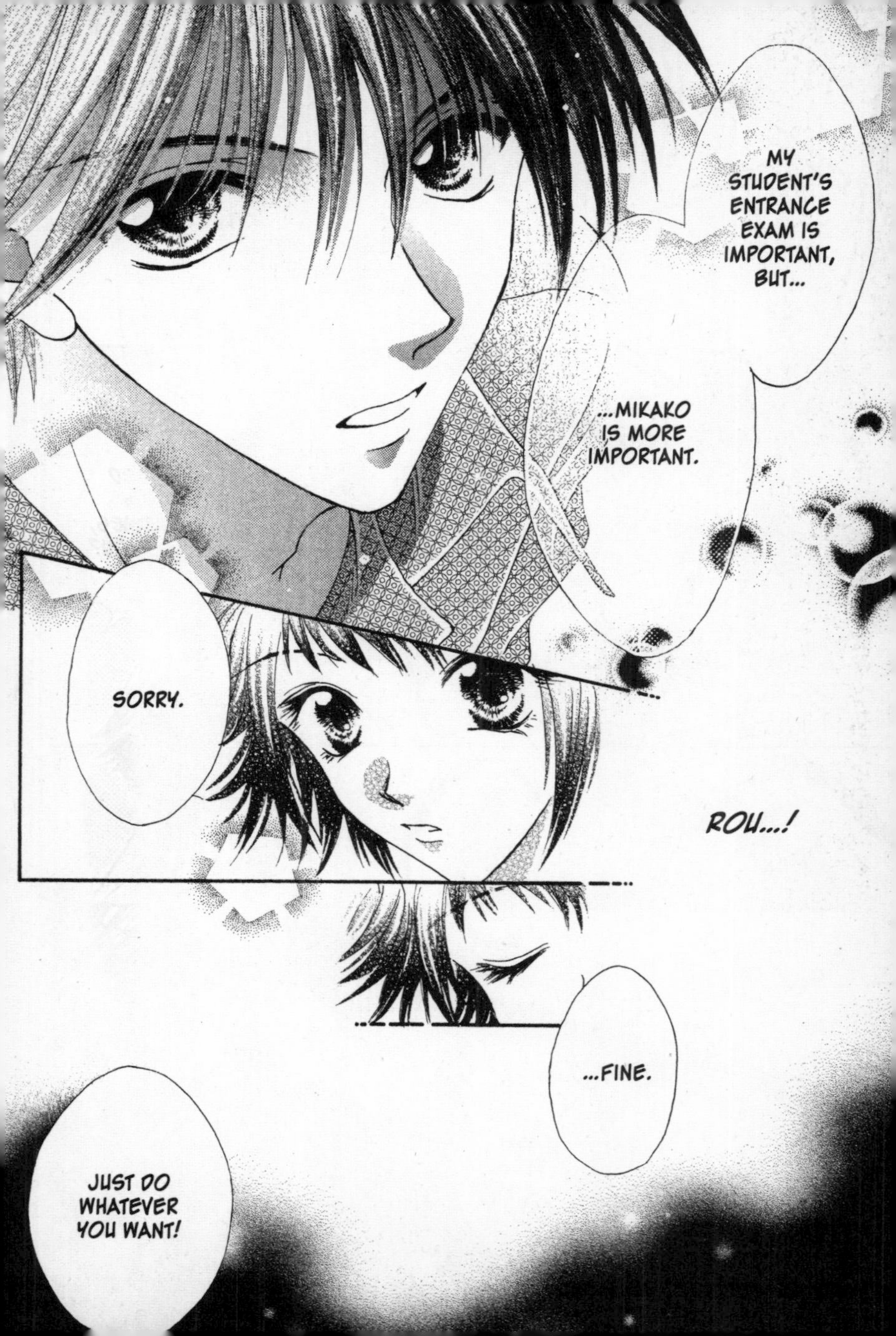
MY STUDENT'S ENTRANCE EXAM IS IMPORTANT, BUT...
...MIKAKO IS MORE IMPORTANT.
ROU...!
SORRY.
...FINE.
JUST DO WHATEVER YOU WANT!

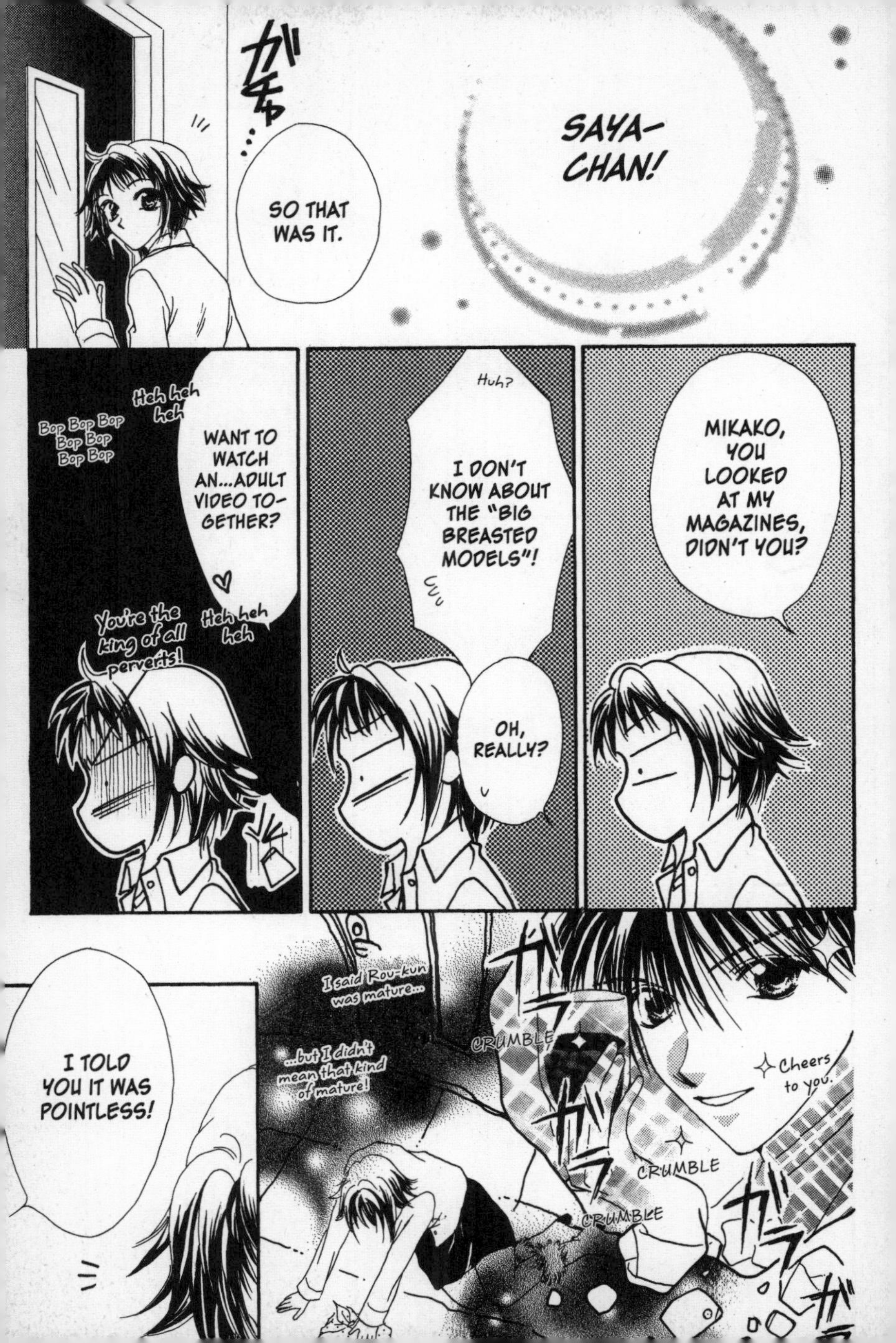
SAYA-CHAN!
SO THAT WAS IT.
MIKAKO, YOU LOOKED AT MY MAGAZINES, DIDN'T YOU?
Huh?
I DON'T KNOW ABOUT THE "BIG BREASTED MODELS"!
OH, REALLY?
WANT TO WATCH AN...ADULT VIDEO TO-GETHER?
Heh heh heh
Bop Bop Bop Bop Bop Bop Bop
You're the king of all perverts!
Heh heh heh
Cheers to you.
CRUMBLE
CRUMBLE
CRUMBLE
I said Rou-kun was mature...
...but I didn't mean that kind of mature!
I TOLD YOU IT WAS POINTLESS!

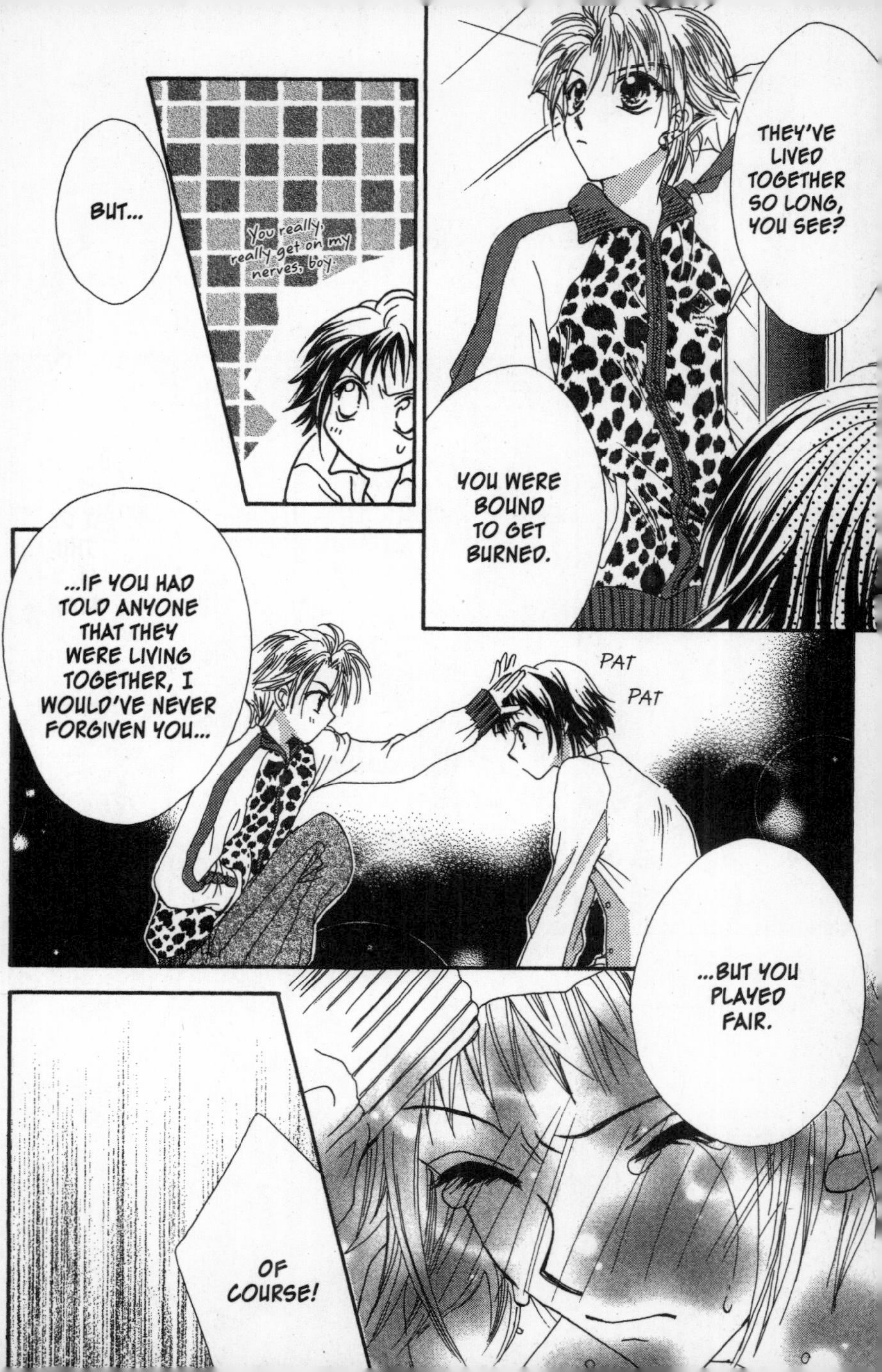
THEY'VE LIVED TOGETHER SO LONG, YOU SEE?
YOU WERE BOUND TO GET BURNED.
BUT...
You really, really get on my nerves, boy.
...IF YOU HAD TOLD ANYONE THAT THEY WERE LIVING TOGETHER, I WOULD'VE NEVER FORGIVEN YOU...
PAT
PAT
...BUT YOU PLAYED FAIR.
OF COURSE!

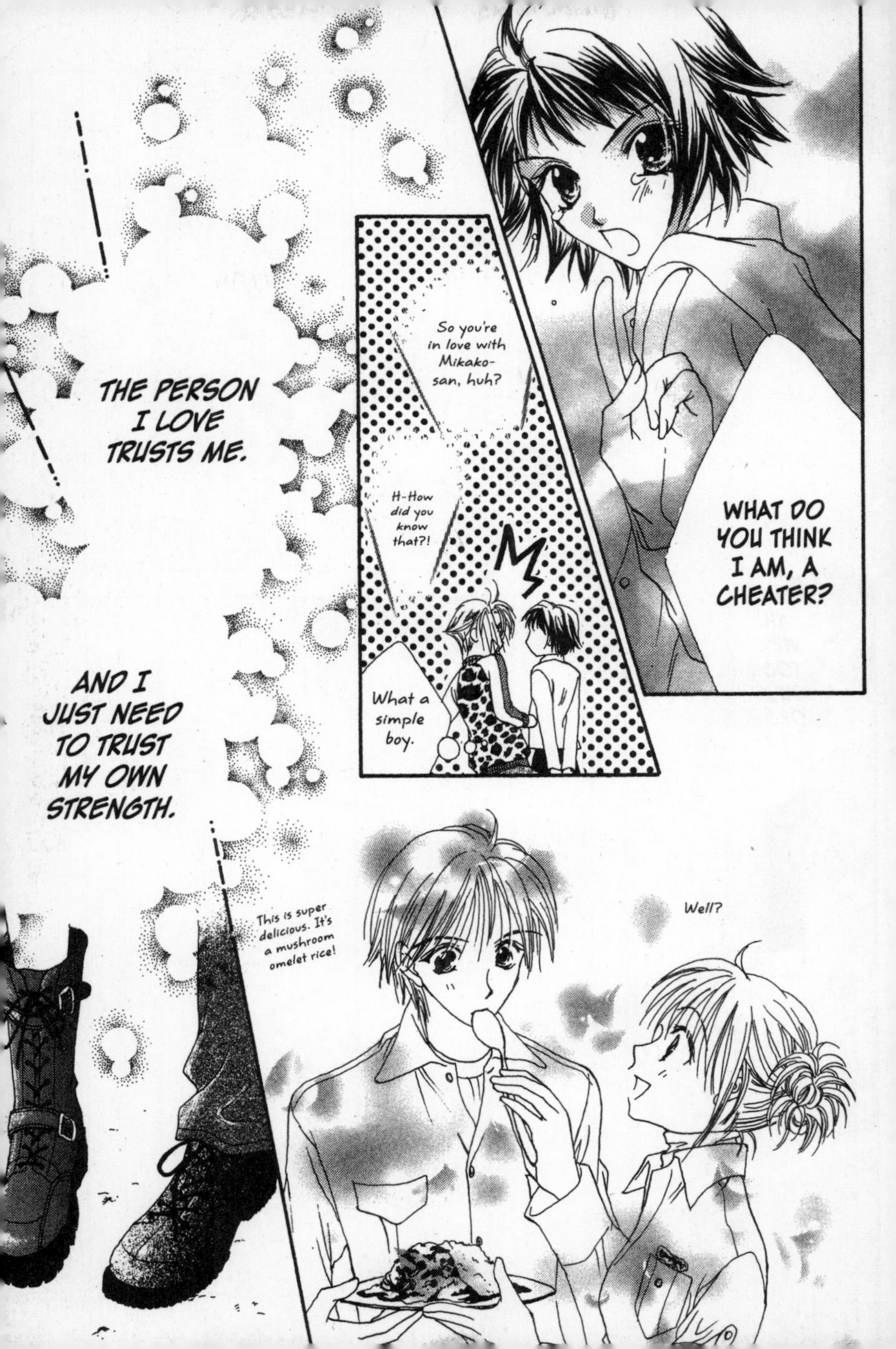
WHAT DO YOU THINK I AM, A CHEATER?
So you're in love with Mikako-san, huh?
H-How did you know that?!
What a simple boy.
THE PERSON I LOVE TRUSTS ME.
AND I JUST NEED TO TRUST MY OWN STRENGTH.
Well?
This is super delicious. It's a mushroom omelet rice!

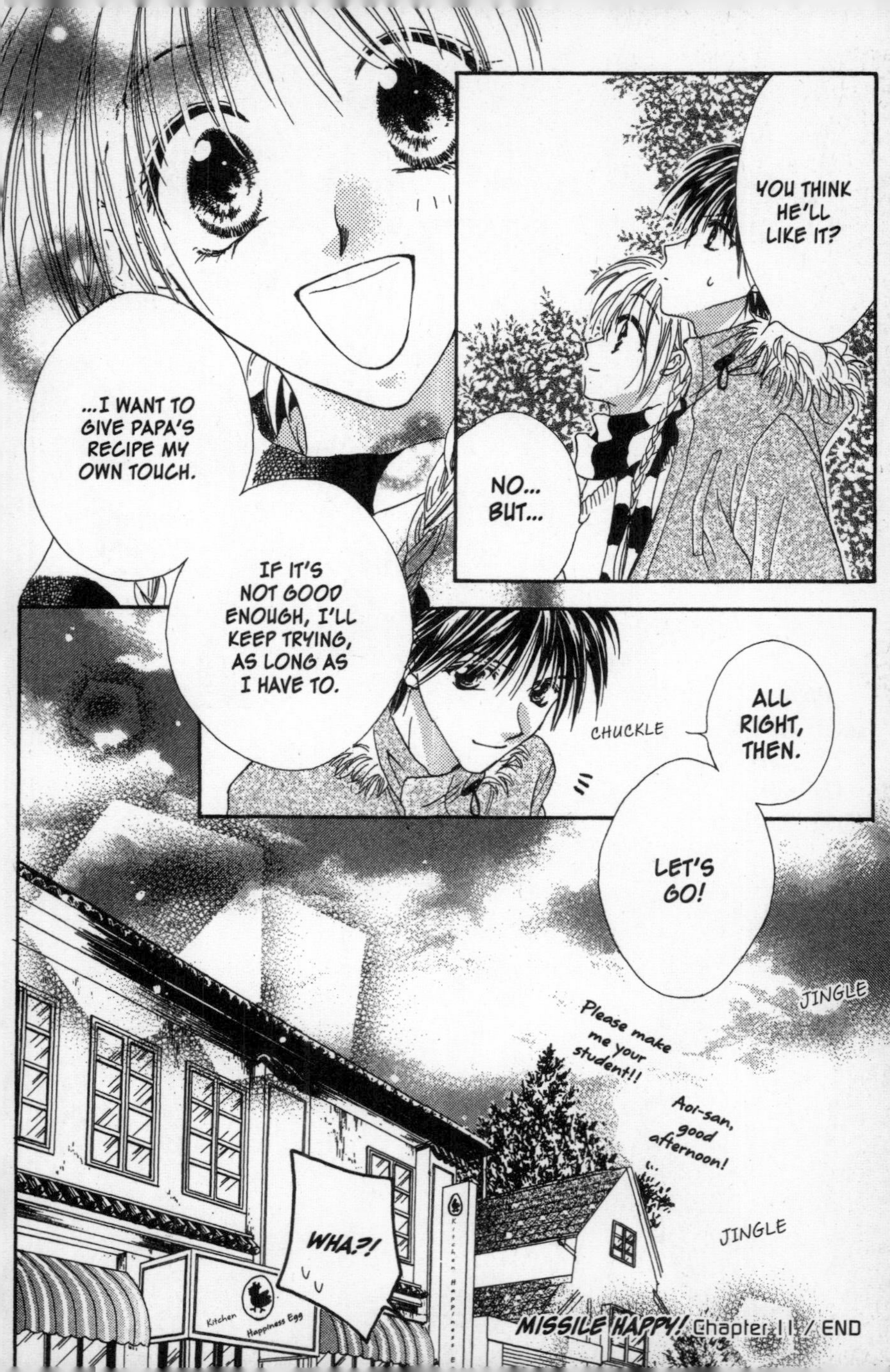
YOU THINK HE'LL LIKE IT?
NO... BUT...
...I WANT TO GIVE PAPA'S RECIPE MY OWN TOUCH.
IF IT'S NOT GOOD ENOUGH, I'LL KEEP TRYING, AS LONG AS I HAVE TO.
CHUCKLE
ALL RIGHT, THEN.
LET'S GO!
JINGLE
Please make me your student!!
Aoi-san, good afternoon!
JINGLE
WHA?!
Kitchen Happiness Egg
MISSILE HAPPY! Chapter 11 / END

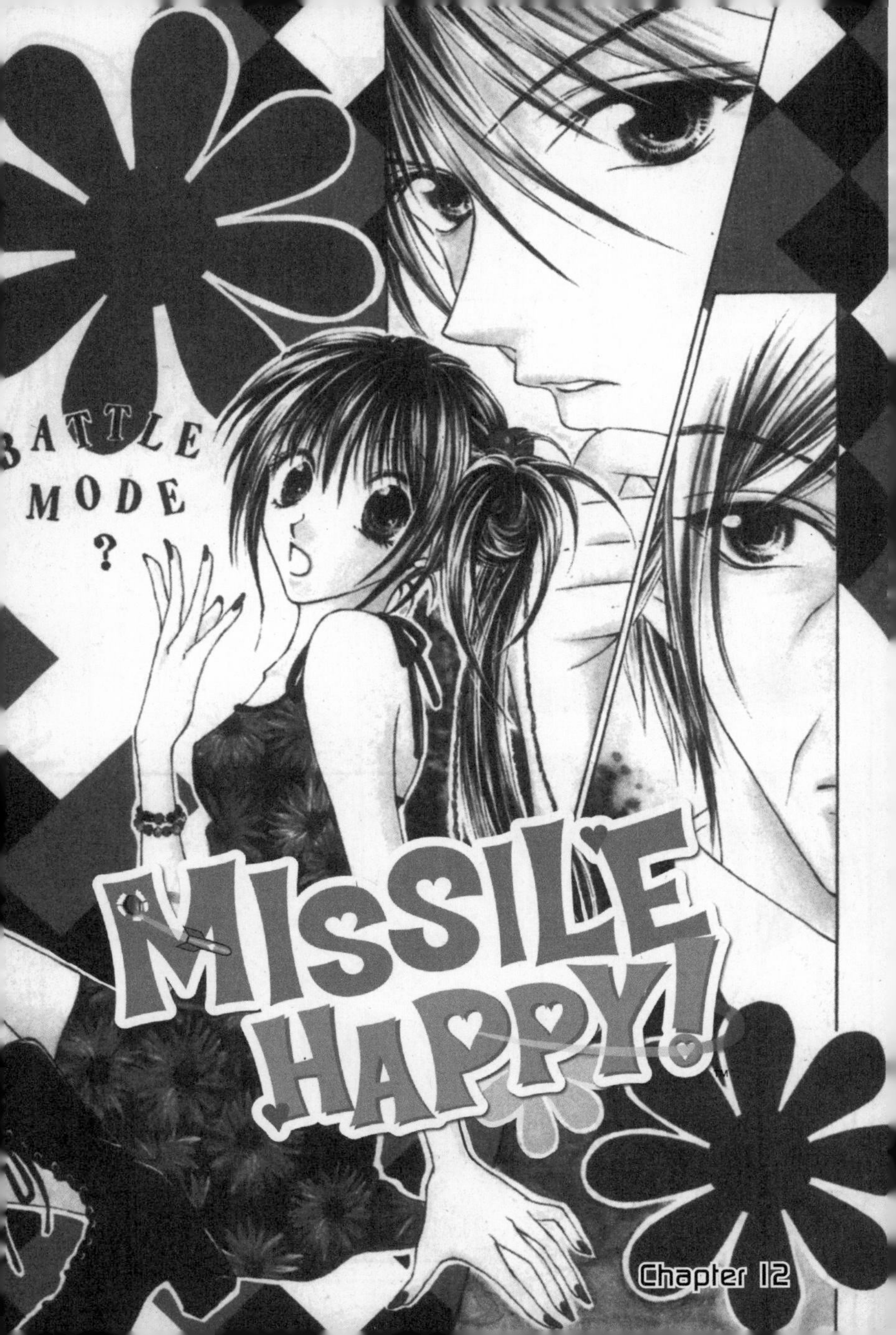
BATTLE MODE ?
MISSILE HAPPY!™
Chapter 12

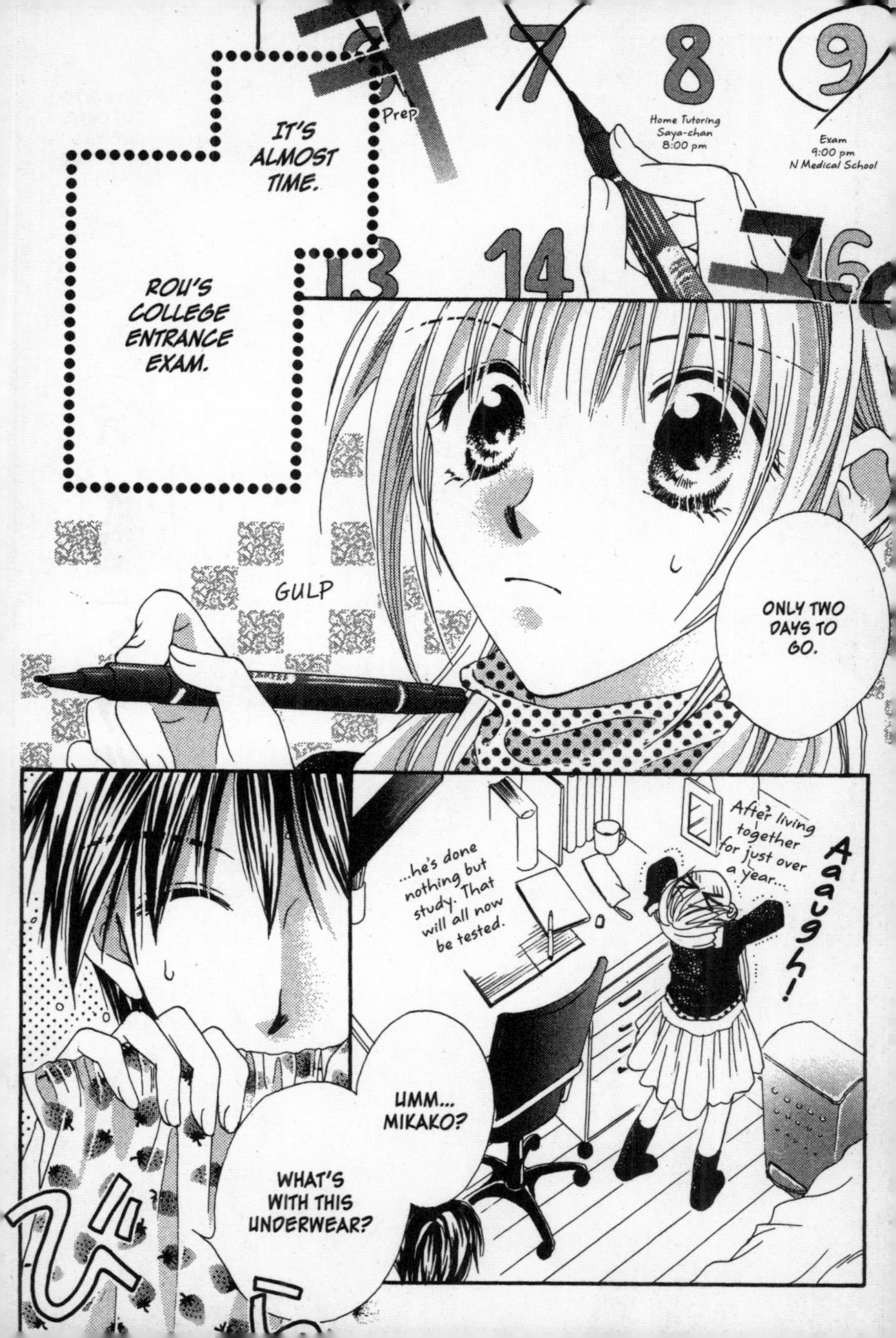
Exam 9:00 pm N Medical School
Home Tutoring Saya-chan 8:00 pm
Prep
IT'S ALMOST TIME.
ROU'S COLLEGE ENTRANCE EXAM.
ONLY TWO DAYS TO GO.
GULP
Aaaugh!
After living together for just over a year...
...he's done nothing but study. That will all now be tested.
UMM... MIKAKO?
WHAT'S WITH THIS UNDERWEAR?

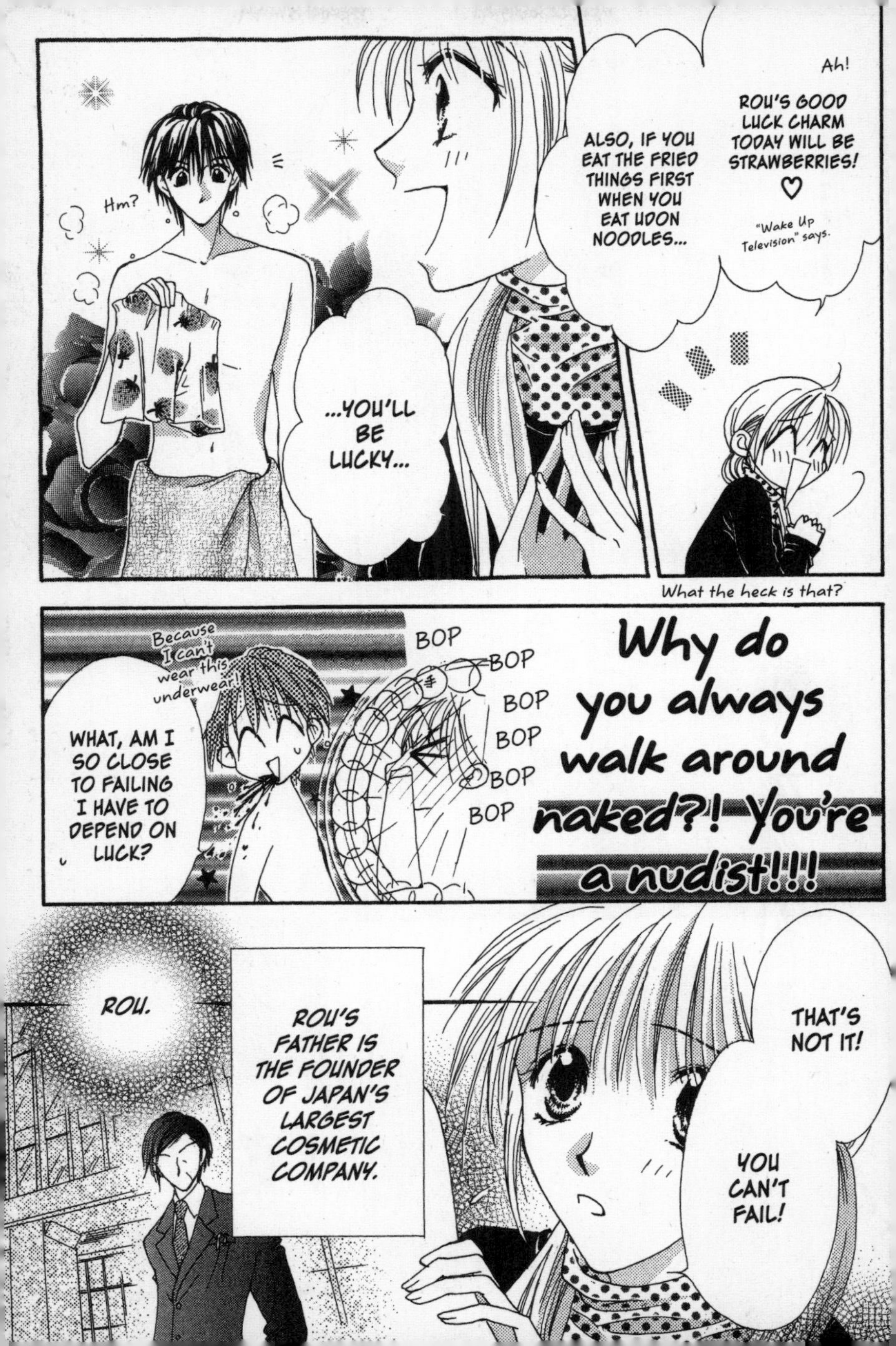

Ah!
ROU'S GOOD LUCK CHARM TODAY WILL BE STRAWBERRIES! ♡
"Wake Up Television" says.
ALSO, IF YOU EAT THE FRIED THINGS FIRST WHEN YOU EAT UDON NOODLES...
...YOU'LL BE LUCKY...
Hm?
What the heck is that?
Why do you always walk around naked?! You're a nudist!!!
BOP
BOP
BOP
BOP
BOP
BOP
WHAT, AM I SO CLOSE TO FAILING I HAVE TO DEPEND ON LUCK?
Because I can't wear this underwear!
THAT'S NOT IT!
YOU CAN'T FAIL!
ROU'S FATHER IS THE FOUNDER OF JAPAN'S LARGEST COSMETIC COMPANY.
ROU.

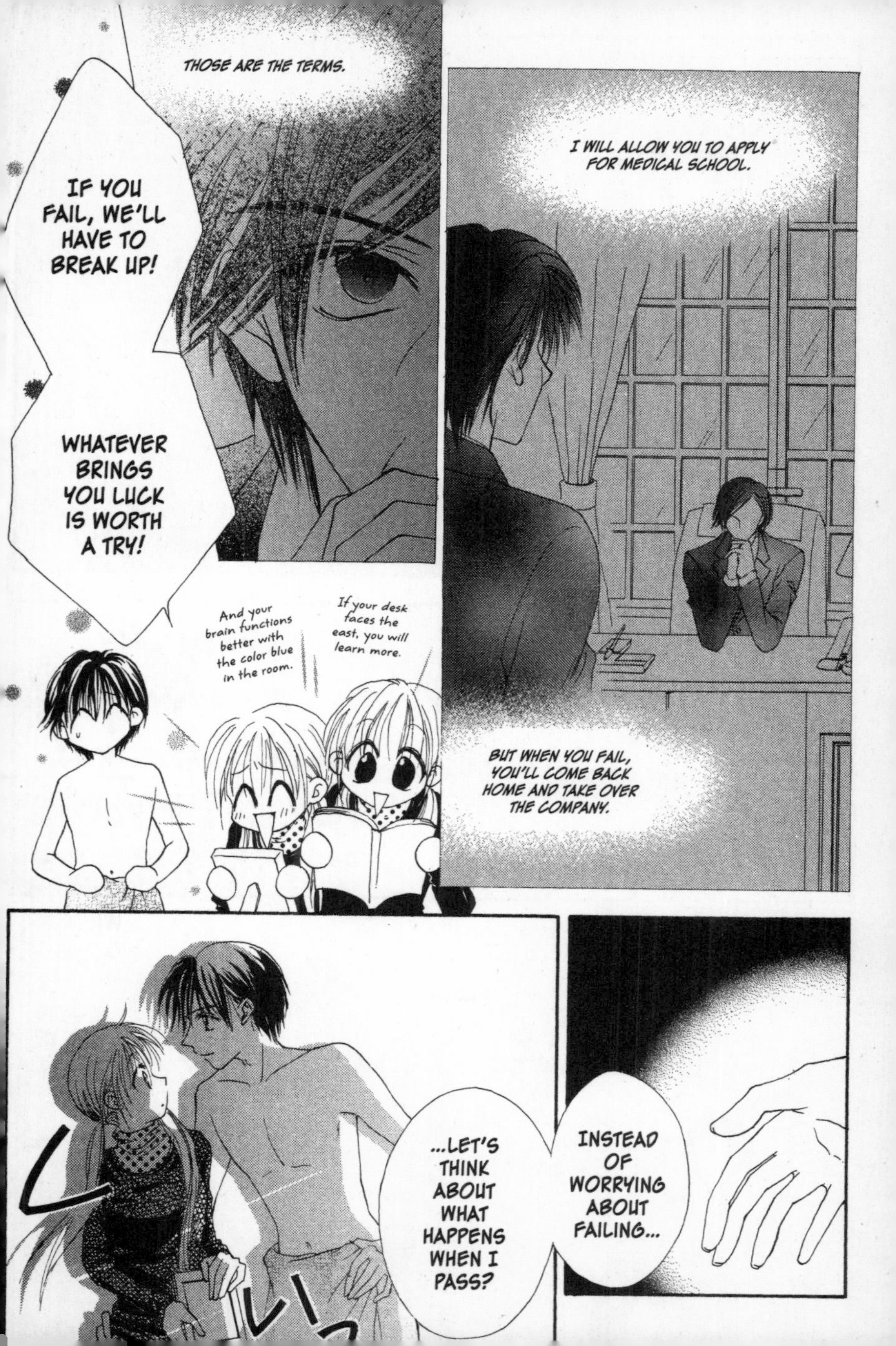
I WILL ALLOW YOU TO APPLY FOR MEDICAL SCHOOL.
BUT WHEN YOU FAIL, YOU'LL COME BACK HOME AND TAKE OVER THE COMPANY.
THOSE ARE THE TERMS.
IF YOU FAIL, WE'LL HAVE TO BREAK UP!
WHATEVER BRINGS YOU LUCK IS WORTH A TRY!
If your desk faces the east, you will learn more.
And your brain functions better with the color blue in the room.
INSTEAD OF WORRYING ABOUT FAILING...
...LET'S THINK ABOUT WHAT HAPPENS WHEN I PASS?

MISSILE IN GERMAN

That's right. In Germany there is a magazine "Daisuki," and Missile is published there in German. It's a great lineup, but even my last editor wasn't sure why my manga was chosen to be in there. It's a mystery to me, too!

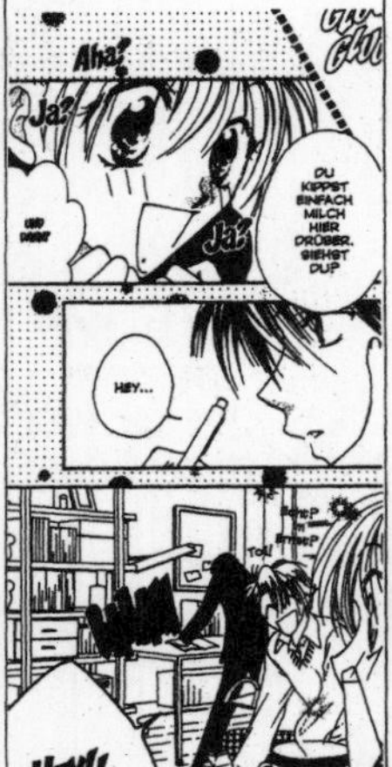
Aha?
Ja?
Ja!
DU KIPPST EINFACH MILCH HIER DRÜBER. SIEHST DU?
HEY...
HEY!!
21.

I like that on this page, the third panel says, "Hey..." and the last panel says, "HEY!!" It's cool.

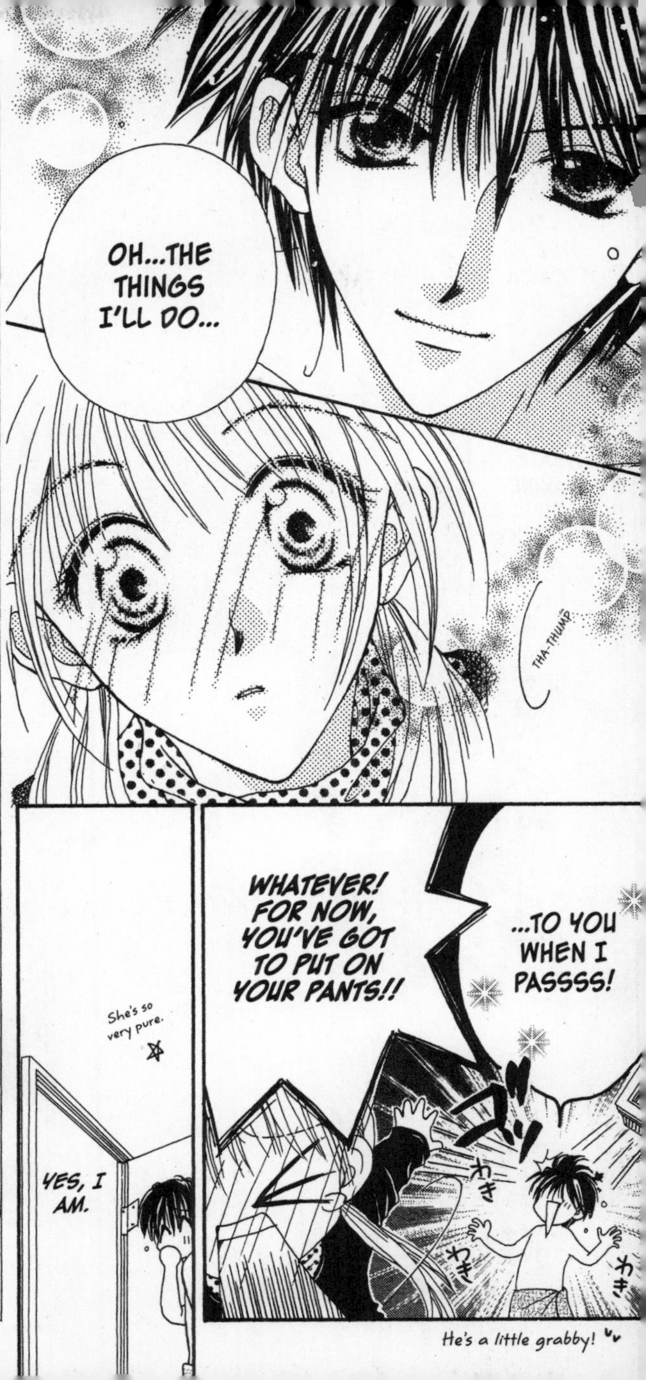
OH...THE THINGS I'LL DO...
THA-THUMP
...TO YOU WHEN I PASSSS!
WHATEVER! FOR NOW, YOU'VE GOT TO PUT ON YOUR PANTS!!
わき
わき
わき
She's so very pure.
YES, I AM.

He's a little grabby!

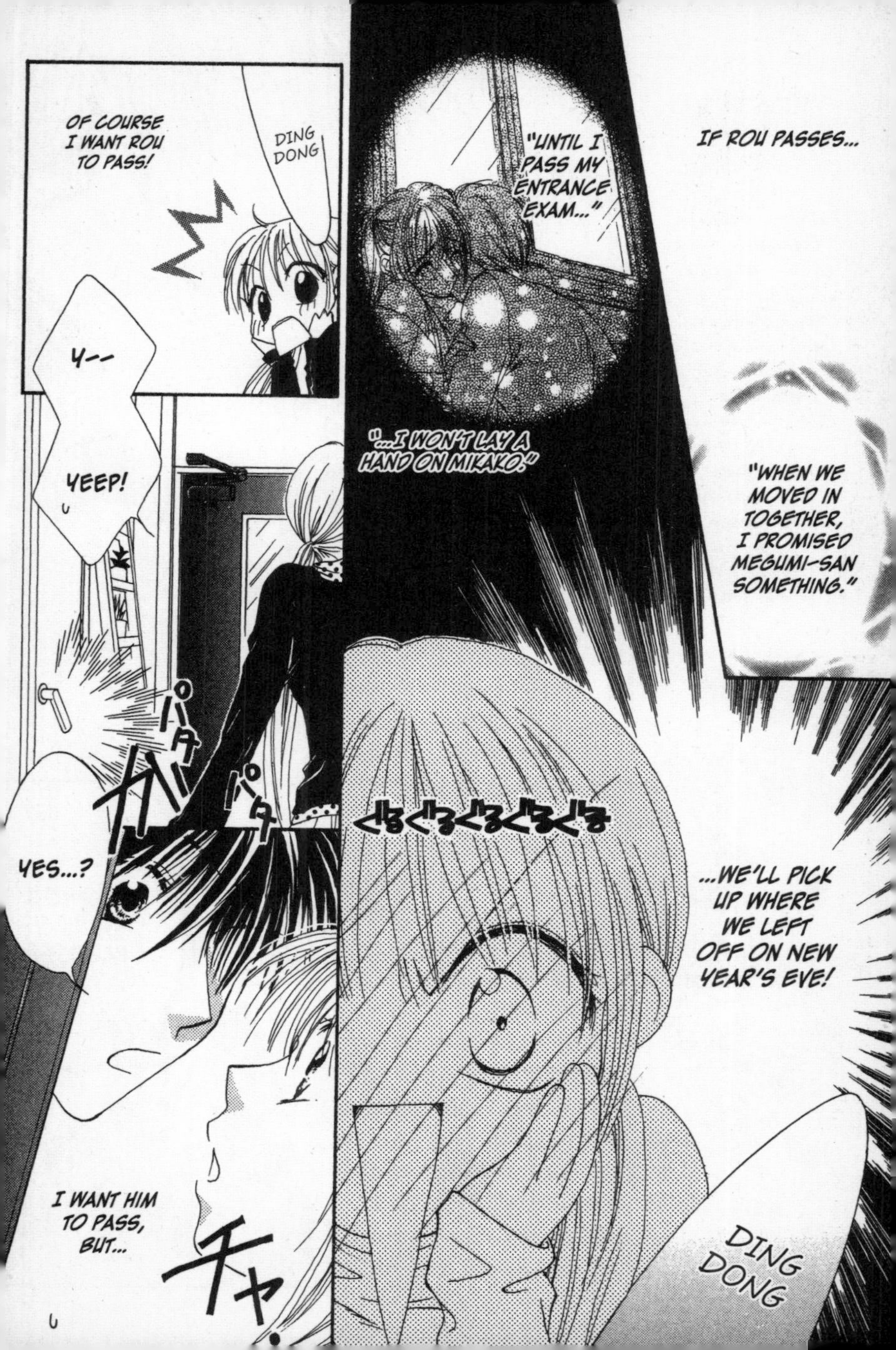
IF ROU PASSES...
"WHEN WE MOVED IN TOGETHER, I PROMISED MEGUMI-SAN SOMETHING."
"UNTIL I PASS MY ENTRANCE EXAM..."
"...I WON'T LAY A HAND ON MIKAKO."
...WE'LL PICK UP WHERE WE LEFT OFF ON NEW YEAR'S EVE!
ぐるぐるぐるぐるぐる
DING DONG
OF COURSE I WANT ROU TO PASS!
DING DONG
Y--
YEEP!
パタ
パタ
YES...?
I WANT HIM TO PASS, BUT...
チャ

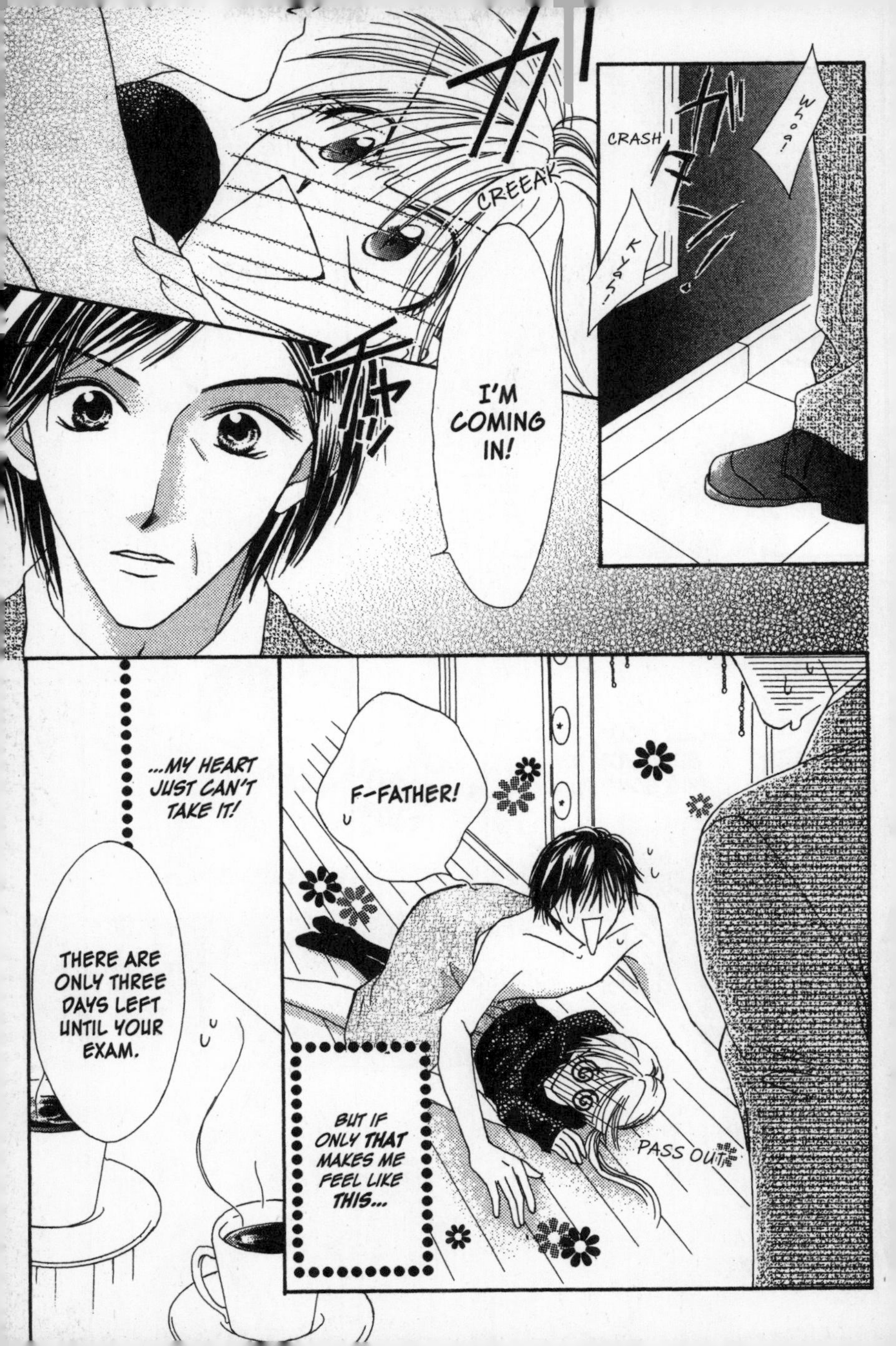
Whoa!
CRASH
Kyaa!
CREEAK
I'M COMING IN!
F-FATHER!
PASS OUT
BUT IF ONLY THAT MAKES ME FEEL LIKE THIS...
...MY HEART JUST CAN'T TAKE IT!
THERE ARE ONLY THREE DAYS LEFT UNTIL YOUR EXAM.

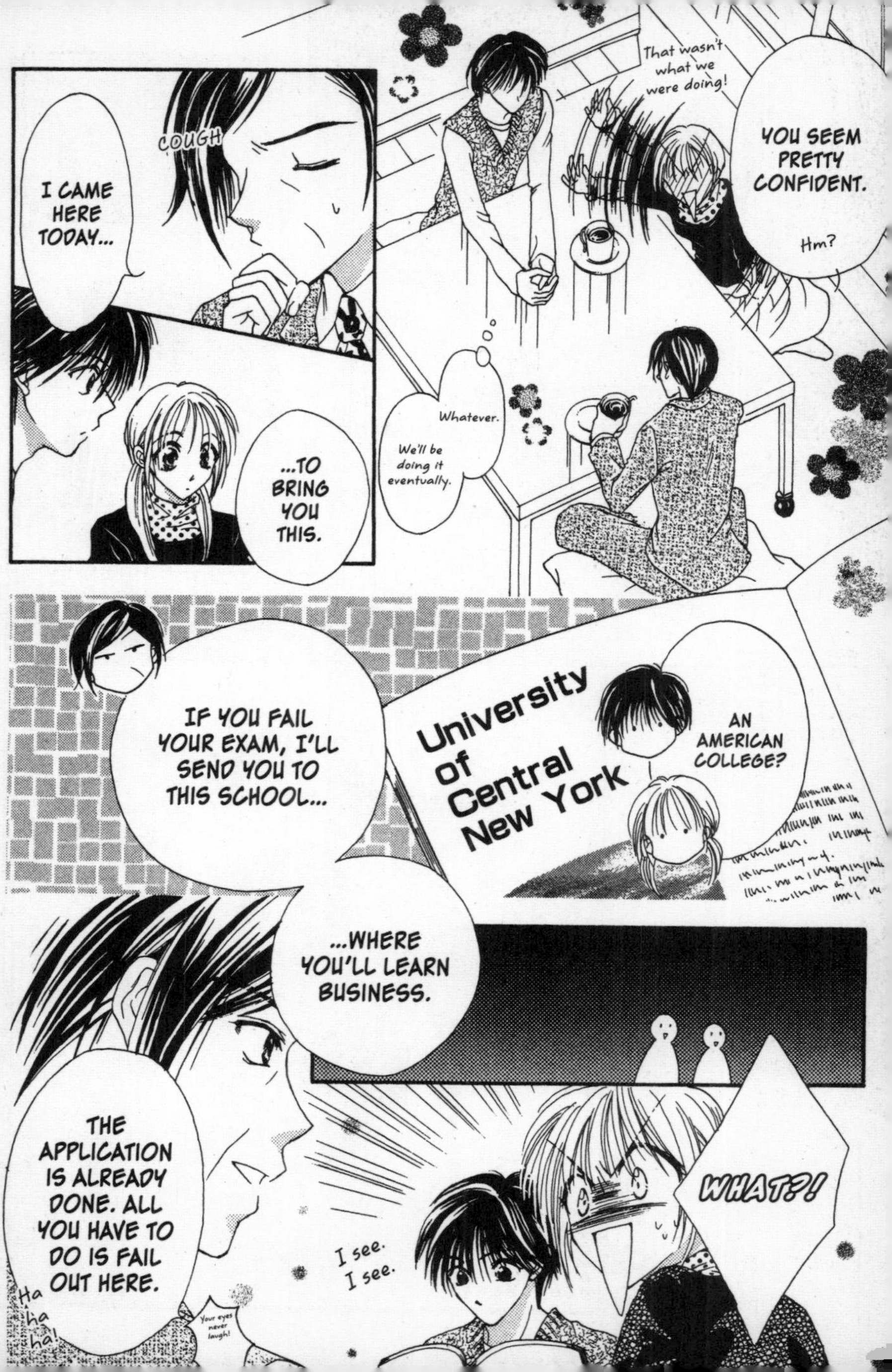
YOU SEEM PRETTY CONFIDENT.
Hm?
That wasn't what we were doing!
Whatever.
We'll be doing it eventually.
COUGH
I CAME HERE TODAY...
...TO BRING YOU THIS.
University of Central New York
AN AMERICAN COLLEGE?
IF YOU FAIL YOUR EXAM, I'LL SEND YOU TO THIS SCHOOL...
...WHERE YOU'LL LEARN BUSINESS.
WHAT?!
I see. I see.
THE APPLICATION IS ALREADY DONE. ALL YOU HAVE TO DO IS FAIL OUT HERE.
Ha ha ha!
Your eyes never laugh!

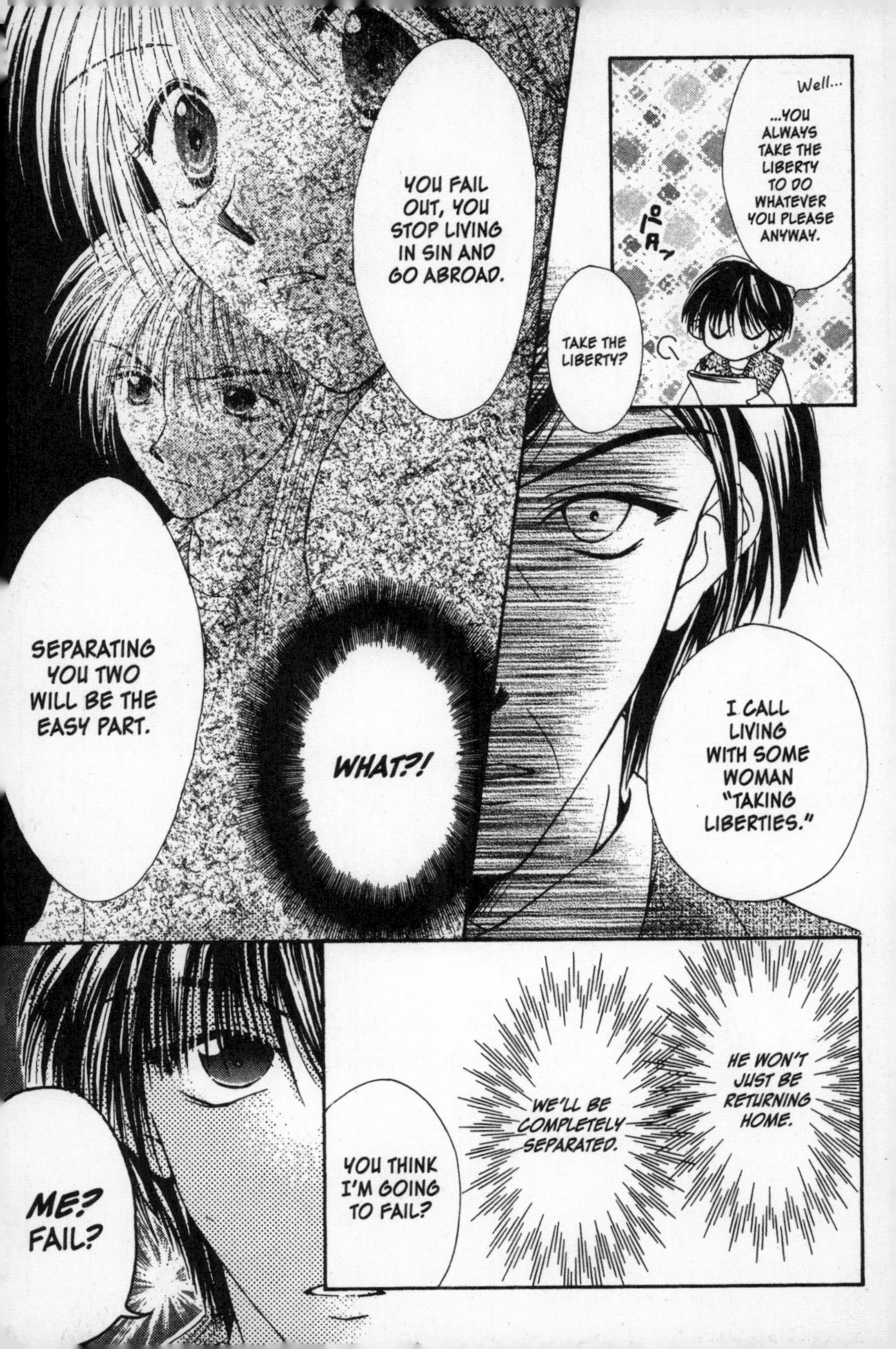
Well...
...YOU ALWAYS TAKE THE LIBERTY TO DO WHATEVER YOU PLEASE ANYWAY.
TAKE THE LIBERTY?
I CALL LIVING WITH SOME WOMAN "TAKING LIBERTIES."
YOU FAIL OUT, YOU STOP LIVING IN SIN AND GO ABROAD.
WHAT?!
SEPARATING YOU TWO WILL BE THE EASY PART.
HE WON'T JUST BE RETURNING HOME.
WE'LL BE COMPLETELY SEPARATED.
YOU THINK I'M GOING TO FAIL?
ME? FAIL?

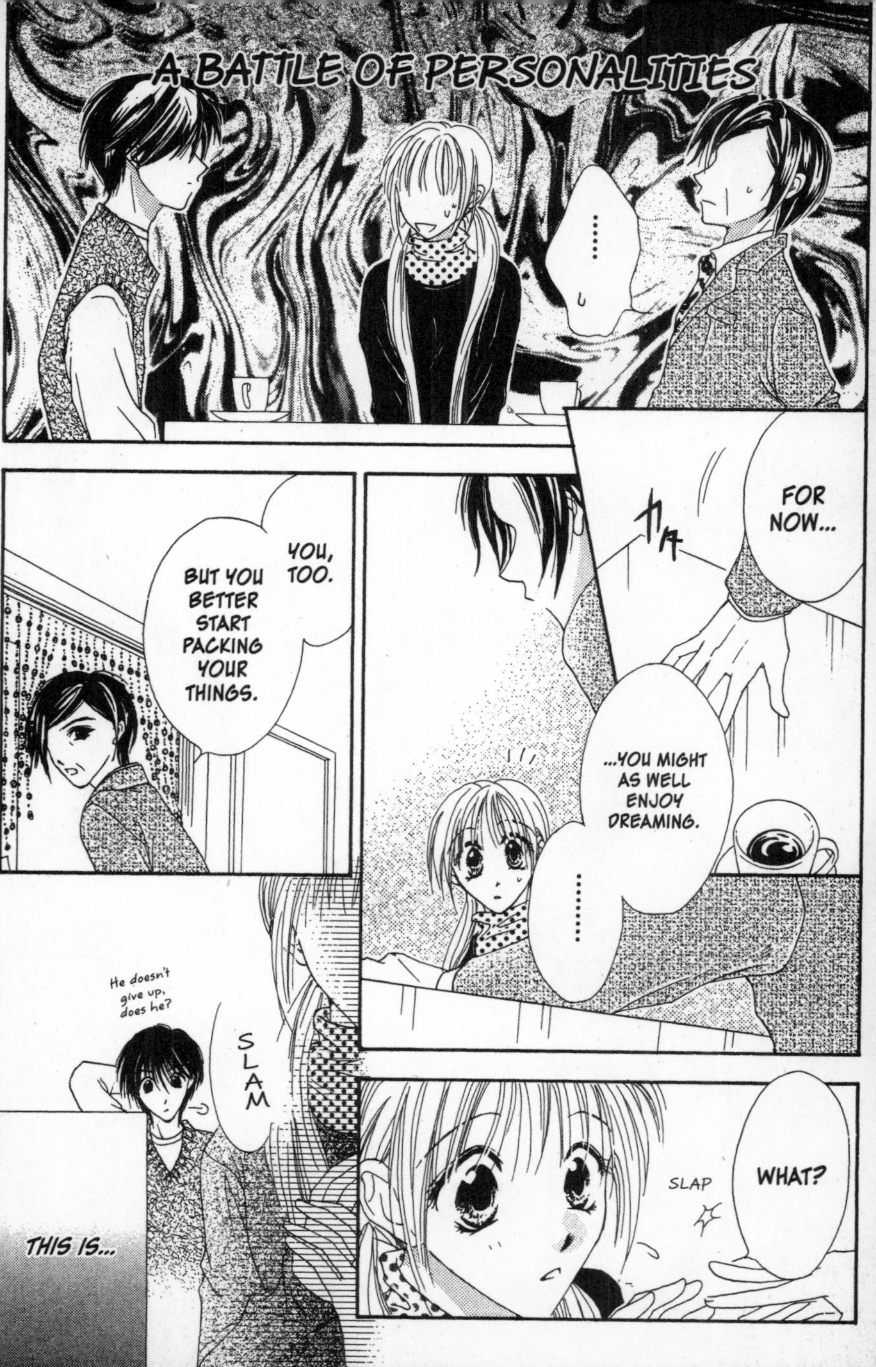
A BATTLE OF PERSONALITIES
......
FOR NOW...
ガタ
...YOU MIGHT AS WELL ENJOY DREAMING.
......
YOU, TOO.
BUT YOU BETTER START PACKING YOUR THINGS.
WHAT?
SLAP
SLAM
He doesn't give up, does he?
THIS IS...

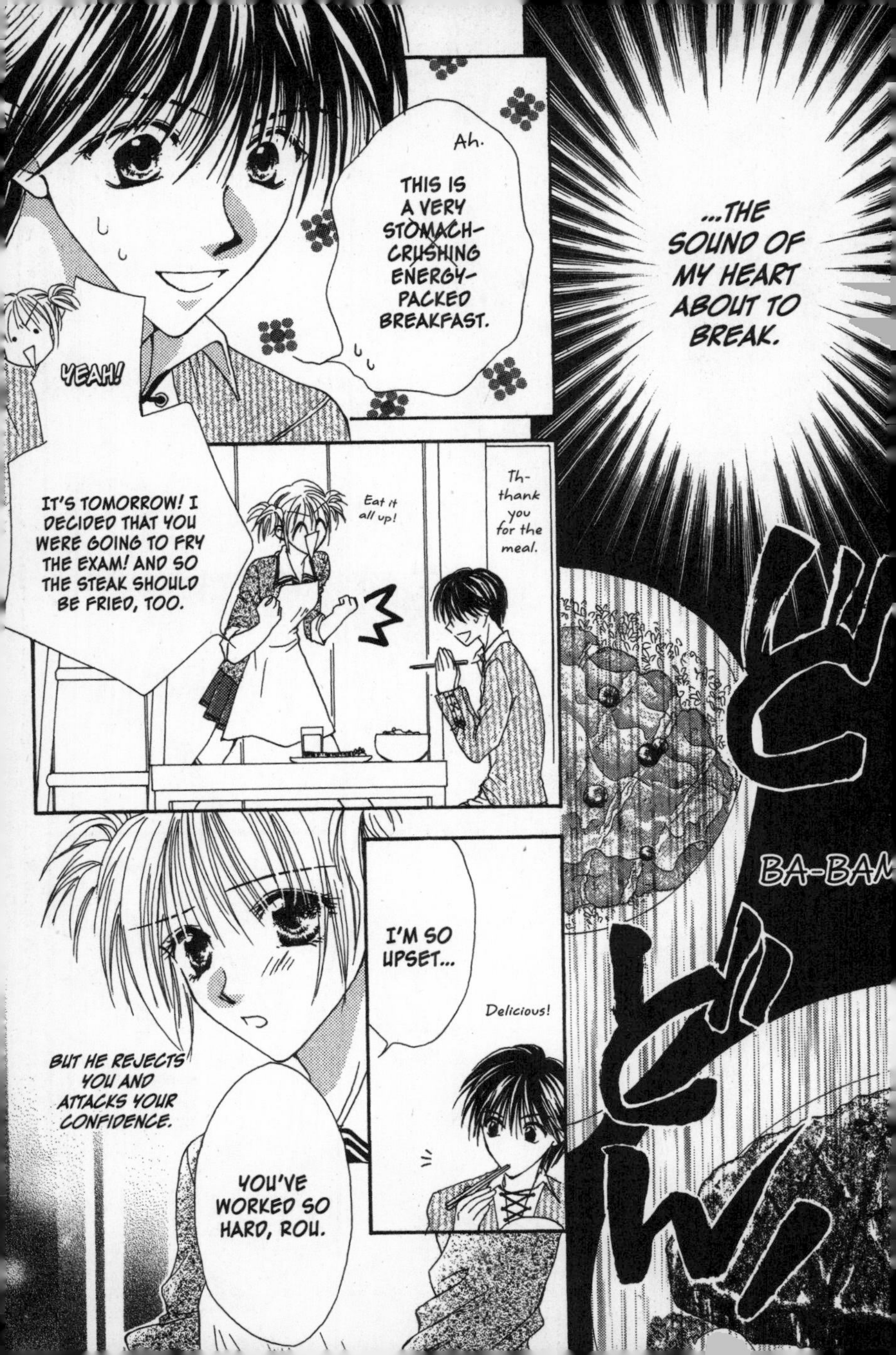
...THE SOUND OF MY HEART ABOUT TO BREAK.
BA-BAM
Ah.
THIS IS A VERY STOMACH-CRUSHING ENERGY-PACKED BREAKFAST.
YEAH!
Th-thank you for the meal.
Eat it all up!
IT'S TOMORROW! I DECIDED THAT YOU WERE GOING TO FRY THE EXAM! AND SO THE STEAK SHOULD BE FRIED, TOO.
I'M SO UPSET...
Delicious!
BUT HE REJECTS YOU AND ATTACKS YOUR CONFIDENCE.
YOU'VE WORKED SO HARD, ROU.

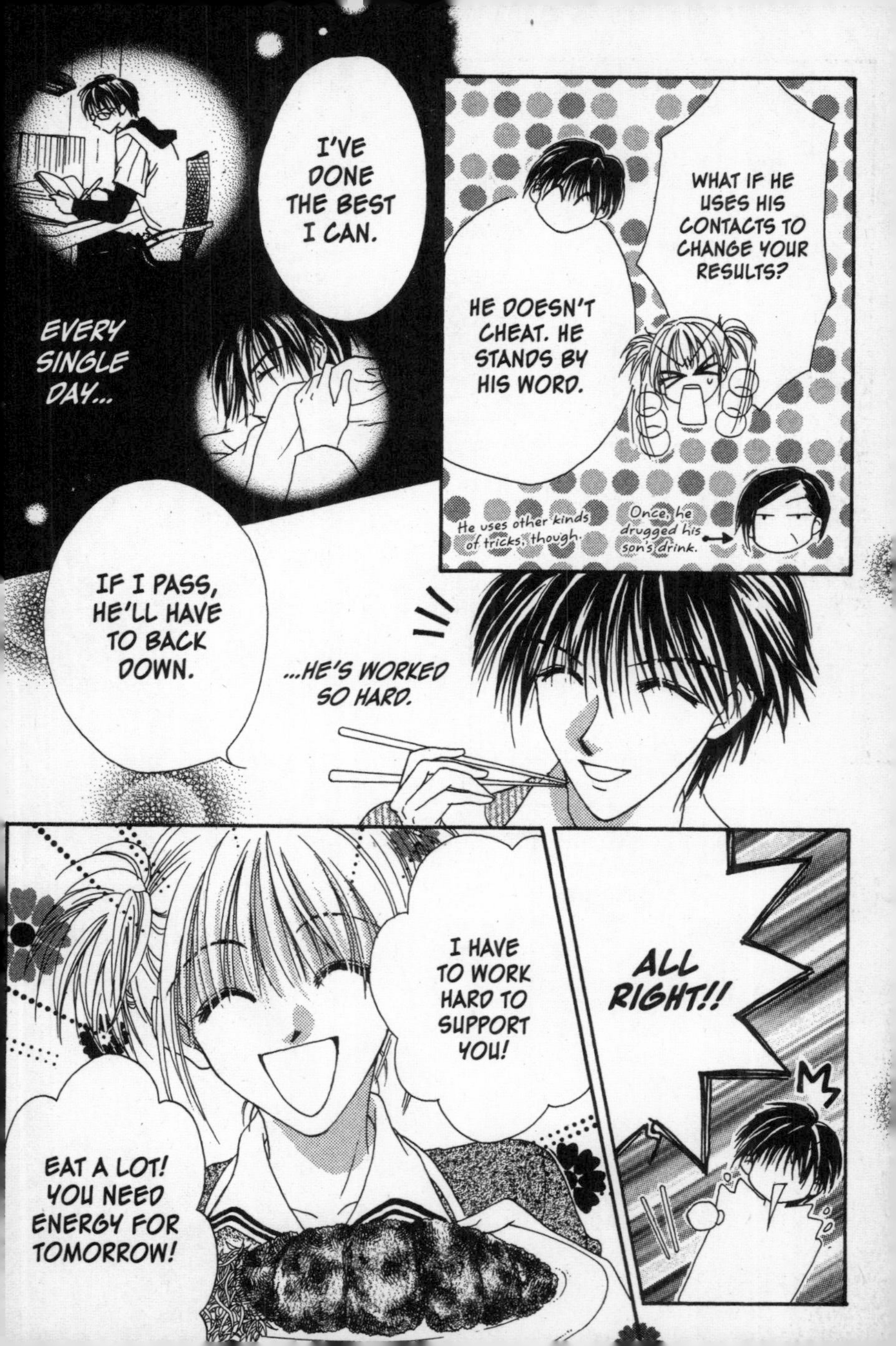
WHAT IF HE USES HIS CONTACTS TO CHANGE YOUR RESULTS?
HE DOESN'T CHEAT. HE STANDS BY HIS WORD.
Once, he drugged his son's drink.
He uses other kinds of tricks, though.
I'VE DONE THE BEST I CAN.
EVERY SINGLE DAY...
IF I PASS, HE'LL HAVE TO BACK DOWN.
...HE'S WORKED SO HARD.
ALL RIGHT!!
I HAVE TO WORK HARD TO SUPPORT YOU!
EAT A LOT! YOU NEED ENERGY FOR TOMORROW!

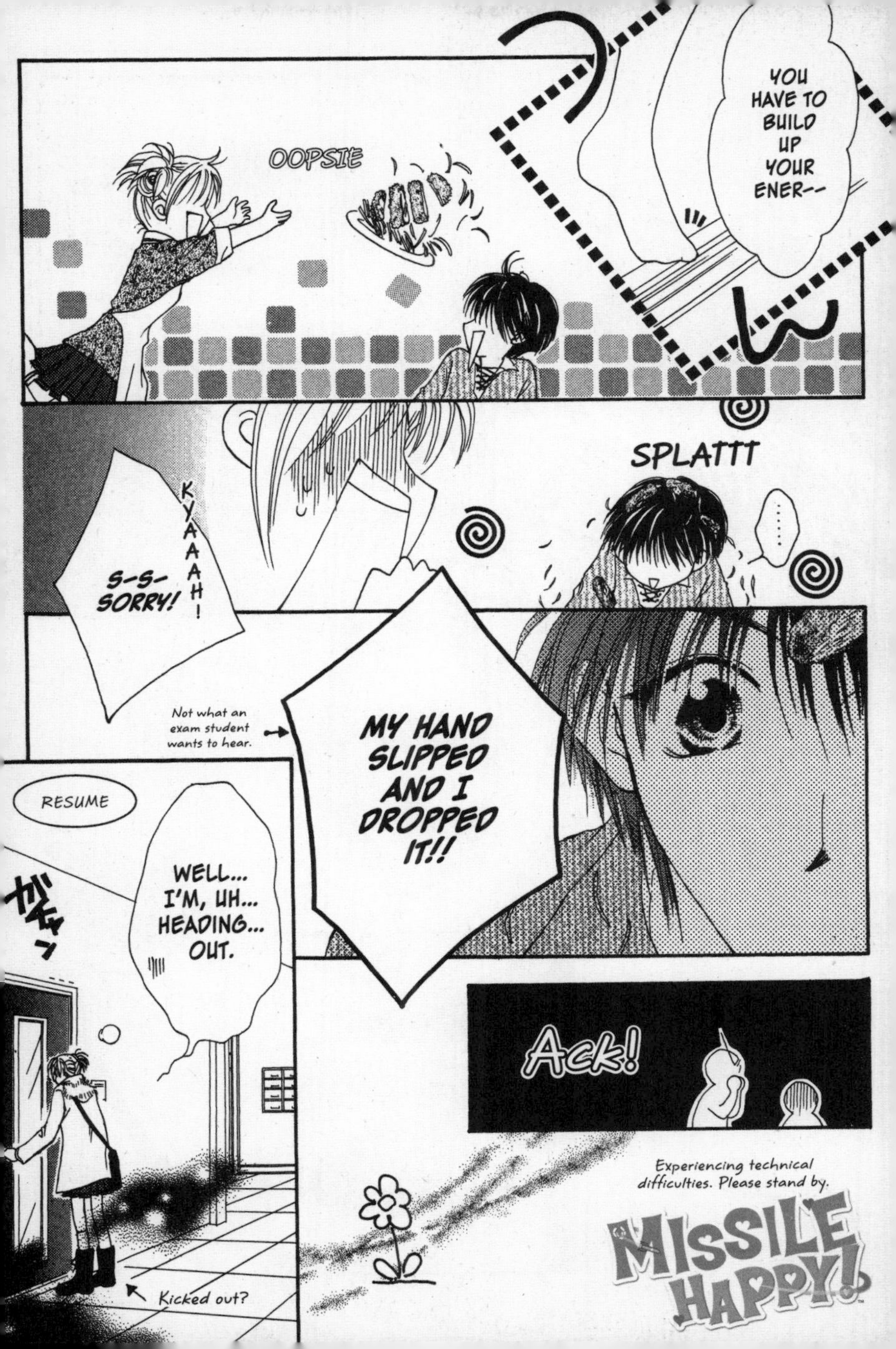

YOU HAVE TO BUILD UP YOUR ENER--
OOPSIE
SPLATTT
......
KYAAAAH!
S-S-SORRY!
MY HAND SLIPPED AND I DROPPED IT!!
Not what an exam student wants to hear.
Ack!
Experiencing technical difficulties. Please stand by.
MISSILE HAPPY!™
RESUME
WELL... I'M, UH... HEADING... OUT.
Kicked out?

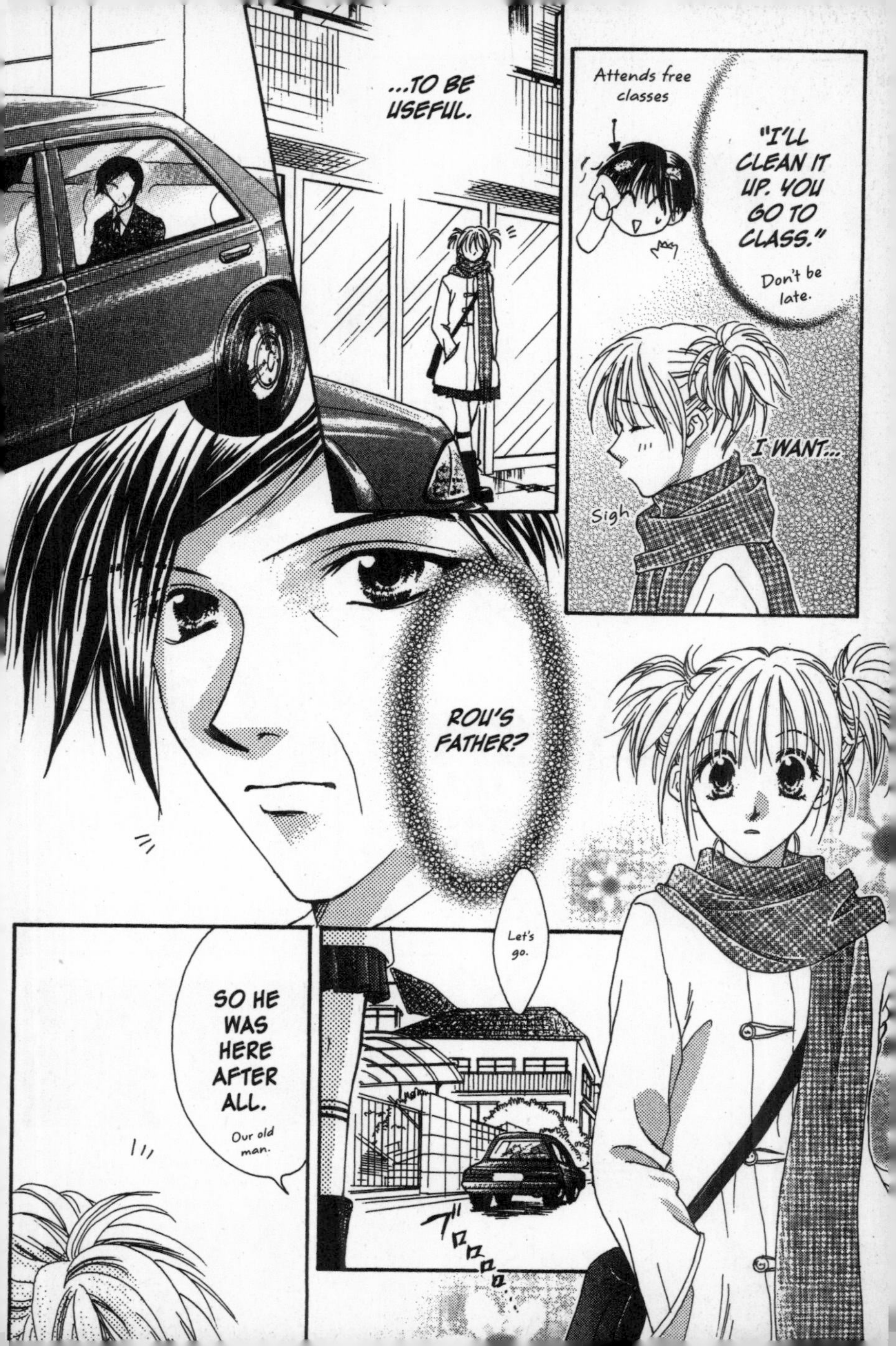
Attends free classes
"I'LL CLEAN IT UP. YOU GO TO CLASS."
Don't be late.
I WANT...
Sigh
...TO BE USEFUL.
ROU'S FATHER?
Let's go.
SO HE WAS HERE AFTER ALL.
Our old man.

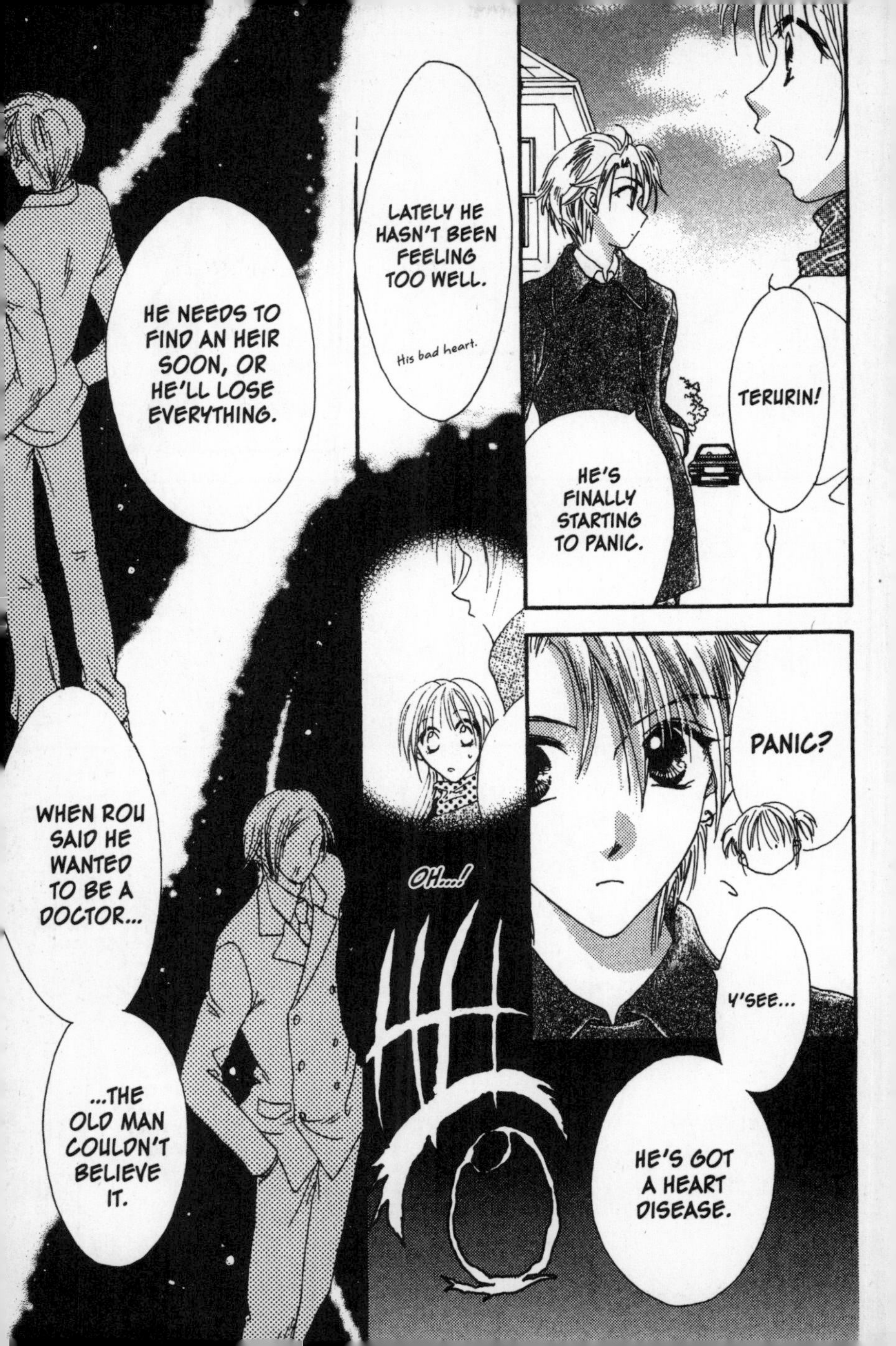
TERURIN!
HE'S FINALLY STARTING TO PANIC.
PANIC?
Y'SEE...
HE'S GOT A HEART DISEASE.
OH...!
LATELY HE HASN'T BEEN FEELING TOO WELL.
His bad heart.
HE NEEDS TO FIND AN HEIR SOON, OR HE'LL LOSE EVERYTHING.
WHEN ROU SAID HE WANTED TO BE A DOCTOR...
...THE OLD MAN COULDN'T BELIEVE IT.

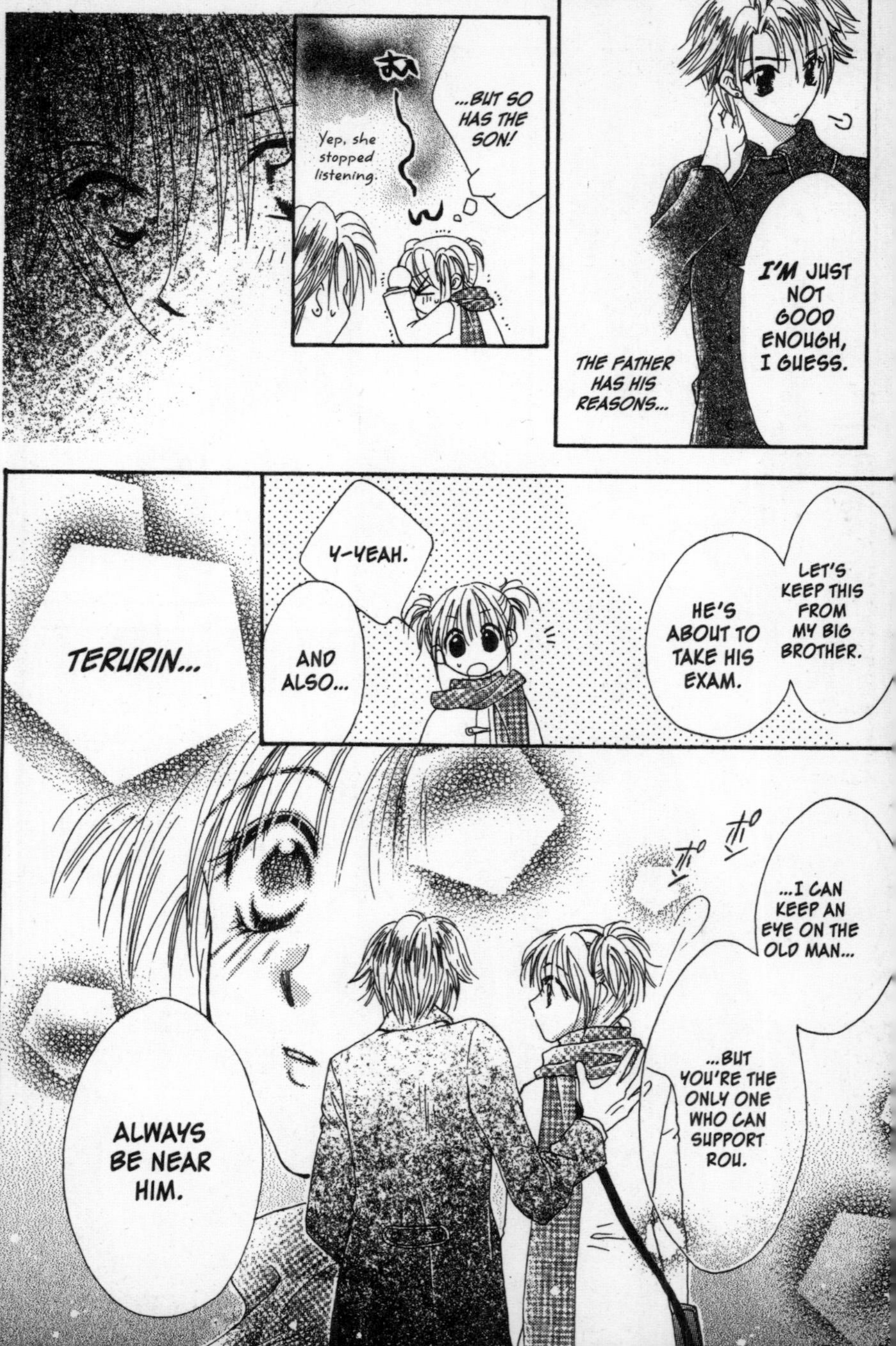
I'M JUST NOT GOOD ENOUGH, I GUESS.
THE FATHER HAS HIS REASONS...
...BUT SO HAS THE SON!
Yep, she stopped listening.
LET'S KEEP THIS FROM MY BIG BROTHER.
HE'S ABOUT TO TAKE HIS EXAM.
Y-YEAH.
AND ALSO...
...I CAN KEEP AN EYE ON THE OLD MAN...
...BUT YOU'RE THE ONLY ONE WHO CAN SUPPORT ROU.
TERURIN...
ALWAYS BE NEAR HIM.

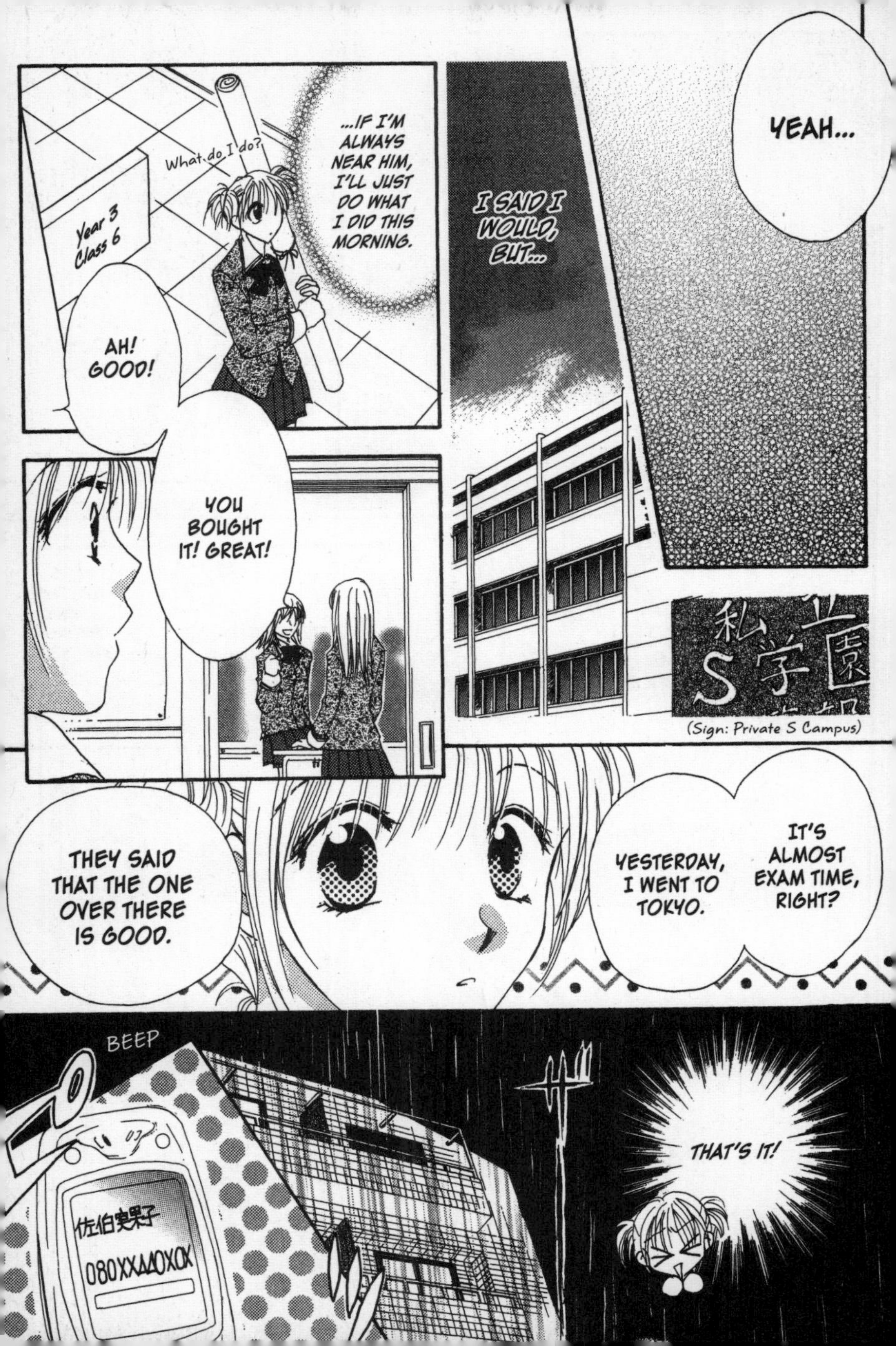
YEAH...
I SAID I WOULD, BUT...
(Sign: Private S Campus)
...IF I'M ALWAYS NEAR HIM, I'LL JUST DO WHAT I DID THIS MORNING.
What do I do?
Year 3 Class 6
AH! GOOD!
YOU BOUGHT IT! GREAT!
IT'S ALMOST EXAM TIME, RIGHT?
YESTERDAY, I WENT TO TOKYO.
THEY SAID THAT THE ONE OVER THERE IS GOOD.
THAT'S IT!
BEEP
佐伯実果子
080XXΔΔOXOX

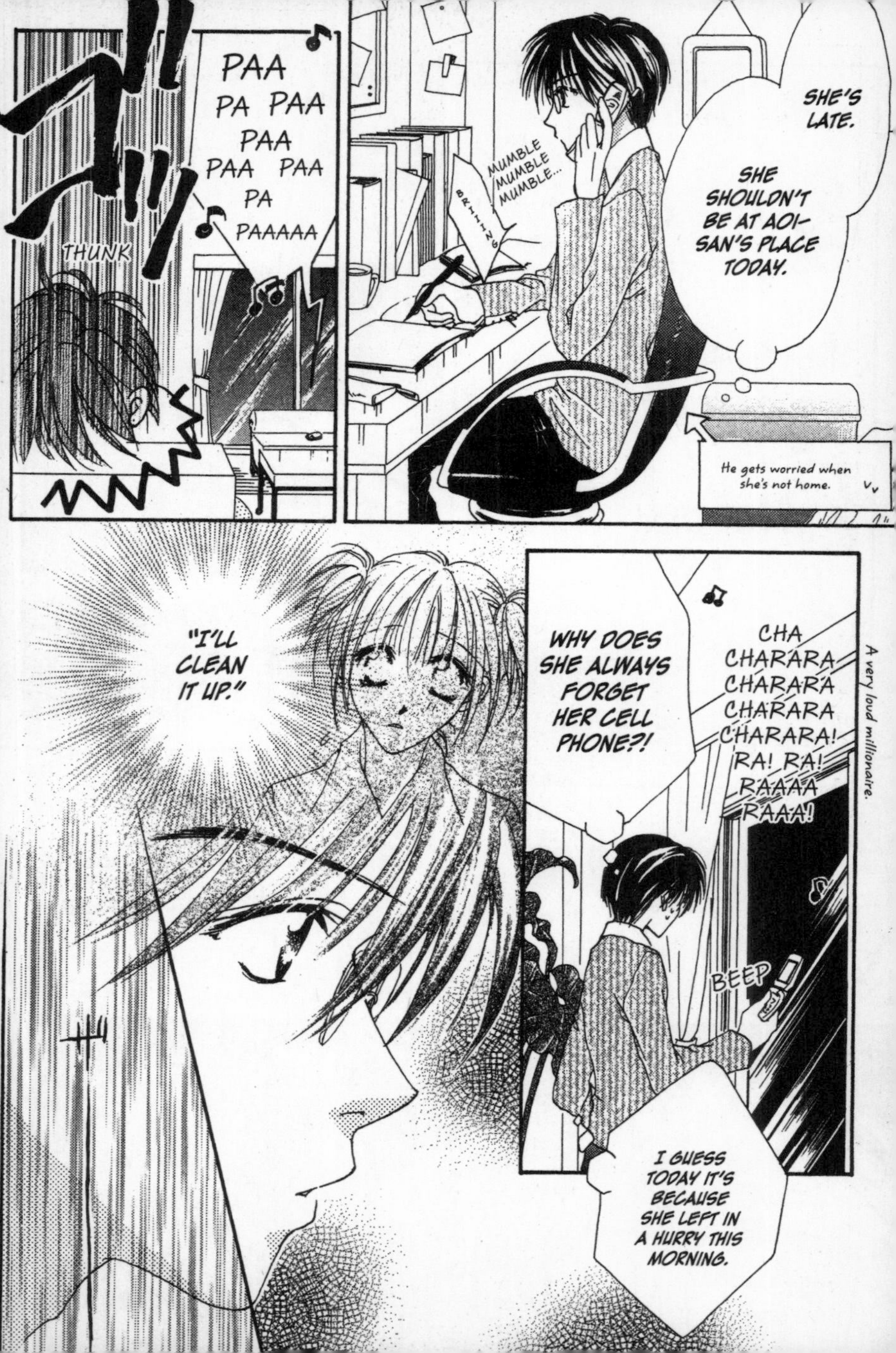
SHE'S LATE.
SHE SHOULDN'T BE AT AOI-SAN'S PLACE TODAY.
MUMBLE MUMBLE MUMBLE...
BRIIIING
He gets worried when she's not home.
PAA PA PAA PAA PAA PAA PA PAAAAA
THUNK
WHY DOES SHE ALWAYS FORGET HER CELL PHONE?!
CHA CHARARA CHARARA CHARARA CHARARA! RA! RA! RAAAA RAAA!
A very loud millionaire.
BEEP
I GUESS TODAY IT'S BECAUSE SHE LEFT IN A HURRY THIS MORNING.
"I'LL CLEAN IT UP."

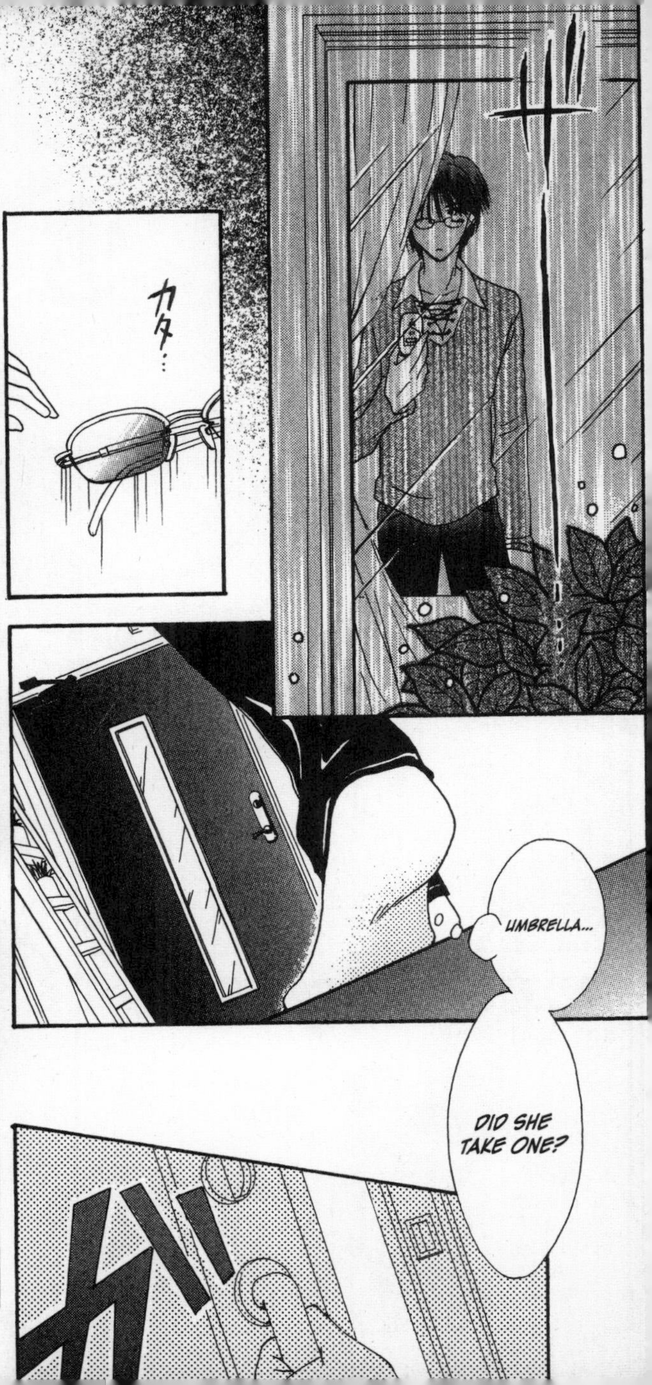
カタ…
UMBRELLA...
DID SHE TAKE ONE?

CHARA INTRO

I'm starting to run out of characters with birthdays!

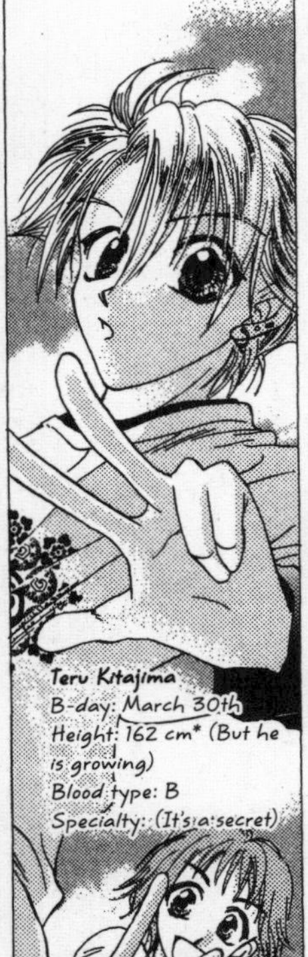

Teru Kitajima
B-day: March 30th
Height: 162 cm* (But he is growing)
Blood type: B
Specialty: (It's a secret)

Seki Arimizu
B-day: August 8th
Height: 161 cm
Blood type: AB
Specialty: Writing

* Approximately 5.3 ft.

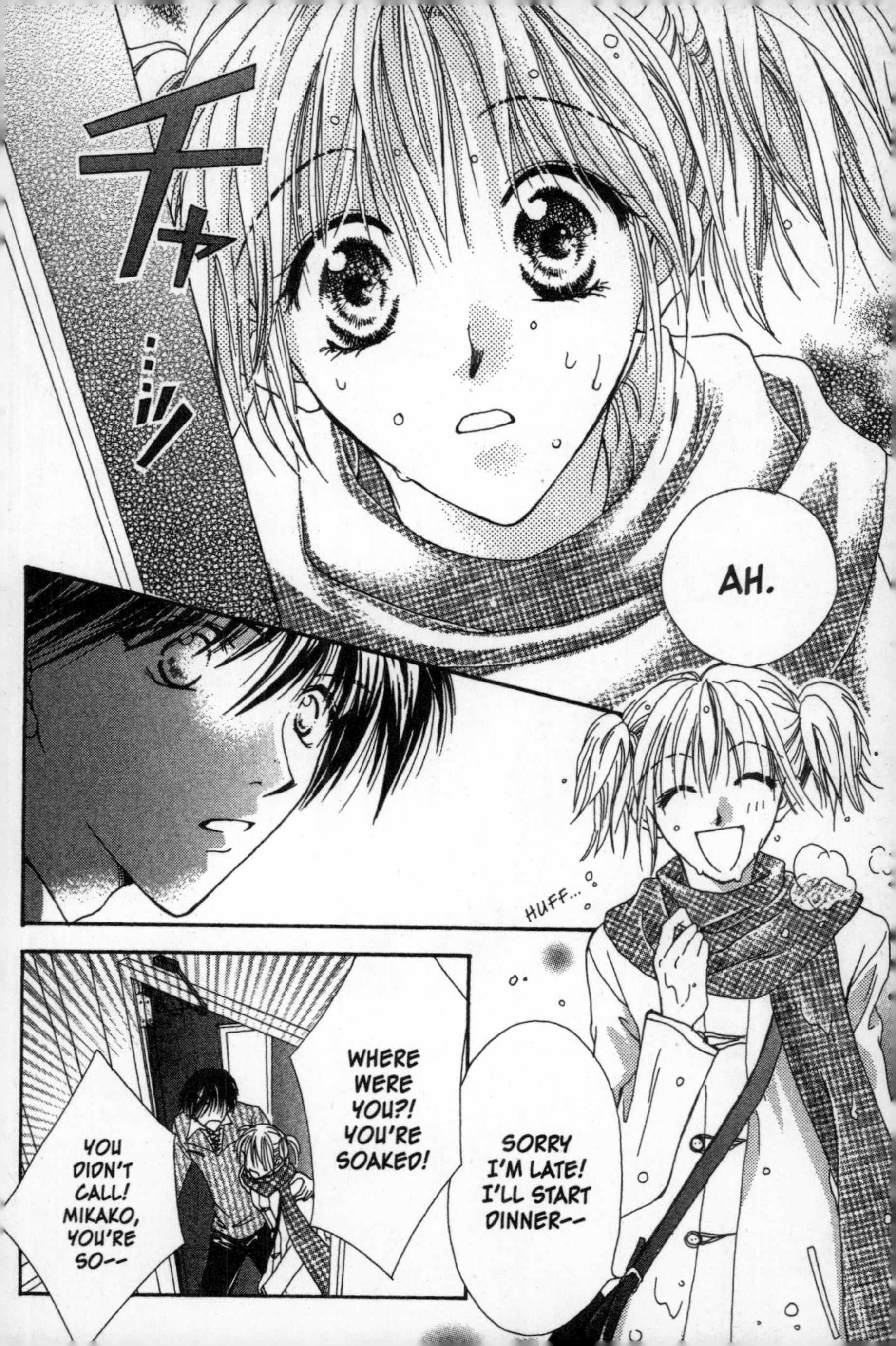
チャ…ッ
AH.
HUFF...
SORRY I'M LATE! I'LL START DINNER--
WHERE WERE YOU?! YOU'RE SOAKED!
YOU DIDN'T CALL! MIKAKO, YOU'RE SO--

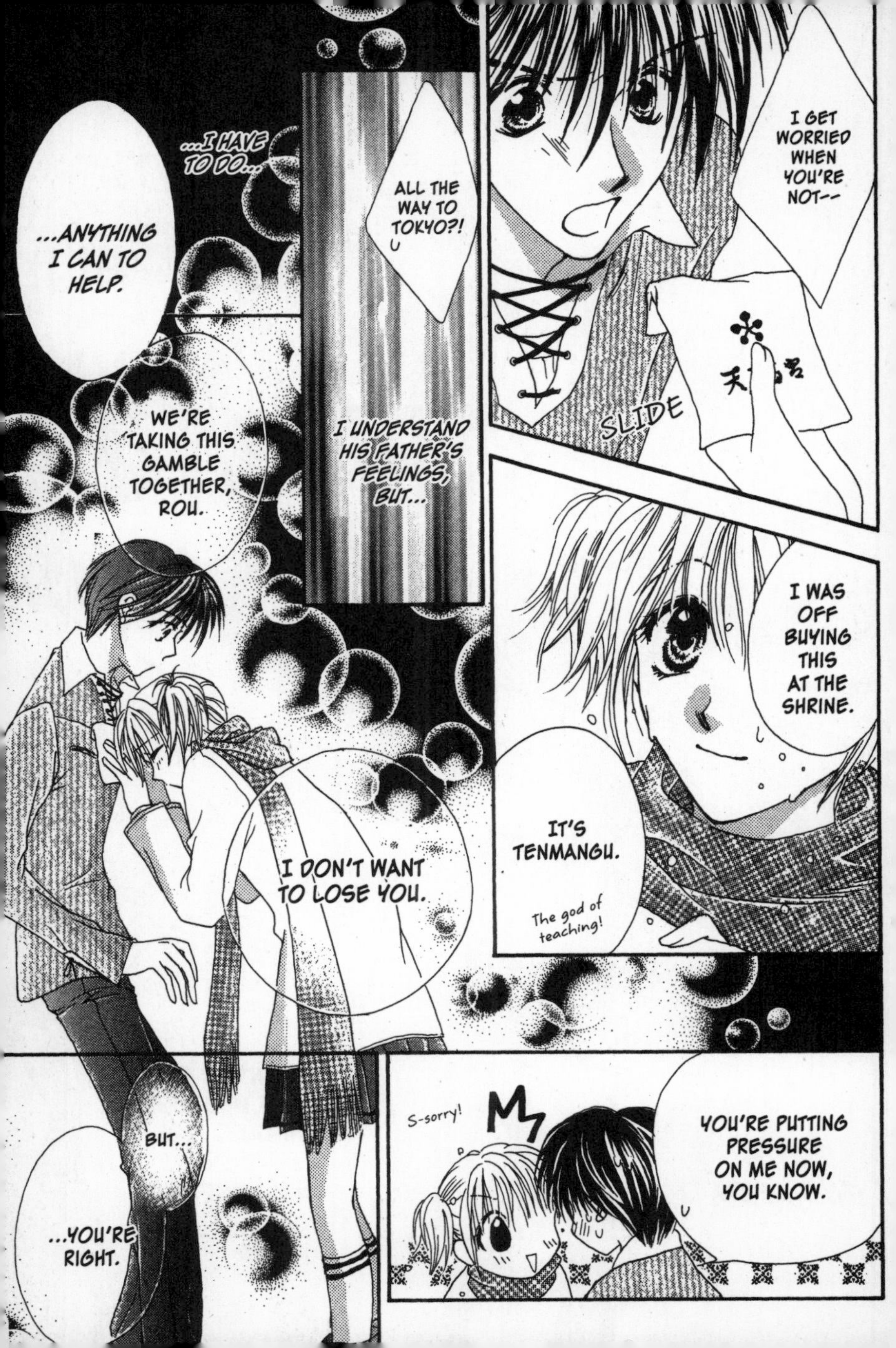

I GET WORRIED WHEN YOU'RE NOT--
SLIDE
I WAS OFF BUYING THIS AT THE SHRINE.
IT'S TENMANGU.
The god of teaching!
ALL THE WAY TO TOKYO?!
I UNDERSTAND HIS FATHER'S FEELINGS, BUT...
...I HAVE TO DO...
...ANYTHING I CAN TO HELP.
WE'RE TAKING THIS GAMBLE TOGETHER, ROU.
I DON'T WANT TO LOSE YOU.
YOU'RE PUTTING PRESSURE ON ME NOW, YOU KNOW.
M
S-sorry!
BUT...
...YOU'RE RIGHT.

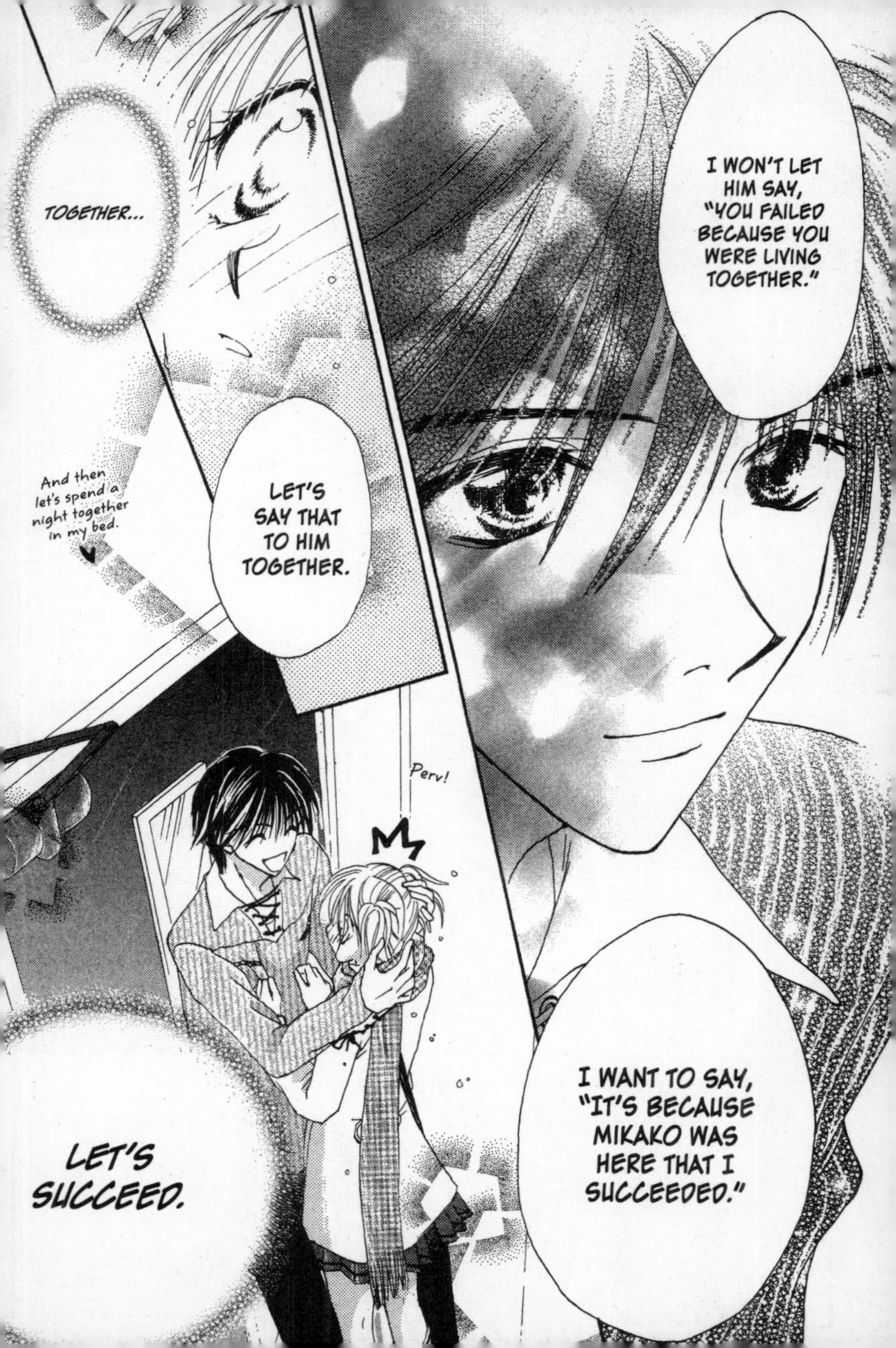
I WON'T LET HIM SAY, "YOU FAILED BECAUSE YOU WERE LIVING TOGETHER."
I WANT TO SAY, "IT'S BECAUSE MIKAKO WAS HERE THAT I SUCCEEDED."
TOGETHER...
LET'S SAY THAT TO HIM TOGETHER.
And then let's spend a night together in my bed.
Perv!
LET'S SUCCEED.

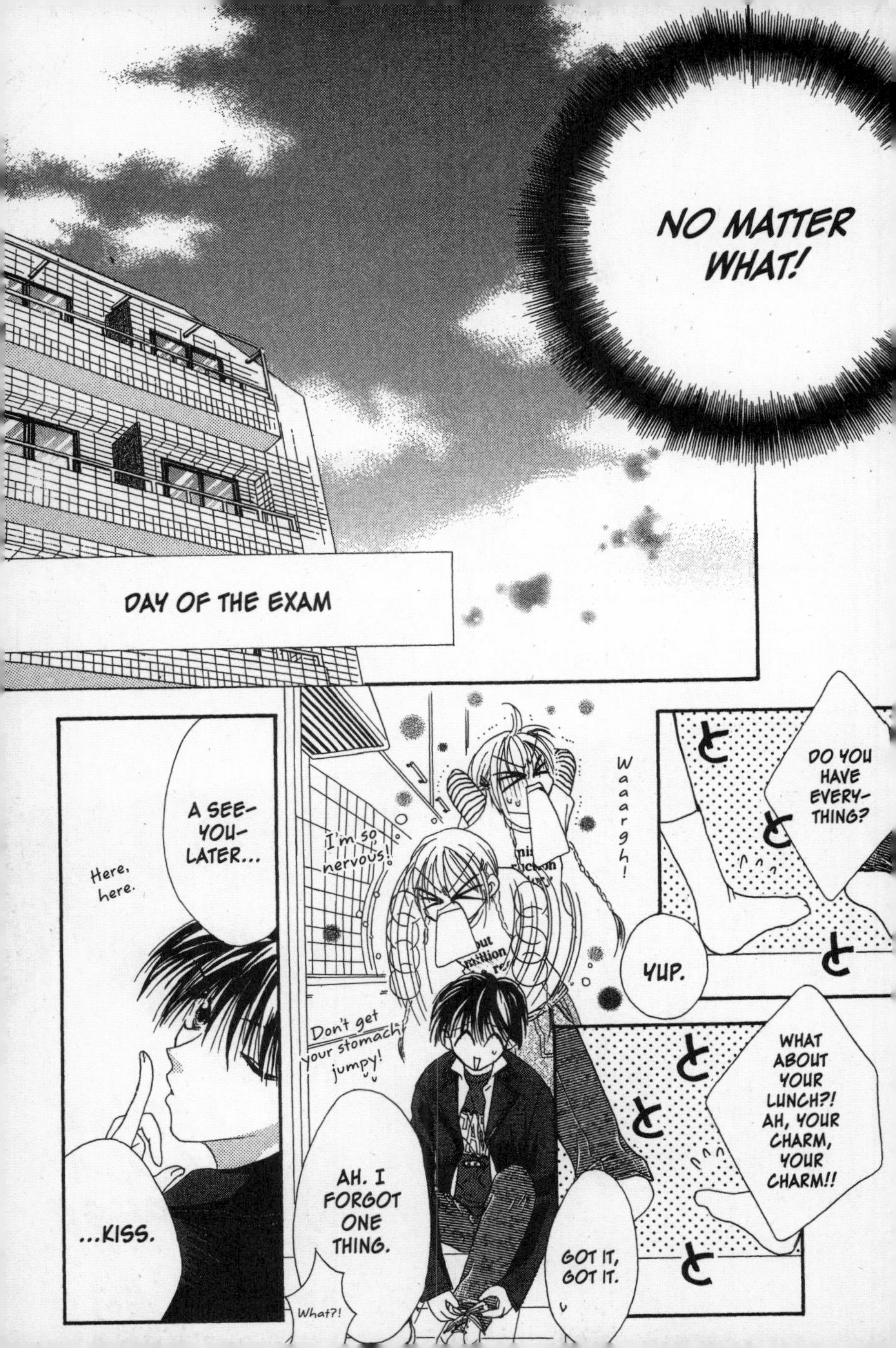
NO MATTER WHAT!
DAY OF THE EXAM
と
と
DO YOU HAVE EVERYTHING?
と
YUP.
と
と
WHAT ABOUT YOUR LUNCH?! AH, YOUR CHARM, YOUR CHARM!!
と
GOT IT, GOT IT.
Waaargh!
I'm so nervous!
Don't get your stomach jumpy!
AH. I FORGOT ONE THING.
What?!
A SEE-YOU-LATER...
Here, here.
...KISS.

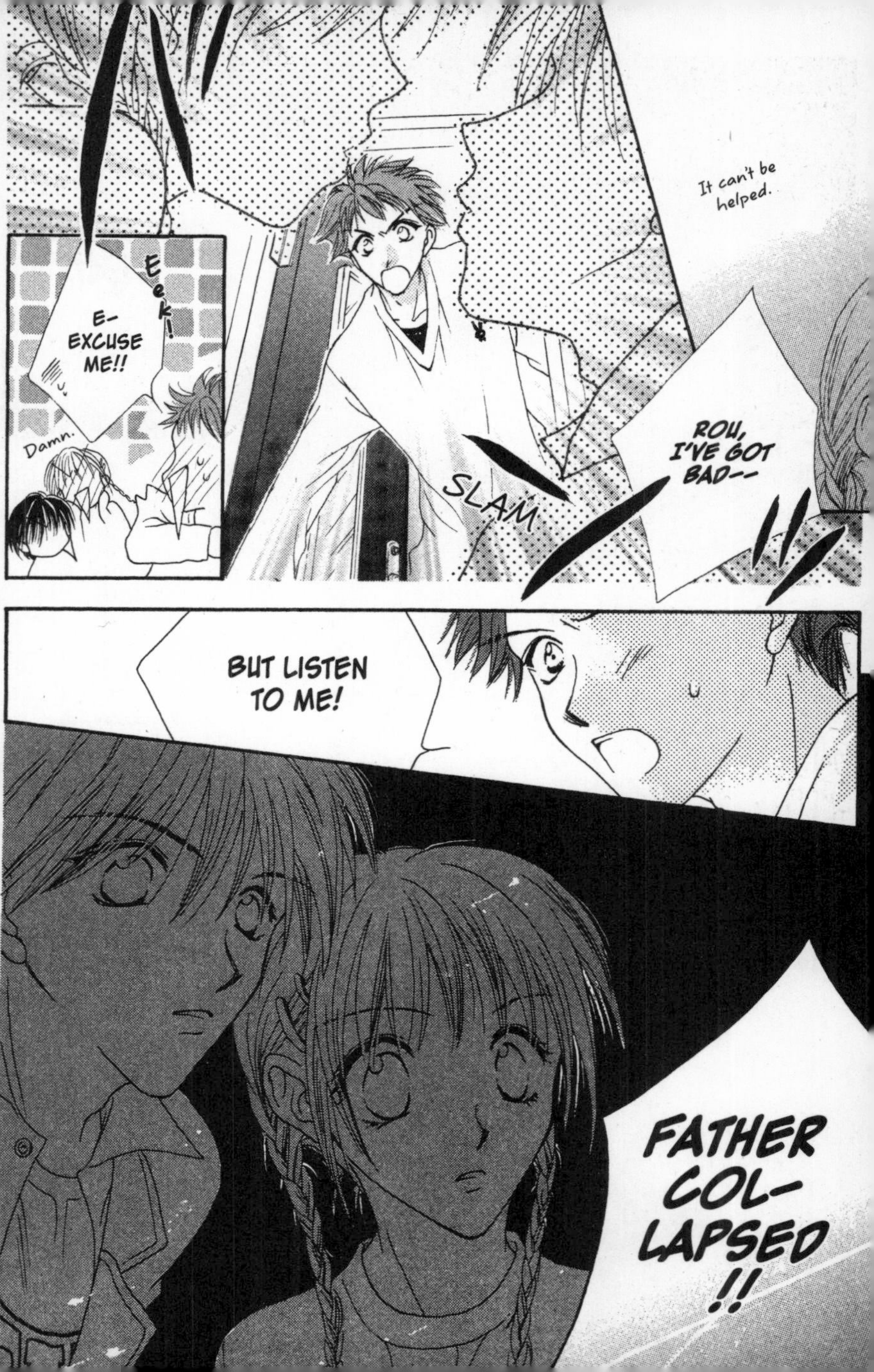
It can't be helped.
ROU, I'VE GOT BAD--
SLAM
Eek!
E-EXCUSE ME!!
Damn.
BUT LISTEN TO ME!
FATHER COL-LAPSED!!

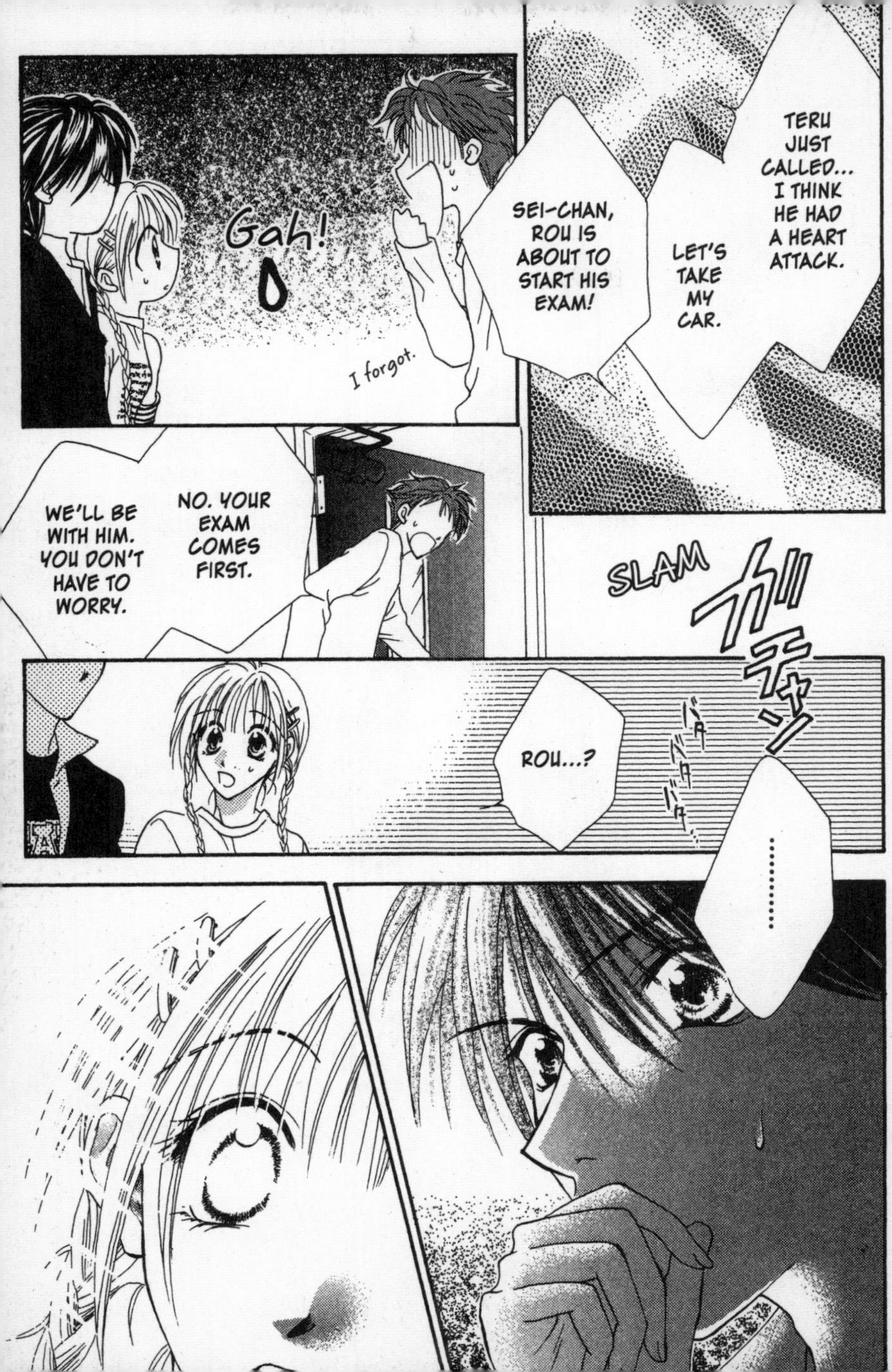
TERU JUST CALLED... I THINK HE HAD A HEART ATTACK.
LET'S TAKE MY CAR.
SEI-CHAN, ROU IS ABOUT TO START HIS EXAM!
Gah!
I forgot.
SLAM
カチャーン
NO. YOUR EXAM COMES FIRST.
WE'LL BE WITH HIM. YOU DON'T HAVE TO WORRY.
バタバタバタ…
ROU...?
......

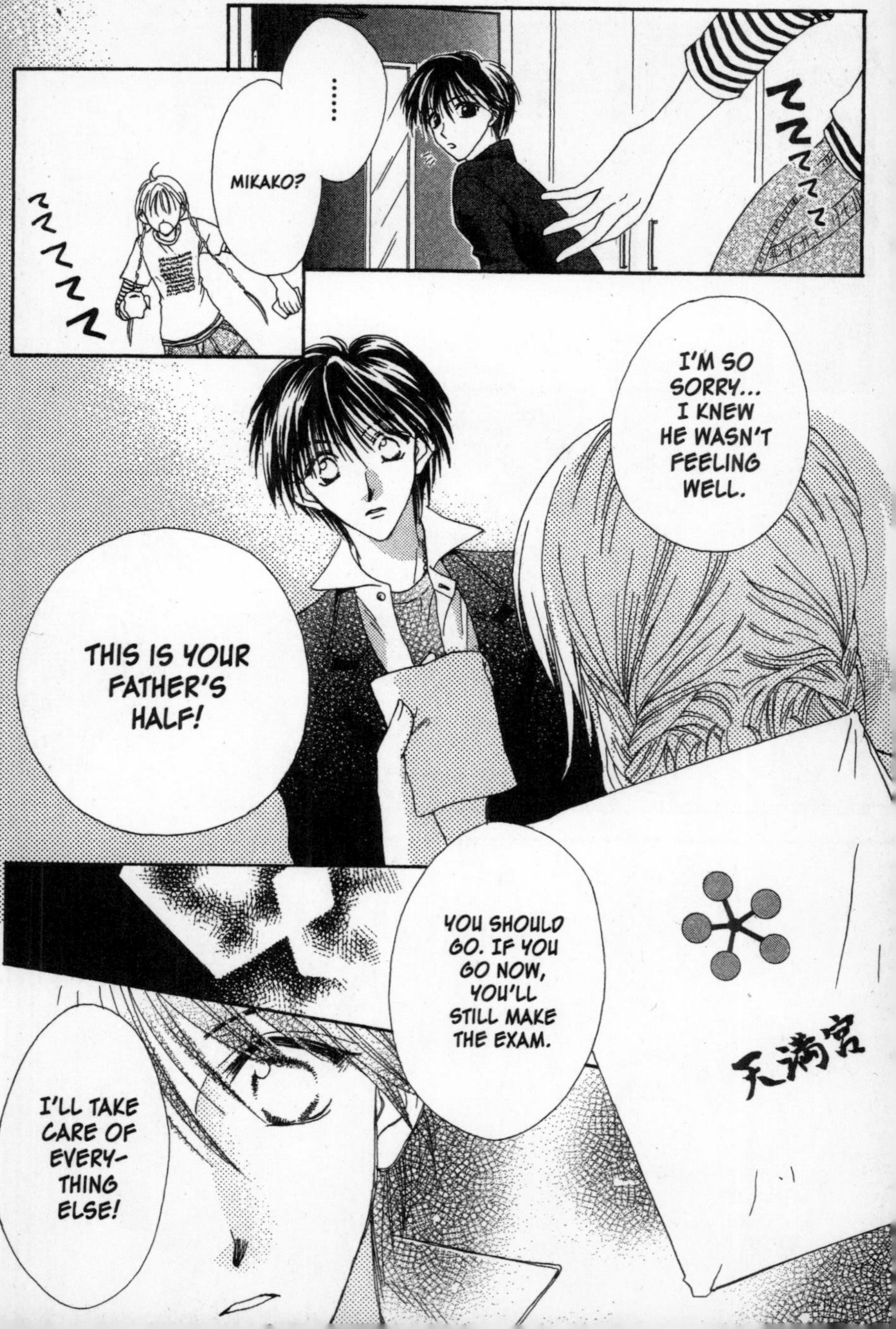

ZZZZZZZ
......
MIKAKO?
ZZZZZZ
I'M SO SORRY... I KNEW HE WASN'T FEELING WELL.
THIS IS YOUR FATHER'S HALF!
天満宮
YOU SHOULD GO. IF YOU GO NOW, YOU'LL STILL MAKE THE EXAM.
I'LL TAKE CARE OF EVERY-THING ELSE!

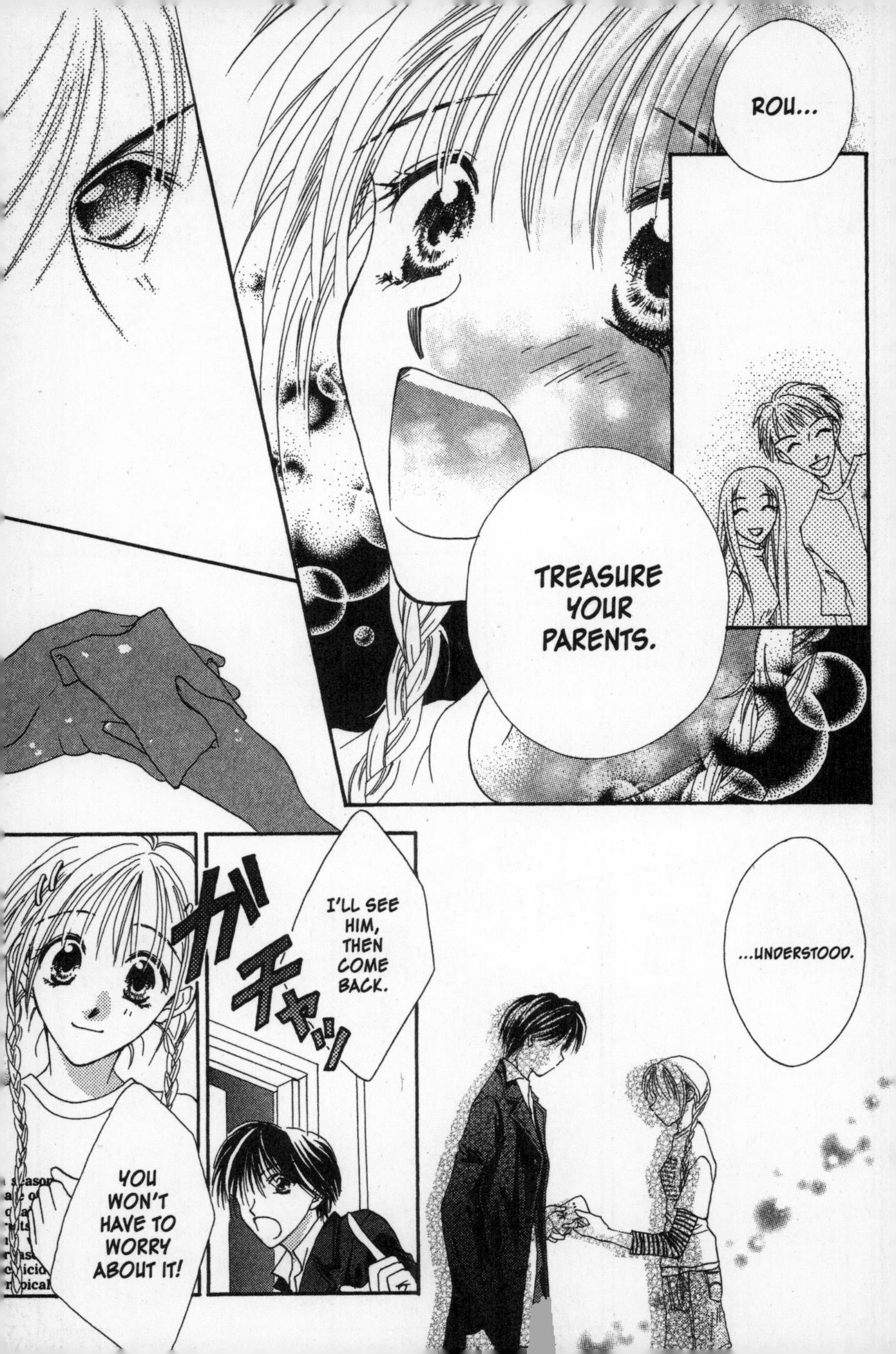
ROU...
TREASURE YOUR PARENTS.
...UNDERSTOOD.
I'LL SEE HIM, THEN COME BACK.
ガチャッ
YOU WON'T HAVE TO WORRY ABOUT IT!

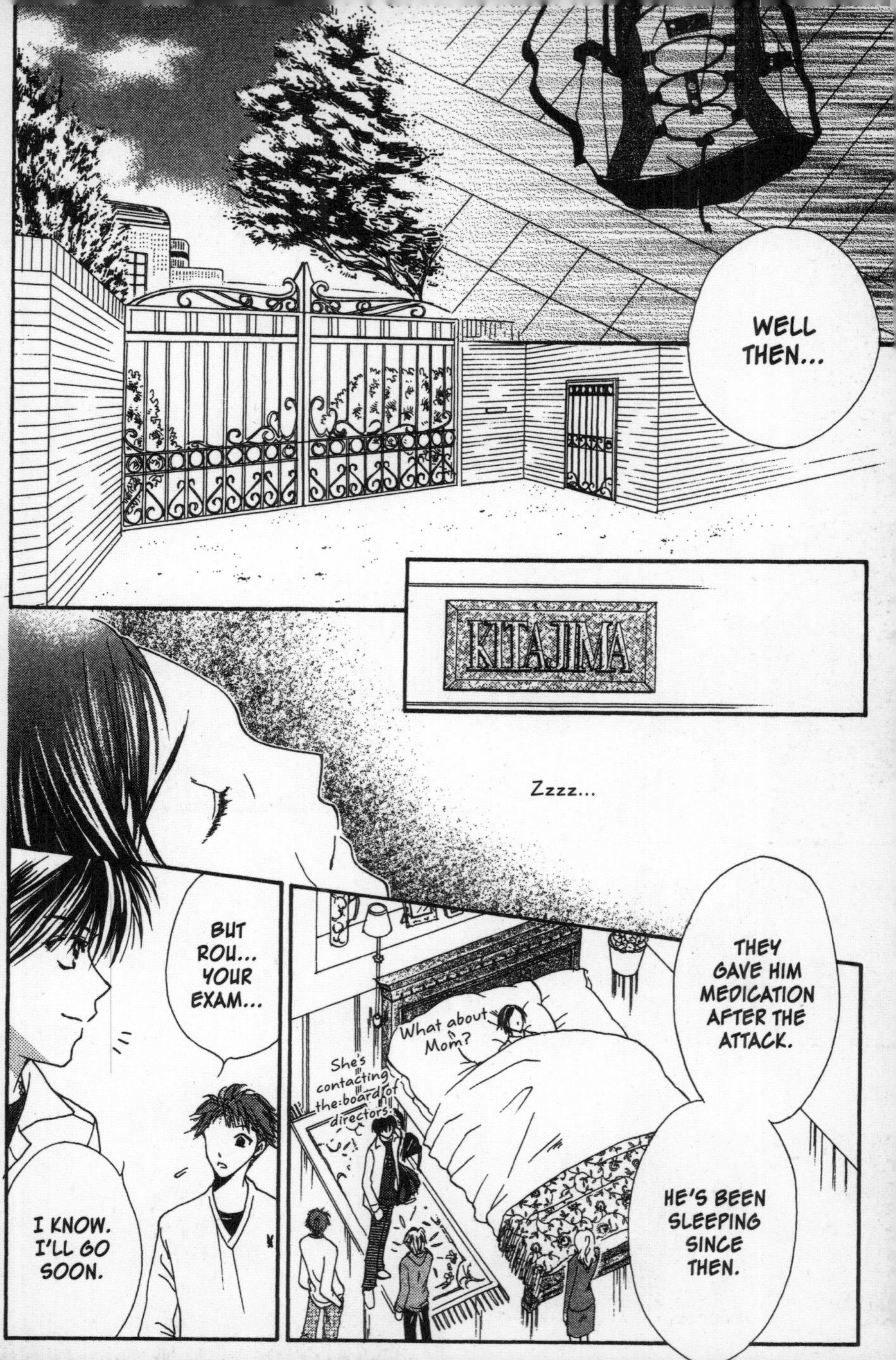
WELL THEN...
KITAJIMA
Zzzz...
THEY GAVE HIM MEDICATION AFTER THE ATTACK.
HE'S BEEN SLEEPING SINCE THEN.
What about Mom?
She's contacting the board of directors.
BUT ROU... YOUR EXAM...
I KNOW. I'LL GO SOON.

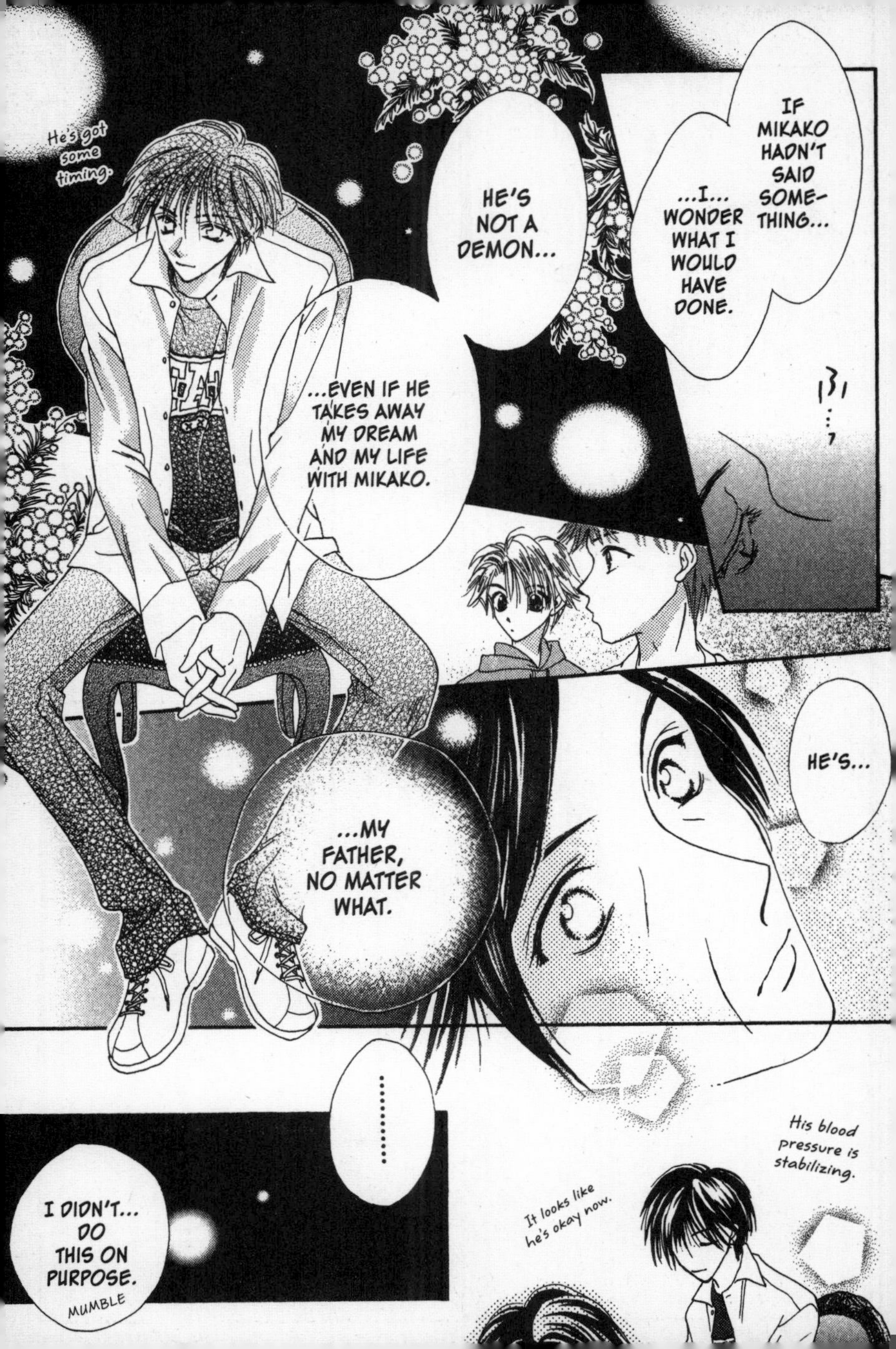
IF MIKAKO HADN'T SAID SOME-THING...
...I... WONDER WHAT I WOULD HAVE DONE.
HE'S NOT A DEMON...
He's got some timing.
...EVEN IF HE TAKES AWAY MY DREAM AND MY LIFE WITH MIKAKO.
HE'S...
...MY FATHER, NO MATTER WHAT.
His blood pressure is stabilizing.
It looks like he's okay now.
......
I DIDN'T... DO THIS ON PURPOSE.
MUMBLE

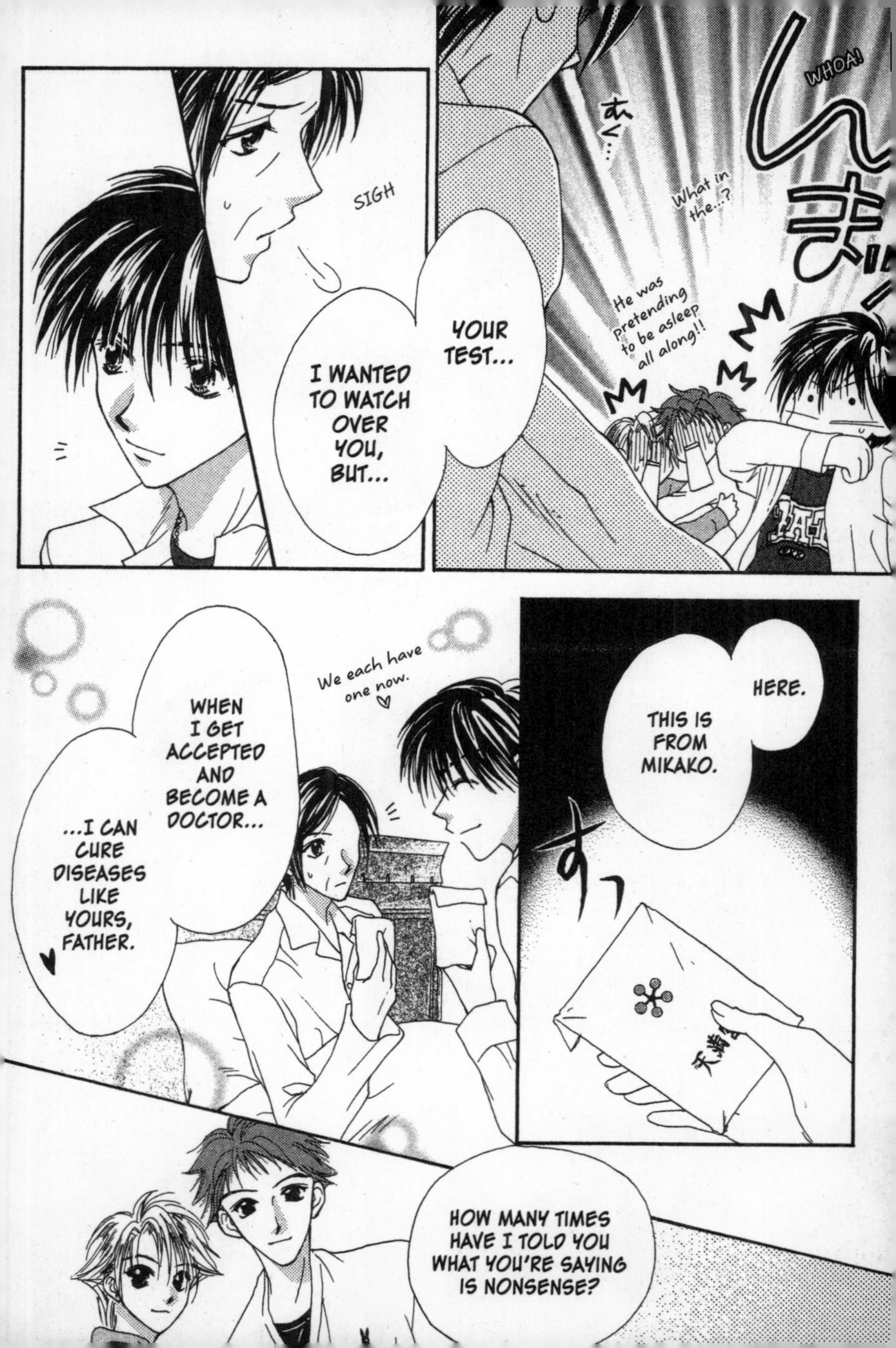

WHOA!
What in the...?
He was pretending to be asleep all along!!
むく…
YOUR TEST...
I WANTED TO WATCH OVER YOU, BUT...
SIGH
HERE.
THIS IS FROM MIKAKO.
すっ
天満宮
We each have one now.
WHEN I GET ACCEPTED AND BECOME A DOCTOR...
...I CAN CURE DISEASES LIKE YOURS, FATHER.
HOW MANY TIMES HAVE I TOLD YOU WHAT YOU'RE SAYING IS NONSENSE?

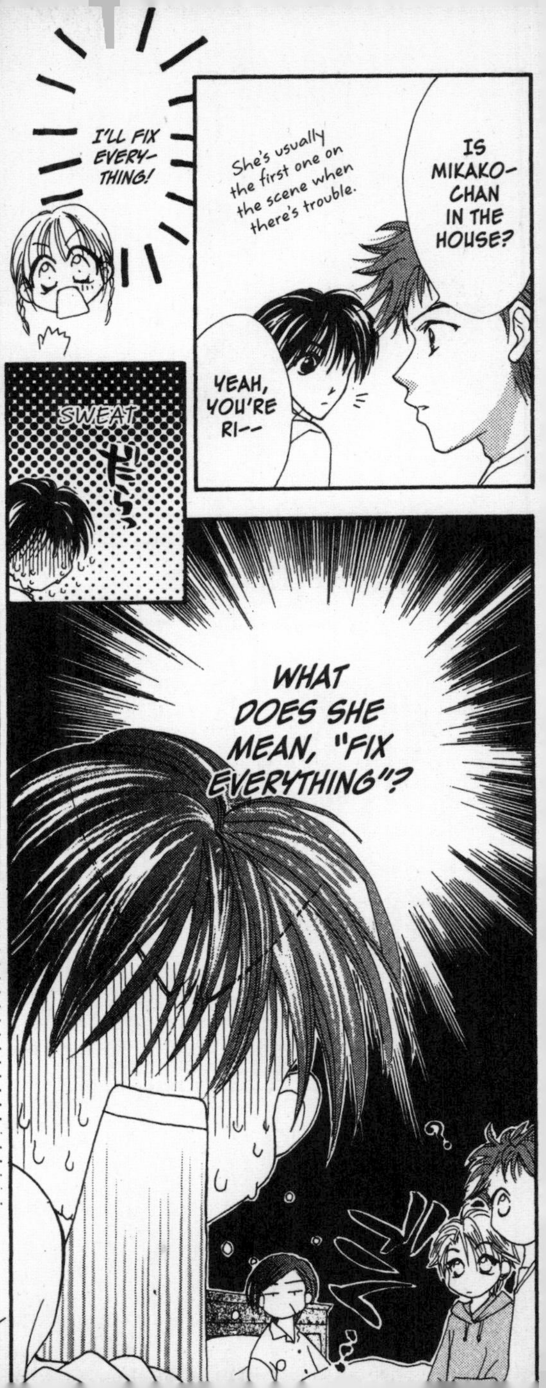
IS MIKAKO-CHAN IN THE HOUSE?
She's usually the first one on the scene when there's trouble.
YEAH, YOU'RE RI--
I'LL FIX EVERY-THING!
SWEAT
WHAT DOES SHE MEAN, "FIX EVERYTHING"?

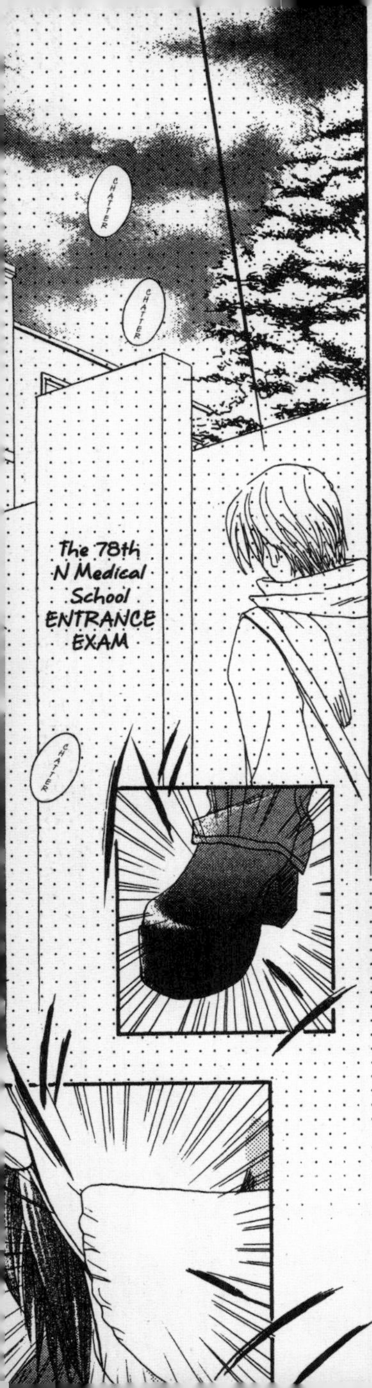
CHATTER
CHATTER
The 78th N Medical School ENTRANCE EXAM
CHATTER

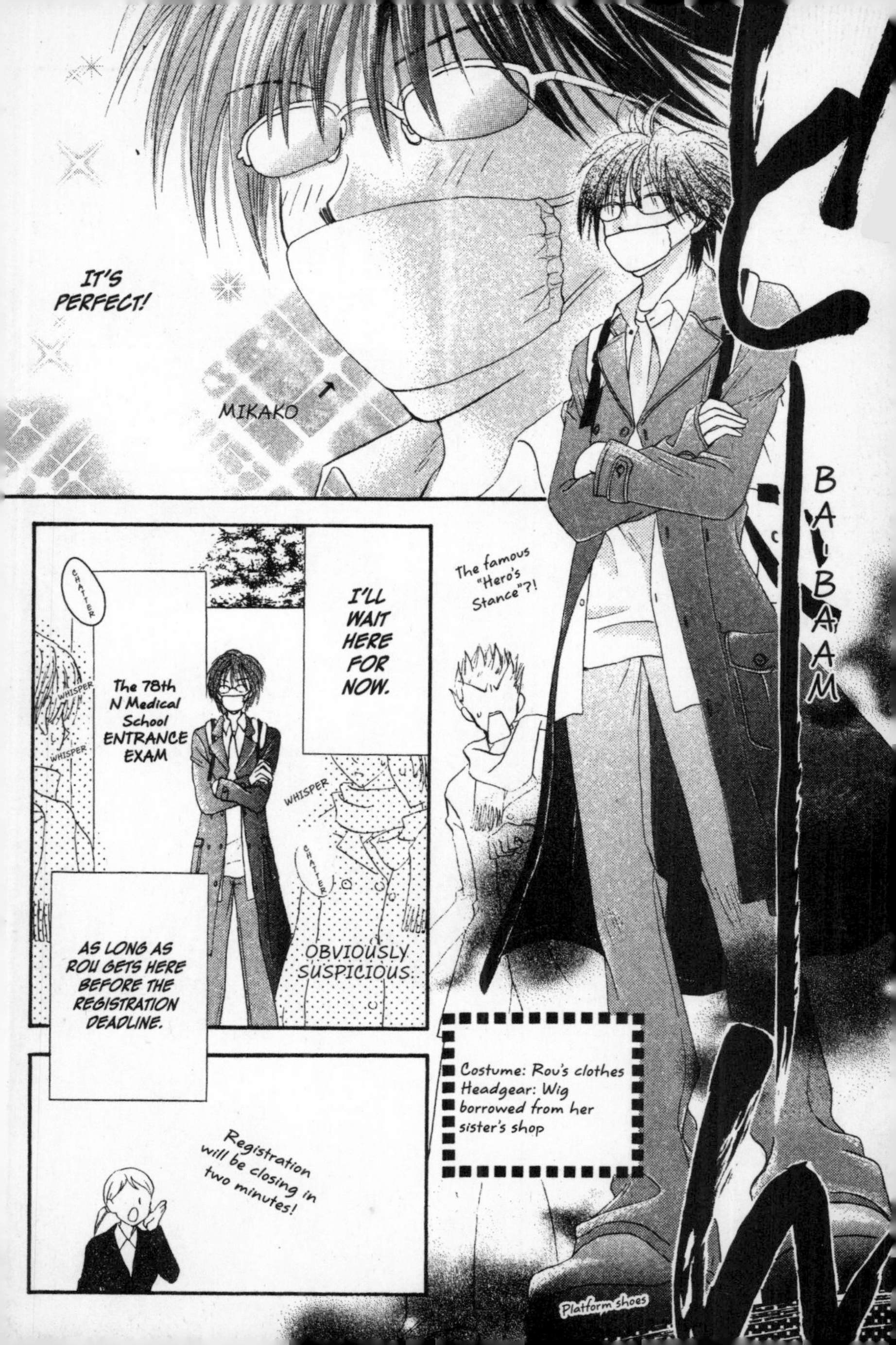
IT'S PERFECT!
MIKAKO
BABAAM
The famous "Hero's Stance"?!
Costume: Rou's clothes
Headgear: Wig borrowed from her sister's shop
Platform shoes
I'LL WAIT HERE FOR NOW.
The 78th N Medical School ENTRANCE EXAM
CHATTER
WHISPER
WHISPER
WHISPER
CHATTER
OBVIOUSLY SUSPICIOUS
AS LONG AS ROU GETS HERE BEFORE THE REGISTRATION DEADLINE.
Registration will be closing in two minutes!

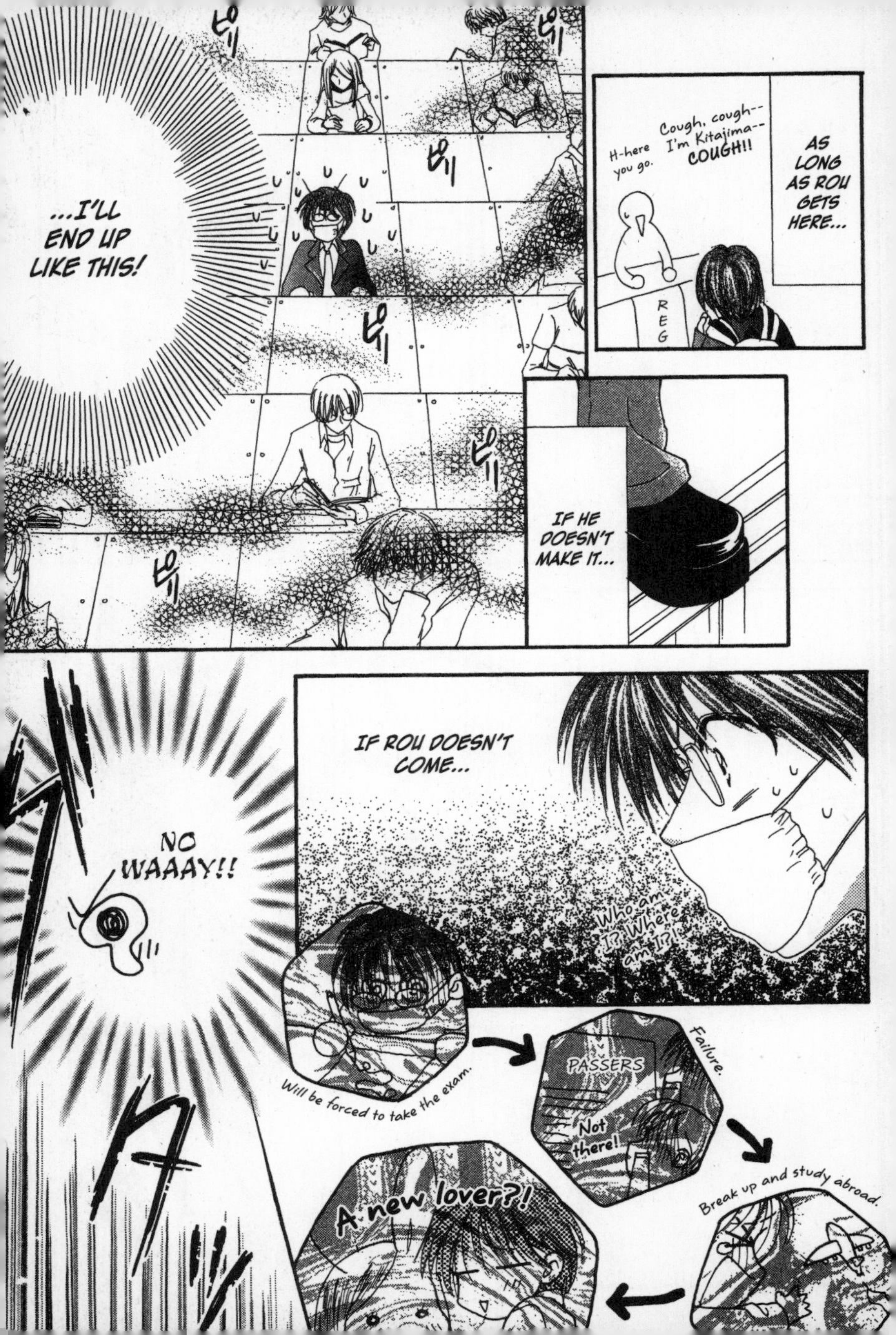
AS LONG AS ROU GETS HERE...
Cough, cough-- I'm Kitajima-- COUGH!!
H-here you go.
REG
IF HE DOESN'T MAKE IT...
...I'LL END UP LIKE THIS!
IF ROU DOESN'T COME...
Who am I?! Where am I?!
Will be forced to take the exam.
PASSERS
Not there!
Failure.
Break up and study abroad.
A new lover?!
NO WAAAY!!

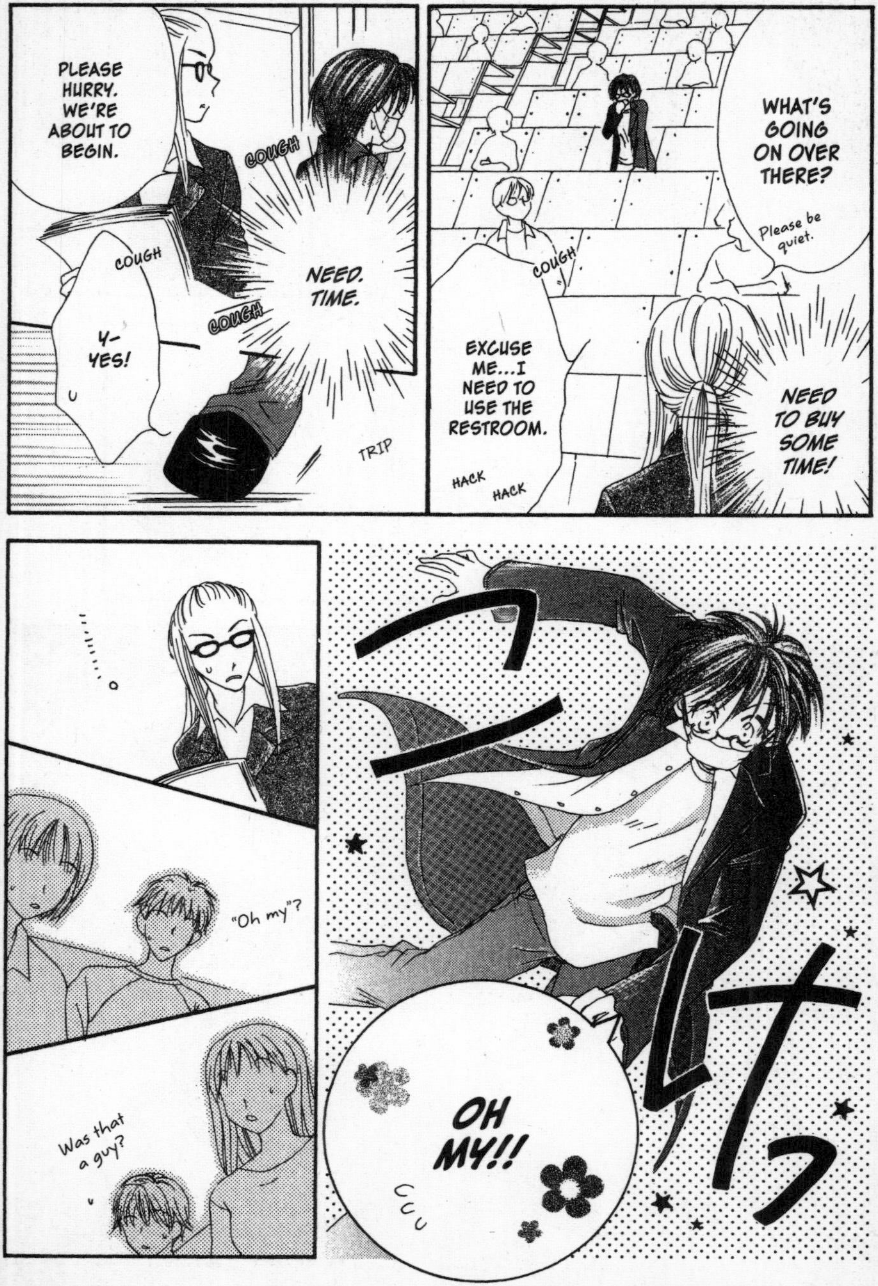
WHAT'S GOING ON OVER THERE?
Please be quiet.
COUGH
EXCUSE ME...I NEED TO USE THE RESTROOM.
HACK HACK
NEED TO BUY SOME TIME!
PLEASE HURRY. WE'RE ABOUT TO BEGIN.
COUGH
NEED. TIME.
COUGH
COUGH
Y-YES!
TRIP
OH MY!!
"Oh my"?
Was that a guy?

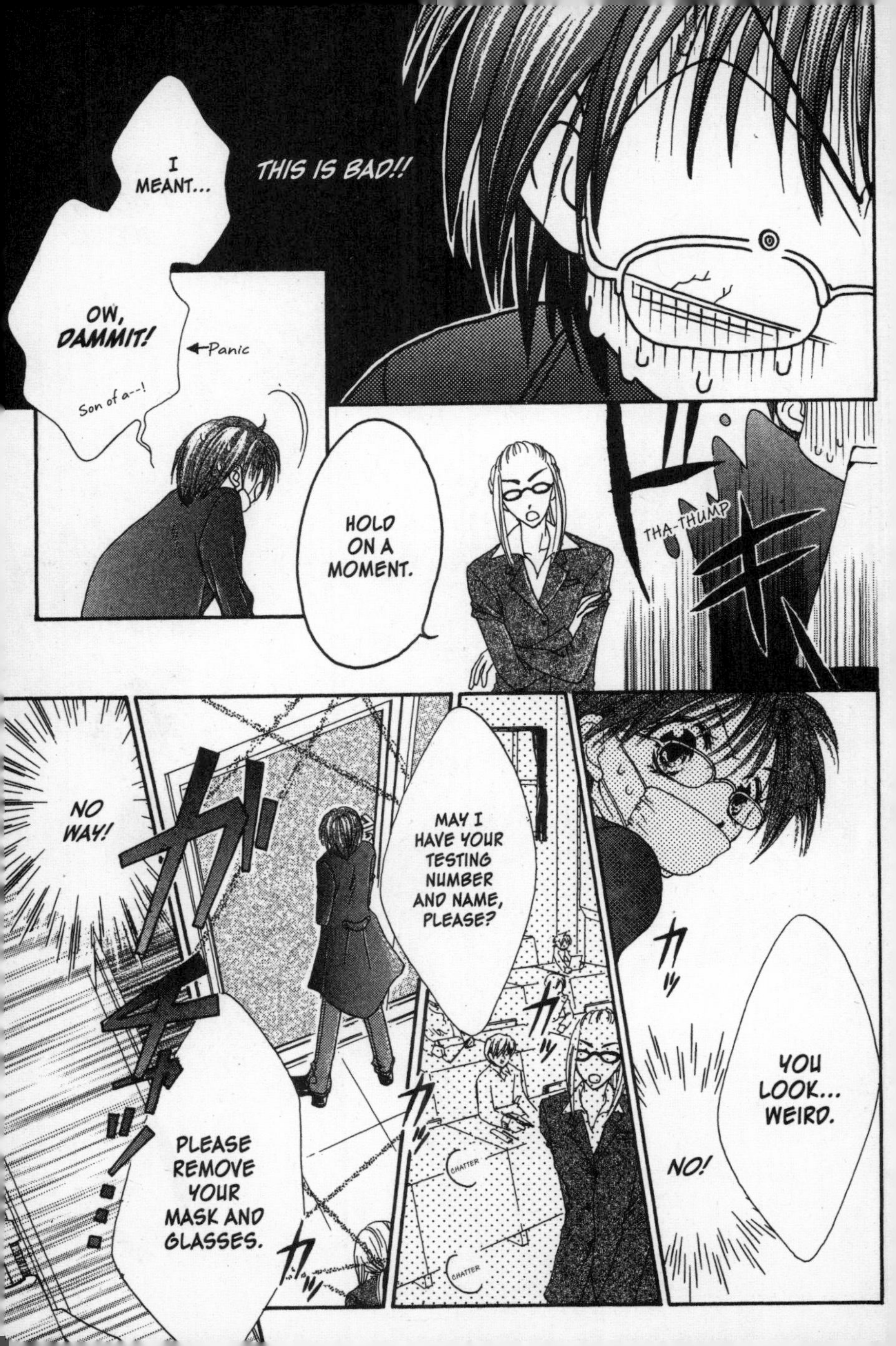
THIS IS BAD!!
THA-THUMP
HOLD ON A MOMENT.
I MEANT...
OW, DAMMIT!
←Panic
Son of a--!
YOU LOOK... WEIRD.
NO!
MAY I HAVE YOUR TESTING NUMBER AND NAME, PLEASE?
CHATTER
CHATTER
NO WAY!
PLEASE REMOVE YOUR MASK AND GLASSES.

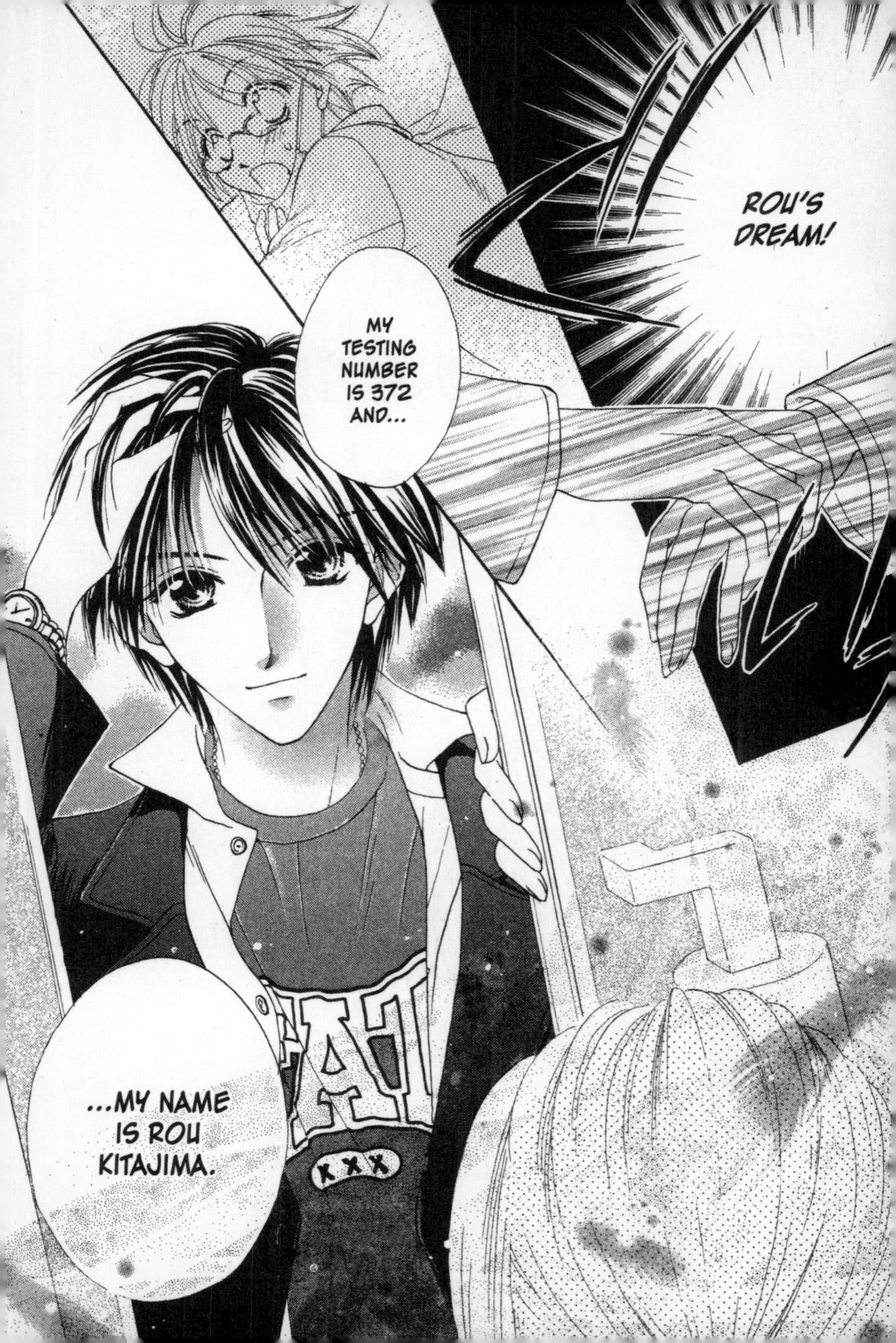
ROU'S DREAM!
MY TESTING NUMBER IS 372 AND...
...MY NAME IS ROU KITAJIMA.

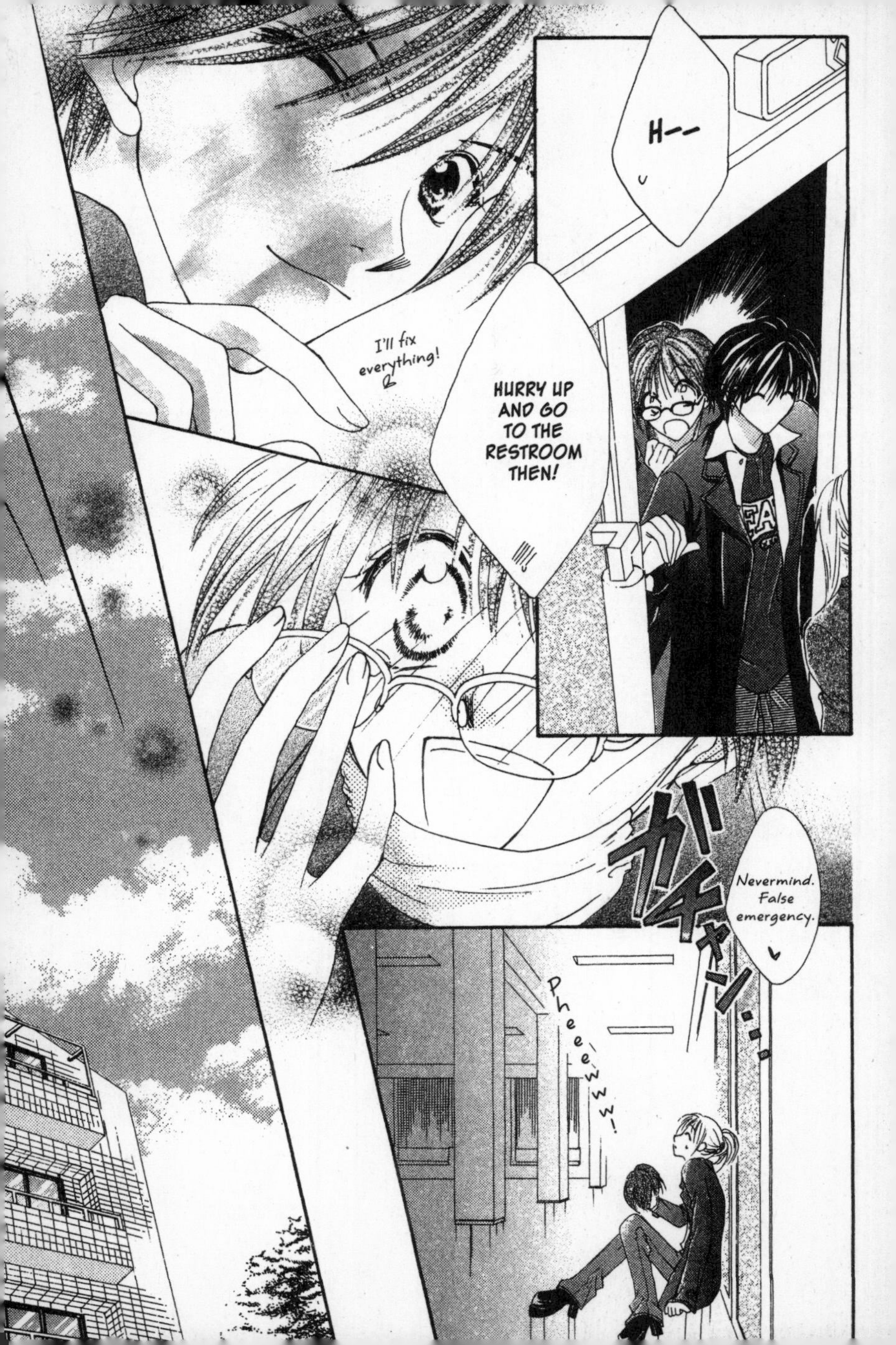
H--
HURRY UP AND GO TO THE RESTROOM THEN!
I'll fix everything!
ガチャン…
Nevermind. False emergency.
Pheeewww!

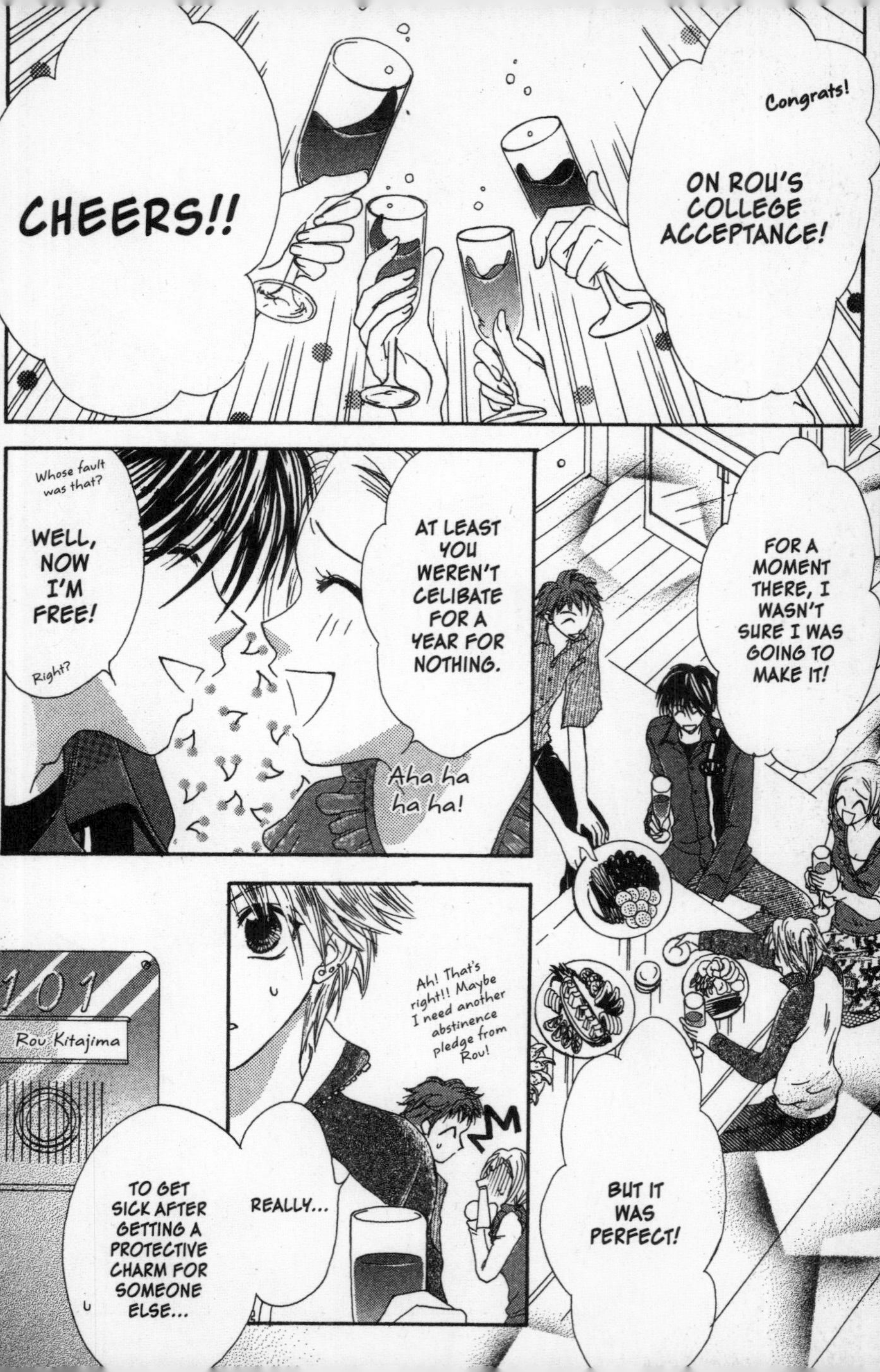
Congrats!
ON ROU'S COLLEGE ACCEPTANCE!
CHEERS!!
FOR A MOMENT THERE, I WASN'T SURE I WAS GOING TO MAKE IT!
BUT IT WAS PERFECT!
AT LEAST YOU WEREN'T CELIBATE FOR A YEAR FOR NOTHING.
Whose fault was that?
WELL, NOW I'M FREE!
Right?
Aha ha ha ha!
Ah! That's right!! Maybe I need another abstinence pledge from Rou!
REALLY...
101
Rou Kitajima
TO GET SICK AFTER GETTING A PROTECTIVE CHARM FOR SOMEONE ELSE...

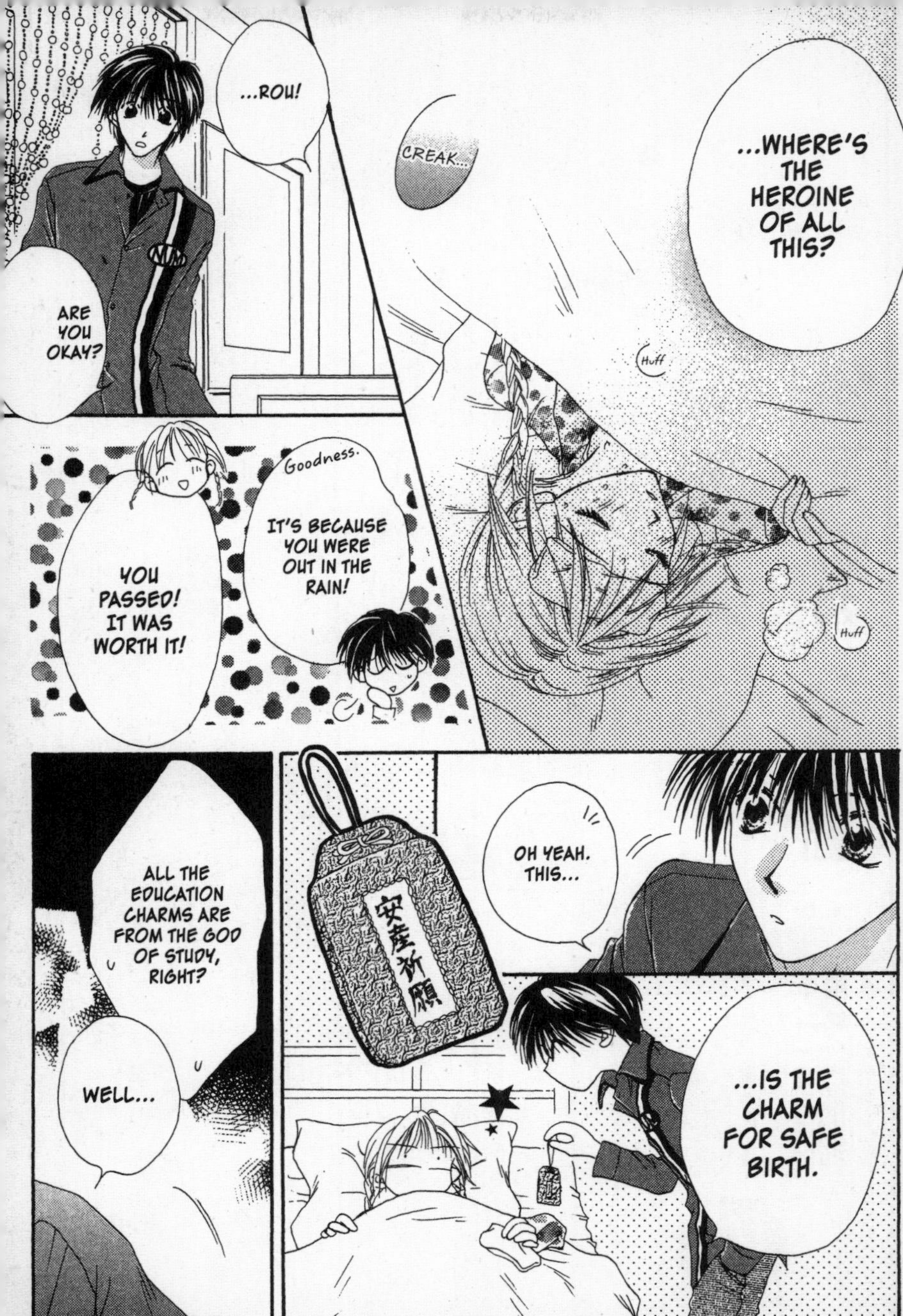

...WHERE'S THE HEROINE OF ALL THIS?
CREAK...
Huff
Huff
...ROU!
ARE YOU OKAY?
Goodness.
IT'S BECAUSE YOU WERE OUT IN THE RAIN!
YOU PASSED! IT WAS WORTH IT!
OH YEAH. THIS...
...IS THE CHARM FOR SAFE BIRTH.
安産祈願
ALL THE EDUCATION CHARMS ARE FROM THE GOD OF STUDY, RIGHT?
WELL...

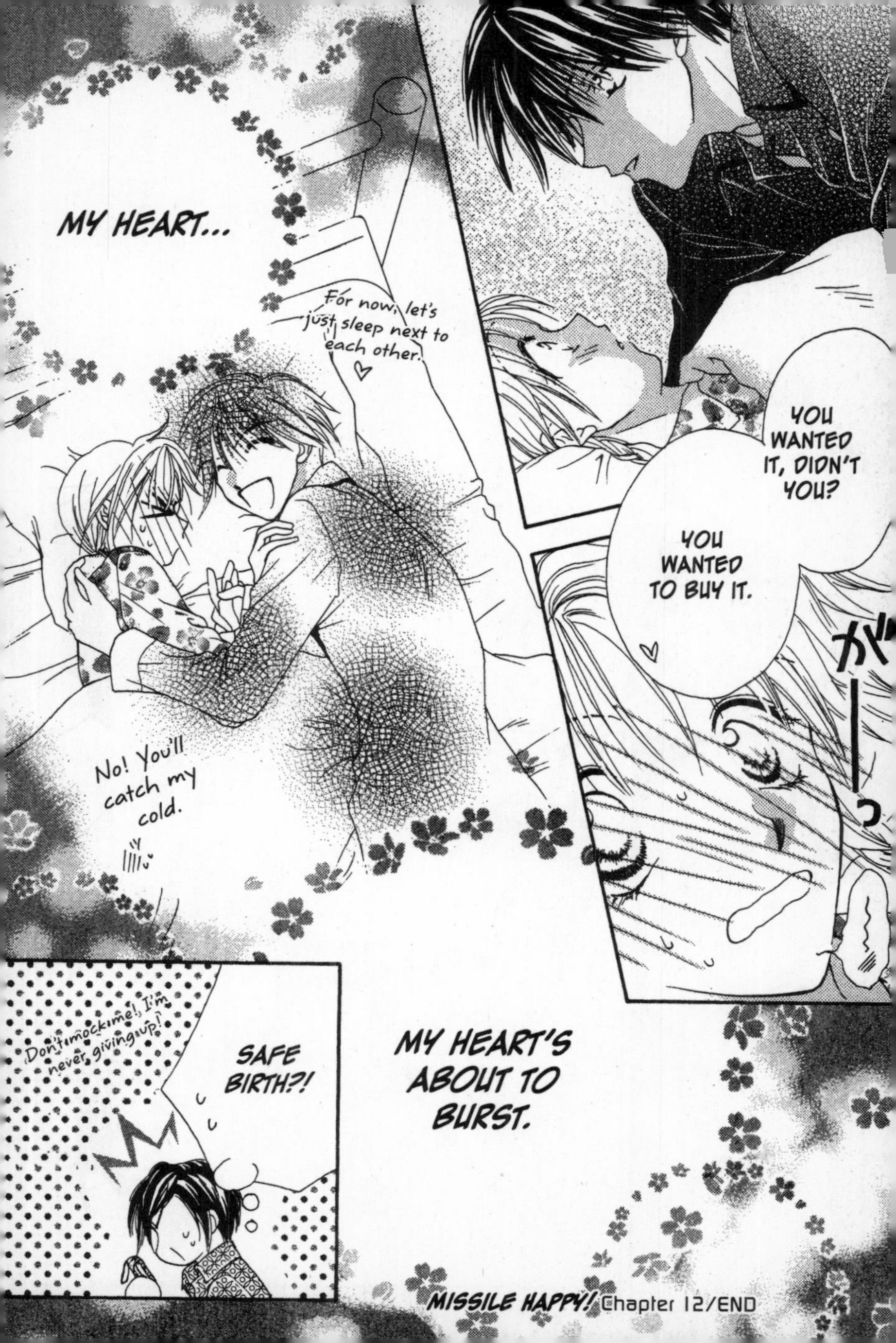
YOU WANTED IT, DIDN'T YOU?
YOU WANTED TO BUY IT.
がーっ
MY HEART...
For now, let's just sleep next to each other.
No! You'll catch my cold.
MY HEART'S ABOUT TO BURST.
SAFE BIRTH?!
Don't mock me! I'm never giving up!
MISSILE HAPPY! Chapter 12/END

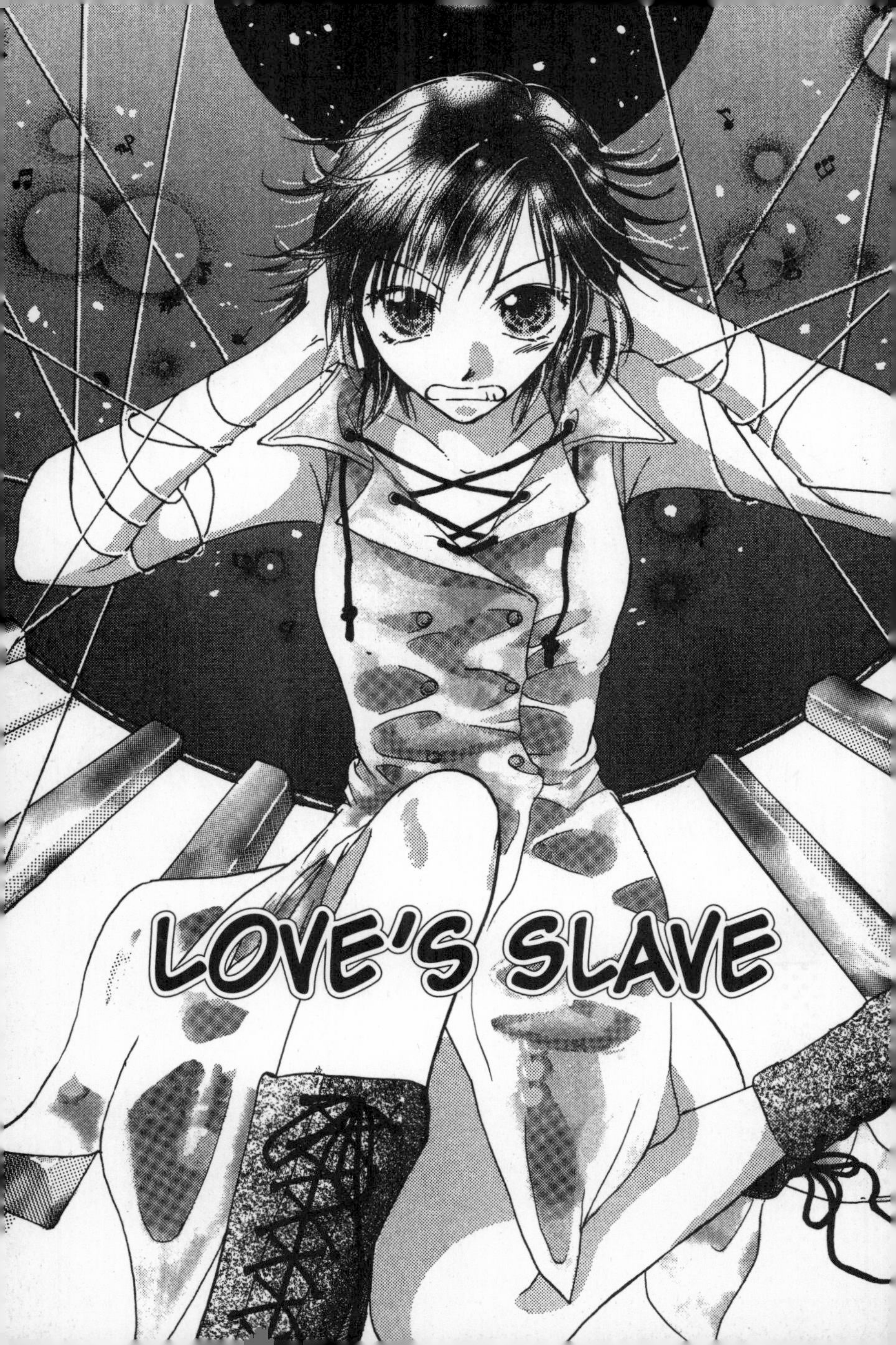
LOVE'S SLAVE

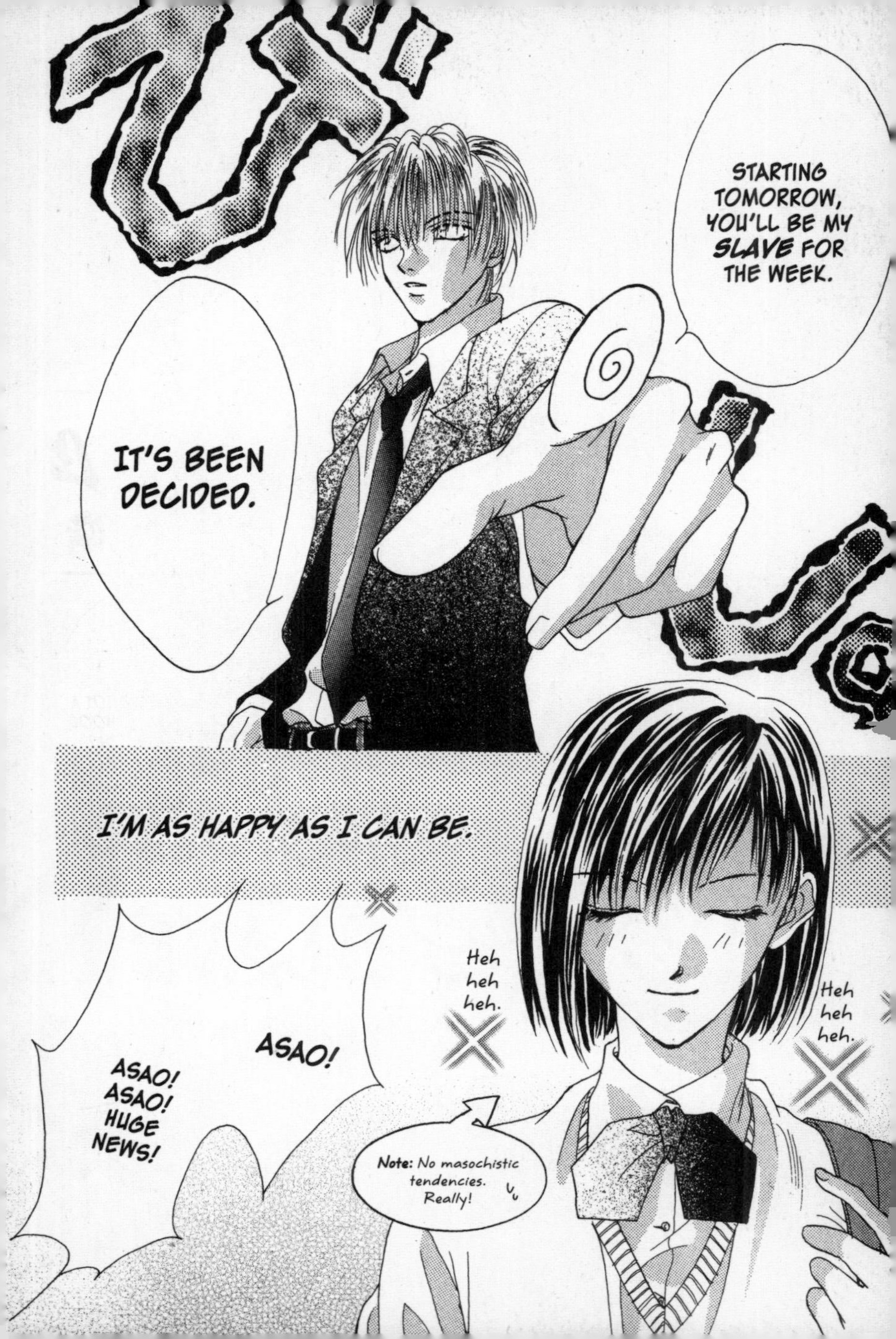
STARTING TOMORROW, YOU'LL BE MY SLAVE FOR THE WEEK.
IT'S BEEN DECIDED.
I'M AS HAPPY AS I CAN BE.
Heh heh heh.
Heh heh heh.
ASAO!
ASAO! ASAO! HUGE NEWS!
Note: No masochistic tendencies. Really!

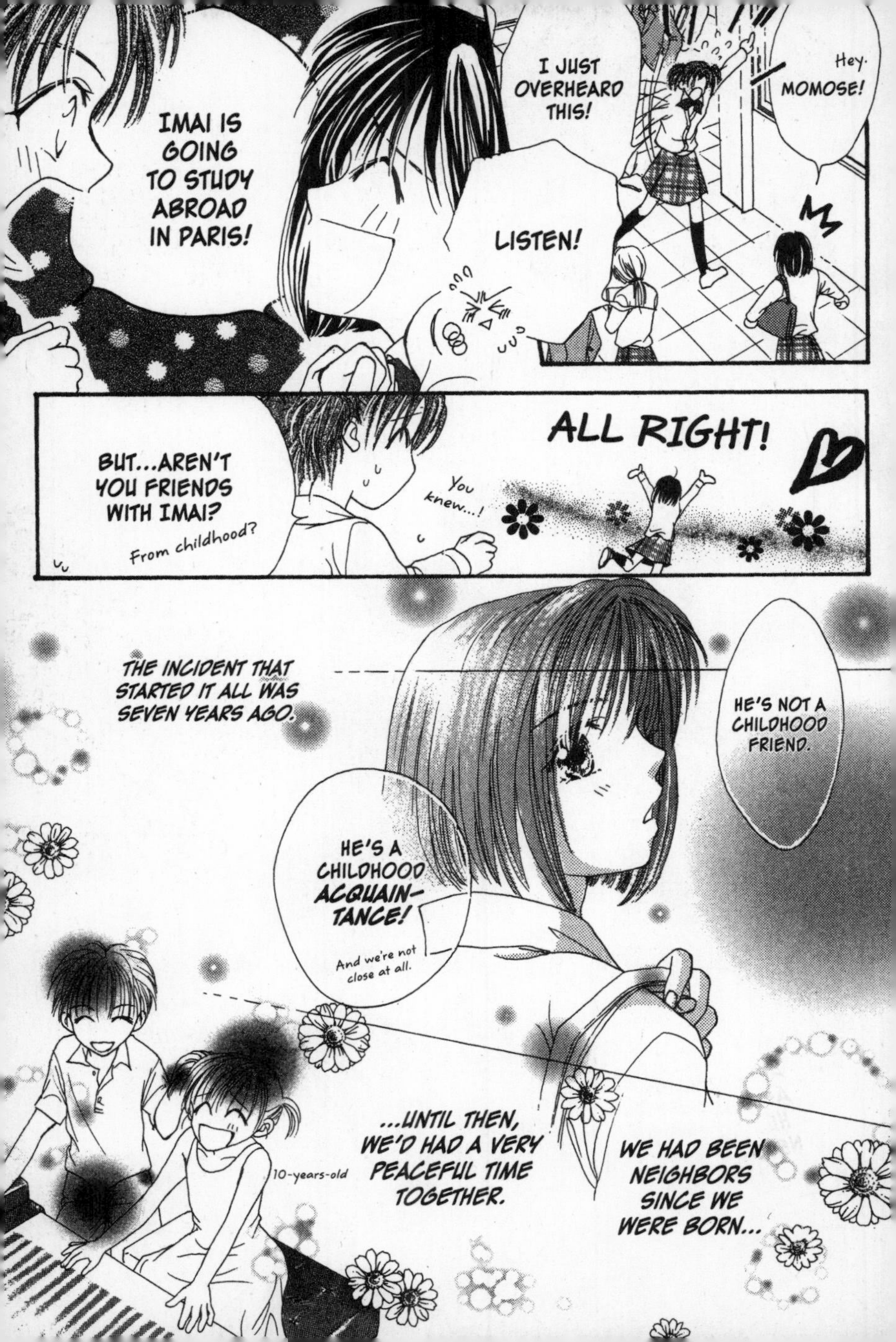
Hey. MOMOSE!
I JUST OVERHEARD THIS!
LISTEN!
IMAI IS GOING TO STUDY ABROAD IN PARIS!
ALL RIGHT!
You knew...!
BUT...AREN'T YOU FRIENDS WITH IMAI?
From childhood?
HE'S NOT A CHILDHOOD FRIEND.
HE'S A CHILDHOOD ACQUAINTANCE!
And we're not close at all.
THE INCIDENT THAT STARTED IT ALL WAS SEVEN YEARS AGO.
WE HAD BEEN NEIGHBORS SINCE WE WERE BORN...
...UNTIL THEN, WE'D HAD A VERY PEACEFUL TIME TOGETHER.
10-years-old

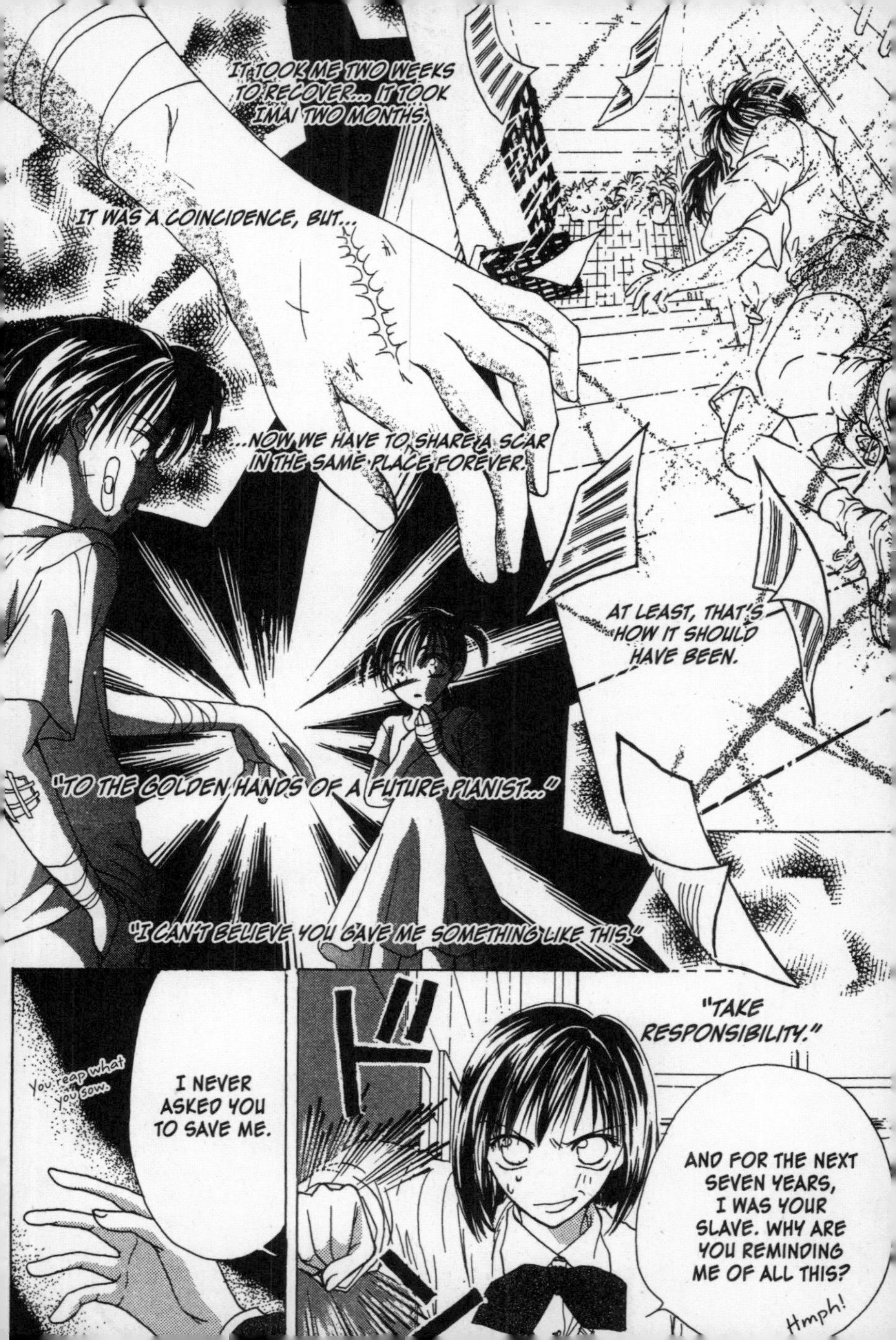
IT TOOK ME TWO WEEKS TO RECOVER... IT TOOK IMAI TWO MONTHS.
IT WAS A COINCIDENCE, BUT...
...NOW WE HAVE TO SHARE A SCAR IN THE SAME PLACE FOREVER.
AT LEAST, THAT'S HOW IT SHOULD HAVE BEEN.
"TO THE GOLDEN HANDS OF A FUTURE PIANIST..."
"I CAN'T BELIEVE YOU GAVE ME SOMETHING LIKE THIS."
"TAKE RESPONSIBILITY."
ド
AND FOR THE NEXT SEVEN YEARS, I WAS YOUR SLAVE. WHY ARE YOU REMINDING ME OF ALL THIS?
Hmph!
I NEVER ASKED YOU TO SAVE ME.
You reap what you sow.

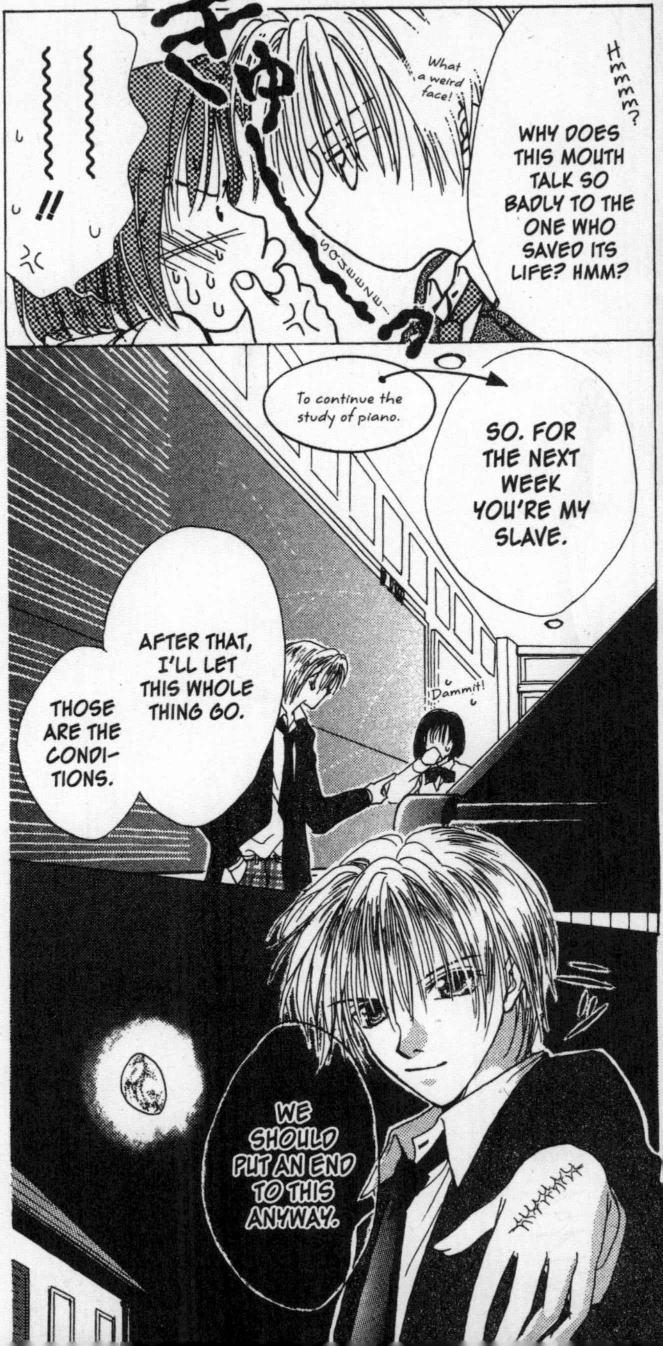
Hmmmm?
WHY DOES THIS MOUTH TALK SO BADLY TO THE ONE WHO SAVED ITS LIFE? HMM?
What a weird face!
SO. FOR THE NEXT WEEK YOU'RE MY SLAVE.
To continue the study of piano.
AFTER THAT, I'LL LET THIS WHOLE THING GO.
THOSE ARE THE CONDITIONS.
Dammit!
WE SHOULD PUT AN END TO THIS ANYWAY.

SPECIAL THANKS

This is the last box. It's the "Thank You" corner.

- To everyone who reads Missile.
- To everyone who helped in the making of volume 3:

T.S-san / Chapters 9, 10, 11
A.H-san / Chapters 10, 11, 12
K.S-san / Chapters 9, 12
E.T-san / Chapter 9
T.M-san / " "
H.T-san / Chapter 10
Y.H-san / Chapter 11
H.I-san / Chapter 12
K.S-san / " "
S.S-san / " "
To Suu-san and Yuki Sakurai-san a huge thanks. From Osaka...

- My old editor, Ms. S, as well as my new editor and everyone at the editing department.
- My friends (let's do another yakiniku/beef BBQ lovers meeting), N-kun (thank you for getting me all those logos), acquaintances, my other relatives and everyone who has met me.
- All of my family.

Thank you very much!

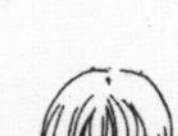

For any comments or criticisms about this book, or if there is something you want Kiritani to know (what's that supposed to mean?) please contact me.

TOKYOPOP
5900 Wilshire Blvd.
Ste 2000
Los Angeles, CA 90036
Attn: Editorial

See you in the extras section!

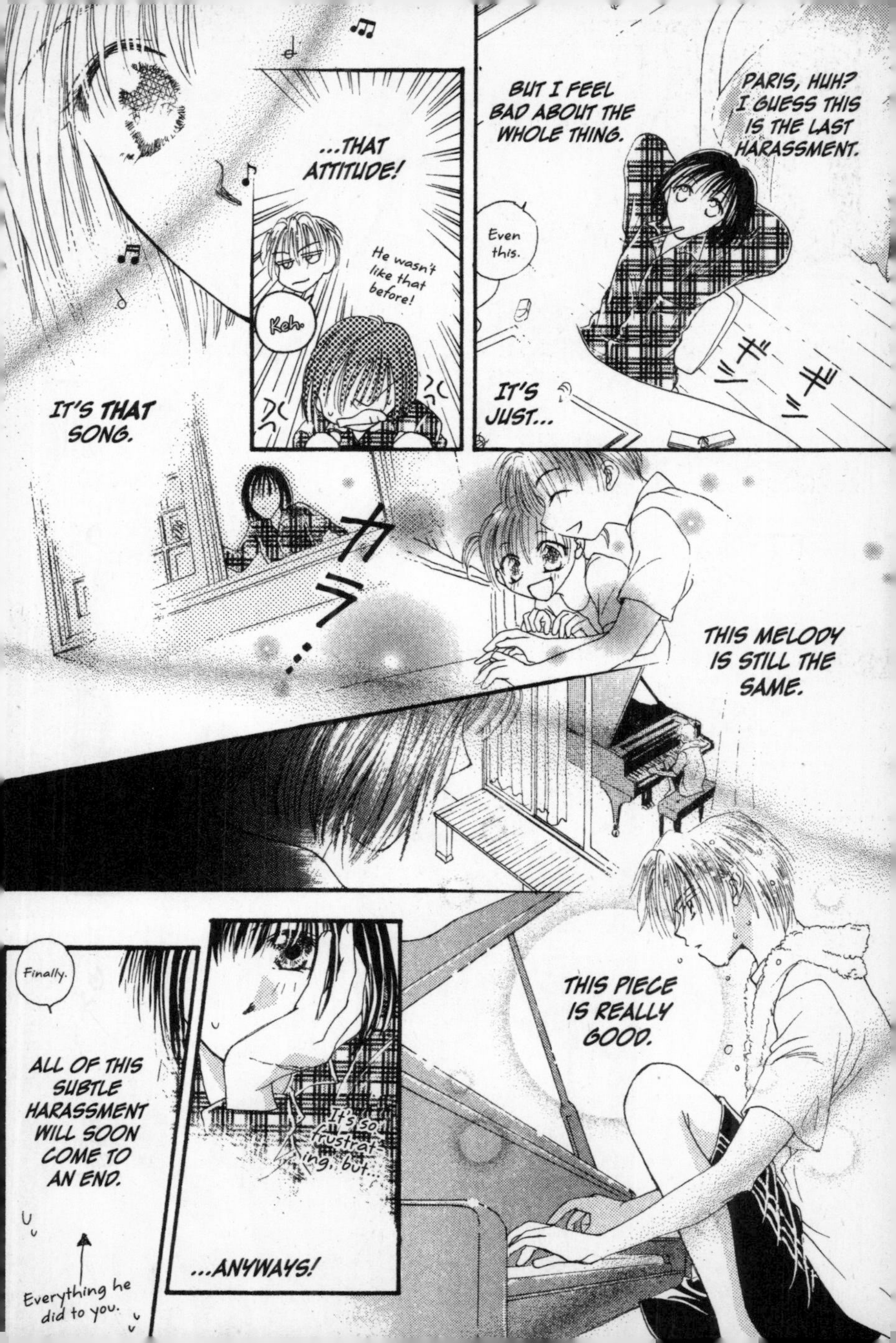
PARIS, HUH? I GUESS THIS IS THE LAST HARASSMENT.
ギシ ギシ
BUT I FEEL BAD ABOUT THE WHOLE THING.
Even this.
IT'S JUST...
...THAT ATTITUDE!
He wasn't like that before!
Keh.
IT'S THAT SONG.
カラ…
THIS MELODY IS STILL THE SAME.
THIS PIECE IS REALLY GOOD.
It's so frustrating, but...
...ANYWAYS!
Finally.
ALL OF THIS SUBTLE HARASSMENT WILL SOON COME TO AN END.
Everything he did to you.

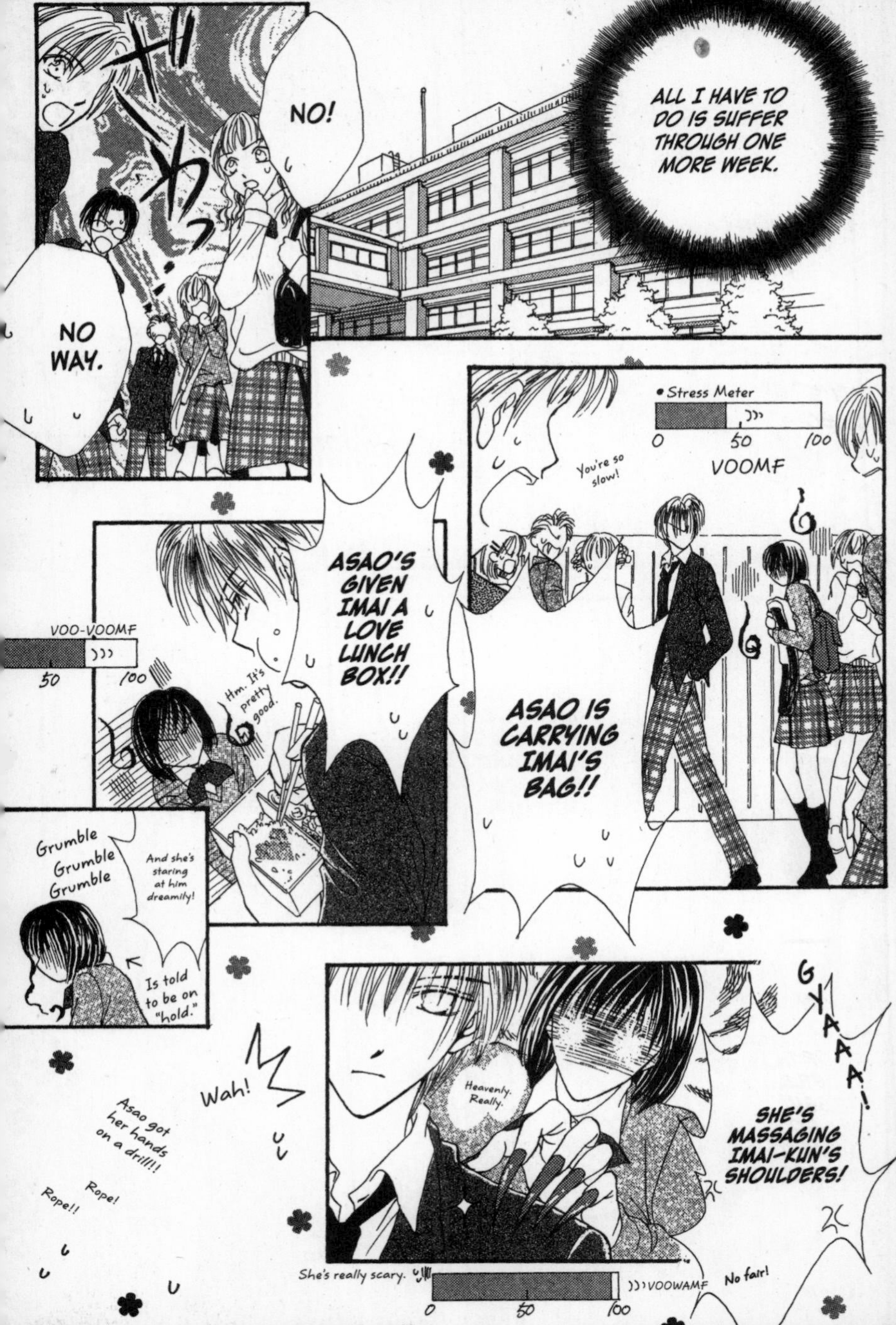
ALL I HAVE TO DO IS SUFFER THROUGH ONE MORE WEEK.
NO!
NO WAY.
Stress Meter
0
50
100
VOOMF
You're so slow!
ASAO IS CARRYING IMAI'S BAG!!
ASAO'S GIVEN IMAI A LOVE LUNCH BOX!!
VOO-VOOMF
50
100
Hm. It's pretty good.
Grumble Grumble Grumble
And she's staring at him dreamily!
Is told to be on "hold."
GYAAAA!
SHE'S MASSAGING IMAI-KUN'S SHOULDERS!
Heavenly. Really.
Wah!
Asao got her hands on a drill!!
Rope!
Rope!!
She's really scary.
VOOWAMF
No fair!
0
50
100

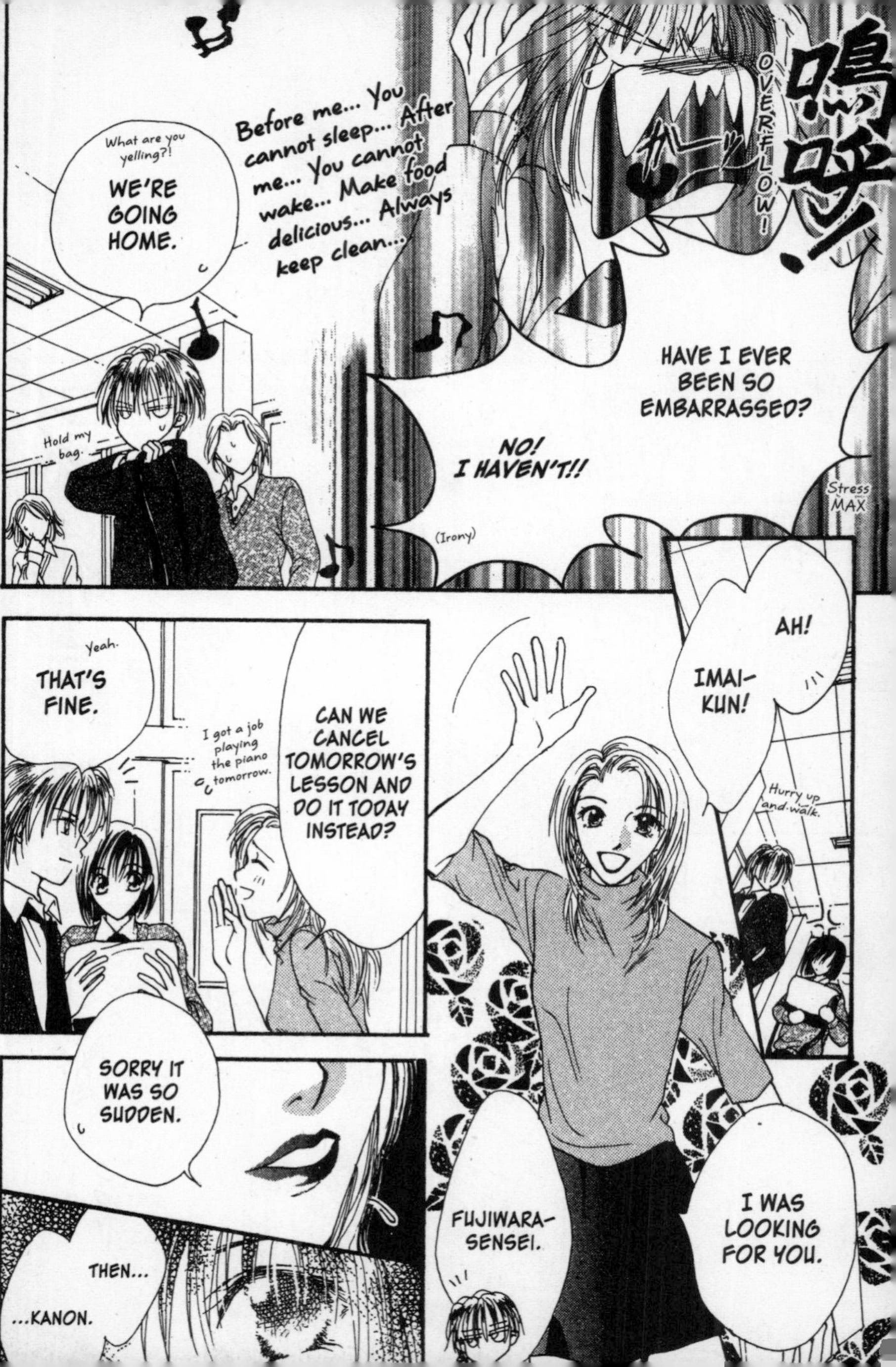
嗚呼!
OVERFLOW!
HAVE I EVER BEEN SO EMBARRASSED?
NO! I HAVEN'T!!
Stress MAX
(Irony)
Before me... You cannot sleep... After me... You cannot wake... Make food delicious... Always keep clean...
What are you yelling?!
WE'RE GOING HOME.
Hold my bag.
AH!
IMAI-KUN!
Hurry up and walk.
I WAS LOOKING FOR YOU.
FUJIWARA-SENSEI.
CAN WE CANCEL TOMORROW'S LESSON AND DO IT TODAY INSTEAD?
I got a job playing the piano tomorrow.
THAT'S FINE.
Yeah.
SORRY IT WAS SO SUDDEN.
THEN...
...KANON.

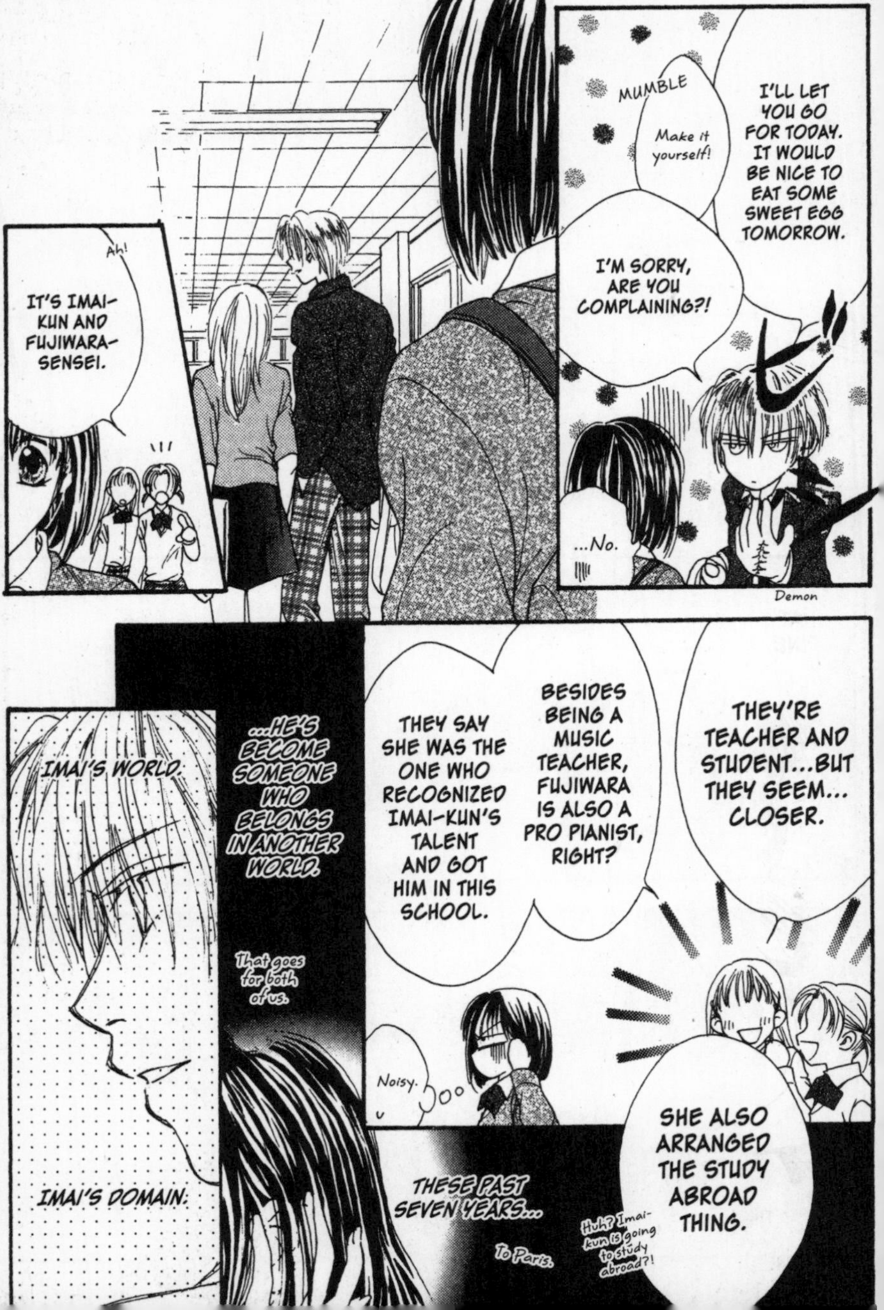

I'LL LET YOU GO FOR TODAY. IT WOULD BE NICE TO EAT SOME SWEET EGG TOMORROW.
MUMBLE
Make it yourself!
I'M SORRY, ARE YOU COMPLAINING?!
...No.
Demon
Ah!
IT'S IMAI-KUN AND FUJIWARA-SENSEI.
THEY'RE TEACHER AND STUDENT...BUT THEY SEEM... CLOSER.
BESIDES BEING A MUSIC TEACHER, FUJIWARA IS ALSO A PRO PIANIST, RIGHT?
THEY SAY SHE WAS THE ONE WHO RECOGNIZED IMAI-KUN'S TALENT AND GOT HIM IN THIS SCHOOL.
Noisy.
SHE ALSO ARRANGED THE STUDY ABROAD THING.
Huh? Imai-kun is going to study abroad?!
THESE PAST SEVEN YEARS...
To Paris.
...HE'S BECOME SOMEONE WHO BELONGS IN ANOTHER WORLD.
That goes for both of us.
IMAI'S WORLD.
IMAI'S DOMAIN:

MY PERSPECTIVE IS BLURRY.

Hang out with me after school today.

Even their seats are next to each other.

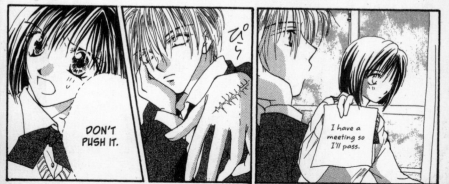

DON'T PUSH IT.

I have a meeting so I'll pass.

She's the school President.

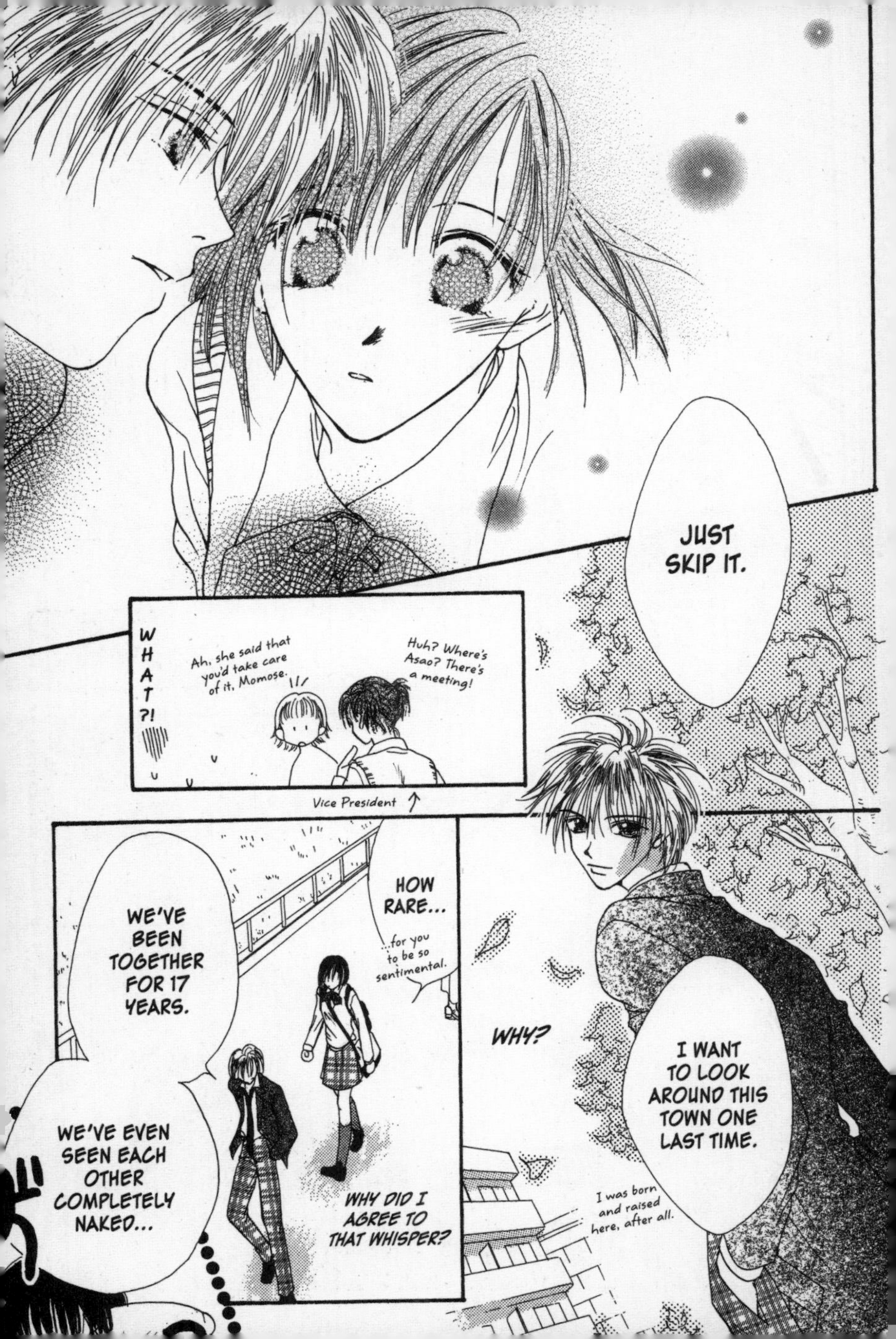
JUST SKIP IT.
WHY?
I WANT TO LOOK AROUND THIS TOWN ONE LAST TIME.
I was born and raised here, after all.
Huh? Where's Asao? There's a meeting!
Ah, she said that you'd take care of it, Momose.
WHAT?!
Vice President
HOW RARE...
...for you to be so sentimental.
WE'VE BEEN TOGETHER FOR 17 YEARS.
WE'VE EVEN SEEN EACH OTHER COMPLETELY NAKED...
WHY DID I AGREE TO THAT WHISPER?

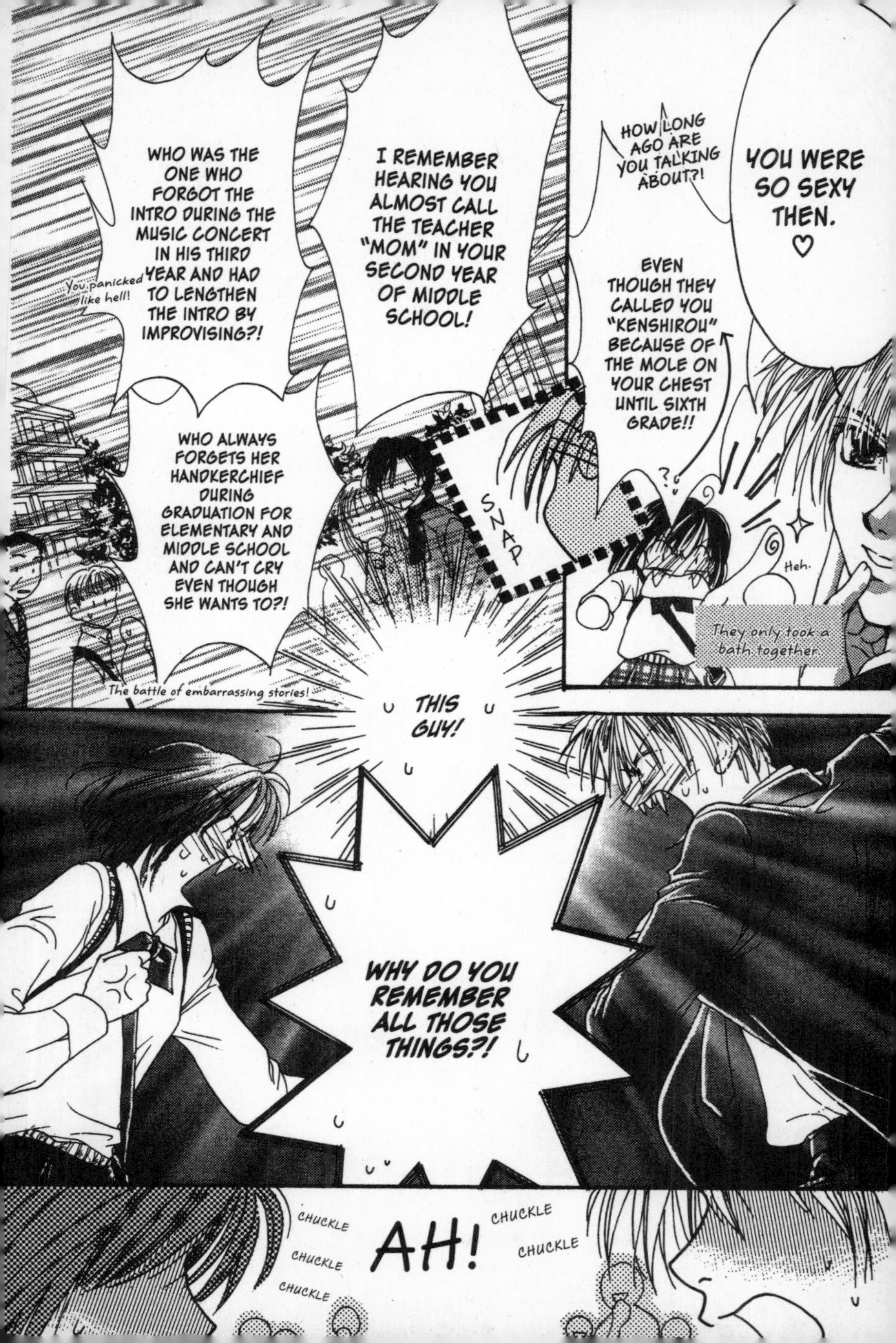
YOU WERE SO SEXY THEN. ♡
HOW LONG AGO ARE YOU TALKING ABOUT?!
EVEN THOUGH THEY CALLED YOU "KENSHIROU" BECAUSE OF THE MOLE ON YOUR CHEST UNTIL SIXTH GRADE!!
Heh.
They only took a bath together.
SNAP
I REMEMBER HEARING YOU ALMOST CALL THE TEACHER "MOM" IN YOUR SECOND YEAR OF MIDDLE SCHOOL!
WHO WAS THE ONE WHO FORGOT THE INTRO DURING THE MUSIC CONCERT IN HIS THIRD YEAR AND HAD TO LENGTHEN THE INTRO BY IMPROVISING?!
You panicked like hell!
WHO ALWAYS FORGETS HER HANDKERCHIEF DURING GRADUATION FOR ELEMENTARY AND MIDDLE SCHOOL AND CAN'T CRY EVEN THOUGH SHE WANTS TO?!
The battle of embarrassing stories!
THIS GUY!
WHY DO YOU REMEMBER ALL THOSE THINGS?!
CHUCKLE
CHUCKLE
AH!
CHUCKLE
CHUCKLE
CHUCKLE

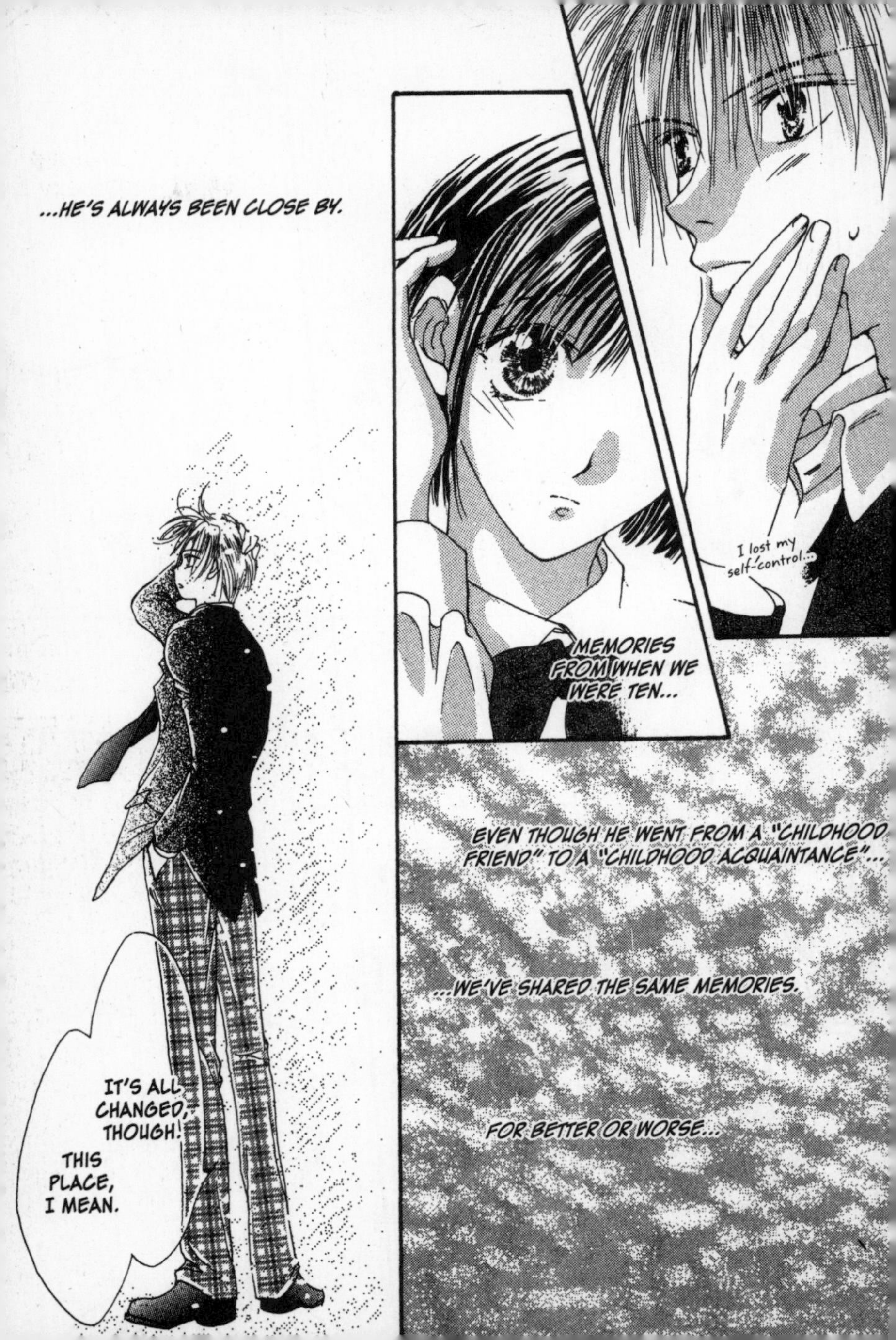
I lost my self-control...
MEMORIES FROM WHEN WE WERE TEN...
EVEN THOUGH HE WENT FROM A "CHILDHOOD FRIEND" TO A "CHILDHOOD ACQUAINTANCE"...
...WE'VE SHARED THE SAME MEMORIES.
FOR BETTER OR WORSE...
...HE'S ALWAYS BEEN CLOSE BY.
IT'S ALL CHANGED, THOUGH!
THIS PLACE, I MEAN.

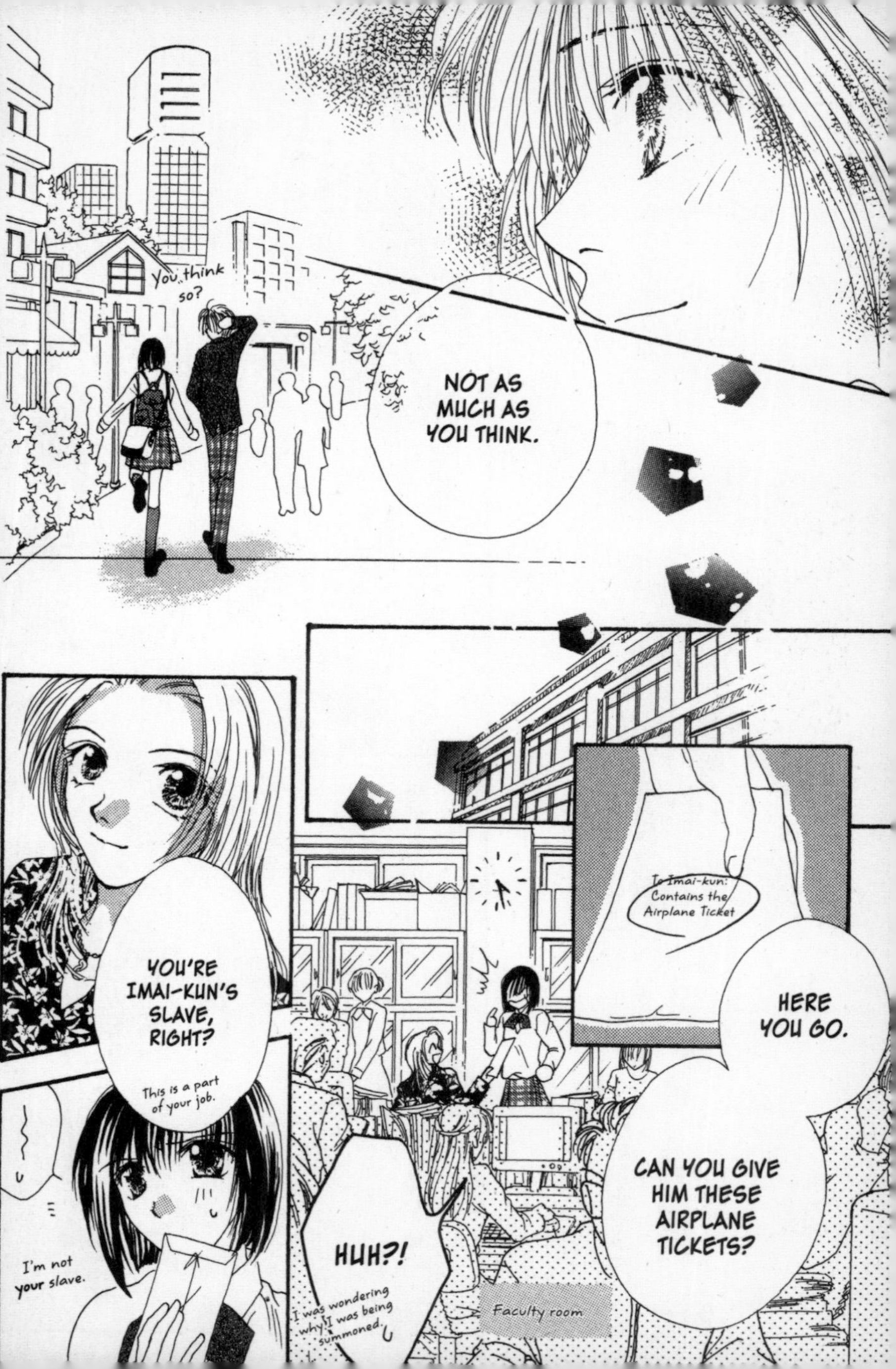
NOT AS MUCH AS YOU THINK.
You think so?
Faculty room
To Imai-kun: Contains the Airplane Ticket
HERE YOU GO.
CAN YOU GIVE HIM THESE AIRPLANE TICKETS?
HUH?!
I was wondering why I was being summoned.
YOU'RE IMAI-KUN'S SLAVE, RIGHT?
This is a part of your job.
I'm not your slave.

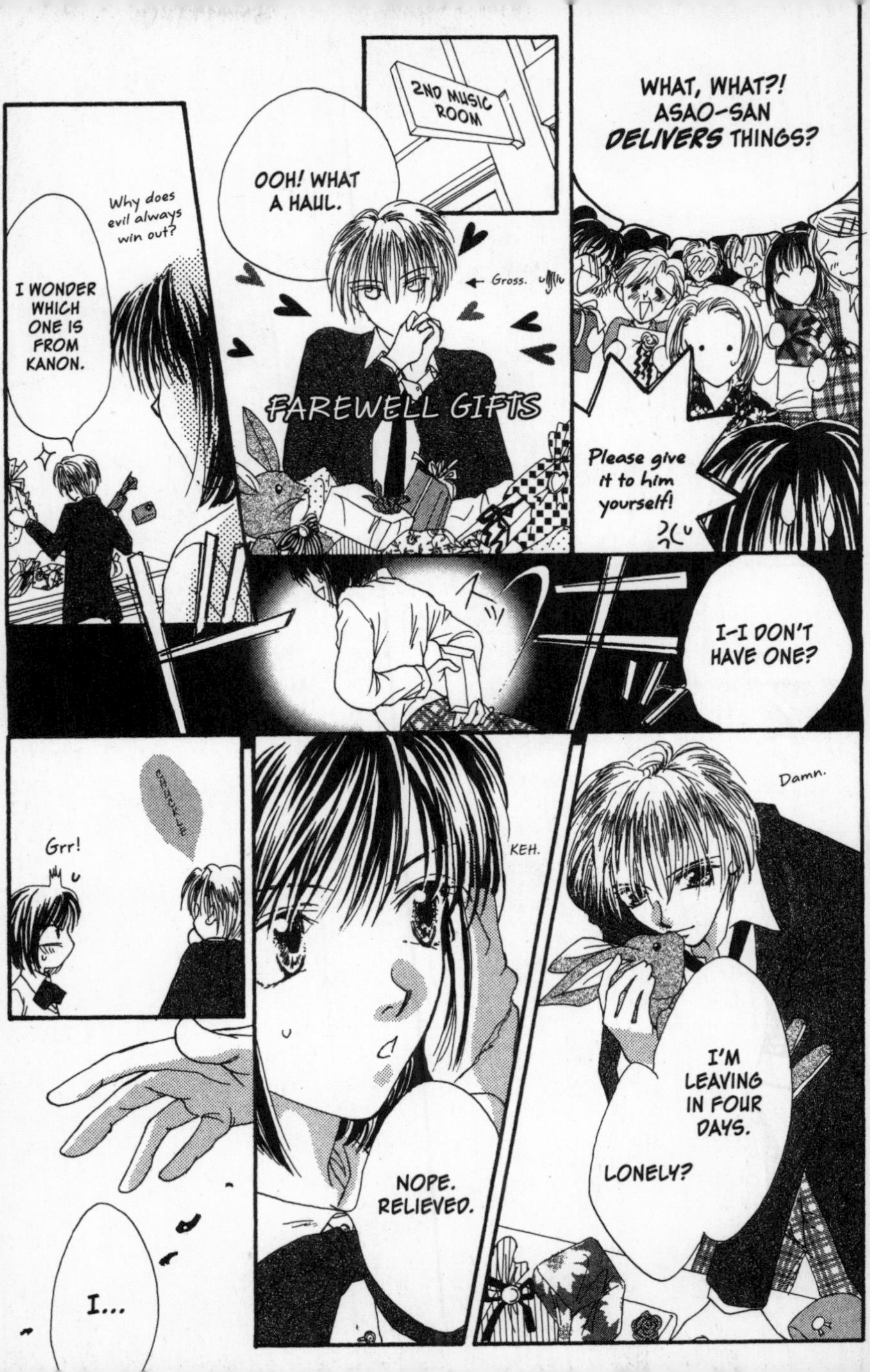
WHAT, WHAT?! ASAO-SAN DELIVERS THINGS?
Please give it to him yourself!
2ND MUSIC ROOM
OOH! WHAT A HAUL.
Gross.
FAREWELL GIFTS
Why does evil always win out?
I WONDER WHICH ONE IS FROM KANON.
I-I DON'T HAVE ONE?
Damn.
I'M LEAVING IN FOUR DAYS.
LONELY?
KEH.
NOPE. RELIEVED.
CHUCKLE
Grr!
I...

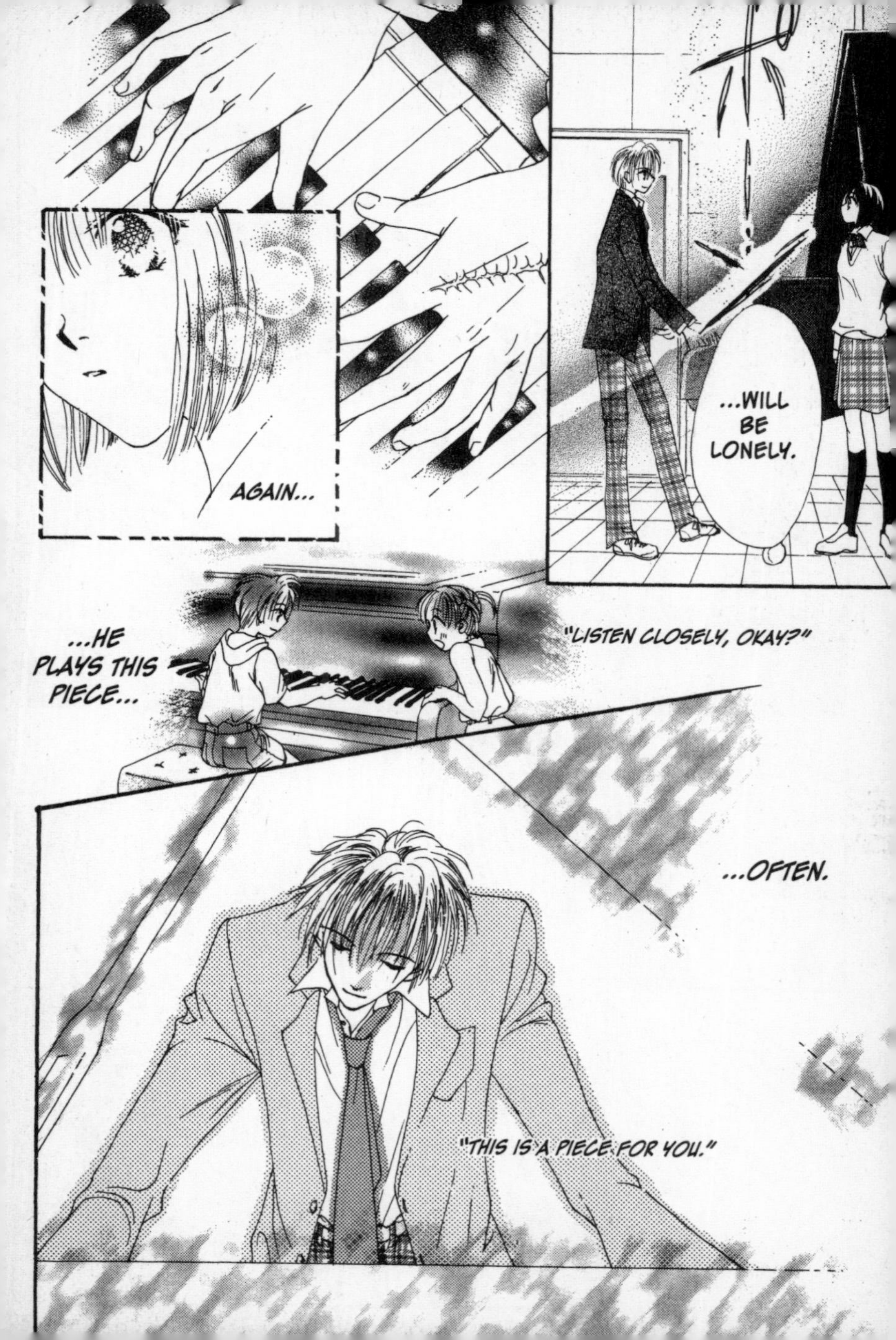
...WILL BE LONELY.
AGAIN...
"LISTEN CLOSELY, OKAY?"
...HE PLAYS THIS PIECE...
...OFTEN.
"THIS IS A PIECE FOR YOU."

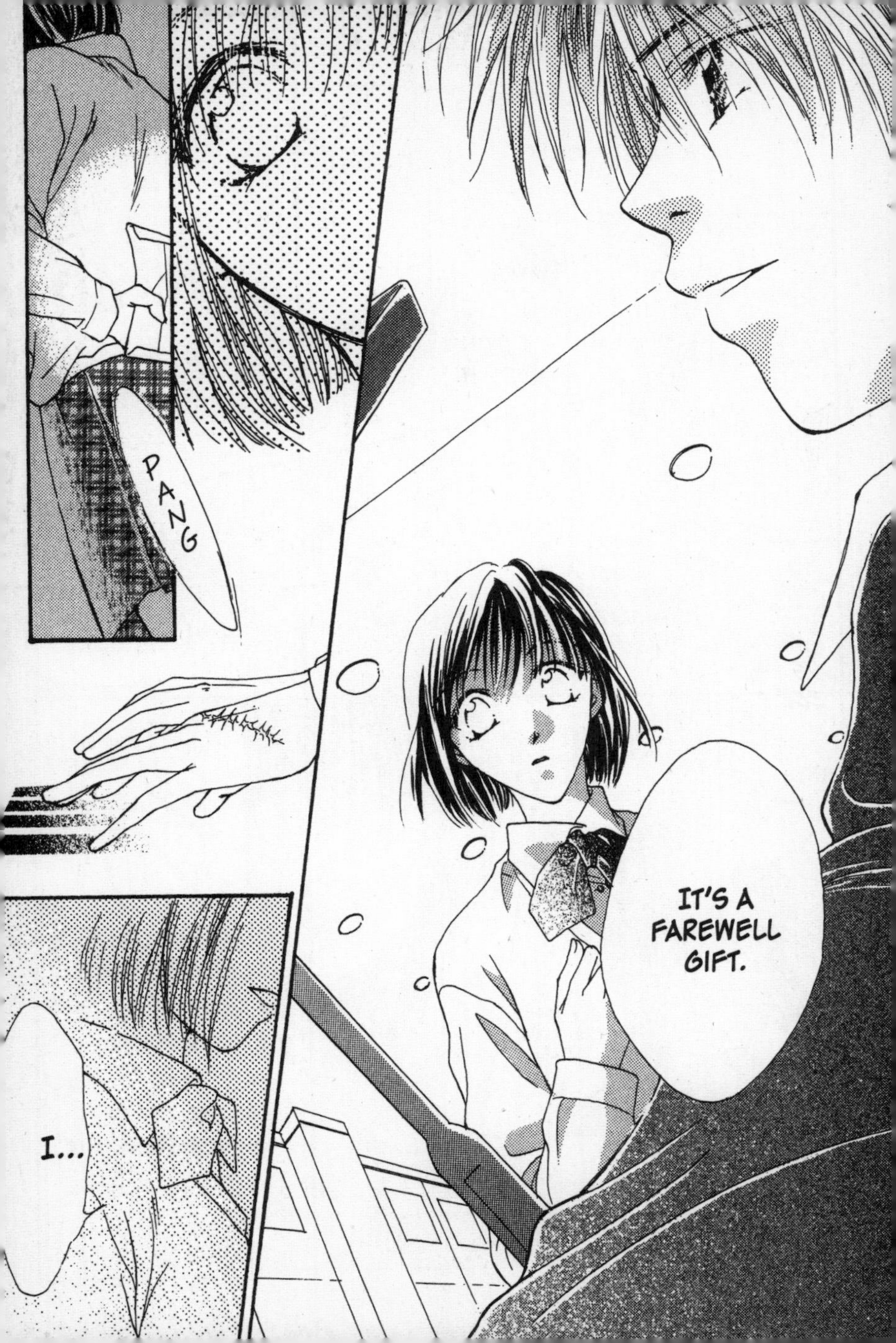
IT'S A FAREWELL GIFT.
PANG
I...

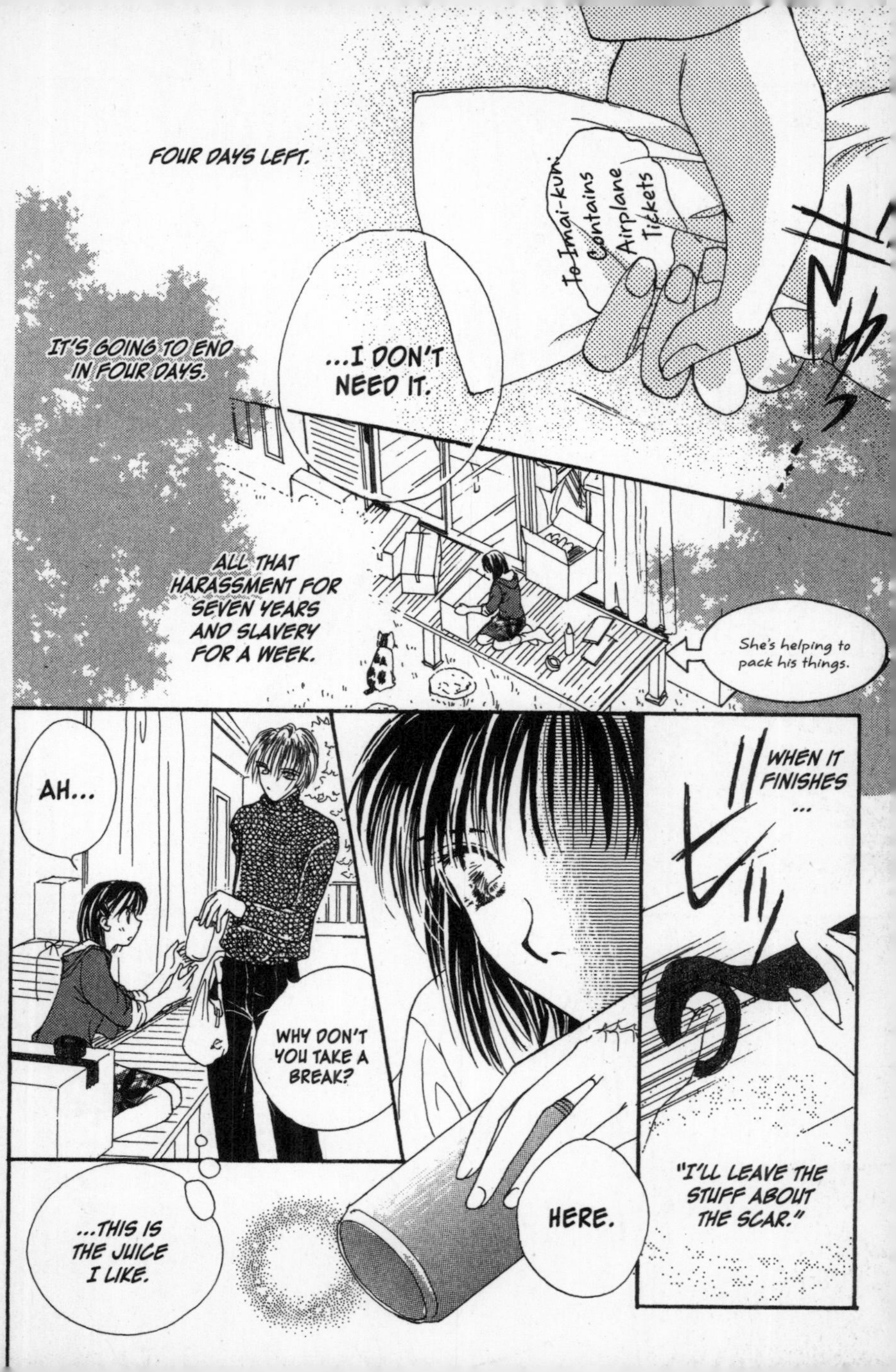
To Imai-kun: Contains Airplane Tickets
FOUR DAYS LEFT.
...I DON'T NEED IT.
IT'S GOING TO END IN FOUR DAYS.
She's helping to pack his things.
ALL THAT HARASSMENT FOR SEVEN YEARS AND SLAVERY FOR A WEEK.
WHEN IT FINISHES ...
"I'LL LEAVE THE STUFF ABOUT THE SCAR."
HERE.
AH...
WHY DON'T YOU TAKE A BREAK?
...THIS IS THE JUICE I LIKE.

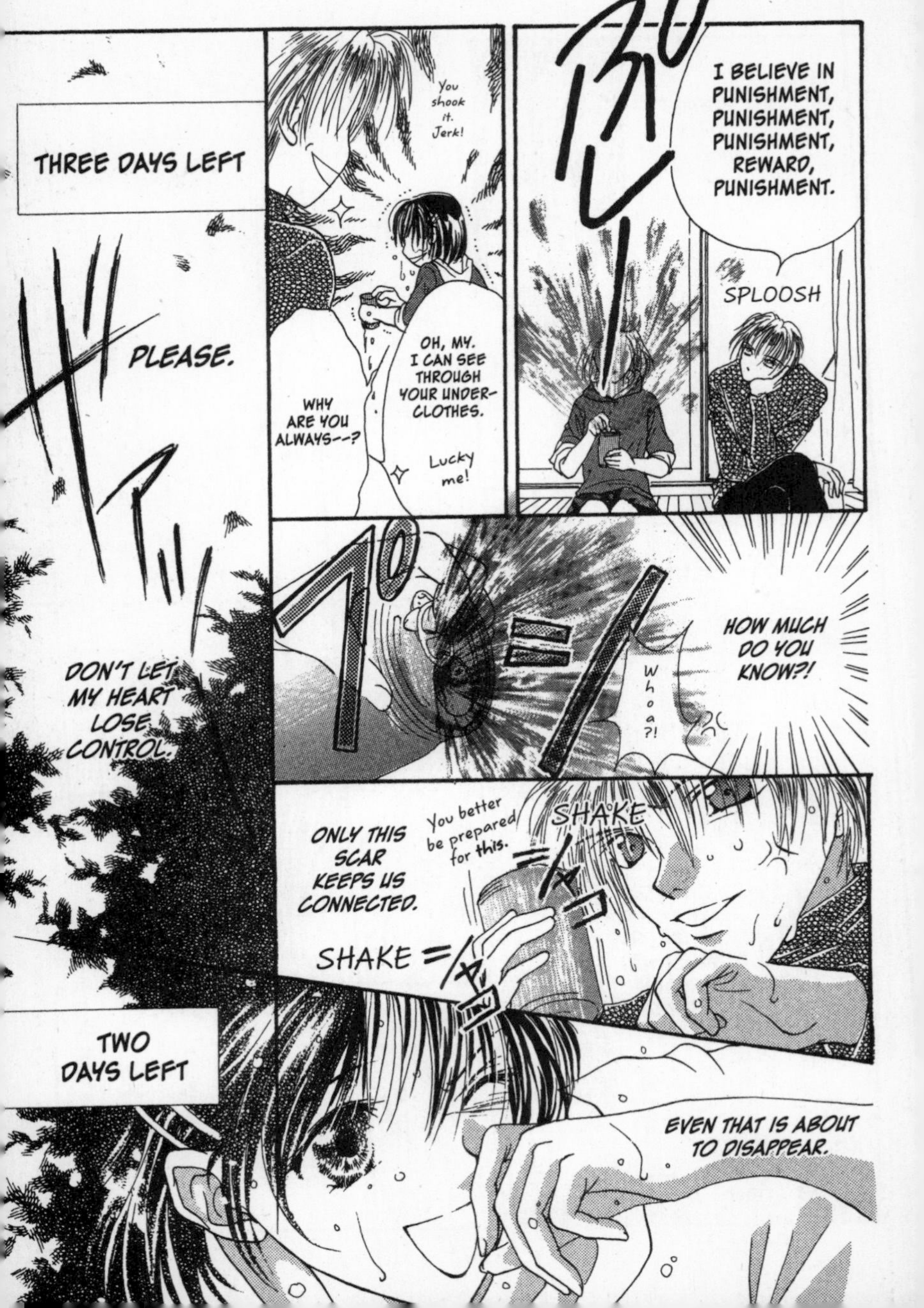
I BELIEVE IN PUNISHMENT, PUNISHMENT, PUNISHMENT, REWARD, PUNISHMENT.
SPLOOSH
You shook it. Jerk!
OH, MY. I CAN SEE THROUGH YOUR UNDER-CLOTHES.
WHY ARE YOU ALWAYS--?
Lucky me!
HOW MUCH DO YOU KNOW?!
Whoa?!
SHAKE
You better be prepared for this.
SHAKE
EVEN THAT IS ABOUT TO DISAPPEAR.
THREE DAYS LEFT
PLEASE.
DON'T LET MY HEART LOSE CONTROL.
ONLY THIS SCAR KEEPS US CONNECTED.
TWO DAYS LEFT

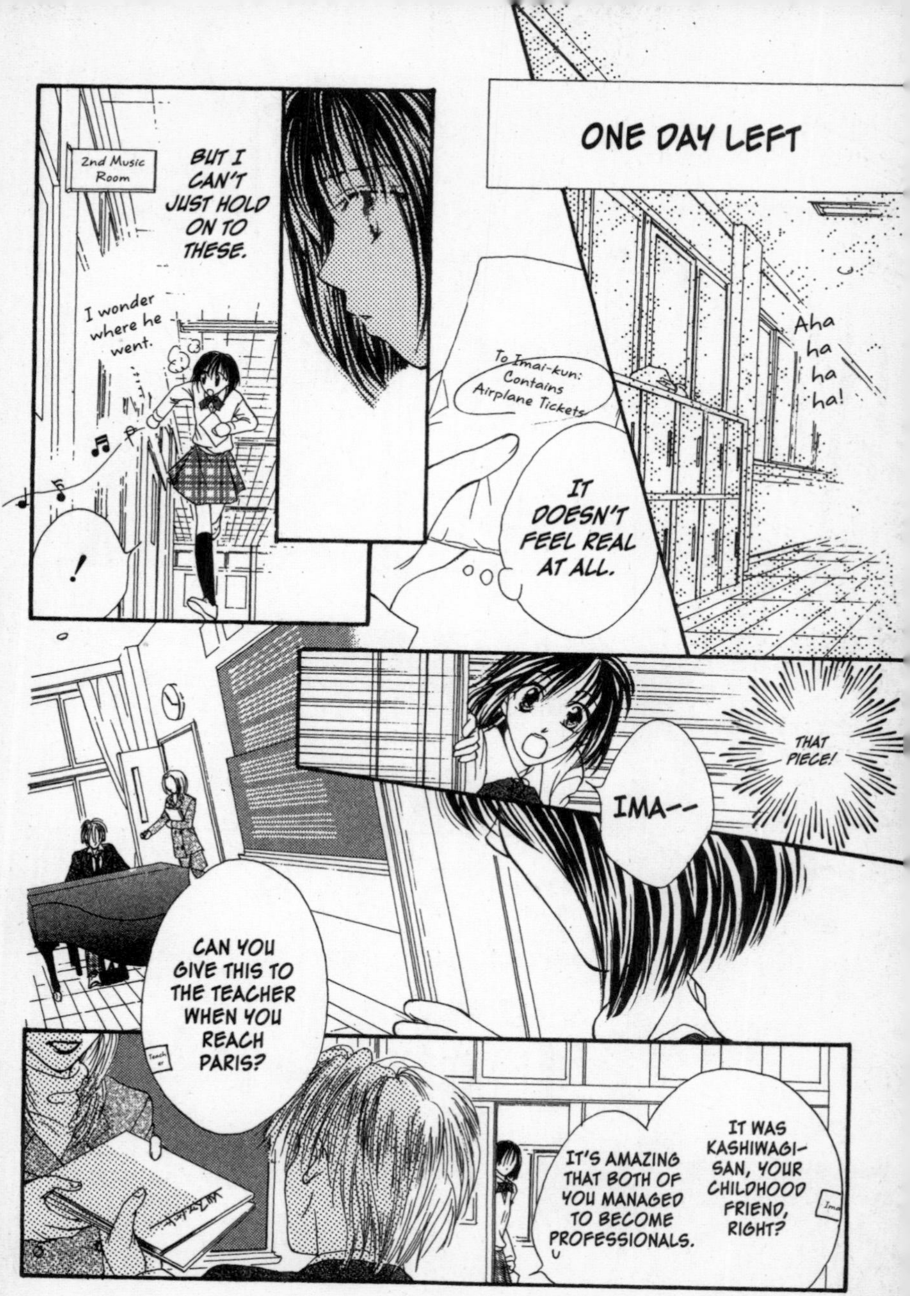
ONE DAY LEFT
Aha ha ha ha!
To Imai-kun: Contains Airplane Tickets
IT DOESN'T FEEL REAL AT ALL.
2nd Music Room
BUT I CAN'T JUST HOLD ON TO THESE.
I wonder where he went.
!
THAT PIECE!
IMA--
CAN YOU GIVE THIS TO THE TEACHER WHEN YOU REACH PARIS?
IT WAS KASHIWAGI-SAN, YOUR CHILDHOOD FRIEND, RIGHT?
IT'S AMAZING THAT BOTH OF YOU MANAGED TO BECOME PROFESSIONALS.

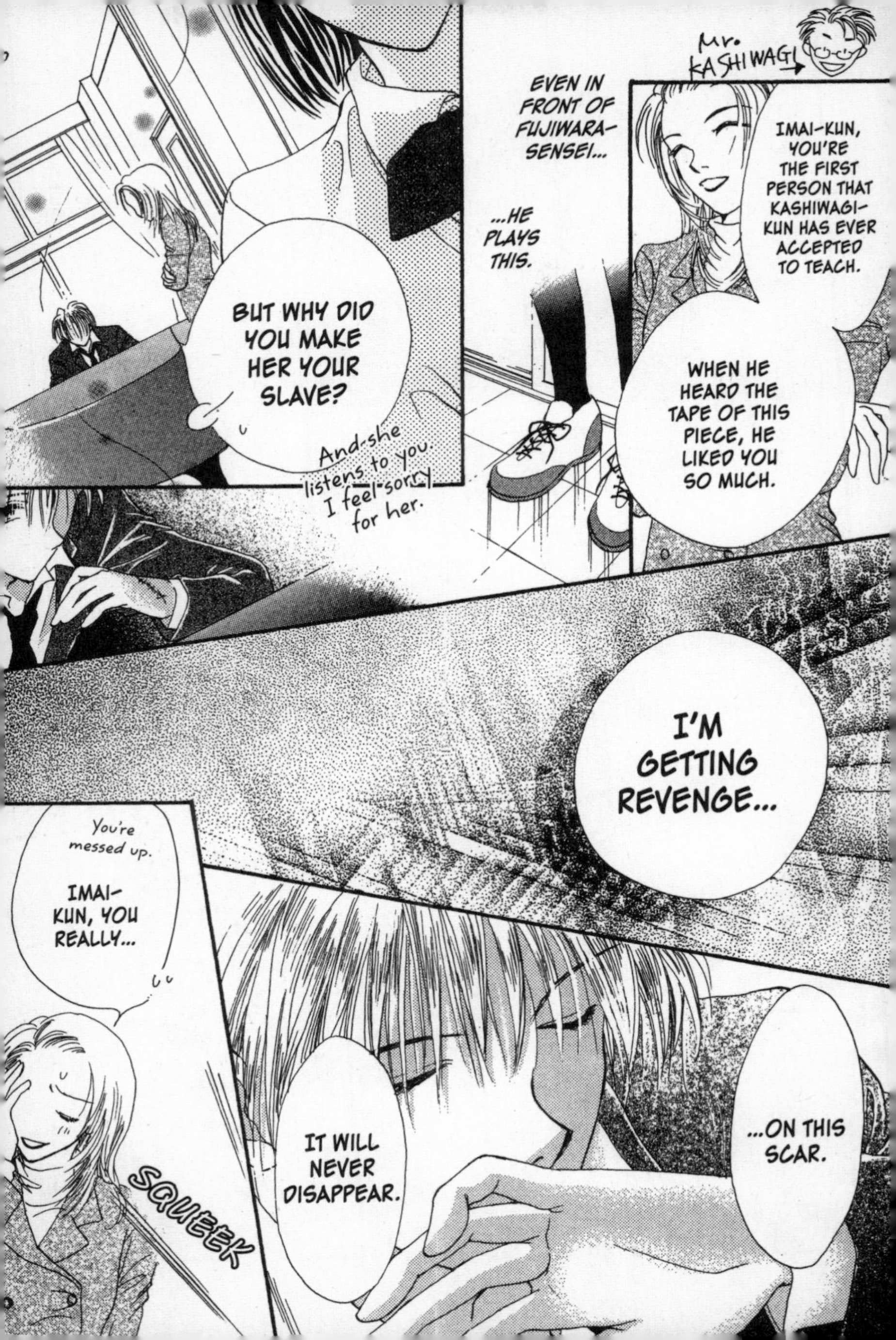
Mr. KASHIWAGI!
IMAI-KUN, YOU'RE THE FIRST PERSON THAT KASHIWAGI-KUN HAS EVER ACCEPTED TO TEACH.
WHEN HE HEARD THE TAPE OF THIS PIECE, HE LIKED YOU SO MUCH.
EVEN IN FRONT OF FUJIWARA-SENSEI...
...HE PLAYS THIS.
BUT WHY DID YOU MAKE HER YOUR SLAVE?
And she listens to you. I feel sorry for her.
I'M GETTING REVENGE...
...ON THIS SCAR.
IT WILL NEVER DISAPPEAR.
You're messed up.
IMAI-KUN, YOU REALLY...
SQUEEK

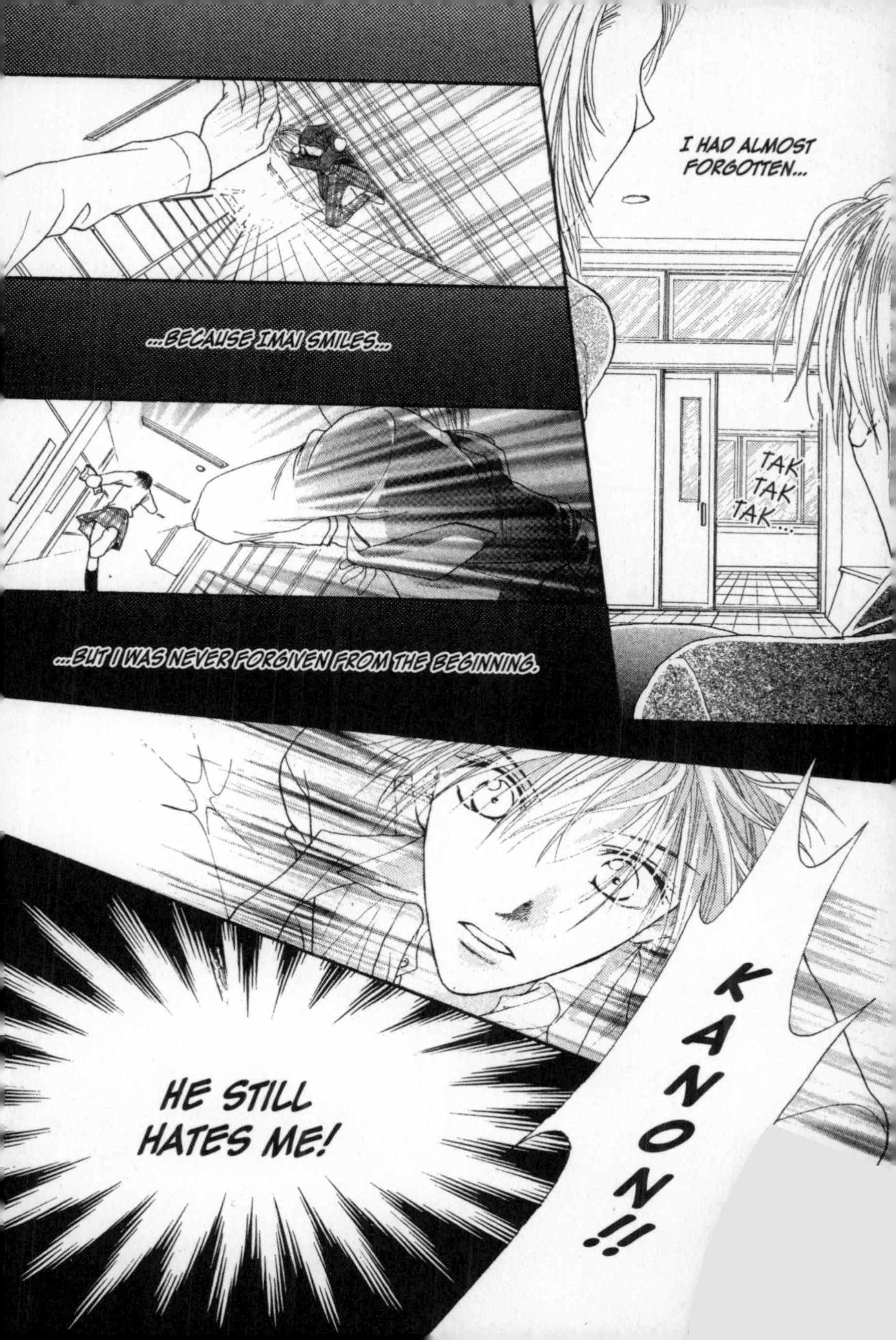
I HAD ALMOST FORGOTTEN...
TAK TAK TAK...
...BECAUSE IMAI SMILES...
...BUT I WAS NEVER FORGIVEN FROM THE BEGINNING.
KANON!!
HE STILL HATES ME!

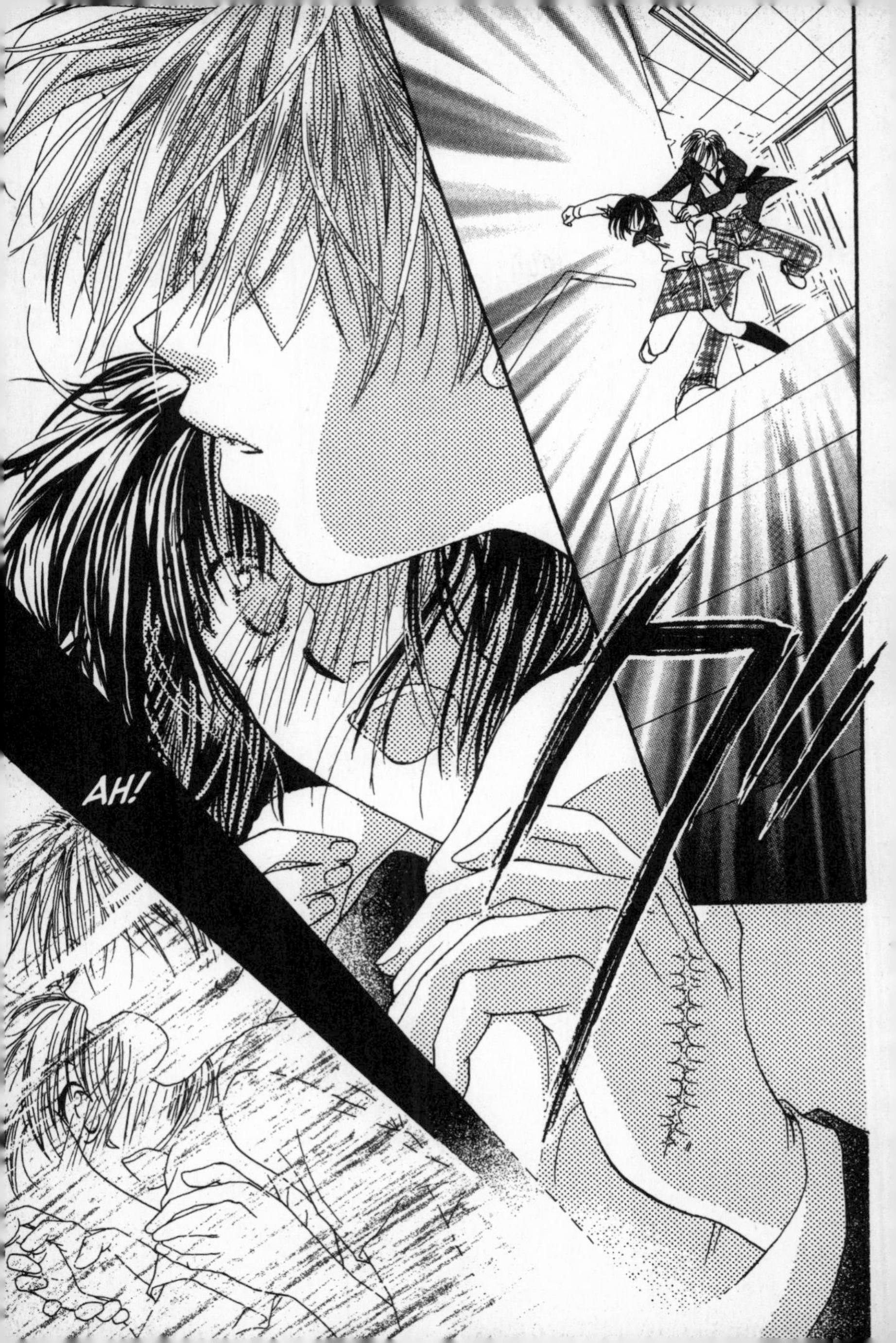
AH!

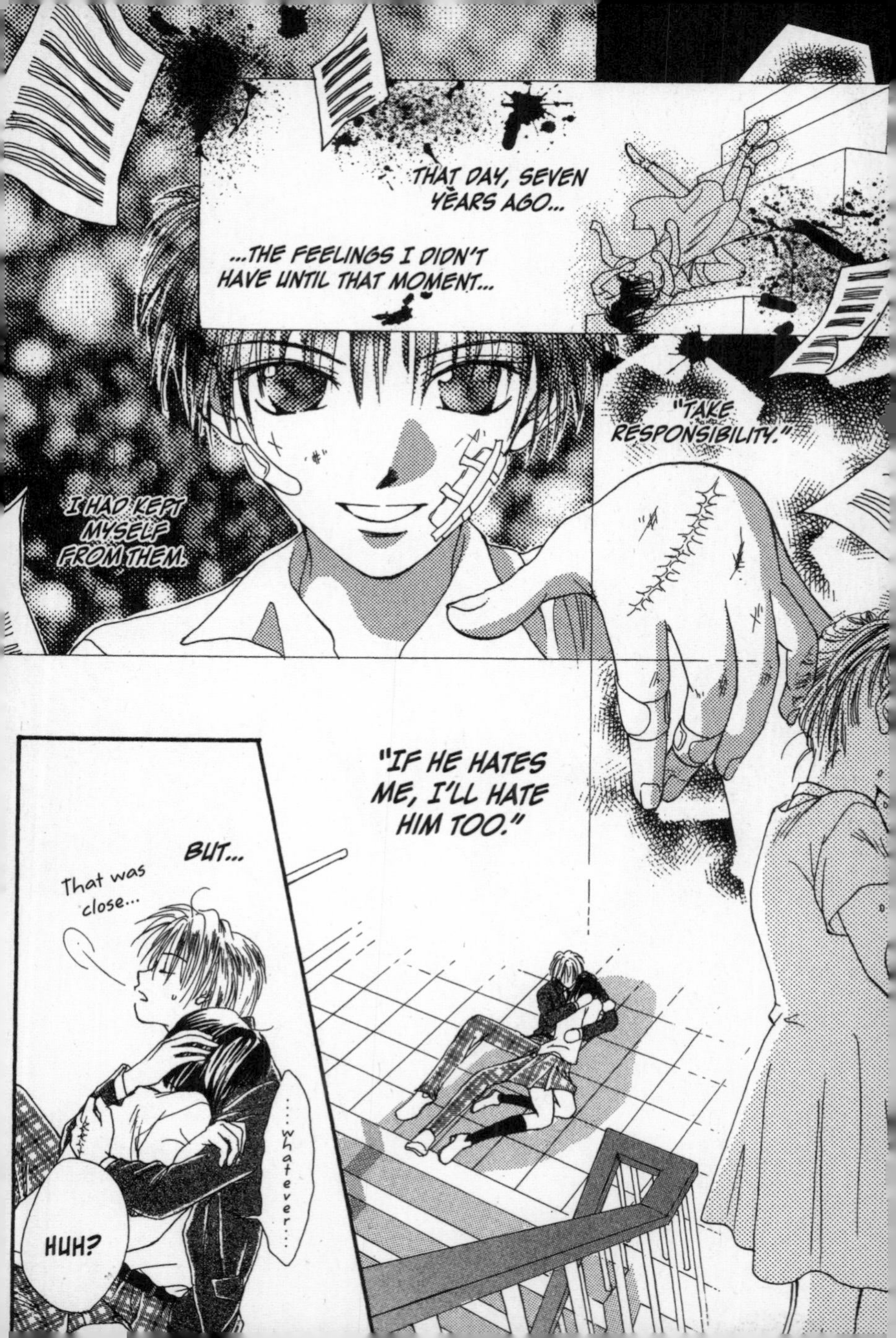
THAT DAY, SEVEN YEARS AGO...
...THE FEELINGS I DIDN'T HAVE UNTIL THAT MOMENT...
"TAKE RESPONSIBILITY."
I HAD KEPT MYSELF FROM THEM.
"IF HE HATES ME, I'LL HATE HIM TOO."
BUT...
That was close...
....whatever...
HUH?

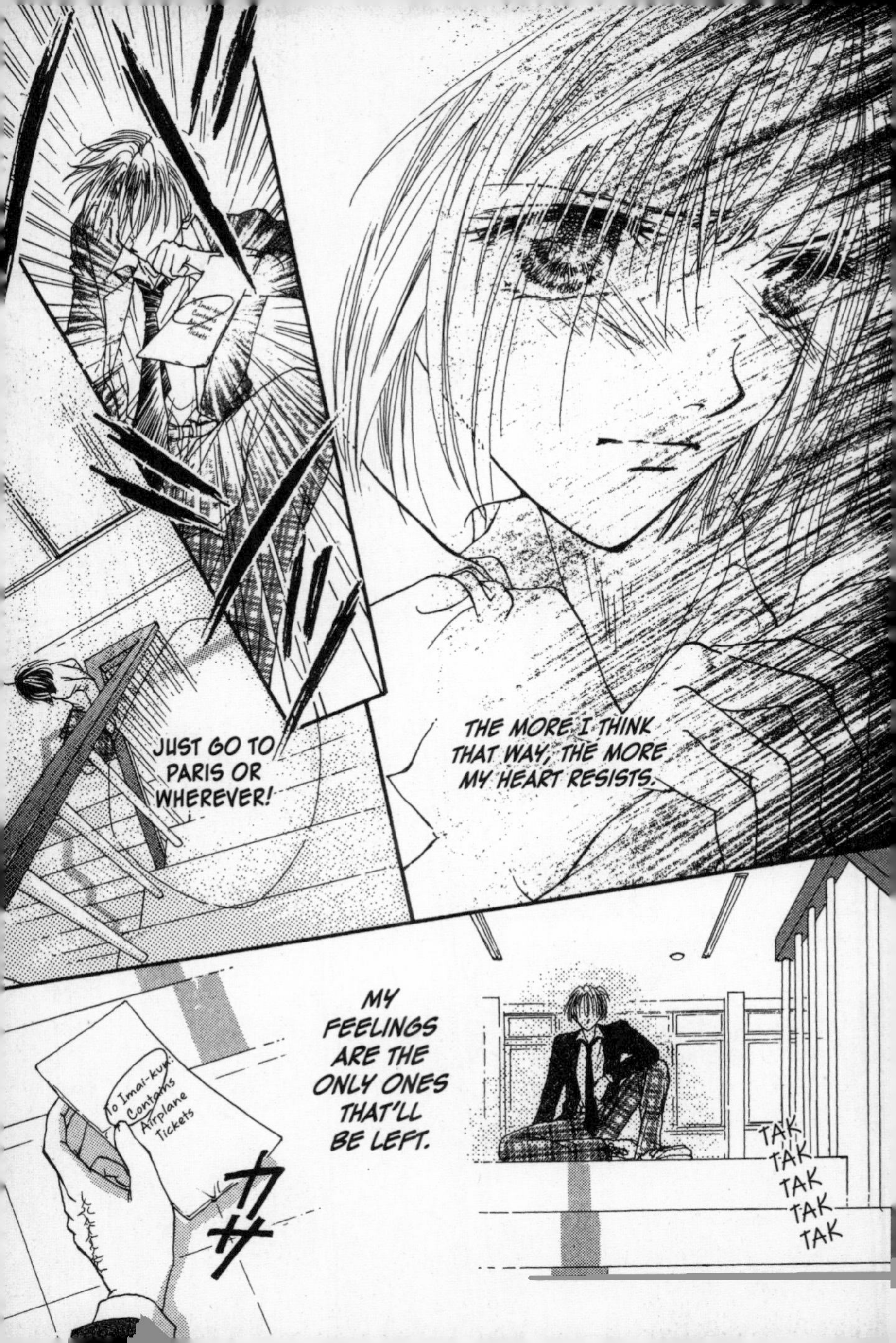
THE MORE I THINK THAT WAY, THE MORE MY HEART RESISTS.
JUST GO TO PARIS OR WHEREVER!
MY FEELINGS ARE THE ONLY ONES THAT'LL BE LEFT.
TAK TAK TAK TAK TAK
To Imai-kun. Contains Airplane Tickets

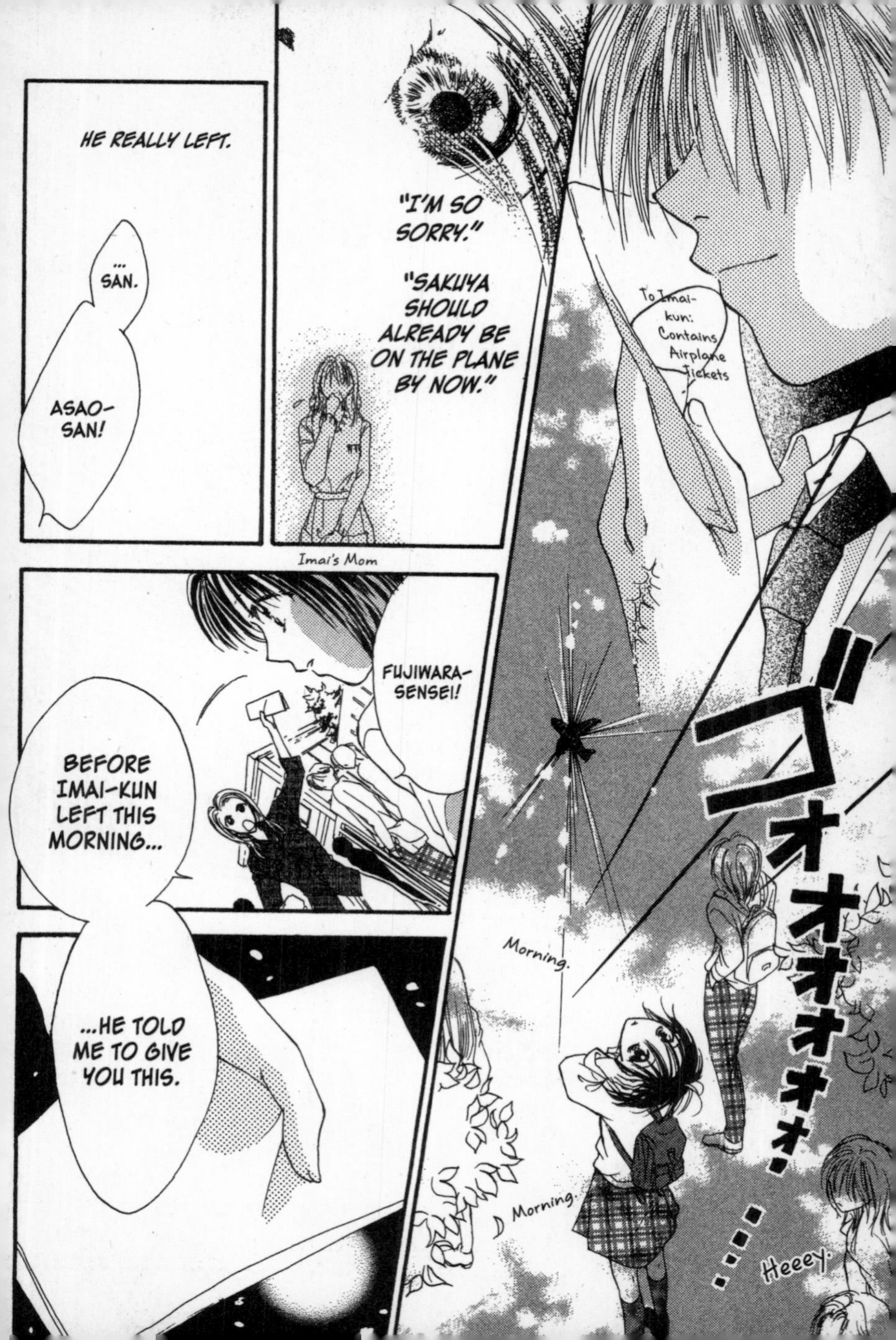
To Imai-kun: Contains Airplane Tickets
ゴォオオオオオ・・・・・・
Morning.
Morning.
Heeey.
"I'M SO SORRY."
"SAKUYA SHOULD ALREADY BE ON THE PLANE BY NOW."
Imai's Mom
HE REALLY LEFT.
... SAN.
ASAO-SAN!
FUJIWARA-SENSEI!
BEFORE IMAI-KUN LEFT THIS MORNING...
...HE TOLD ME TO GIVE YOU THIS.

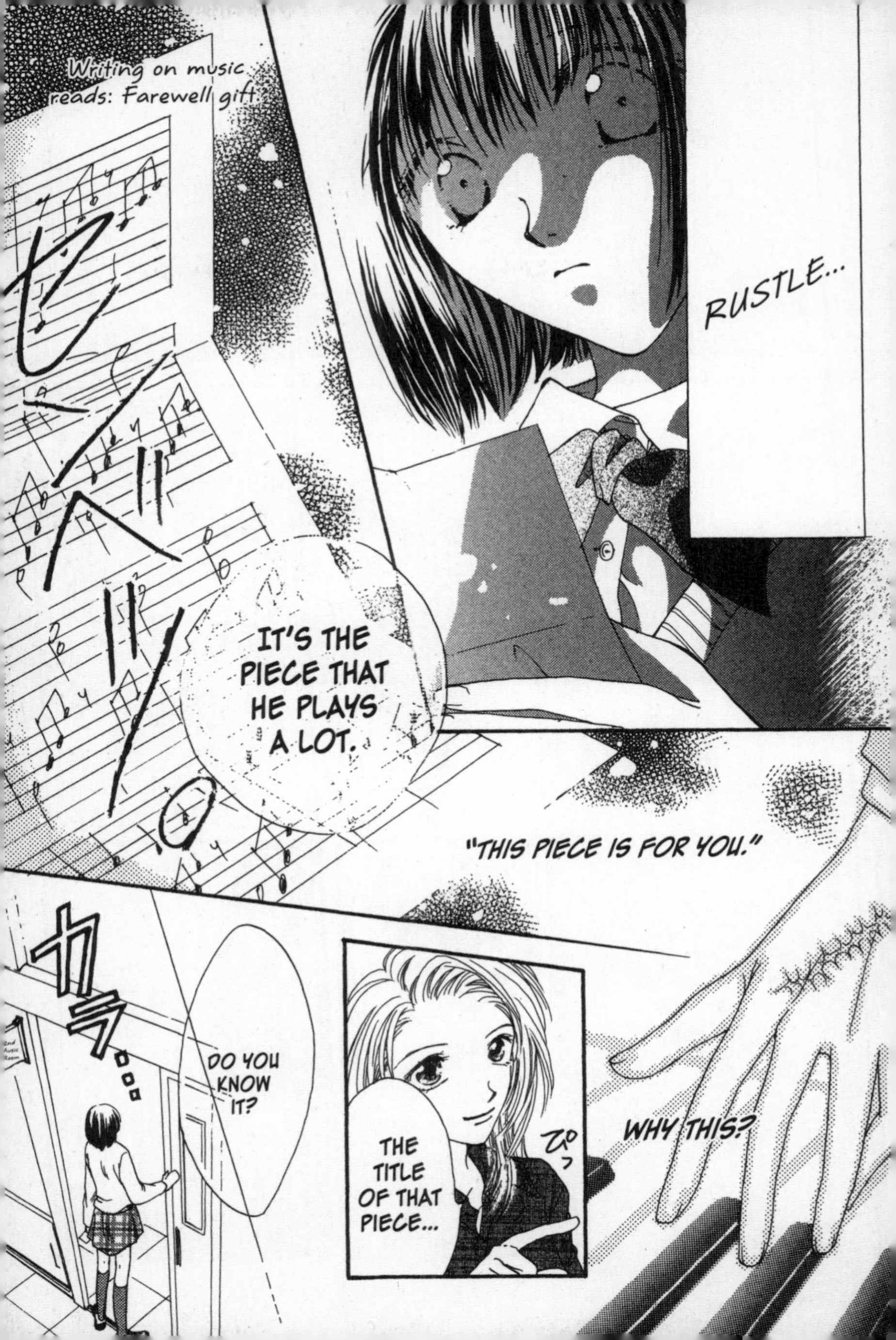
RUSTLE...
Writing on music reads: Farewell gift.
IT'S THE PIECE THAT HE PLAYS A LOT.
"THIS PIECE IS FOR YOU."
WHY THIS?
ぴっ
THE TITLE OF THAT PIECE...
DO YOU KNOW IT?
カラ

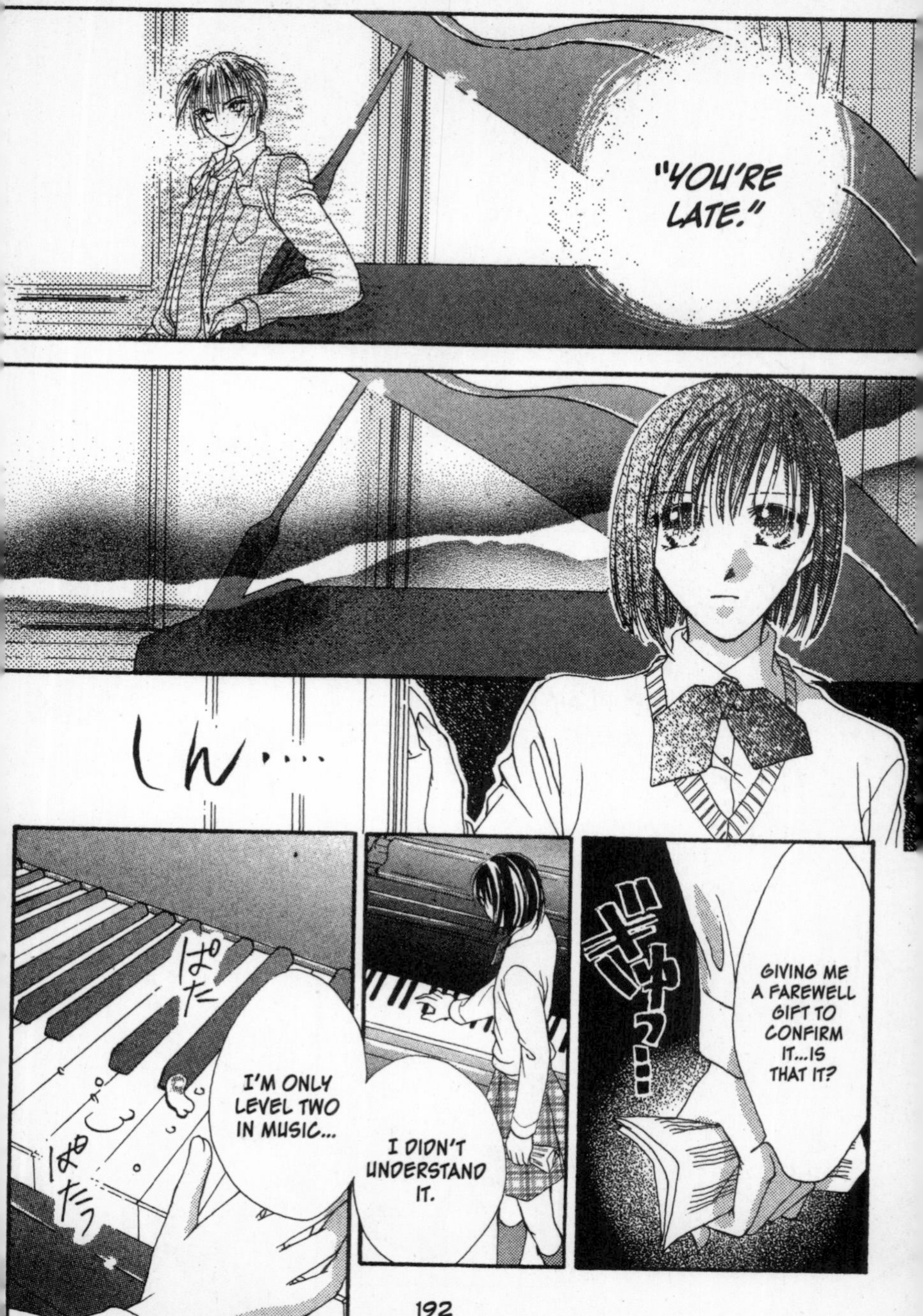
"YOU'RE LATE."
しん….
ぎゅっ…
GIVING ME A FAREWELL GIFT TO CONFIRM IT...IS THAT IT?
I DIDN'T UNDERSTAND IT.
ぱた
ぱたっ
I'M ONLY LEVEL TWO IN MUSIC...

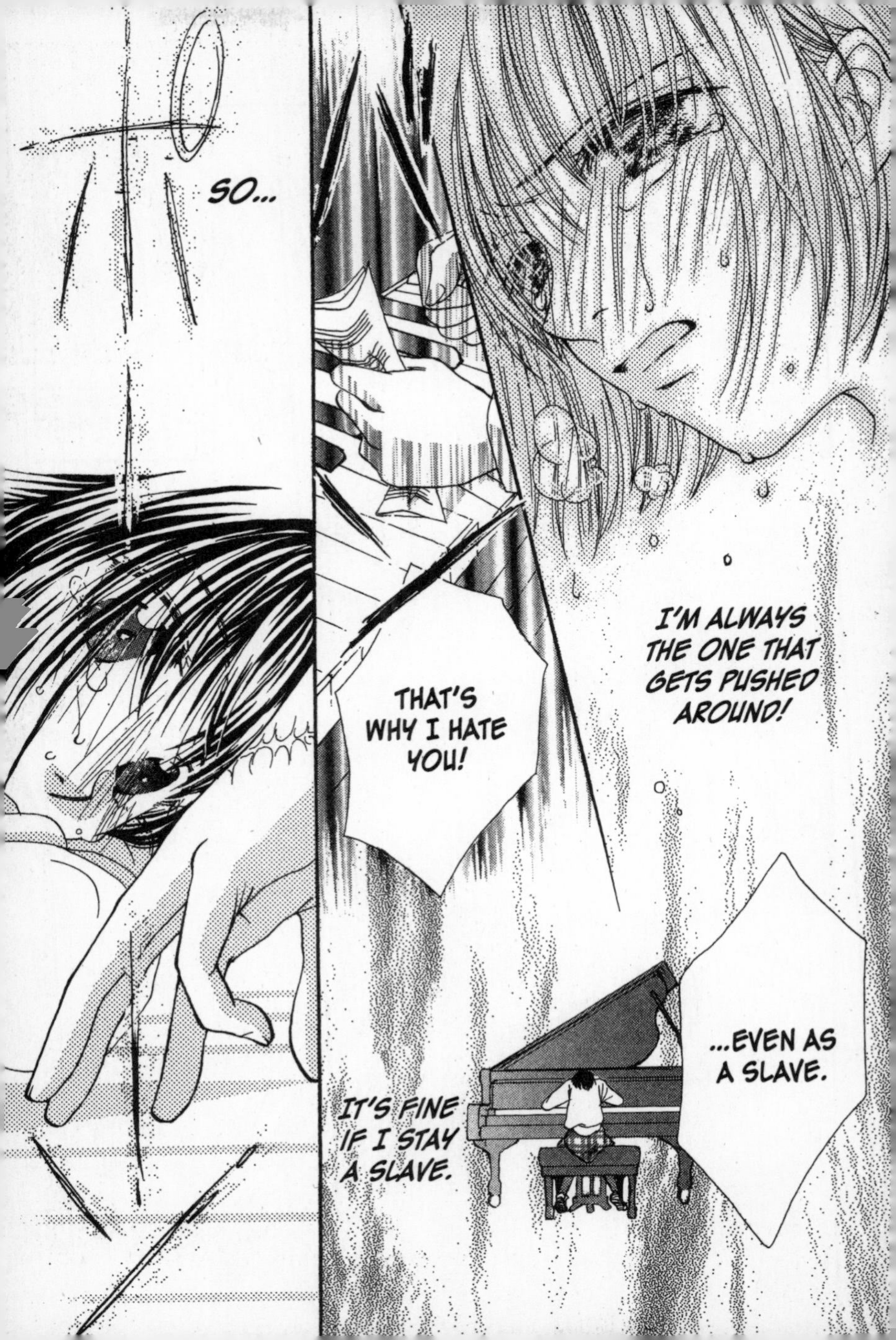
I'M ALWAYS THE ONE THAT GETS PUSHED AROUND!
THAT'S WHY I HATE YOU!
...EVEN AS A SLAVE.
IT'S FINE IF I STAY A SLAVE.
SO...

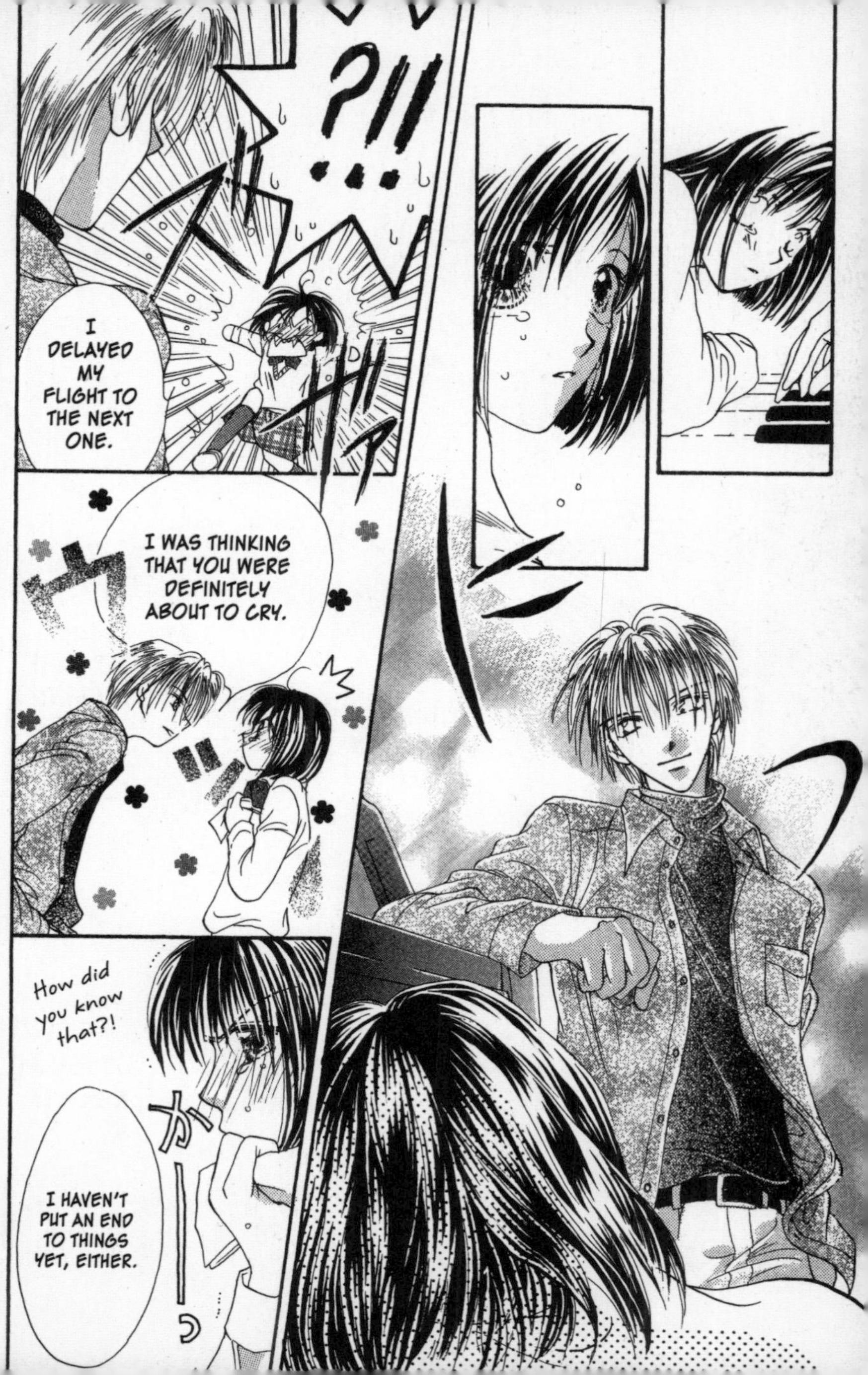
?!!
I DELAYED MY FLIGHT TO THE NEXT ONE.
I WAS THINKING THAT YOU WERE DEFINITELY ABOUT TO CRY.
How did you know that?!
I HAVEN'T PUT AN END TO THINGS YET, EITHER.

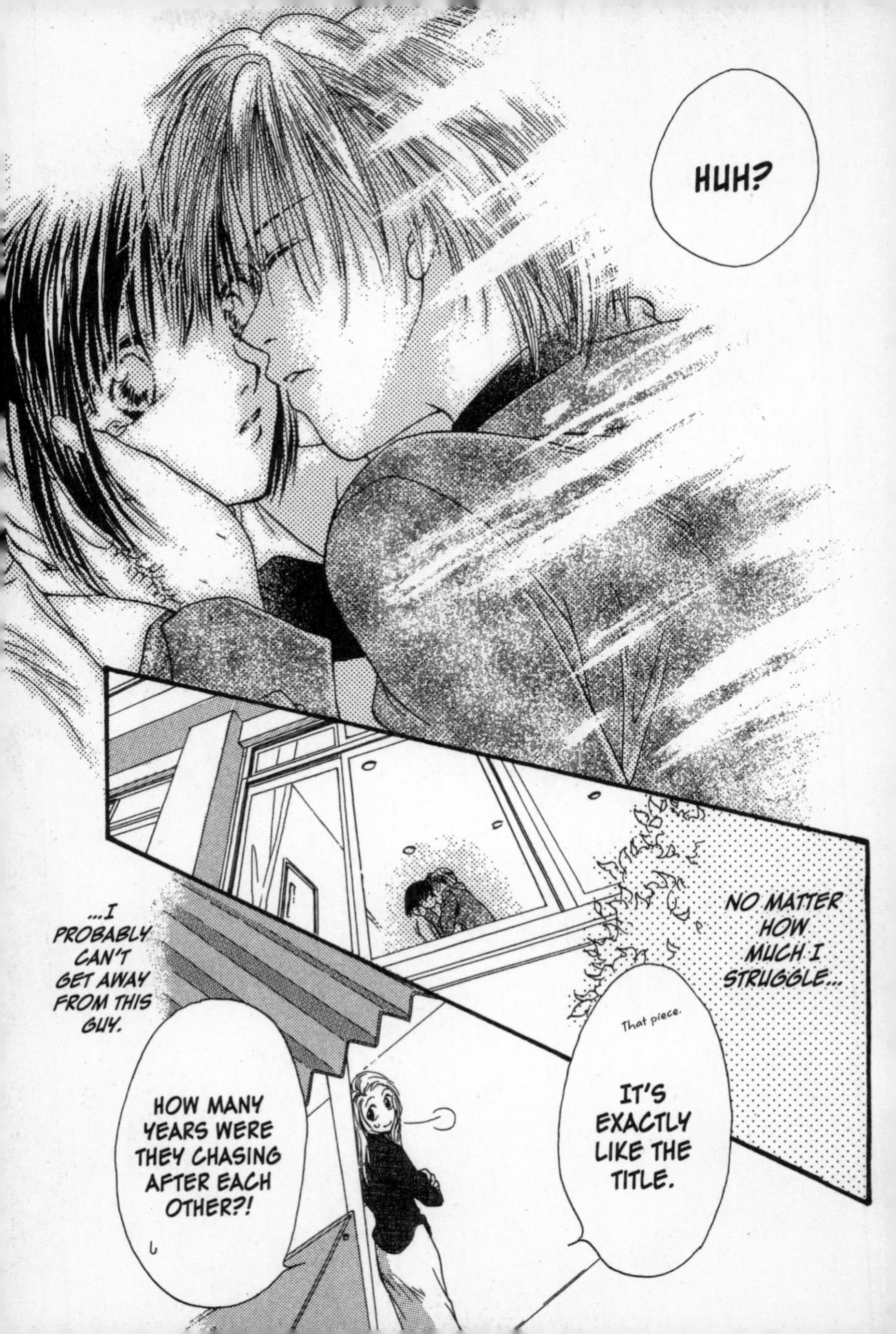
HUH?
NO MATTER HOW MUCH I STRUGGLE...
...I PROBABLY CAN'T GET AWAY FROM THIS GUY.
That piece.
IT'S EXACTLY LIKE THE TITLE.
HOW MANY YEARS WERE THEY CHASING AFTER EACH OTHER?!

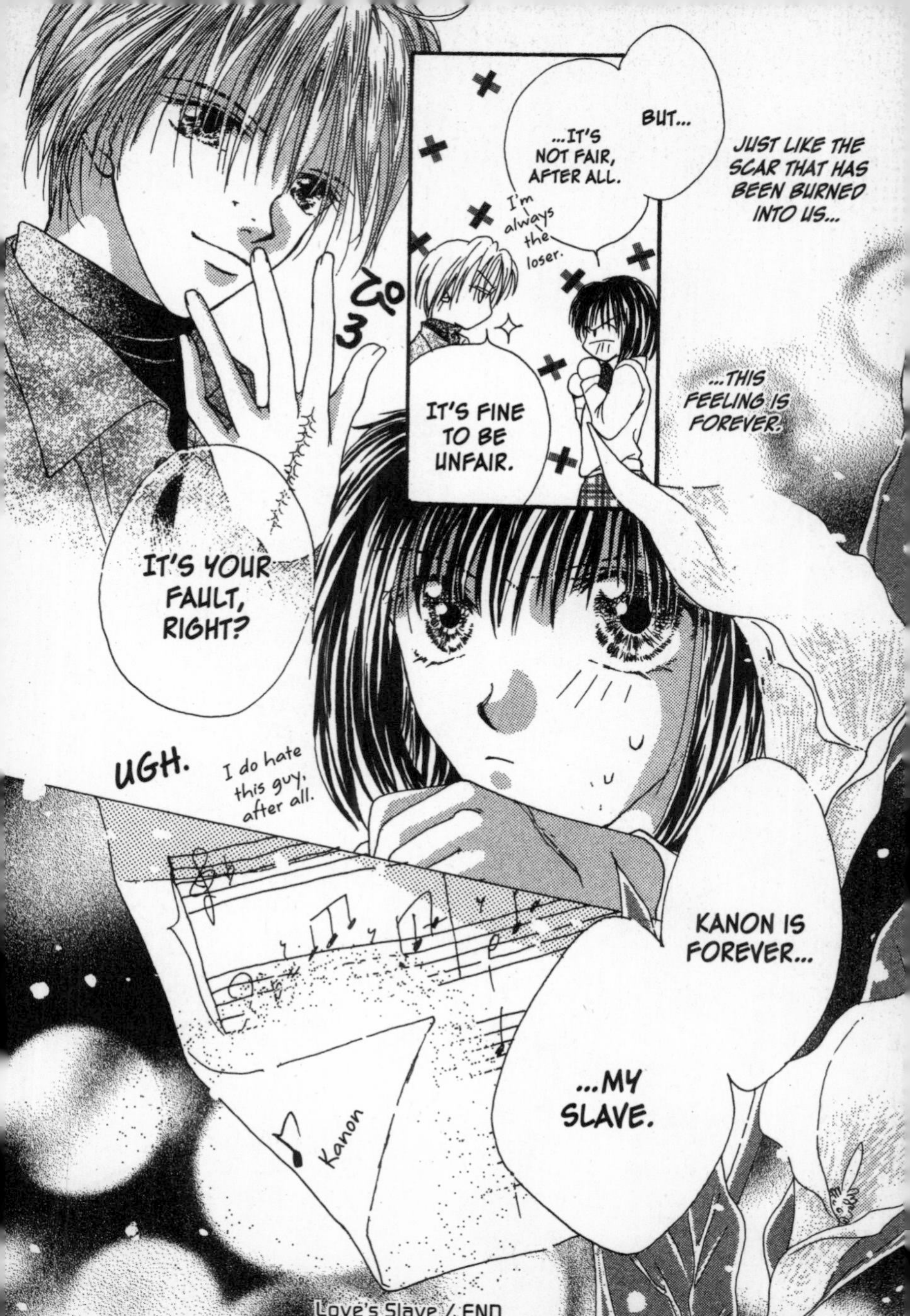
JUST LIKE THE SCAR THAT HAS BEEN BURNED INTO US...
BUT...
...IT'S NOT FAIR, AFTER ALL.
I'm always the loser.
IT'S FINE TO BE UNFAIR.
...THIS FEELING IS FOREVER.
IT'S YOUR FAULT, RIGHT?
KANON IS FOREVER...
...MY SLAVE.
UGH.
I do hate this guy, after all.
Kanon

Love's Slave / END

EXTRA: THE SLEEPING AFTERWORD

KIRIKIRI MY ROOM

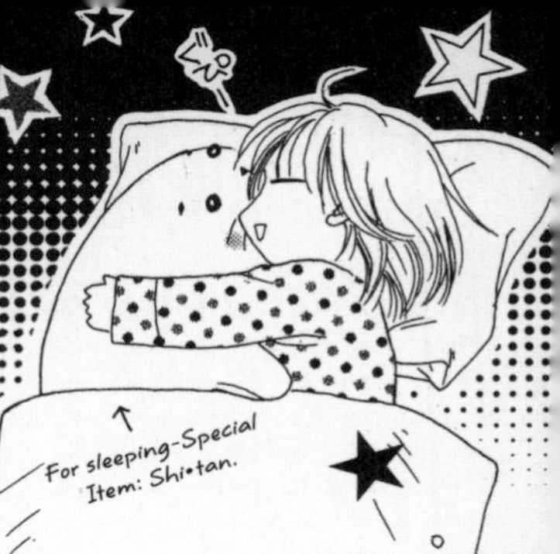

For sleeping-Special Item: Shi•tan.

MISSILE HAPPY! CHAPTER 9

It was very embarrassing to draw chapter 9...

Please read about the "Case of the Mandarin Oranges" in the quarter section. It was really funny and I didn't have enough space to express the event in words only.

I'm so glad that I was able to use the phrase "Neglect Play." It's a habit of mine lately. It's a bit of SM play where you ignore your partner so that they want you more. Using the phrase was a small happiness.

A PLACE TO INTRODUCE OR NOT INTRODUCE CERTAIN EVENTS IN THE MAKING OF VOLUME THREE.

THINGS LIKE THIS AND THAT HAD HAPPENED. I HAVEN'T HEARD THAT SONG SINCE I GRADUATED ELEMENTARY SCHOOL. I WAS THE ONLY ONE...

...who was crying so loudly.

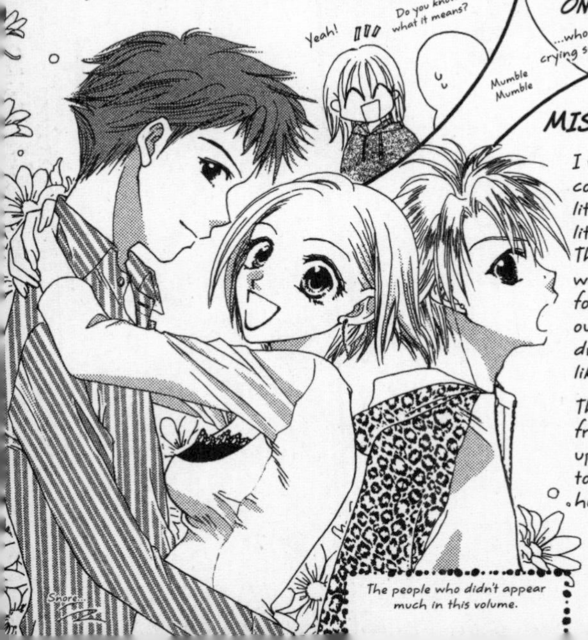

Do you know what it means?
Yeah!
Mumble Mumble
Snore...

The people who didn't appear much in this volume.

MISSILE HAPPY! CHAPTER 10

I went to the convenience store to copy the illustration for this with my little sister, and on the way back my little sister only had the copy of it. That's the type of panicked moment we had during this chapter. I can't forget when all the blood drained out of her face. Thank goodness the drawing was still there. (Sounds like it's about someone else!)

The kanji for Aoi-san's Aoi was used from what someone else had thought up. By the way, his last name was to be set with "Tomitabayashi". So his name is Aoi Tondabayashi.

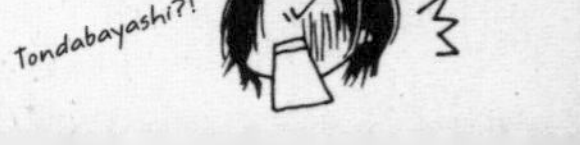

It doesn't match well!
Tondabayashi?!

MISSILE HAPPY! CHAPTER 11

I used the illustration for this chapter as the cover illustration this time, but it seems that lately I haven't had much luck with "color" and for the volume of the second cover, Rou would not look like Rou, or when I was close to finishing the inking for this volume I spilt ink all over the page, and even the illustration for chapter 12 (which is used as the illustration in the sleeve this time) I had to re-draw three times.

MISSILE HAPPY! CHAPTER 12

This is the first chapter that I made with my new editor, Mr. I. Even while talking about pointless things, the plot for this chapter came out rather quickly (although coming up with the title took a while!) Even though I've lived in the Kanagawa prefecture, we've never had the chance to meet up personally. It was a new experience.

But in the café we said things like, "are we going to have them do it?" "No, if we have them do it as soon as he passes the exam it's too fast!" We got strange looks from the waitress.

Mr. I did make a comment about my bottom being too big. Thanks for being so rude.

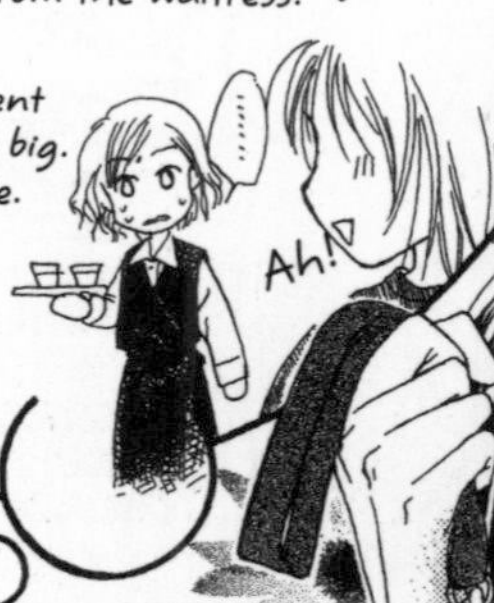
Ah!

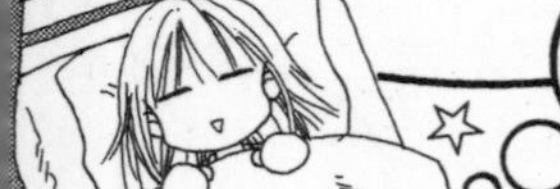

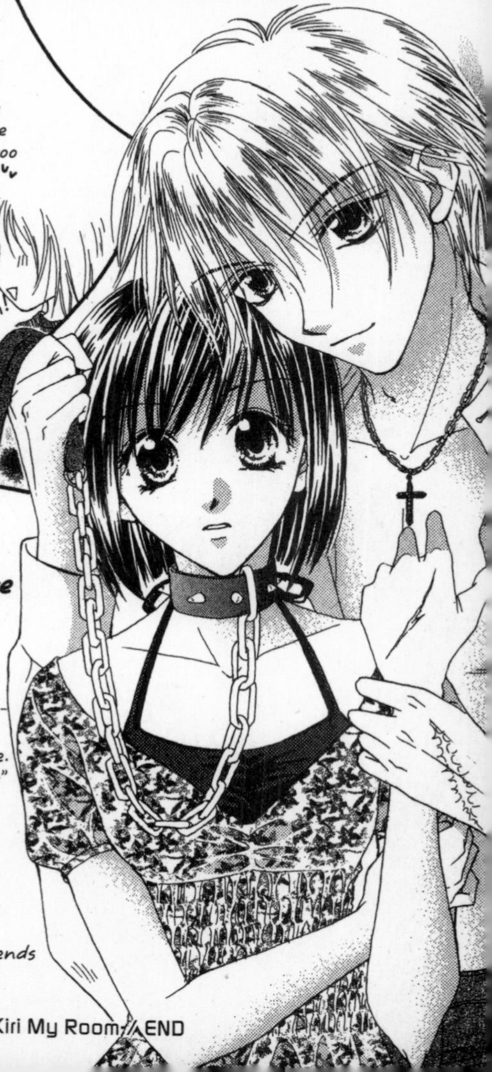

Love's Slave

How many years ago was this one-shot drawn? I can only give you my opinion of it in its present state. This piece was a "small monument" that I had accomplished at the time. During the making of this, a lot of painful things happened to me. But making this story helped me feel much better. It is a very sentimental piece for me.

Well, then, *Missile* Volume 3 ends here. Thank you very much!!
9/1/2003 Miki Kiritani

Extra: The Sleeping Afterword, KiriKiri My Room//END

MISSILE HAPPY!™

NEXT MISSILE... READY TO LAUNCH...

NOW THAT ROU'S FINALLY IN COLLEGE, MIKAKO'S HAPPY...
YOU WOULD THINK. BUT WITH ROU'S NEW LIFE AS A COLLEGE
STUDENT, THE HAPPY COUPLE FEEL THEMSELVES BEING
PULLED APART FROM EACH OTHER. TO REMEDY THE SITUATION,
ROU SUGGESTS A COZY VACATION FOR TWO. WILL IT DO THE
TRICK? AND WHAT'S THIS ABOUT ROU'S HIDDEN CHILD?!

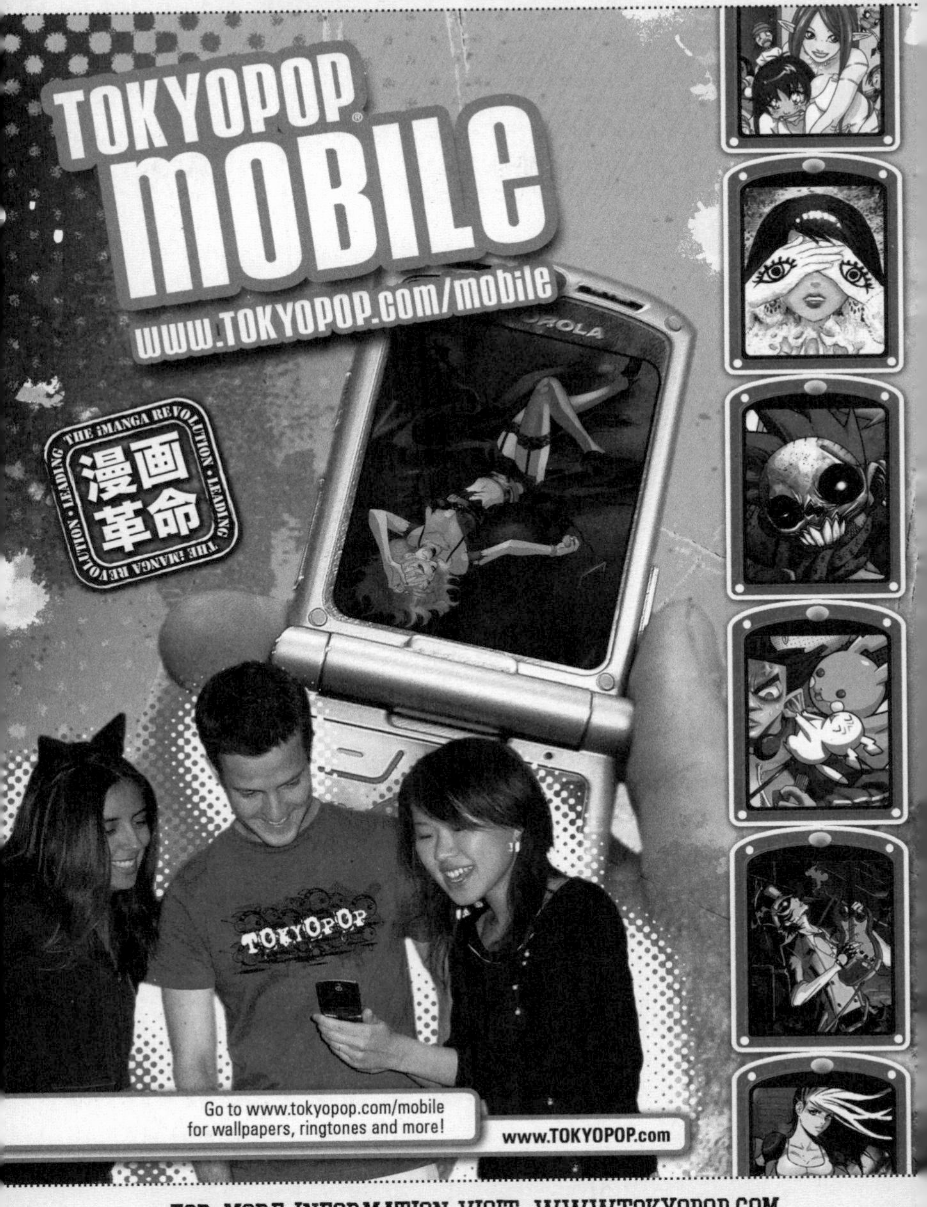
TOKYOPOP® MOBILE
www.TOKYOPOP.com/mobile
THE iMANGA REVOLUTION · LEADING THE iMANGA REVOLUTION · LEADING
漫画革命
TOKYOPOP
Go to www.tokyopop.com/mobile
for wallpapers, ringtones and more!
www.TOKYOPOP.com

FOR MORE INFORMATION VISIT: WWW.TOKYOPOP.COM

Fruits Basket

By Natsuki Takaya

Volume 20

Can Tohru deal with the truth?

After running away from his feelings and everyone he knows, Kyo is back with the truth about his role in the death of Tohru's mother. But how will he react when Tohru says that she still loves him?

Winner of the American Anime Award for Best Manga!

The #1 selling shojo manga in America!

FOR MORE INFORMATION VISIT: WWW.TOKYOPOP.COM

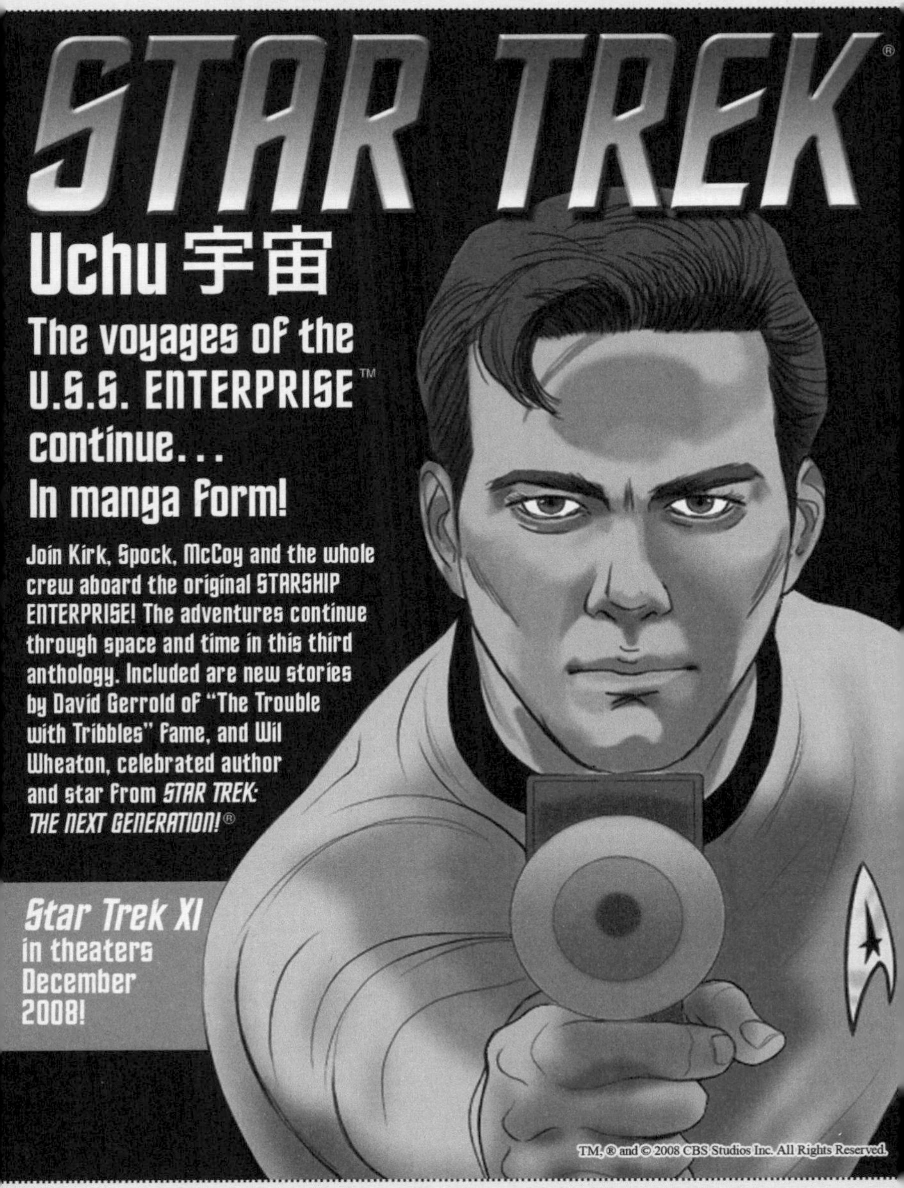
STAR TREK®
Uchu 宇宙
The voyages of the U.S.S. ENTERPRISE™ continue...
In manga form!
Join Kirk, Spock, McCoy and the whole crew aboard the original STARSHIP ENTERPRISE! The adventures continue through space and time in this third anthology. Included are new stories by David Gerrold of "The Trouble with Tribbles" fame, and Wil Wheaton, celebrated author and star from STAR TREK: THE NEXT GENERATION!®
Star Trek XI in theaters December 2008!
TM, ® and © 2008 CBS Studios Inc. All Rights Reserved.

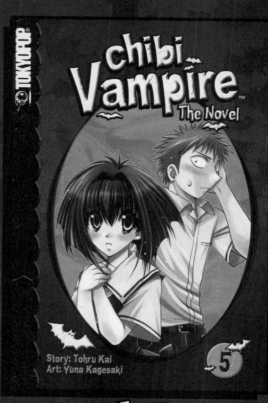

CHIBI VAMPIRE
MANGA BY YUNA KAGESAKI, NOVEL BY TOHRU KAI AND YUNA KAGESAKI

The HILARIOUS adventures of

As Karin and Kenta's official first date continues, Anju shows up to keep an eye on the clumsy couple. When Kenta tells Karin how he really feels, will it destroy their relationship? Also, the new girl in town, Yuriya, begins snooping around in search of vampires. Why is she trying to uncover Karin's identity, and what secrets of her own is she hiding?

chibi Vampire™ ⤙ Inspired the

FOR MORE INFORMATION VISIT:

BIZENGHAST

BY M. ALICE LEGROW, NOVEL BY SHAWN THORGERSEN

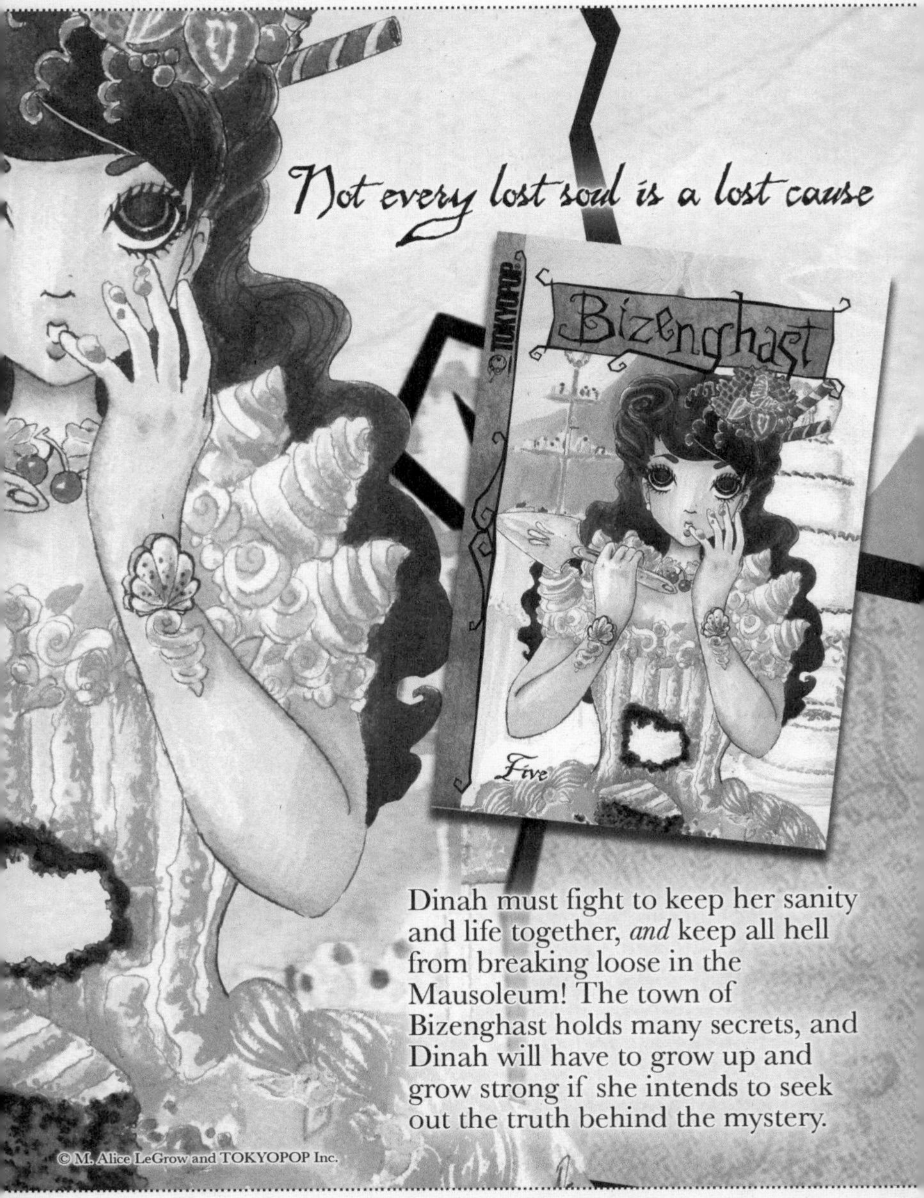
Not every lost soul is a lost cause
TOKYOPOP
Bizenghast
Five

Dinah must fight to keep her sanity and life together, *and* keep all hell from breaking loose in the Mausoleum! The town of Bizenghast holds many secrets, and Dinah will have to grow up and grow strong if she intends to seek out the truth behind the mystery.

FOR MORE INFORMATION VISIT:

STOP!

This is the back of the book.
You wouldn't want to spoil a great ending!

This book is printed "manga-style," in the authentic Japanese right-to-left format. Since none of the artwork has been flipped or altered, readers get to experience the story just as the creator intended. You've been asking for it, so TOKYOPOP® delivered: authentic, hot-off-the-press, and far more fun!

DIRECTIONS

1
2
3
4
5
6
7
8
9
10

If this is your first time reading manga-style, here's a quick guide to help you understand how it works.

It's easy... just start in the top right panel and follow the numbers. Have fun, and look for more 100% authentic manga from TOKYOPOP®!

THE MANGA REVOLUTION · LEADING · THE MANGA REVOLUTION · LEADING
漫画革命

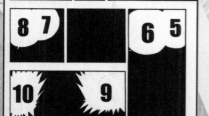

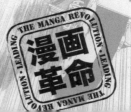